JEWELS FROM
JOHN NEWTON

John Newton

JEWELS FROM
JOHN NEWTON

*Daily Readings from the
Works of John Newton*

Selected by
Miller Ferrie

THE BANNER OF TRUTH TRUST

THE BANNER OF TRUTH TRUST
3 Murrayfield Road, Edinburgh EH12 6EL, UK
P.O. Box 621, Carlisle, PA 17013, USA

*

© The Banner of Truth Trust 2016

*

ISBN
Print: 978 1 84871 555 4
Epub: 978 1 84871 556 1
Kindle: 978 1 84871 557 8

*

Typeset in 11/13 pt Adobe Garamond Pro
at The Banner of Truth Trust, Edinburgh

Printed in the USA by
Versa Press, Inc.,
East Peoria, IL

The Saviour calls his people sheep
    And bids them on his love rely;
For he alone their souls can keep,
    And he alone their wants supply.

Editor's Preface

JOHN NEWTON (1725–1807) was a trophy of God's grace. His transformation from a blasphemous slave trader to a much loved minister of the gospel is a testimony to the powerful, life-changing grace of God in Jesus Christ. His hymns, letters, and other writings have been a source of strength and comfort to Christian believers for centuries.

I have been greatly blessed by the writings of John Newton and for this reason desired to put together a book of daily devotional readings selected from his *Works*. What impresses me about this man is his honesty in readily admitting his struggles, sinfulness, and failures. This aspect of his writings has been such an encouragement to me personally, for it gave me the assurance that my own daily battles and humiliations are not unique. In addition, he repeatedly reminds his readers of God's trustworthiness, no matter what circumstances they might be facing.

The inscription on his tombstone reads,

John Newton, Clerk, once an infidel and libertine, a servant of slaves in Africa, was, by the rich mercy of our Lord and Saviour Jesus Christ, preserved, restored, pardoned, and appointed to preach the faith he had long laboured to destroy.

He never ceased to be amazed at God's grace in the gospel, and it was this grace that he sought to proclaim till his dying day.

The material included in this book is largely drawn from Newton's prolific correspondence, and covers a wide variety of topics. Although written more than two hundred years ago, it remains as relevant and edifying as ever. I hope these selections from his writings will prove to be a blessing and a source of help and encouragement to each reader.

I want to give a special word of thanks to the Banner of Truth Trust for republishing *The Works of John Newton* in six volumes in 1985 and reprinting them again in 2007.[1] These volumes are the treasure chest out of which these jewels have been taken.

Thanks also to my husband Paul for his loving encouragement and support for this project.

MILLER FERRIE
Leith, North Dakota
November 2015

---

[1] In 2015 the Trust published a new four-volume edition of Newton's *Works*. These volumes have been completely re-typeset and include material not found in the old six-volume set. See Publisher's Note on page xi for information on locating the source of the daily readings within the *Works*.

About John Newton

BORN in London in 1725, deprived of the godly influence of his mother before he was seven years old, John Newton was but two years at school before he went, at the age of eleven, on his first voyage with his father, a sea captain. From that time till the age of thirty, when his health was broken by a stroke, Newton endured the wild rigours of a life before the mast, including being press-ganged aboard a naval vessel and flogged when captured after desertion. Only his love for the youthful Mary Catlett preserved him from suicide. He was released from the navy only to join in the slave traffic across the Atlantic, and was reduced almost to death on the Guinea coast before being delivered by a friend of his father's.

Throughout these sad events there ran a Divine purpose; and while Newton forgot the Saviour whom his mother had so often commended to him in childhood, and while he became, like one of old, a 'blasphemer and injurious,' it was all leading to a day—in the midst of a tremendous storm at sea—when he was brought to say: 'I stood in need of an Almighty Saviour, and such a one I found described in the New Testament. The Lord had wrought a marvellous thing.'

After his seafaring days he became tide-surveyor in Liverpool, a thriving slave port with a population of 22,000. It was here that Newton became acquainted with the great evangelist, George Whitefield, and soon he also came to know other leaders of the Evangelical Revival such as William Grimshaw and Henry Venn.

His own thoughts were now turned to the ministry, and after several disappointments he was at length settled in 1764 in the Buckinghamshire parish of Olney – a name immortalized by the hymns which he and the poet William Cowper wrote for the mid-week meetings of the church.

In his sixteen years at Olney, Newton found a good field for exercising his gift as 'the letter writer *par excellence* of the Evangelical Revival.' The dreadful condition from which he had been saved, the long struggle he went through before he came to a clear understanding of the gospel, and the years of patient waiting for an opening in the Church, all served to prepare Newton for this work. He was given a thorough knowledge of the workings of the human heart and of the Lord's dealings with his people.

Newton became minister of St. Mary Woolnoth, London, in 1779, where he continued to preach until almost the end of his life in 1807. Being advised by Richard Cecil in 1806 to discontinue preaching, he gave the memorable reply. 'I cannot stop. What! shall the old African blasphemer stop while he can speak?'

Publisher's Note

Page references to the Banner of Truth six-volume reprints (1985, 2007), mentioned in the Editor's Preface, have been provided at the bottom of each page in square brackets. The second set of page references at the bottom of each page relate to the Trust's re-typeset four-volume edition of Newton's *Works* (2015).

The Lord is my Shepherd.—Psa. 23:1.

A SHEPHERD is a relative name; it has reference to a flock. This great and good Shepherd has a flock, whom he loved from everlasting, and whom having loved, he will love to the end ... he humbled himself for their sakes, submitted to partake of their nature and their sorrows, took upon him the form of a servant, and was made in the likeness of sinful flesh. He died for his sheep, 'the just for the unjust', to redeem them from the curse of the law, from the guilt and dominion of sin, from the power of Satan, and to bring them to God. They, by nature, are all 'gone astray, every one to his own way'; but having thus bought them with his blood, in his own appointed time he seeks, finds, and restores his sheep. By the power of his word and Spirit, he makes himself known to their hearts, causes them to hear and understand his voice, and guides them into his fold. Then they become his sheep... They are under his immediate protection and government.

Considered as individuals, they are fitly described by the name of sheep. A sheep is a weak, defenceless, improvident creature; prone to wander, and if once astray, is seldom known to return of its own accord. A sheep has neither strength to fight with the wolf, nor speed to escape from him; nor has it the foresight of the ant, to provide its own sustenance. Such is our character, and our situation: unable to take care of ourselves, prone to wander from our resting-place, exposed to enemies which we can neither withstand nor avoid, without resource in ourselves, and taught, by daily experience, the insufficiency of everything around us. Yet, if this Shepherd be our Shepherd, weak and helpless as we are, we may be of good courage. If we can say with David, 'The Lord is my Shepherd', we may make the same inferences which he did, 'Therefore I shall not want: therefore I need not fear.'

Messiah: The Great Shepherd, [4:152]; 3:121

Behold the Lamb of God.—John 1:29.

GOD has so loved rebellious, ungrateful sinners, as to appoint them a Saviour in the person of his only Son. The prophets foresaw his manifestation in the flesh, and foretold the happy consequences—that his presence would change the wilderness into a fruitful field, that he was coming to give sight to the blind, and life to the dead; to set the captive at liberty; to unloose the heavy burden; and to bless the weary with rest. But this change was not to be wrought merely by a word of power, as when he said, 'Let there be light, and there was light.' It was great, to speak the world from nothing; but far greater, to redeem sinners from misery. The salvation, of which he is the Author though free to us, must cost him dear. Before the mercy of God can be actually dispensed to such offenders, the rights of his justice, the demands of his law, and the honour of his government, must be provided for. The early institution and long-continued use of sacrifices, had clearly pointed out the necessity of an atonement; but the real and proper atonement could be made only by MESSIAH. The blood of slaughtered animals could not take away sin, nor display the righteousness of God in pardoning it. This was the appointed covenanted work of MESSIAH, and he alone could perform it. With this in view he had said, 'Lo, I come.' And it was in this view, when John saw him, that he pointed him out to his disciples, saying, 'Behold, the Lamb of God!'

This title, therefore, 'The Lamb of God,' refers to his voluntary substitution for sinners, that by his sufferings and death they who deserved to die might obtain eternal life through him, and for his sake.

Messiah: The Lamb of God, the Great Atonement, [4:186]; 3:146

I gave my back to the smiters, and my cheeks to them that plucked off the hair: I hid not my face from shame and spitting.—Isa. 50:6.

WE may observe, from the words, that the humiliation of MESSIAH was *voluntary*, and that it was *extreme*.

With respect to his engagement, as the Mediator between God and sinners, a great work was given him to do, and he became responsible; and therefore, in this sense, bound, and under obligation. But his compliance was likewise *voluntary*, for he gave himself up freely to suffer, the just for the unjust. Could he have relinquished our cause, and left us to the deserved consequence of our sins, in the trying hour when his enemies seized upon him, legions of angels, had they been wanted, would have appeared for his rescue. But if he was determined to save others, then his own sufferings were unavoidable. Men, in the prosecution of their designs, often meet with unexpected difficulties in their way, which, though they encounter with some cheerfulness, in hope of surmounting them, and carrying their point at last, are considered as impediments; but the sufferings of MESSIAH were essentially necessary to the accomplishment of his great designs, precisely determined, and present to his view beforehand; so that ... there was not a single circumstance that happened to him unawares. He knew that no blood but his own could make atonement for sin; that nothing less than his humiliation could expiate our pride; that if he did not *thus* suffer, sinners must inevitably perish; and therefore (such was his love!) he cheerfully and voluntarily 'gave his back to the smiters, and his cheeks to them that plucked off the hair'. Two designs of vast importance filled his mind, the completion of them was that joy set before him, for the sake of which, 'he made himself of no reputation, endured the cross, and despised the shame'. These were, the glory of God, and the salvation of sinners.

Messiah: Voluntary Suffering, [4:211]; 3:165

And Enoch walked with God.—Gen. 5:22, 24.

IT is a believer's privilege to walk with God in the exercise of faith, and by the power of his Spirit, to mortify the whole body of sin, to gain a growing victory over the world and self, and to make daily advances in conformity to the mind that was in Christ.

Faith, then in its practical exercise, has for its object the whole word of God, and forms its estimate of all things with which the soul is at present concerned, according to the standard of Scripture. Like Moses, it 'endures, as seeing him who is invisible'. When our Lord was upon earth, and conversed with his disciples, their eyes and hearts were fixed upon him. In danger he was their defender; their guide when in perplexity; and to him they looked for the solution of all their doubts, and the supply of all their wants. He is now withdrawn from our eyes; but faith sets him still before us, for the same purposes, and according to its degree, with the same effects, as if we actually saw him. His spiritual presence, apprehended by faith, is a restraint from evil, an encouragement to every service, and affords a present refuge and help in every time of trouble. To this is owing the delight a believer takes in ordinances, because there he meets his Lord: and to this, likewise, it is owing, that his religion is not confined to public occasions; but he is the same person in secret as he appears to be in the public assembly; for he worships him who sees in secret; and dares appeal to his all-seeing eye for the sincerity of his desires and intentions. By faith he is enabled to use prosperity with moderation; and knows and feels, that what the world calls good is of small value, unless it is accompanied with the presence and blessings of him whom his soul loveth.

Of the Practical Influence of Faith, [1:168]; 1:111

But without faith it is impossible to please him.—Heb. 11:6.

AND [the believer's] faith upholds him under all trials, by assuring him, that every dispensation is under the direction of his Lord; that chastisements are a token of his love; that the season, measure, and continuance of his sufferings, are appointed by infinite wisdom, and designed to work for his everlasting good; and that grace and strength shall be afforded him, according to his day. Thus, his heart being fixed, trusting in the Lord, to whom he has committed all his concerns; and knowing that his best interests are safe; he is not greatly afraid of evil tidings, but enjoys a stable peace in the midst of a changing world. For, though he cannot tell what a day may bring forth, he believes that he who has invited and enabled him to cast all his cares upon him, will suffer nothing to befall him but what shall be made subservient to his chief desire,—the glory of God in the sanctification and final salvation of his soul. And if, through the weakness of his flesh, he is liable to be startled by the first impression of a sharp and sudden trial, he quickly flees to his strong refuge, remembers it is the Lord's doing, resigns himself to his will, and patiently expects a happy issue.

By the same principle of faith, a believer's conduct is regulated towards his fellow creatures; and in the discharge of the several duties and relations of life, his great aim is to please God, and to let his light shine in the world. He believes and feels his own weakness and unworthiness, and lives upon the grace and pardoning love of his Lord. This gives him an habitual tenderness and gentleness of spirit. Humbled under a sense of much forgiveness to himself, he finds it easy to forgive others, if he has aught against any.

Of the Practical Influence of Faith, [1:169]; 1:112

*For whatsoever is born of God overcometh the world: and this is the
victory that overcometh the world, even our faith.*—1 John 5:4.

FAITH is of daily use as a preservative from a compliance with the
corrupt customs and maxims of the world. The believer, though
in the world, is not *of* it; by faith he triumphs over its smiles and
enticements: he sees that all that is in the world, suited to gratify the
desires of the flesh or the eye, is not only to be avoided as sinful, but
as incompatible with his best pleasures. He will mix with the world so
far as is necessary, in the discharge of the duties of that station of life
in which the providence of God has placed him, but no further. His
leisure and inclinations are engaged in a different pursuit. They who
fear the Lord are his chosen companions: and the blessings he derives
from the word, and throne, and ordinances of grace, make him look
upon the poor pleasures and amusements of those who live without
God in the world with a mixture of disdain and pity. And by faith he
is proof against its frowns. He will obey God rather than man; he will
'have no fellowship with the unfruitful works of darkness, but will
rather reprove them'. And if, upon this account, he should be despised
and injuriously treated, whatever loss he suffers in such a cause, he
accounts his gain, and esteems such disgrace his glory.

I am not aiming to draw a perfect character, but to show the
proper effects of that faith which justifies, which purifies the heart,
worketh by love, and overcomes the world. An habitual endeavour to
possess such a frame of spirit, and thus to adorn the gospel of Christ,
and that with growing success, is what I am persuaded you are not
a stranger to; and I am afraid that they who can content themselves
with aiming at anything short of this in their profession, are too much
strangers to themselves, and to the nature of that liberty wherewith
Jesus has promised to make his people free.

Of the Practical Influence of Faith, [1:171]; 1:114

My son, give me thine heart.—Prov. 23:26.

WE know how we are often affected when in the presence of a fellow worm: if he is one on whom we depend, or who is considerably our superior in life, how careful we are to compose our behaviour, and to avoid whatever might be deemed improper or offensive! Is it not strange, that those who have taken their ideas of the Divine majesty, holiness, and purity, from the Scriptures and are not wholly insensible of their inexpressible obligations to regulate all they say or do by his percepts, should upon many occasions be betrayed into improprieties of behaviour from which the presence of a nobleman or prince, would have effectually restrained them, yea, sometimes perhaps even the presence of a child? Even in the exercise of prayer, by which we profess to draw near the Lord, the consideration that his eye is upon us has little power to engage our attention, or prevent our thoughts from wandering, like the fool's eyes, to the ends of the earth. What should we think of a person, who, being admitted into the king's presence upon business of the greatest importance, should break off in the midst of his address, to pursue a butterfly? Could such an instance of weakness be met with, it would be but a faint emblem of the inconsistencies which they who are acquainted with their own hearts can often charge themselves with in prayer. They are not wholly ignorant in what a frame of spirit it becomes a needy dependent sinner to approach that God, before whom the angels are represented as veiling their faces; yet, in defiance of their better judgment, their attention is diverted from him with whom they have to do, to the merest trifles; they are not able to realize that presence with which they believe themselves to be surrounded, but speak as if they were speaking into the air.

On the Inefficacy of Our Knowledge, [1:246]; 1:170

> *Behold, he taketh away, who can hinder him?*
> *who will say unto him, What doest thou?*—Job 9:12.

FURTHER, if our sense that God is always present was in any good measure answerable to the conviction of our judgment, would it not be an effectual preservative from the many importunate though groundless fears with which we are harassed? He says, 'Fear not I am with thee'; he promises to be a shield and a guard to those who put their trust in him; yet, though we profess to believe his word, and to hope that he is our protector, we seldom think ourselves safe, even in the path of duty, a moment longer than danger is kept out of our view. Little reason have we to value ourselves upon our knowledge of this indisputable truth, when it has no more effective and habitual influence upon our conduct.

The doctrine of God's sovereignty likewise... This humiliating doctrine concludes as strongly for submission to the will of God, under every circumstance of life, as it does for our acquiescing in his purpose to have mercy on whom he will have mercy. But alas! how often do we find ourselves utterly unable to apply it, so as to reconcile our spirits to those afflictions which he is pleased to allot us! So far as we are enabled to say, when we are exercised with poverty, or heavy losses or crosses, 'I was dumb and opened not my mouth, because thou didst it', so far, and no further, are we truly convinced that God has a sovereign right to dispose of us as he pleases... What an inconsistence, that, while we think God is just and righteous in withholding from others the things which pertain to their everlasting peace, we should find it so hard to submit to his dispensations to ourselves in matters of unspeakably less importance!

On the Inefficacy of Our Knowledge, [1:247]; 1:170

Hath God forgotten to be gracious?
hath he in anger shut up his tender mercies? Selah.—Psa. 77:9.

B UT the Lord's appointments, to those who fear him, are not only sovereign, but wise and gracious. He has connected their good with his own glory, and is engaged, by promise, to make all things work together for their advantage. He chooses for his people better than they could choose for themselves: if they are in heaviness, there is a need-be for it, and he withholds nothing from them but what, upon the whole, it is better they should be without. Thus the Scriptures teach, and thus we profess to believe. Furnished with these principles, we are at no loss to suggest motives of patience and consolation to our brethren that are afflicted: we can assure them, without hesitation, that, if they are interested in the promises, their concerns are in safe hands; that the things which at present are not joyous, but grievous, shall in due season yield the peaceable fruits of righteousness; and that their trials are as certainly mercies as their comforts. We can prove to them, from the history of Joseph, David, Job, and other instances recorded in Scripture, that, notwithstanding any present dark appearances, it shall certainly be well with the righteous; that God can and will make crooked things straight; and that he often produces the greatest good from those events which we are apt to look upon as evil. From hence we can infer, not only the sinfulness, but the folly, of finding fault with any of his dispensations. We can tell them, that, at the worst, the sufferings of the present life are not worthy to be compared with the glory that shall be revealed; and that therefore, under the greatest pressures, they should so weep as those who expect in a little time to have all their tears wiped away. But when the case is our own, when we are troubled on every side, or touched in the tenderest part, how difficult is it to feel the force of these reasonings, though we know they are true to a demonstration! Then, unless we are endued with fresh strength from on high, we are as liable to complain and despond, as if we thought our afflictions sprung out of the ground, and the Lord had forgotten to be gracious.

On the Inefficacy of Knowledge, [1:249]; 1:172

What is man?—Psa. 8:4.

MAY we not say, with the psalmist, 'Lord, what is man!' yea, what an enigma, what a poor inconsistent creature, is a believer! In one view, how great is his character and privilege! He knows the Lord; he knows himself. His understanding is enlightened to apprehend and contemplate the great mysteries of the gospel. He has just ideas of the evil of sin, the vanity of the world, the beauties of holiness, and the nature of true happiness. He was once 'darkness, but now he is light in the Lord'. He has access to God by Jesus Christ; to whom he is united, and in whom he lives by faith. While the principles he has received are enlivened by the agency of the Holy Spirit, he can do all things. He is humble, gentle, patient, watchful, faithful. He rejoices in afflictions, triumphs over temptation, lives upon the foretastes of eternal glory, and counts not his life dear, so he may glorify God his Saviour, and finish his course with joy. But his strength is not his own; he is absolutely dependent; and is still encompassed with infirmities, and burdened with a depraved nature. If the Lord withdraws his power, he becomes weak as another man, and drops, as a stone sinks to the earth by its own weight... Without renewed and continual communications from the Spirit of grace, he is unable to withstand the smallest temptation, to endure the slightest trial, to perform the least service in a due manner, or even to think a good thought. He knows this, and yet he too often forgets it. But the Lord reminds him of it frequently, by suspending that assistance without which he can do nothing. Then he feels what he is, and is easily prevailed upon to act in contradiction to his better judgment. Thus repeated experience of his own weakness teaches him by degrees where his strength lies; that it is not in anything he has already attained, or can call his own, but in the grace, power, and faithfulness of his Saviour.

On the Inefficacy of Our Knowledge, [1:251]; 1:173

There was given to me a thorn in the flesh ... lest I should be exalted above measure.—2 Cor. 12:7.

A S you intimate, that you are in the main favoured with liberty and usefulness in the pulpit, give me leave to ask you, what you would do if you did not find yourself occasionally poor, insufficient, and, as you express it, stupid, at other times? Are you aware of what might be the possible, the probable, the almost certain consequences, if you always found your spirit enlarged, and your frames lively and comfortable? Would you not be in great danger of being puffed up with spiritual pride? Would you not be less sensible of your absolute dependence upon the power of Christ, and of your continual need of his blood, pardon, and intercession? Would you not be quite at a loss to speak suitably and feelingly to the case of many gracious souls, who are groaning under those effects of a depraved nature, from which, upon that supposition, you would be exempted? How could you speak properly upon the deceitfulness of the heart, if you did not feel the deceitfulness of your own; or adapt yourself to the changing experiences through which your hearers pass, if you yourself were always alike, or nearly so? Or how could you speak pertinently of the inward warfare, the contrary principles of flesh and spirit fighting one against another, if your own spiritual desires were always vigorous and successful, and met with little opposition?

The Apostle Paul, though favoured with a singular eminency in grace, felt at times that he had no sufficiency in himself so much as to think a good thought; and he saw there was a danger of his being exalted above measure, if the Lord had not wisely and graciously tempered his dispensations to prevent it. By 'being exalted above measure', perhaps there may be a reference not only to his spirit, lest he should think more highly of himself than he ought, but likewise to his preaching, lest, not having the same causes of complaint and humiliation in common with others, he should shoot over the heads of his hearers, confine himself chiefly to speak of such comforts and privileges as he himself enjoyed, and have little to say for the refreshment of those who were discouraged and cast down by a continual conflict with indwelling sin.

On a Believer's Frames, [1:253]; 1:175

But I am poor and needy; yet the Lord thinketh upon me.—Psa. 40:17.

THOUGH our desires of comfort, and what we call lively frames, cannot be too importunate while they are regulated by a due submission to his will, yet they may be inordinate for want of such submission. Sinful principles may, and too often do, mix with and defile our best desires. I have often detected the two vile abominations self-will and self-righteousness insinuating themselves into this concern: like Satan, who works by them, they can occasionally assume the appearance of an angel of light. I have felt an impatience in my spirit, utterly unsuitable to my state as a sinner and a beggar, and to my profession of yielding myself and all my concerns to the Lord's disposal. He has mercifully convinced me that I labour under a complication of disorders, summed up in the word *sin*; he has graciously revealed himself to me as the infallible physician; and has enabled me, as such, to commit myself to him, and to expect my cure from his hand alone. Yet how often, instead of thankfully accepting his prescriptions, have I foolishly and presumptuously ventured to prescribe to him, and to point out how I would have him deal with me! How often have I thought something was necessary which he saw best to deny, and that I could have done better without those dispensations which his wisdom appointed to work for my good! He is God, and not man, or else he would have been weary of me, and left me to my own management long ago. How inconsistent! To acknowledge that I am blind, to entreat him to lead me, and yet to want to choose my own way, in the same breath! I have limited the Holy One of Israel, and not considered that he magnifies his wisdom and grace in working by contraries, and bringing good out of seeming evil.

On a Believer's Frames, [1:257]; 1:178

But of him are ye in Christ Jesus, who of God is made unto us wisdom,
and righteousness, and sanctification, and redemption.—1 Cor. 1:30.

AGAIN: self-righteousness has had a considerable hand in dictating many of my desires for an increase of comfort and spiritual strength. I have wanted some stock of my own. I have been wearied of being so perpetually beholden to him, necessitated to come to him always in the same strain, as a poor miserable sinner. I could have liked to have done something for myself in common, and to have depended upon him chiefly upon extraordinary occasions. I have found indeed, that I could do nothing without his assistance, nor anything even with it, but what I have reason to be ashamed of. If this had only humbled me and led me to rejoice in his all-sufficiency, it would have been well. But it has too often had a different effect, to make me sullen, angry, and discontented, as if it was not best and most desirable that he should have all the glory of his own work, and I should have nothing to boast of, but that in the Lord I have righteousness and strength. I am now learning to glory only in my infirmities, that the power of Christ may rest upon me; to be content to be nothing that he may be All in All. But I find this a hard lesson; and when I seem to have made some proficiency, a slight turn in my spirit throws me back, and I have to begin all again.

There can be no effect without a cause, no active cause without a proportionable effect. Now indwelling sin is an active cause; and therefore, while it remains in our nature, it will produce effects according to its strength. Why then should I be surprised, that, if the Lord suspends his influence for a moment, in that moment sin will discover itself?… Humbled I ought to be, to find I am totally depraved; but not discouraged, since Jesus is appointed to me of God, wisdom, righteousness, sanctification, and redemption; and since I find that, in the midst of all this darkness and deadness, he keeps alive the principle of grace which he has implanted in my heart.

On a Believer's Frames, [1:258]; 1:179

That ye may be blameless and harmless, the sons of God, without rebuke,
in the midst of a crooked and perverse nation, among whom ye shine
as lights in the world.—Phil. 2:15.

IT is not necessary, perhaps it is not lawful, wholly to renounce the society of the world. A mistake of this kind took place in the early ages of Christianity, and men (at first, perhaps, with a sincere desire of serving God without distraction) withdrew into deserts and uninhabited places, and wasted their lives at a distance from their fellow creatures. But unless we could flee from ourselves likewise, this would afford us no advantage; so long as we carry our own wicked hearts with us, we shall be exposed to temptation, go where we will. Besides, this would be thwarting the end of our vocation. Christians are to be the salt and the lights of the world, conspicuous as cities set upon a hill; they are commanded to let their light shine before men, that they, beholding their good works, may glorify their Father who is in heaven. This injudicious deviation from the paths of nature and providence, gave occasion at length to the vilest abominations; and men who withdrew from the world, under pretence of retirement, became the more wicked and abandoned as they lived more out of public view and observation.

Nor are we at liberty, much less are we enjoined, to renounce the duties of relative life, so as to become careless in the discharge of them. Allowances should, indeed, be made for the distresses of persons newly awakened, or under the power of temptation, which may for a time so much engross their thoughts as greatly to indispose them for their bounden duty. But, in general, the proper evidence of true Christians is, not merely that they can talk about divine things, but that, by the grace of God, they live and act agreeable to the rules of his word, in the state in which his providence has placed them, whether as masters or servants, husbands or wives, parents or children; bearing rule, or yielding obedience, as in his sight.

On Conformity to the World, [1:276]; 1:192

*And be not conformed to this world: but be ye transformed
by the renewing of your mind.*—Rom. 12:2.

DILIGENCE and fidelity in the management of temporal concernments, though observable in the practice of many worldly men, may be maintained without a sinful conformity to the world.

Neither are we required to refuse a moderate use of the comforts and conveniences of life, suitable to the station which God has appointed us in the world. The spirit of self-righteousness and will-worship works much in this way, and supposes that there is something excellent in long fastings, in abstaining from pleasant food, in wearing meaner clothes than is customary with those in the same rank of life, and in many other austerities and singularities not commanded by the word of God. And many persons, who are in the main sincere, are grievously burdened with scruples respecting the use of lawful things. It is true, there is need of a constant watch, lest what is lawful in itself become hurtful to us by its abuse. But these outward strictnesses may be carried to great lengths, without a spark of true grace, and even without the knowledge of the true God. The mortifications and austerities practiced by the Bramins in India (if the accounts we have of them be true) are vastly more severe than the most zealous effects of modern superstition in our country. There is a strictness which arises rather from ignorance than knowledge, is wholly conversant about externals, and gratifies the spirit of self as much in one way as it seems to retrench it in another. A man may almost starve his body to feed his pride: but to those who fear and serve the Lord, every creature of God is good, and nothing to be refused, if it be received with thanksgiving, for it is sanctified by the word of God and prayer.

Notwithstanding these limitations, the precept is very extensive and important. 'Be not conformed to the world.' As believers, we are strangers and pilgrims upon earth. Heaven is our country, and the Lord is our King. We are to be known and noticed as his subjects; and therefore it is his pleasure, that we do not speak the language, or adopt the customs, of the land in which we sojourn.

On Conformity to the World, [1:277]; 1:193

For where your treasure is, there your heart will be also.—Matt. 6:21.

WE must not conform to the spirit of the world. As members of society, we have a part to act in it, in common with others. But if our business is the same, our principles and ends are to be entirely different. Diligence in our respective callings is, as I have already observed, commendable, and our duty; but not with the same views which stimulate the activity of the men of the world. If they rise early, and take rest late, their endeavours spring from and terminate in self, to establish and increase their own importance, to add house to house, and field to field, that, like the builders of Babel, they may get themselves a name, or provide means for the gratification of their sinful passions. If they succeed, they sacrifice to their own net; if they are crossed in their designs, they are filled with anxiety and impatience; they either murmur or despond. But a Christian is to pursue his lawful calling with an eye to the providence of God, and with submission to his wisdom. Thus, so far as he acts in the exercise of faith, he cannot be disappointed. He casts his care upon his heavenly Father who has promised to take care of him. What he gives, he receives with thankfulness, and is careful as a faithful steward to improve it for the furtherance of the cause of God, and the good of mankind; and if he meets with losses and crosses, he is not disconcerted, knowing that all his concerns are under a Divine direction; that the Lord whom he serves, chooses for him better than he could choose for himself; and that his best treasure is safe, out of the reach of the various changes to which all things in the present state are liable.

On Conformity to the World, [1:278]; 1:194

What communion hath light with darkness?—2 Cor. 6:14.

WE must not conform to the maxims of the world. The world in various instances calls evil good, and good evil. But we are to have recourse to the law and to the testimony, and to judge of things by the unerring word of God, uninfluenced by the determination of the great, or the many. We are to obey God rather than man, though upon this account we may expect to be despised or reviled, to be made a gazing-stock or a laughing-stock to those who set his authority at defiance. We must bear our testimony to the truth as it is in Jesus, avow the cause of his despised people, and walk in the practice of universal obedience, patiently endure reproaches, and labour to overcome evil with good. Thus we shall show that we are not ashamed of him. And there is an hour coming when he will not be ashamed of us, who have followed him, and borne his cross in the midst of a perverse generation, but will own our worthless names before the assembled world.

We must not conform to the world in their amusements and diversions. We are to mix with the world so far as our necessary and providential connections engage us, so far as we have a reasonable expectation of doing or getting good and no further. 'What fellowship hath light with darkness, or what concord hath Christ with Belial?' What call can a believer have into those places and companies, where everything tends to promote a spirit of dissipation; where the fear of God has no place; where things are purposely disposed to inflame or indulge corrupt and sinful appetites and passions, and to banish all serious thoughts of God and ourselves? If it is our duty to redeem time, to walk with God, to do all things in the name of our Lord Jesus Christ, to follow the example which he set us when he was upon the earth, and to work out our salvation with fear and trembling; it must of course be our duty to avoid a conformity with the world in those vain and sensual diversions, which stand in as direct contradiction to a spiritual frame of mind as darkness to light.

On Conformity to the World, [1:279]; 1:195

Let us hold fast the profession of our faith without wavering;
(for he is faithful that promised;)—Heb. 10:23.

UNBELIEF is continually starting objections, magnifying and multiplying difficulties. But faith in the power and promises of God inspires a noble simplicity, and casts every care upon him, who is able and has engaged to support and provide. Thus, when Abraham, at the Lord's call, forsook his country and his father's house, the Apostle observes, 'he went out, not knowing whither he went'. It was enough that he knew *whom he followed:* the all-sufficient God was his guide, his shield, and his exceeding great reward. So, when exercised with long waiting for the accomplishment of a promise, he staggered not—he did not dispute or question—but simply depended upon God, who had spoken, and was able to perform. So likewise, when he received the hard command to offer up his son, of whom it was said, 'in Isaac shall thy seed be called', he simply obeyed, and depended upon the Lord to make good his own word: Hebrews 11:18-19. In this spirit David went forth to meet Goliath, and overcame him: and thus the three worthies were unawed by the threats of Nebuchadnezzar, and rather chose to be cast into a burning furnace than to sin against the Lord. And thus Elijah, in a time of famine, was preserved from anxiety and want, and supported by extraordinary methods; 1 Kings 17. In these times we do not expect miracles, in the strict sense of the word; but they who simply depend upon the Lord, will meet with such tokens of his interposition in a time of need, as will, to themselves at least, be a satisfying proof that he careth for them. How comfortable is it to us, as well as ornamental to our profession to be able to trust the Lord in the path of duty! To believe that he will supply our wants, direct our steps, plead our cause, and control our enemies! Thus he has promised, and it belongs to gospel simplicity to take his word against all discouragements.

On Simplicity and Godly Sincerity, [1:301]; 1:211

For our rejoicing is this, the testimony of our conscience, that in simplic-ity and godly sincerity, not with fleshly wisdom, but by the grace of God, we have had our conversation in the world.—2 Cor. 1:12.

I NEED not take time to prove, that the effect of simplicity will be sincerity. For they who love the Lord above all, who prefer the light of his countenance to thousands of gold and silver, who are enabled to trust him with all their concerns, and would rather be at his disposal than at their own, will have but little temptation to insincerity. The principles and motives upon which their conduct is formed, are the same in public as in private. Their behaviour will be all of a piece because they have but one *design.* They will speak the truth in love, observe a strict punctuality in their dealings, and do unto others as they would others should do unto them; because these things are essential to their great aim of glorifying and enjoying their Lord. A fear of dishonouring his name, and of grieving his Spirit, will teach them not only to avoid gross and known sins, but to abstain from all appearance of evil. Their conduct will therefore be consist-ent; and they will be enabled to appeal to all who know them, 'that in simplicity and godly sincerity, not in fleshly wisdom, but by the grace of God, they have had their conversation in the world'.

To a sincere Christian, that craft and cunning which passes for wisdom in the world, appears to be not only unlawful but unneces-sary. He has no need of the little reserves, evasions, and disguises, by which designing men endeavour (though often in vain) to conceal their proper characters, and to escape deserved contempt. He is what he seems to be, and therefore not afraid of being *found out.* He walks by the light of the wisdom that is from above, and leans upon the arm of Almighty Power; therefore he walks at liberty, trusting in the Lord, whom he serves with his spirit in the gospel of his Son.

On Simplicity and Godly Sincerity, [1:303]; 1:213

But now in Christ Jesus ye who sometimes were far off are made nigh by the blood of Christ.—Eph. 2:13.

COMMUNION presupposes union. By nature we are strangers, yea, enemies to God; but we are reconciled, brought nigh, and become his children, by faith in Christ Jesus. We can have no true knowledge of God, desire towards him, access unto him, or gracious communications from him, but in and through the Son of his love. He is the medium of this inestimable privilege: for he is the way, the only way, of intercourse between heaven and earth; the sinner's way to God, and God's way of mercy to the sinner. If any pretend to know God, and to have communion with him, otherwise than by the knowledge of Jesus Christ, whom he hath sent, and by faith in his name, it is a proof that they neither know God nor themselves. God, if considered abstracted from the revelation of himself in the person of Jesus, is a consuming fire; and if he should look upon us without respect to his covenant of mercy established in the Mediator, we could expect nothing from him but indignation and wrath. But when his Holy Spirit enables us to receive the record which he has given of his Son, we are delivered and secured from condemnation; we are accepted in the Beloved; we are united to him in whom all the fulness of the Godhead substantially dwells, and all the riches of Divine wisdom, power, and love, are treasured up. Thus in him, as the temple wherein the glory of God is manifested, and by him, as the representative and high priest of his people, and through him, as the living head of his mystical body the church, believers maintain communion with God. They have meat to eat which the world knows not of, honour which cometh of God only, joy which a stranger intermeddleth not with. They are, for the most part, poor and afflicted, frequently scorned and reproached, accounted hypocrites or visionaries, knaves or fools; but this one thing makes amends for all, 'They have fellowship with the Father, and with his Son Jesus Christ.'

On Communion with God, [1:306]; 1:215

For the creature was made subject to vanity, not willingly, but by reason
of him who hath subjected the same in hope.—Rom. 8:20.

GOD, the righteous judge, subjected the creature to vanity, as the just consequence and desert of man's disobedience. But he has subjected it *in hope*; with a reserve in favour of his own people, by which, though they are liable to trouble, they are secured from the penal desert of sin, and the vanity of the creature is by his wisdom over-ruled to wise and gracious purposes. The earth, and all in it, was made for the sake of man; for his sin it was first cursed, and afterwards destroyed by water; and sin at last shall set it on fire. But God, who is rich in mercy, appointed a people to himself out of the fallen race; for their sakes, and as a theatre whereon to display the wonders of his providence and grace, it was renewed after the flood, and still continues; but not in its original state: there are marks of the evil of sin, and of God's displeasure against it, wherever we turn our eyes. This truth is witnessed to by everything without us, and within us. But there shall be a deliverance to those who fear him; and, by his word and Spirit, he teaches them to receive instruction and benefit even from this root of bitterness. Even now they are the sons of God; but it doth not yet appear what they will be when he shall appear, and be admired in all them that believe. Then they shall be manifested, and then the creature also shall be delivered from the bondage of corruption.

How blind, then, are they who expect happiness from the creature, which is itself subject to vanity, and who are meanly content with the present state of things! It is because they are estranged from God, have no sense of his excellency, no regard for his glory, no knowledge of their own proper good! ... Fire and hail, wind and storm, fulfil the word of God, though we poor mortals dare to disobey it. But if the secret voice of the whole creation desires the consummation of all things, surely they who have the light of God's word and Spirit will look forward, and long for that glorious day.

Thoughts on Romans 8:19-21, [1:338]; 1:239

I know that in me (that is, in my flesh,) dwelleth no good thing.
—Rom. 7:18.

WE cannot at present conceive how much we owe to the guardian care of Divine Providence, that any of us are preserved in peace and safety for a single day in such a world as this. Live where we will, we have those near us, who, both by nature, and by the power which Satan has over them, are capable of the most atrocious crimes. But he whom they know not, restrains them, so that they cannot do the things that they would. When he suspends the restraint, they act immediately; then we hear of murders, rapes, and outrages. But did not the Lord reign with a strong hand, such evils would be perpetrated every hour, and no one would be safe in the house or in the field. His ordinance of civil government is one great means of preserving the peace of society; but this is in many cases inadequate. The heart of man, when fully bent upon evil, will not be intimidated or stopped by gibbets and racks.

How wonderful is the love of God in giving his Son to die for such wretches! And how strong and absolute is the necessity of a new birth, if we would be happy! ... The due consideration of this subject is likewise needful to preserve believers in an humble, thankful, watchful frame of spirit. Such we once were, and such, with respect to the natural principle remaining in us, which the Apostle calls the flesh, or the old man, we still are. The propensities of the fallen nature are not eradicated in the children of God, though by grace they are made partakers of a new principle, which enables them, in the Lord's strength, to resist and mortify the body of sin, so that it cannot reign in them. Yet they are liable to sad surprisals; and the histories of Aaron, David, Solomon, and Peter, are left on record, to teach us what evil is latent in the hearts of the best men, and what they are capable of doing if left but a little to themselves. 'Lord, what is man!'

On Man in his Fallen Estate, [1:369]; 1:262

And of his fulness have all we received, and grace for grace.—John 1:16.

IF I was to describe [a believer] from the Scripture character, I should say, he is one whose heart is athirst for God, for his glory, his image, his presence; his affections are fixed upon an unseen Saviour; his treasures, and consequently his thoughts, are on high, beyond the bounds of sense. Having experienced much forgiveness, he is full of bowels of mercy to all around; and having been often deceived by his own heart, he dares trust it no more, but lives by faith in the Son of God, for wisdom, righteousness, and sanctification, and derives from him grace for grace; sensible that without him he has not sufficiency even to think a good thought.

But was I to describe him from experience, especially at some times, how different would the picture be? Though he knows that communion with God is his highest privilege, he too seldom finds it so... He takes up the Bible, conscious that it is the fountain of life and true comfort; yet perhaps, while he is making the reflection, he feels a secret distaste, which prompts him to lay it down, and give his preference to a newspaper. He needs not to be told of the vanity and uncertainty of all beneath the sun; and yet is almost as much elated or cast down by a trifle, as those who have their portion in this world. He believes that all things shall work together for his good, and that the most high God appoints, adjusts, and overrules all his concerns; yet he feels the risings of fear, anxiety, and displeasure, as though the contrary was true.

How can these things be, or why are they permitted? ... By these exercises he teaches us more truly to know and feel the utter depravity and corruption of our whole nature, that we are indeed defiled in every part. His method of salvation is likewise hereby exceedingly endeared to us: we see that it is and must be of grace, wholly of grace; and that the Lord Jesus Christ, and his perfect righteousness, is and must be our all in all.

Cardiphonia: Letters to a Nobleman, [1:433]; 1:312

For he knoweth our frame; he remembereth that we are dust.
—Psa. 103:14.

I DAILY groan under a desultory, ungovernable imagination, and a palpable darkness of understanding, which greatly impede me in my attempts to contemplate the truths of God… Now it costs us much pains to acquire a *pittance* of solid and useful knowledge; and the ideas we have collected are far from being at the disposal of judgment, and, like men in a crowd, are perpetually clashing and interfering with each other. But it will not be so when we are completely freed from the effects of sin. Confusion and darkness will not follow us into the world where light and order reign. Then, and not till then, our knowledge will be perfect, and our possession of it uninterrupted and secure.

Since the radical powers of the soul are thus enfeebled and disordered, it is not to be wondered at that the best of men, and under their highest attainments, have found cause to make acknowledgement of the Apostle, 'When I would do good, evil is present with me.' But, blessed be God, though we must feel hourly cause for shame and humiliation for what we are in ourselves, we have cause to rejoice continually in Christ Jesus, who, as he is revealed unto us under the various names, characters, relations, and offices, which he bears in the Scripture, holds out to our faith a balm for every wound, a cordial for every discouragement, and a sufficient answer to every objection which sin or Satan can suggest against our peace. If we are guilty, he is our Righteousness; if we are sick, he is our infallible Physician; if we are weak, helpless and defenceless, he is the compassionate and faithful Shepherd who has taken charge of us, and will not suffer anything to disappoint our hopes, or to separate us from his love. He knows our frame, he remembers that we are but dust, and has engaged to guide us by his counsel, support us by his power, and at length to receive us to his glory, that we may be with him forever.

Cardiphonia: Letters to a Nobleman, [1:438]; 1:315

For the good that I would I do not.—Rom. 7:19.

HE [the believer] would willingly enjoy God in prayer. He knows that prayer is his duty; but, in his judgment, he considers it likewise as his greatest honour and privilege... By prayer, he can say, You have liberty to cast all your cares upon him that careth for you. By one hour's intimate access to the throne of grace, where the Lord causes his glory to pass before the soul that seeks him, you may acquire more true spiritual knowledge and comfort, than by a day or a week's converse with the best of men... But, alas! How seldom can he do as he would! How often does he find this privilege a mere task, which he would be glad of a just excuse to omit? ... The like may be said of reading the Scripture. He believes it to be the word of God he admires the wisdom and grace of the doctrines, the beauty of the precepts... and therefore, with David, he accounts it preferable to thousands of gold and silver, and sweeter than honey or the honeycomb. Yet, while he thus thinks of it, and desires that it may dwell in him richly, and be his meditation night and day, he cannot do as he would. It will require some resolution to persist in reading a portion of it every day; and even then his heart is often less engaged than when reading a pamphlet.

He would willingly have abiding, admiring thoughts of the person and love of the Lord Jesus Christ. Glad he is, indeed, of those occasions which recall the Saviour to his mind; and with this view, notwithstanding all discouragements, he perseveres in attempting to pray and read, and waits upon the ordinances. Yet he cannot do as he would... Ah! what trifles are capable of shutting *him* out of our thoughts, of whom we say, he is the Beloved of our souls... But though we aim at this good, evil is present with us; we find we are renewed but in part, and have still cause to plead the Lord's promise, To take away the heart of stone and give us a heart of flesh.

Cardiphonia: Letters to a Nobleman, [1:440]; 1:317

> *But I see another law in my members,*
> *warring against the law of my mind.*—Rom. 7:23.

HE [the believer] would willingly acquiesce in all the dispensations of Divine Providence. He believes that all events are under
the direction of infinite wisdom and goodness, and shall surely issue
in the glory of God and the good of those who fear him. He doubts
not but the hairs of his head are all numbered; that blessings of every
kind which he possesses, were bestowed upon him, and are preserved
to him, by the bounty and special favour of the Lord whom he
serves;—that afflictions spring not out of the ground, but are fruits
and tokens of Divine love, no less than his comforts; that there is a
need-be, whenever for a season he is in heaviness. Of these principles
he can no more doubt than of what he sees with his eyes; and there
are seasons when he thinks they will prove sufficient to reconcile him
to the sharpest trials. But often, when he aims to apply them in an
hour of *present* distress, he cannot do what he would. He feels a law in
his members warring against the law in his mind; so that, in defiance
of the clearest convictions, seeing as though he perceived not, he is
ready to complain, murmur, and despond. Alas! how vain is man in
his best estate! how much weakness and inconsistency even in those
whose hearts are right with the Lord! and what reason have we to
confess that we are unworthy, unprofitable servants!

But, blessed be God, we are not under the law, but under grace.
And even these distressing effects of the remnants of indwelling sin
are overruled for good. By these experiences the believer is weaned
more from self, and taught more highly to prize and more absolutely
to rely on him, who is appointed to us of God, Wisdom, Righteousness, Sanctification, and Redemption. The more vile we are in our
own eyes, the more precious he will be to us; and a deep repeated
sense of the evil of our hearts is necessary to preclude all boasting,
and to make us willing to give the whole glory of our salvation where
it is due.

Cardiphonia: Letters to a Nobleman, [1:442]; 1:319

I shall not die, but live, and declare the works of the LORD.—Psa. 118:17.

MY heart is like a highway, like a city without walls or gates: nothing so false, so frivolous, so absurd, so impossible, or so horrid, but it can obtain access, and that at any time, or in any place; neither the study, the pulpit, nor even the Lord's table, exempt me from their intrusion.

In defiance of my best judgment, and best wishes, I find something within me which cherishes and cleaves to these evils, from which I ought to start and flee, as I should if a toad or a serpent was put in my food, or in my bed. Ah! how vile must the heart (at least my heart) be, that can hold a parley with such abominations, when I so well know their nature and their tendency!

I would not be influenced by a principle of self on any occasion; yet this evil I often do… The pride of others often offends me, and makes me studious to hide my own; because their good opinion of me depends much on their not perceiving it.

That the Judge of all the earth will do right, is to me as evident and necessary as two and two make four. I believe that he has a sovereign right to do what he will with his own, and that this sovereignty is but another name for the unlimited exercise of wisdom and goodness. But my reasonings are often such, as if I had never heard of these principles, or had formally renounced them.

I am invited to take the water of life *freely*, yet often discouraged, because I have nothing wherewith to pay for it. If I am at times favoured with some liberty from the above-mentioned evils, it rather gives me a more favourable opinion of myself, than increases my admiration of the Lord's goodness to so unworthy a creature.

This … is only a faint sketch of my heart; … But though my disease is grievous, it is not desperate; I have a gracious and infallible Physician. I shall not die, but live, and declare the works of the Lord.

Cardiphonia: Letters to a Nobleman, [1:444]; 1:320

We shall be like him; for we shall see him as he is.—1 John 3:2.

IF the evils we feel were not capable of being overruled for good, he would not permit them to remain in us.

As to the remedy, neither our state nor his honour are affected by the workings of indwelling sin, in the hearts of those whom he has taught to wrestle, strive, and mourn on account of what they feel. Though sin wars, it shall not reign; and though it breaks our peace, it cannot separate from his love. Nor is it inconsistent with his holiness and perfection, to manifest his favour to such poor defiled creatures, or to admit them to communion with himself; for they are not considered as in themselves, but as one with Jesus, to whom they have fled for refuge, and by whom they live a life of faith. They are accepted in the Beloved, they have an Advocate with the Father, who once made an atonement for their sins, and ever lives to make intercession for their persons. Though they cannot fulfil the law, he has fulfilled it for them; though the obedience of the members is defiled and imperfect, the obedience of the Head is spotless and complete; and though there is much evil in them, there is something good, the fruit of his own gracious Spirit. They act from a principle of love, they aim at no less than his glory, and their habitual desires are supremely fixed upon himself. There is a difference in kind between the feeblest efforts of faith in a real believer, while he is covered with shame at the thoughts of his miscarriages, and the highest and most specious attainments of those who are wise in their own eyes, and prudent in their own sight. Nor shall this conflict remain long, or the enemy finally prevail over them. They are supported by Almighty power, and led on to certain victory. They shall not always be as they are now; yet a little while, and they shall be freed from this vile body, which, like the leprous house, is incurably contaminated, and must be entirely taken down. Then they shall see Jesus as he is, and be like him and with him forever.

Cardiphonia: Letters to a Nobleman, [1:448]; 1:323

Where is boasting then? It is excluded.—Rom. 3:27.

THE gracious purposes to which the Lord makes the sense and feeling of our depravity subservient, are manifold. Hereby his own power, wisdom, faithfulness, and love, are more signally displayed. His power, in maintaining his own work in the midst of such opposition, like a spark burning in the water, or a bush unconsumed in the flames. His wisdom, in defeating and controlling all the devices which Satan, from his knowledge of the evil of our nature, is encouraged to practice against us... The unchangeableness of the Lord's love, and the riches of his mercy, are likewise more illustrated by the multiplied pardons he bestows upon his people, than if they needed no forgiveness at all.

Hereby the Lord Jesus Christ is more endeared to the soul; all boasting is effectually excluded, and the glory of a full and free salvation is ascribed to him alone... But when, after a long experience of their own deceitful hearts, after repeated proofs of their weakness, wilfulness, ingratitude, and insensibility, they find that none of these things can separate them from the love of God in Christ, Jesus becomes more and more precious to their souls. They love much, because much has been forgiven them. They dare not, they will not ascribe anything to themselves, but are glad to acknowledge, that they must have perished (if possible) a thousand times over, if Jesus had not been their Saviour, their Shepherd, and their Shield. When they were wandering he brought them back, when fallen he raised them, when wounded he healed them, when fainting he revived them. By him, out of weakness they have been made strong; he has taught their hands to war, and covered their heads in the day of battle. In a word, some of the clearest proofs they have had of his excellence, have been occasioned by the mortifying proofs they have had of their own vileness. They would not have known so much of him, if they had not known so much of themselves.

Cardiphonia: Letters to a Nobleman, [1:449]; 1:324

The sacrifices of God are a broken spirit: a broken and a contrite heart,
O God, thou wilt not despise.—Psa. 51:17.

A BROKEN and contrite spirit is pleasing to the Lord, he has promised to dwell with those who have it: and experience shows, that the exercise of all our graces is in proportion to the humbling sense we have of the depravity of our nature. But that we are so totally depraved, is a truth which no one ever truly learned by being only told it. Indeed, if we could receive, and habitually maintain, a right judgment of ourselves, by what is plainly declared in Scripture, it would probably save us many a mournful hour; but experience is the Lord's school, and they who are taught by him usually learn that they have no wisdom, by the mistakes they make; and that they have no strength, by the slips and falls they meet with... Thus by degrees they are weaned from leaning to any supposed wisdom, power, or goodness in themselves; they feel the truth of our Lord's words, 'without me ye can do nothing'; and the necessity of crying with David, 'O lead me and guide me for thy name's sake.' ... [Says God], 'The knowledge of my free and full forgiveness of thy innumerable back-slidings and transgressions, shall make thee ashamed, and silence the unruly working of thine heart; thou shalt open thy mouth in praise; but thou shalt no more boast in thyself, or censure others, or repine at my dispensations.' ... Whoever is truly humbled will not be easily angry, will not be positive and rash, will be compassionate and tender to the infirmities of his fellow sinners, knowing, that, if there be a difference, it is grace that has made it, and that he has the seeds of every evil in his own heart; and, under all trials and afflictions, he will look to the hand of the Lord, and lay his mouth in the dust, acknowledging that he suffers much less than his iniquities have deserved. These are some of the advantages and good fruits which the Lord enables us to obtain from that bitter root, indwelling sin.

Cardiphonia: Letters to a Nobleman, [1:451]; 1:325

The LORD *is my portion, saith my soul.*—Lam. 3:24.

I DO not plead for an absolute indifference to temporal blessings: he gives us all things richly to enjoy; and a capacity of relishing them is his gift likewise; but then the consideration of his love in bestowing should exceedingly enhance the value, and a regard to his will should regulate their use. Nor can they all supply the want of *that* which we can only receive immediately from himself. This principle likewise moderates that inordinate fear and sorrow to which we are liable upon the prospect or the occurrence of great trials, for which there is a sure support and resource provided in the all-sufficiency of infinite goodness and grace. What a privilege is this, to possess God *in all things* while we have them, and all things in God when they are taken from us.

An acquiescence in the Lord's will, founded in a persuasion of his wisdom, holiness, sovereignty, and goodness.—This is one of the greatest privileges and brightest ornaments of our profession. So far as we attain to this, we are secure from disappointment. Our own limited views and short-sighted purposes and desires, may be, and will be, often overruled; but then our main and leading desire, that the will of the Lord may be done, must be accomplished. How highly does it become us, both as creatures and as sinners, to submit to the appointments of our Maker! And how necessary is it to our peace! This great attainment is too often unthought of, and overlooked: we are prone to fix our attention upon the second causes and immediate instruments of events; forgetting that whatever befalls us is according to his purpose, and therefore must be right and seasonable in itself, and shall in the issue be productive of good. From hence arise impatience, resentment, and secret repinings, which are not only sinful, but tormenting: whereas, if all things are in his hand; if the very hairs of our head are numbered; if every event, great and small, is under the direction of his providence and purpose; and if he has a wise, holy, and gracious end in view, to which everything that happens is subordinate and subservient; then we have nothing to do, but with patience and humility to follow as he leads, and cheerfully to expect a happy issue.

Cardiphonia: Letters to a Nobleman, [1:455]; 1:328

Most gladly therefore will I rather glory in my infirmities, that the power
of Christ may rest upon me.—2 Cor. 12:9.

THE Lord can design nothing short of his own glory, nor should we. The constraining love of Christ has a direct and marvellous tendency, in proportion to the measure of faith, to mortify the corrupt principle *self*, which for a season is the grand spring of our conduct, and by which we are too much biased after we know the Lord. But as grace prevails, self is renounced. We feel that we are not our own, that we are bought with a price; and that it is our duty, our honour, and our happiness, to be the servants of God and of the Lord Jesus Christ. To devote soul and body, every talent, power, and faculty, to the service of his cause and will; to let our light shine (in our several situations) to the praise of his grace; to place our highest joy in the contemplation of his adorable perfections; to rejoice even in tribulations and distresses, in reproaches and infirmities, if thereby the power of Christ may rest upon us, and be magnified in us; to be content, yea glad, to be nothing, that he may be all in all; to obey him, in opposition to the threats or solicitations of men; to trust him, though all outward appearances seem against us; to rejoice in him, though we should (as will sooner or later be the case) have nothing else to rejoice in; to live above the world, and to have our conversation in heaven; to be like the angels, finding our own pleasure in performing his:—This ... is the prize, the mark of our high calling, to which we are encouraged with a holy ambition continually to aspire. It is true, we shall still fall short; we shall find that, when we would do good, evil will be present with us. But the attempt is glorious, and shall not be wholly in vain. He that gives us thus to will, will enable us to perform with growing success, and teach us to profit even by our mistakes and imperfections.

Cardiphonia: Letters to a Nobleman, [1:456]; 1:329

He that is slow to anger is better than the mighty; and he that ruleth his spirit than he that taketh a city.—Prov. 16:32.

O BLESSED man! that thus fears the Lord, that delights in his word, and derives his principles, motives, maxims, and consolations, from that unfailing source of light and strength. He shall be like a tree planted by the rivers of water, whose leaf is always green, and fruit abundant. The wisdom that is above shall direct his plans, inspire his counsels; and the power of God shall guard him on every side and prepare his way through every difficulty; he shall see mountains sink into plains, and streams spring up in the dry wilderness... The conduct of such a one, though in a narrow and retired sphere of life, is of more real excellence and importance, than the most splendid actions of kings and conquerors, which fill the annals of history, Prov. 16:32. And if the God whom he serves is pleased to place him in a more public light, his labours and cares will be amply compensated, by the superior opportunities afforded him of manifesting the power and reality of true religion, and promoting the good of mankind.

I hope I *may* say, that I *desire* to be thus entirely given up to the Lord; I am sure I *must* say, that what I have written is far from being my actual experience. Alas! I might be condemned out of my own mouth, were the Lord strict to mark what is amiss. But, O the comfort! we are not under the law, but under grace. The gospel is a dispensation for sinners, and we have an Advocate with the Father. *There* is the unshaken ground of hope. A reconciled Father, a prevailing Advocate, a powerful Shepherd, a compassionate Friend, a Saviour who is able and willing to save to the uttermost. He knows our frame; he remembers that we are but dust; and has opened for us a new and blood-besprinkled way of access to the throne of grace, that we may obtain mercy, and find grace to help in every time of need.

Cardiphonia: Letters to a Nobleman, [1:457]; 1:330

He hath done all things well.—Mark 7:37.

FOR five or six weeks past I have been a good deal indisposed. The ground of my complaint was a cold, attended with a slight fever, and for some time with a cough ... to this succeeded a deafness, so great as to cut me off from conversation... But the Lord has mercifully removed the fever and cough, opened my ears, and I am now nearly as well as usual. I had cause to be thankful, especially for two things, under this dispensation. First, that I was enabled, though sometimes with a little difficulty, to go on with my public work... My other great mercy was, that the Lord was pleased to preserve me in a peaceful, resigned frame... This was the effect of his goodness: for though I know enough of his sovereignty, wisdom, and faithfulness, of his right to do what he pleases, and the certainty that he does all things well, to furnish me with arguments enough to prove that submission to his will is our absolute duty; yet I am sensible, that when the trial actually comes, notwithstanding all the advice I may have offered to others, I should myself toss like a wild bull in a net; rebel and repine; forget that I am a sinner, and that he is sovereign: this, I say, would always and invariably be the case, unless he was graciously pleased to fulfil his word, that strength shall be according to the day. I hope my deafness has been instructive to me. The exercise of our senses is so easily and constantly performed, that it seems a thing of course; but I was then reminded how precarious the tenure is by which we hold those blessings which seem most our own, and which are most immediately necessary to the comfortable enjoyment of life... This alone is the proper ground of glory and joy, If we know the Lord... Then, whatever changes may affect our temporal concernments, our best interests and hopes are secured beyond the reach of change; and whatever we may lose or suffer during this little span of time, will be abundantly compensated in that glorious state of eternity which is just at hand.

Cardiphonia: Letters to a Nobleman, [1:459]; 1:331

*To the praise of the glory of his grace, wherein he hath made us
accepted in the beloved.*—Eph. 1:6.

WHEN we are justified by faith, and accepted in the Beloved,
we become heirs of everlasting life; but we cannot know the
full value of our privileges until we enter upon the state of glory. For
this, most who are converted have to wait some time after they are
partakers of grace. Though the Lord loves them, hates sin, and teaches
them to hate it, he appoints them to remain a while in a sinful world,
and to groan under the burden of a depraved nature. He could put
them in immediate possession of the heaven for which he has given
them a meetness, but he does not. He has a service for them here; an
honour which is worth all they can suffer, and for which eternity will
not afford an opportunity, namely, to be instruments of promoting
his designs, and manifesting his grace in the world. Strictly speaking,
this is the whole of our business here, the only reason why life is
prolonged, or for which it is truly desirable, that we may fill up our
connections and situations, improve our comforts and our crosses, in
such a manner as that God may be glorified in us and by us. As he is
a bountiful Master and a kind Father, he is pleased to afford a variety
of temporal blessings, which sweeten our service, and as coming
from his hand are very valuable, but are by no means worth living
for, considered in themselves, as they can neither satisfy our desires,
preserve us from trouble, or support us under it. That light of God's
countenance, which can pervade the walls and dissipate the gloom of
a dungeon, is unspeakably preferable to all that can be enjoyed in a
palace without it. The true end of life is, to live not to ourselves, but
to him who died for us; and while we devote ourselves to his service
upon earth, to rejoice in the prospect of being happy with him for
ever in heaven.

Cardiphonia: Letters to a Nobleman, [1:465]; 1:336

My counsel shall stand, and I will do all my pleasure.—Isa. 46:10.

THE government is upon his shoulders; and though he is concealed by a veil of second causes from common eyes, so that they can perceive only the means, instruments, and contingencies by which he works, and therefore think he does nothing; yet, in reality, he does *all*, according to his own counsel and pleasure, in the armies of heaven, and among the inhabitants of the earth.

If we consider the heavens, the work of his fingers, the moon and the stars which he has ordained; if we call in the assistance of astronomers and glasses to help us in forming a conception of the number, distances, magnitudes, and motions of the heavenly bodies; the more we search, the more we shall be confirmed that these are but a portion of his ways. But he calls them all by their names, upholds them by his power, and without his continual energy they would rush into confusion, or sink into nothing.—If we speak of intelligences, he is the life, the joy, the sun of all that are capable of happiness. Whatever may be signified by the thrones, principalities, and powers in the world of light, they are all dependent upon his power, and obedient to his command: it is equally true of angels as of men, that without him they can do nothing. The powers of darkness are likewise under his subjection and control. Though but little is said of them in Scripture, we read enough to assure us that their number must be immensely great, and that their strength, subtlety, and malice are such as we may tremble to think of them as our enemies and probably should, but for our strange insensibility to whatever does not fall under the cognizance of our outward senses. But he holds them all in a chain, so that they can do or attempt nothing but by his permission; and whatever he permits them to do (though they mean nothing less) has its appointed subserviency in accomplishing his designs.

Cardiphonia: Letters to a Nobleman, [1:473]; 1:342

In him we live, and move, and have our being.—Acts 17:28.

BEFORE this blessed and only Potentate, all the nations of the earth are but as the dust upon the balance, and the small drop of a bucket, and might be thought (if compared with the immensity of his works) scarcely worthy of his notice: yet here he presides, pervades, provides, protects, and rules. In him his creatures live, move, and have their being: from him is their food and preservation. The eyes of all are upon him: what he gives they gather, and can gather no more; and at his word they sink into the dust. There is not a worm that crawls upon the ground, or a flower that grows in the pathless wilderness, or a shell upon the sea-shore, but bears the impress of his wisdom, power, and goodness. With respect to men, he reigns with uncontrolled dominion over every kingdom, family, and individual. Here we may be astonished at his wisdom in employing free agents, the greater part of whom are his enemies, to accomplish his purposes: but, however reluctant, they all serve him. His patience likewise is wonderful. Multitudes, yes nearly our whole species, spend the life and strength which he affords them, and abuse all the bounties he heaps upon them, in the ways of sin. His commands are disregarded, his name blasphemed, his mercy disdained, his power defied—yet still he spares. It is an eminent part of his government, to restrain the depravity of human nature, and in various ways to check its effects, which, if left to itself, without his providential control, would presently make earth the very image of hell: for the vilest men are not suffered to perpetrate a thousandth part of the evil which their hearts would prompt them to. The earth, though lying in the wicked one, is filled with the goodness of the Lord.

Cardiphonia: Letters to a Nobleman, [1:474]; 1:343

For I the LORD thy God will hold thy right hand, saying unto thee,
Fear not, I will help thee.—Isa. 41:13.

ALL the abilities, powers, and instincts, that are found amongst creatures, are emanations from his fulness. All changes, successes, disappointments—all that is memorable in the annals of history, all the risings and falls of empires, all the turns in human life—take place according to his plan. In vain men contrive and combine to accomplish their own counsels, unless they are parts of his counsel likewise: the efforts of their utmost strength and wisdom are crossed and reversed by the feeblest and most unthought-of circumstances. But when he has a work to accomplish, and his time is come, however inadequate and weak the means he employs may seem to a carnal eye, the success is infallibly secured: for all things serve him, and are in his hands as clay in the hands of the potter. Great and marvellous are thy works, Lord God Almighty! Just and true are thy ways, thou King of saints!

This is the God whom we adore. This is he who invites us to lean upon his almighty arm, and promises to guide us with his unerring eye. He says to you … and even to me, 'Fear not, I am with thee; be not dismayed, I am thy God; I will strengthen thee, yea I will help thee, yea I will uphold thee, with the right hand of my righteousness.' Therefore, while in the path of duty, and following his call, we may cheerfully pass on, regardless of apparent difficulties; for the Lord, whose we are, and who has taught us to make his glory our highest end, will go before us, and at his word crooked things become straight, light shines out of darkness, and mountains sink into plains. Faith may and must be exercised; experience must and will confirm what his word declares, that the heart is deceitful, and that man in his best estate is vanity: but his promises to them that fear him shall be confirmed likewise, and they shall find him, in all situations, a sun, a shield, and an exceeding great reward.

Cardiphonia: Letters to a Nobleman, [1:476]; 1:344

For we have not followed cunningly devised fables.—2 Pet. 1:16.

THOUGH the grand evidence of those truths upon which our hopes are built arises from the authority of God speaking them in his word, and revealing them by his Spirit to the awakened heart (for, till the heart is awakened, it is incapable of receiving this evidence); yet some of these truths are so mysterious, so utterly repugnant to the judgment of depraved nature, that, through the remaining influence of unbelief and vain reasoning, the temptations of Satan, and the subtle arguments with which some men, reputed wise, attack the foundations of our faith, the minds even of believers are sometimes capable of being shaken. I know no better corroborating evidence for the relief of the mind under such assaults than the testimony of dying persons... Permit me ... to relate, upon this occasion, some things which exceedingly struck me in the conversation I had with a young woman, whom I visited in her last illness, about two years ago. She was a sober, prudent person, of plain sense, could read her Bible, but had read little beside. Her knowledge of the world was nearly confined to the parish; for I suppose she was seldom, if ever, twelve miles from home in her life. She had known the gospel about seven years before the Lord visited her with a lingering consumption, which at length removed her to a better world. A few days before her death, I had been praying by her bed-side, and in my prayer I thanked the Lord that he gave her now to see that she had not followed cunningly devised fables. When I finished, she repeated that word. 'No', she said, 'not cunningly devised fables: these are realities indeed; I feel their truth; I feel their comfort. O tell my friends, tell my acquaintance, tell inquiring souls, tell poor sinners, tell all the daughters of Jerusalem ... what Jesus has done for my soul. Tell them, that now, in the time of need, I find him my Beloved and my Friend, and as such I commend him to them.'

Cardiphonia: Letters to a Nobleman, [1:479]; 1:347

Being filled with the fruits of righteousness, which are by Jesus Christ,
unto the glory and praise of God.—Phil. 1:11.

WHAT a mercy it is to be separated in spirit, conversation, and interest, from the world that knows not God! Where all are alike by nature, grace makes a happy and unspeakable difference. Believers were once under the same influence of that spirit who still worketh in the children of disobedience; pursuing different paths, but all equally remote from truth and peace... These two general heads, of mischief and vanity, include all the schemes, aims, and achievements of which man is capable, till God is pleased to visit the heart with his grace. The busy part of mankind are employed in multiplying evils and miseries; the more retired, speculative and curious, are amusing themselves with what will hereafter appear as unsubstantial, unstable, and useless, as a cobweb. Death will soon sweep away all that the philosophers, the virtuosi, the mathematicians, the antiquarians, and other learned triflers, are now weaving with so much self-applauded address. Nor will the fine-spun dresses, in which the moralist and the self-righteous clothe themselves, be of more advantage to them, either for ornament or defence, than the produce of a spider. But it is given to a few to know their present state and future destination. These build upon the immovable Rock of Ages for eternity: these are trees springing from a living root, and bear the fruits of righteousness, which are by Jesus Christ, to the glory and praise of God... O for a thousand tongues, to proclaim in the ears of the thoughtless mortals that important aphorism of our Lord, 'One thing is needful!' Yet a thousand tongues would be, and are, employed in vain, unless so far as the Lord is pleased to send the watchman's warning, by the power and agency of his own Spirit... It is of grace that any are saved; and in the distribution of that grace, he does what he will with his own, a right which most are ready enough to claim in their own concerns, though they are so unwilling to allow it to the Lord of all.

Cardiphonia: Letters to a Nobleman, [1:483]; 1:350

He that believeth on the Son of God hath the witness in himself: he that
believeth not God hath made him a liar; because he believeth not
the record that God gave of his Son.—1 John 5:10.

WHAT a comfort, what an honour is this, that worms have liberty to look up to God! And that he, the high and holy One, who inhabiteth eternity, is pleased to look down upon us, to maintain our peace, to supply our wants, to guide us with his eye, and to inspire us with wisdom and grace suitable to our occasions! They who profess to know something of this intercourse, and to depend upon it, are, by the world, accounted enthusiasts, who know not what they mean; or perhaps hypocrites, who pretend to what they have not, in order to cover some base designs. But we have reason to bear their reproaches with patience… Well then may the believer say, Let them laugh, let them rage; let them, if they please point at me for a fool as I walk the streets: if I do but take up the Bible, or run over in my mind the inventory of the blessings with which the Lord has enriched me, I have sufficient amends. Jesus is mine: in him I have wisdom, righteousness, sanctification … and redemption, an interest in all the promises and in all the perfections of God: he will guide me by his counsel, support me by his power, comfort me with his presence, while I am here; and afterwards, when flesh and heart fail, he will receive me to his glory.

If all the blind men in the kingdom should endeavour to bear me down, that the sun is not bright, or that the rainbow has no colours, I would still believe my own eyes. I have seen them both: they have not. I cannot prove to their satisfaction what I assert, because they are destitute of sight, the necessary medium; yet their exceptions produce no uncertainty in my mind: they would not, they could not hesitate a moment, if they were not blind. Just so, they who have been taught of God, who have tasted that the Lord is gracious, have an experimental perception of the truth, which renders them proof against all the sophistry of infidels.

Cardiphonia: Letters to a Nobleman, [1:487]; 1:353

Know ye that the LORD he is God: it is he that hath made us, and not we ourselves; we are his people, and the sheep of his pasture.—Psa. 100:3.

HOW astonishing the thought,—that the Maker of heaven and earth, the Holy One of Israel, before whose presence the earth shook, the heavens dropped, when he displayed a faint emblem of his majesty upon Sinai, should afterwards appear in the form of a servant, and hang upon a cross, the sport and scorn of wicked men! I cannot wonder that to the wise men of the world this appears absurd, unreasonable, and impossible; yet to right reason, to reason enlightened and sanctified, however amazing the proposition be, yet it appears true and necessary, upon a supposition that a holy God is pleased to pardon sinners in a way suited to display the awful glories of his justice. The same arguments which prove the blood of bulls and goats insufficient to take away sin, will conclude against the utmost doings or sufferings of men or angels. The Redeemer of sinners must be mighty; he must have a personal dignity, to stamp such a value upon his undertakings, as that thereby God may appear just, as well as merciful, in justifying the ungodly for his sake; and he must be all-sufficient to bless, and almighty to protect, those who come to him for safety and life.

Such a one is our Shepherd. This is he of whom we, through grace, are enabled to say, we are *his* people, and the sheep of *his* pasture. We are his by every tie and right: he made us, he redeemed us, he reclaimed us from the hand of our enemies; and we are his by our own voluntary surrender of ourselves; for though we once slighted, despised, and opposed him, he made us willing in the day of his power: he knocked at the door of our hearts; but we (at least I) barred and fastened it against him as much and as long as possible: but when he revealed his love, we could stand out no longer.

Cardiphonia: Letters to a Nobleman, [1:494]; 1:358

The LORD is longsuffering, and of great mercy.—Num. 14:18.

HOW wonderful is the patience of God towards sinful men! In him they live, and move, and have their being; and if he were to withdraw his support for a single moment, they must perish. He maintains their lives, guards their persons, supplies their wants, while they employ the powers and faculties they receive from him in a settled course of opposition to his will. They trample upon his laws, affront his government, and despise his grace; yet still he spares. To silence all his adversaries in a moment, would require no extraordinary exertion of his power; but his forbearance towards them manifests his glory, and gives us cause to say, Who is a God like unto thee?

Sometimes, however, there are striking instances of his displeasure against sin. When such events take place immediately upon a public and premeditated contempt offered to him that sitteth in the heavens, I own they remind me of the danger of standing, if I may so speak, in the Lord's way: for though his long-suffering is astonishing, and many dare him to his face daily, with seeming impunity; yet he sometimes strikes an awful and unexpected blow, and gives an illustration of that solemn word, 'Who ever hardened himself against the Lord and prospered?' But who am I, to make this observation? I ought to do it with the deepest humiliation, remembering that I once stood (according to my years and ability) in the foremost rank of his avowed opposers; and with a determined and unwearied enmity renounced, defied, and blasphemed him. 'But he will have mercy on whom he will have mercy'; and therefore I was spared, and reserved to speak of his goodness.

While we lament the growth and pernicious effects of infidelity, and see how wicked men and seducers wax worse and worse, deceiving, and being deceived; what gratitude should fill our hearts to him, who has been pleased to call us out of the horrid darkness in which multitudes are bewildered and lost, into the glorious light of his gospel!

Cardiphonia: Letters to a Nobleman, [1:497]; 1:361

For what is your life? It is even a vapour, that appeareth for a little time, and then vanisheth away.—James 4:14.

I HAVE an imperfect remembrance of an account I read, when I was a boy, of an ice palace, built one winter at Petersburgh. The walls, the roof, the floors, the furniture, were all of ice, but finished with taste; and everything that might be expected in a royal palace was to be found there; the ice, while in the state of water, being previously coloured, so that to the eye all seemed formed of proper materials; but all was cold, useless, and transient. Had the frost continued till now, the palace might have been standing; but with the returning spring it melted away, like the baseless fabric of a vision. Methinks there should have been one stone in the building, to have retained the inscription, *Sic transit gloria mundi!* ['So the world's glory vanishes!'] for no contrivance could exhibit a fitter illustration of the vanity of human life. Men build and plan as if their work were to endure for ever; but the wind passes over them, and they are gone. In the midst of all their preparations, or at the farthest when they think they have just completed their designs, their breath goeth forth, they return to their earth; in that very day their thoughts perish.

Yet this ice-house had something of a leisurely dissolution; though, when it began to decay, all the art of man was unable to prop it; but often death comes hastily, and, like the springing of a mine, destroys the very foundations without previous notice. Then all we have been concerned in here (all, but the consequences of our conduct, which will abide to eternity) will be no more to us than the remembrance of a dream. This truth is too plain to be denied; but the greater part of mankind act as if they were convinced it was false: they spend their days in vanity, and in a moment they go down to the grave. What cause of thankfulness have they who are delivered from this delusion; and who, by the knowledge of the glorious gospel, have learned their true state and end; are saved from the love of the present world, from the heart-distressing fear of death; and know, that, if their earthly house were *dissolved*, like the ice-palace, they have a house not made with hands, eternal in the heavens.

Cardiphonia: Letters to a Nobleman, [1:501]; 1:364

Without me ye can do nothing.—John 15:5.

I ASSENT to our Lord's declaration, 'Without me ye can do nothing'; not only upon the authority of the speaker, but from the same irresistible and experimental evidence, as if he had told me, that I cannot make the sun to shine, or change the course of the seasons. Though my pen and my tongue sometimes move freely, yet the total incapacity and stagnation of thought I labour under at other times, convinces me, that in myself I have not sufficiency to think a good thought; and I believe the case would be the same, if that little measure of knowledge and abilities, which I am too prone to look upon as my own, were a thousand times greater than it is. For every new service, I stand in need of a new supply, and can bring forth nothing of my supposed store into actual exercise, but by his immediate assistance. His gracious influence is that, to those who are best furnished with gifts, which the water is to the mill, or the wind to the ship, without which the whole apparatus is motionless and useless. I apprehend that we lose much of the comfort which might arise from a sense of our continual dependence upon him, and of course, fall short of acknowledging as we ought what we receive from him, by mistaking the manner of his operation. Perhaps we take it too much for granted, that communications from himself must bear some kind of sensible impression that they are *his*, and therefore are ready to give our own industry or ingenuity credit for those performances in which we can perceive no such impression; yet it is very possible that we may be under his influence when we are least aware... This gracious assistance is afforded in a way imperceptible to ourselves, to hide pride from us, and to prevent us from being indolent and careless with respect to the use of appointed means; and it would be likewise more abundantly, and perhaps more sensibly afforded, were our spirits more simple in waiting upon the Lord.

Cardiphonia: Letters to a Nobleman, [1:505]; 1:368

And he humbled thee, and suffered thee to hunger,
and fed thee with manna. —Deut. 8:3.

HOW great and honourable is the privilege of a true believer! That he has neither wisdom nor strength in himself, is no disadvantage; for he is connected with infinite wisdom and almighty power... The Lord, whom he serves, engages to proportion his strength to his day, whether it be a day of service or of suffering: and though he be fallible and short-sighted, exceeding liable to mistake and imposition; yet, while he retains a sense that he is so, and with the simplicity of a child asks counsel and direction of the Lord, he seldom takes a wrong step, at least not in matters of consequence; and even his inadvertencies are overruled for good. If he forgets his true state, and thinks himself to be something, he presently finds he is indeed nothing; but if he is content to be nothing, and to have nothing, he is sure to find a seasonable and abundant communication of all that he wants. Thus he lives, like Israel in the wilderness, upon mere bounty; but then it is a bounty unchangeable, unwearied, inexhaustible, and all-sufficient. Moses when speaking of the methods the Lord took to humble Israel, mentions his feeding them with manna, as one method. I could not understand this for a time. I thought they were rather in danger of being proud, when they saw themselves provided for in such an extraordinary way. But the manna would not keep; they could not hoard it up, and were therefore in a state of absolute dependence from day to day: this appointment was well suited to humble them. Thus it is with us in spirituals. We should be better pleased, perhaps, to be set up with a stock or sufficiency at once; such an inherent portion of wisdom and power, as we might depend upon, at least for common occasions, without being constrained, by a sense of indigence, to have a continual recourse to the Lord for everything we want. But his way is best. His own glory is most displayed, and our safety best secured, by keeping us quite poor and empty in ourselves, and supplying us from one minute to another, according to our need.

Cardiphonia: Letters to a Nobleman, [1:509]; 1:370

But it is good for me to draw near to God.—Psa. 73:28.

REAL communion with the Lord, in his appointed means of grace, is likewise an important branch of this blessedness... They who have tasted it can say, It is good for me to draw nigh to God. The soul thus refreshed by the water of life, is preserved from thirsting after the vanities of the world; thus instructed in the sanctuary, comes down from the mount filled with heavenly wisdom, anointed with a holy unction, and thereby qualified to judge, speak, and act in character, in all the relations and occasions of secular life. In this way, besides the pleasure, a spiritual taste is acquired, something analogous to the meaning of the word taste when applied to music or good-breeding; by which discords and improprieties are observed and avoided, as it were by instinct; and what is right is felt and followed, not so much by the force of rules, as by a habit insensibly acquired, and in which the substance of all necessary rules are, if I may so say, digested. O that I knew more of this blessedness, and more of its effects!

Another branch of blessedness, is a power of reposing ourselves and our concerns upon the Lord's faithfulness and care; and may be considered in two respects:—a reliance upon him that he will surely provide for us, guide us, protect us; be our help in trouble, our shield in danger; so that, however poor, weak, and defenceless in ourselves, we may rejoice in his all-sufficiency as our own;—and further, in consequence of this, a peaceful, humble submission to his will, under all events which, upon their first impression, are contrary to our own views and desires. Surely, in a world like this, where everything is uncertain, where we are exposed to trials on every hand, and know not but a single hour may bring forth something painful, yea dreadful, to our natural sensations, there can be no blessedness, but so far as we are thus enabled to entrust and resign all to the direction and faithfulness of the Lord our Shepherd.

Cardiphonia: Letters to a Nobleman, [1:522]; 1:380

And lead us not into temptation.—Matt. 6:13.

THAT wonderful power which we call the imagination, is, I suppose, rather the medium of the soul's perceptions during its present state of union with the body, than a spiritual faculty, strictly speaking; but it partakes largely of the depravity which sin has brought upon our whole frame and affords Satan an avenue for assaulting us with the most terrifying, if not the most dangerous, of his temptations. At the best, we have but an indifferent command over it. We cannot, by an act of our own will, exclude a thousand painful, wild, inconsistent, and hurtful ideas, which are ever ready to obtrude themselves upon our minds... We are fearfully and wonderfully made; and, with all our boasted knowledge of other things, can form no conception of what is so vastly interesting to us, the mysterious connection between soul and body, and the manner in which they are mutually affected by each other. The effects we too sensibly feel. The wisest of men would be accounted fools or mad, were they to express in words a small part of what passes within them; and it would appear that much of the soberest life is little better than a waking dream; but how dreadful are the consequences when the Lord permits some hidden pin in the human machine to be altered! Immediately a door flies open, which no hand but his can shut, and the enemy pours in, like a flood, falsehood and horror, and the blackness of darkness; the judgment is borne down and disabled, and the most distressing illusions seize us with all the apparent force of evidence and demonstration... All the Lord's people are not called to navigate in these deep waters of soul distress; but all are liable. Ah! if we knew what some suffer ... surely we should be more earnest and frequent in praying, 'Lead us not into temptation.' From some little sense I have of the malice and subtlety of our spiritual enemies, and the weakness of those barriers which we have to prevent their assaults, I am fully persuaded that nothing less than the continual exertion of that Almighty power which preserves the stars in their orbits, can maintain our peace of mind for an hour or a minute.

Cardiphonia: Letters to a Nobleman, [1:529]; 1:385

Watch and pray, that ye enter not into temptation: the spirit indeed is willing, but the flesh is weak.—Matt. 26:41.

BUT our Lord, who knows and considers our weakness, of which we are so little aware, allows and directs us to pray, 'Lead us not into temptation.' We are not to expect an absolute freedom from temptation; we are called to be soldiers, and must sometimes meet with enemies, and perhaps with wounds; yet, considering this prayer as provided by him who knows what we are, and where we are, it may afford us both instruction and consolation.

It calls to a constant reflection upon our own weakness. Believers, especially young ones, are prone to rest too much in grace received. They feel their hearts warm; and, like Peter, are ready to please themselves with thinking how they would act in such or such a state of trial. It is as if the Lord had said, Poor worms, be not high-minded, but fear and pray, that if it may be, you may be kept from learning by bitter experience how weak your supposed strength is. It sweetly intimates, that all our ways, and all our enemies, are in the hands of our great Shepherd. He knows our path. We are short-sighted, and cannot tell what an hour may bring forth: but we are under his protection; and if we depend upon him, we need not be anxiously afraid. He will be faithful to the trust we repose in him, and will suffer no temptation to overtake us, but what he will support us under and bring us through. But it becomes us to beware of security and presumption, to keep our eyes upon him and not to think ourselves safe a moment longer than our spirits feel and breathe the meaning of this petition.

It implies, likewise, the duty of watchfulness on our part; as our Lord joins them elsewhere, 'watch and pray'. If we desire not to be led into temptation, surely we are not to run into it … and though we cannot wholly shut Satan out of our imaginations, we should be cautious that we do not wilfully provide fuel for his flame; but entreat the Lord to set a watch upon our eyes and our ears, and to teach us to reject the first motions and the smallest appearance of evil.

Cardiphonia: Letters to a Nobleman, [1:531]; 1:387

*Therefore if any man be in Christ, he is a new creature:—*2 Cor. 5:17.

WHAT are the effects, which (making allowance for the unavoidable infirmities attending upon the present state of mortality) may be expected from a real experimental knowledge of the gospel? I would not insinuate that none are Christians who do not come up to the character I would describe; for then I fear I should unchristian myself: but only to consider what the Scripture encourages us to aim at as the prize of our high calling in this life.

The Christian is a new creature, born and taught from above. He has been convinced of his guilt and misery as a sinner, has fled for refuge to the hope set before him, has seen the Son and believed on him; his natural prejudices against the glory and grace of God's salvation have been subdued and silenced by Almighty power; he has accepted the Beloved, and is made acceptable in him; he now knows the Lord; has renounced the confused, distant, uncomfortable notions he once formed of God; and beholds him in Christ, who is the way, the truth, and the life, the only door by which we can enter to any true satisfying knowledge of God, or communion with him. But he sees God in Christ, reconciled, a Father, a Saviour and a Friend, who has freely forgiven him all his sins, and given him the Spirit of adoption: he is now no longer a servant, much less a stranger, but a son; and because a son, an heir already interested in all the promises, admitted to the throne of grace, and an assured expectant of eternal glory. The gospel is designed to give us not only a peradventure, or a probability, but a certainty both of our acceptance and our persever-ance, till death shall be swallowed up in life. And though many are sadly fluctuating and perplexed upon this head, and perhaps all are so for a season; yet there are those who can say, we know that we are of God; and therefore they are steadfast and unmoveable in his way; because they are confident that their labour shall not be in vain, but that, when they shall be absent from the body, they shall be present with their Lord.

Cardiphonia: Letters to a Nobleman, [1:533]; 1:389

But where sin abounded, grace did much more abound.—Rom. 5:20.

THE Christian's temper God-ward is evidenced by *humility*. He has received from Gethsemane and Golgotha such a sense of the evil of sin, and of the holiness of God, combined with his matchless love to sinners, as has deeply penetrated his heart: he has an affecting remembrance of the state of rebellion and enmity in which he once lived against this holy and good God; and he has a quick perception of the defilements and defects which still debase his best services. His mouth is therefore stopped as to boasting; he is vile in his own eyes, and is filled with wonder that the Lord should visit such a sinner with such a salvation. He sees so vast a disproportion between the obligations he is under to grace, and the returns he makes, that he is disposed, yea constrained, to adopt the apostle's words without affectation, and to account himself less than the least of all saints; and knowing his own *heart*, while he sees only the outside of others, he is not easily persuaded there can be a believer upon earth so faint, so unfruitful, so unworthy as himself. Yet, though abased, he is not discouraged, for he enjoys *peace*. The dignity, offices, blood, righteousness, faithfulness, and compassion of the Redeemer, in whom he rests, trusts, and lives, for wisdom, righteousness, sanctification, and redemption, are adequate to all his wants and wishes, provide him with an answer to every objection, and give him no less confidence in God, than if he were sinless as an angel: for he sees, that, though sin has abounded in him, grace has much more abounded in Jesus. With respect to the past, all things are become new; with respect to the present and future, he leans upon an Almighty arm, and relies upon the word and power which made and upholds the heavens and the earth.

Cardiphonia: Letters to a Nobleman, [1:535]; 1:390

If ye love me, keep my commandments.—John 14:15.

THE truth of [the believer's] love is manifested by *submission*. This is twofold, and absolute and without reserve in each. He submits to his revealed will, as made known to him by precept, and by his own example. He aims to tread in his Saviour's footsteps, and makes conscience of *all* his commandments, without exception and without hesitation. Again, he submits to his providential will: he yields to his sovereignty, acquiesces in his wisdom; he knows he has no *right* to complain of anything, because he is a sinner; and he has no *reason*, because he is sure the Lord does all things well. Therefore this submission is not forced, but is an act of *trust*. He knows he is not more unworthy than he is unable to choose for himself, and therefore rejoices that the Lord has undertaken to manage for him; and were he compelled to make his own choice, he could only choose that all his concerns should remain in that hand to which he has already committed them. And thus he judges of *public* as well as of his personal affairs. He cannot be an unaffected spectator of national sins, nor without apprehension of their deserved consequences; he feels, and almost trembles, for others, but he himself dwells under the shadow of the Almighty, in a sanctuary that cannot be forced; and therefore, should he see the earth shaken, and the mountains cast into the midst of the sea, his heart would not be greatly moved, for God is his refuge; the Lord reigns. He sees his Saviour's hand directing every dark appearance, and overruling all to the accomplishment of his own great purposes; this satisfies him; and though the winds and waves should be high, he can venture his own little bark in the storm, for he has an infallible and almighty Pilot on board with him.

Cardiphonia: Letters to a Nobleman, [1:537]; 1:392

Take heed, and beware of covetousness: for a man's life consisteth not in the abundance of the things which he possesseth.—Luke 12:15.

SATAN will not often tempt a believer to gross crimes: our greatest snares and sorest conflicts are usually found in things lawful in themselves, but hurtful to us by their abuse, engrossing too much of our time, or of our hearts, or somehow indisposing us for communion with the Lord. The Christian will be jealous of anything that might entangle his affections, damp his zeal, or straiten him in his opportunities of serving his Saviour. He is likewise content with his situation, because the Lord chooses it for him; his spirit is not eager for additions and alterations in his circumstances. If Divine Providence points out and leads to a change, he is ready to follow, though it should be what the world would call from a better to a worse; for he is a pilgrim and a stranger here, and a citizen of heaven. As people of fortune sometimes, in travelling, submit cheerfully to inconvenient accommodations, very different from their homes, and comfort themselves with thinking that they are not always to live so; so the Christian is not greatly solicitous about externals. If he has them, he will use them moderately. If he has but little of them, he can make a good shift without them: he is but upon a journey, and will soon be home. If he be rich, experience confirms our Lord's words, Luke 12:15, and satisfies him, that a large room, a crowd of servants, and twenty dishes upon his table, add nothing to the real happiness of life: therefore he will not have his heart set upon such things. If he be in a humbler state, he is more disposed to pity than to envy those above him; for he judges they must have many encumbrances from which he is freed. However, the will of God, and the light of his countenance, are the chief things the Christian, whether rich or poor, regards; and therefore his moderation is made known unto all men.

Cardiphonia: Letters to a Nobleman, [1:539]; 1:393

Blessed are the meek: for they shall inherit the earth.—Matt. 5:5.

A THIRD branch of the Christian's temper respects his fellow creatures... We have, in this degenerate day, among those who claim and are allowed the name of Christian, too many of a narrow, selfish, mercenary spirit; but in the beginning it was not so. The gospel is designed to cure such a spirit, but gives no indulgence to it. A Christian has the mind of Christ, who went about doing good, who makes his sun to shine upon the good and the evil, and sendeth rain on the just and the unjust. His Lord's example forms him to the habit of diffusive benevolence; he breathes a spirit of goodwill to mankind, and rejoices in every opportunity of being useful to the souls and bodies of others, without respect to parties or interests. He commiserates, and would if possible alleviate, the miseries of all around him; and if his actual services are restrained by want of ability, yet all share in his sympathy and prayers. Acting in the spirit of his Master, he frequently meets with a measure of the like treatment; but if his good is requited with evil, he labours to overcome evil with good. He feels himself a sinner, and needs much forgiveness: this makes him ready to forgive. He is not haughty, captious, easily offended, or hard to be reconciled; for at the feet of Jesus he has learned meekness; and when he meets with unkindness or injustice, he considers, that, though he has not deserved such things from men, they are instruments employed by his heavenly Father (from whom he has deserved to suffer much more), for his humiliation and chastisement; and is therefore more concerned for their sins, than for his own sufferings, and prays, after the pattern of his Saviour, 'Father, forgive them, for they know not what they do!'

Cardiphonia: Letters to a Nobleman, [1:540]; 1:394

I thank my God ... Hearing of thy love and faith, which thou hast toward the Lord Jesus, and toward all saints.—Philem. 4-5.

A Christian ... knows he is frail; and therefore dares not be censorious. As a member of society, he is just, punctual in the discharge of every relative duty, faithful to his engagements and promises, rendering to all their dues, obedient to lawful authority, and acting to all men according to the golden rule, of doing as he would be done by. His conduct is simple, devoid of artifice, and consistent, attending to every branch of duty: and in the closet, the family, the church, and in the transactions of common life, he is the same man; for in every circumstance he serves the Lord, and aims to maintain a conscience void of offence in his sight. No small part of the beauty of his profession in the sight of men, consists in the due government of his tongue. The law of truth, and kindness, and purity, is upon his lips. He abhors lying; and is so far from inventing a slander, that he will not repeat a report to the disadvantage of his neighbour, however true, without a proper call. His converse is cheerful, but inoffensive; and he will no more wound another with his wit (if he has a talent that way), than with a knife. His speech is with grace, seasoned with salt, and suited to promote the peace and edification of all around him.

Such is the Christian in civil life. But though he loves all mankind, he stands in a nearer relation, and bears an especial brotherly love, to all who are partakers of the faith and hope of the gospel. This regard is not confined within the pale of a denomination, but extended to all who love the Lord Jesus Christ with sincerity... He rejoices in the image of God, wherever he sees it and in the work of God, wherever it is carried on. Though tenacious of the truths which the Lord has taught him, his heart is open to those who differ from him in less essential points, and allows to others that right of private judgment which he claims for himself, and is disposed to hold communion in love with all who hold the Head.

Cardiphonia: Letters to a Nobleman, [1:540]; 1:394

Let all those that seek thee rejoice and be glad in thee: let such as love thy salvation say continually, The LORD be magnified.—Psa. 40:16.

THERE is no doubt but first religious impressions are usually mingled with much of a legal spirit; and that conscience at such a time is not only tender, but misinformed and scrupulous; and I believe … that when the mind is more enlightened, and we feel a liberty from many fetters we had imposed upon ourselves, we are in danger of verging too far towards the other extreme. It seems to me that no one person can adjust the medium, and draw the line exactly for another. There are so many particulars in every situation, of which a stranger cannot be a competent judge, and the best human advices and models are mixed with such defects, that it is not *right* to expect others to be absolutely guided by our rules, nor is it *safe* for us implicitly to adopt the decisions or practices of others. But the Scripture undoubtedly furnishes sufficient and infallible rules for every person, however circumstanced; and the throne of grace is appointed for us to wait upon the Lord for the best exposition of his precepts. Thus David often prays to be led in the right way, in the path of judgment. By frequent prayer and close acquaintance with the Scripture, and an habitual attention to the frame of our hearts, there is a certain delicacy of spiritual taste and discernment to be acquired… Love is the clearest and most persuasive casuist; and when our love to the Lord is in lively exercise, and the rule of his word is in our eye, we seldom make great mistakes. And I believe the over-doings of a young convert, proceeding from an honest simplicity of heart, and a desire of pleasing the Lord, are more acceptable in his sight, than a certain coolness of conduct which frequently takes place afterward, when we are apt to look back with pity upon our former weakness, and secretly to applaud ourselves for our present greater attainments in knowledge, though perhaps (alas that it should ever be so!) we may have lost as much in warmth, as we have gained in light.

Cardiphonia: Letters to a Nobleman, [1:544]; 1:396

He doeth according to his will in the army of heaven, and among the
inhabitants of the earth: and none can stay his hand,
or say unto him, What doest thou?—Dan. 4:35.

I HAVE lately read Robertson's history of Charles V, which, like most other histories, I consider as a comment upon those passages of Scripture which teach us the depravity of man, the deceitfulness of the heart, the ruinous effects of sin, and the powerful, though secret, rule of Divine Providence, moving, directing, controlling the designs and actions of men, with an unerring hand, to the accomplishment of his own purposes, both of mercy and judgment. Without the clue and the light which the word of God affords, the history of mankind, of any, of every age, only presents to view a labyrinth and a chaos; a detail of wickedness and misery to make us tremble; and a confused jumble of interfering incidents, as destitute of stability, connection, or order, as the clouds which fly over our heads... But with the Scripture key, all is plain, all is instructive. Then I see, verily there is a God, who governs the earth, who pours contempt upon princes, takes the wise in their own craftiness, overrules the wrath and pride of man to bring his own designs to pass, and restrains all that is not necessary to that end; blasting the best concerted enterprises at one time, by means apparently slight, and altogether unexpected, and at other times producing the most important events from instruments and circumstances which are at first thought too feeble and trivial to deserve notice... What an empty phantom do the great men of the world pursue, while they wage war with the peace of mankind, and butcher (in the course of their lives) perhaps hundreds of thousands, to maintain the shadow of authority over distant nations, whom they can reach with no other influence than that of oppression and devastation!

But though the effects of this principle of self are more extensive and calamitous in proportion as those who are governed by it are more elevated, the principle itself is deep-rooted in every heart, and is the spring of every action, till grace infuses a new principle, and self, like Dagon, falls before the Lord of hosts.

Cardiphonia: Letters to a Nobleman, [1:552]; 1:403

The fruit of the righteous is a tree of life;
and he that winneth souls is wise.—Prov. 11:30.

HE that winneth souls is wise; wise in the choice of the highest end he can propose to himself in this life, wise in the improvement of the only means by which this desirable end can be attained. Wherever we cast our eyes, the bulk of the people are ignorant, immoral, careless. They live without God in the world; they are neither awed by his authority, nor affected by his goodness, nor enabled to trust to his promises, nor disposed to aim at his glory. If, perhaps, they have a serious interval, or some comparative sobriety of character, they ground their hopes upon their own doings, endeavours, or purposes; and treat the inexpressible love of God revealed in Christ, and the gospel method of salvation by faith in his name, with neglect, often with contempt. They have preachers, whom perhaps they hear with some pleasure, because they neither alarm their consciences by insisting on the spirituality and sanction of the Divine law, nor offend their pride by publishing the humiliating doctrines of that gospel, which is the power of God through faith unto salvation. Therefore what they do speak, they speak in vain; the world grows worse and worse under their instructions; infidelity and profligacy abound more and more: for God will own no other doctrine but what the apostle calls the truth as it is in Jesus; that doctrine which drives the sinner from all his vain pleas and points out the Lord Jesus Christ as the only ground of hope, the supreme object of desire, as appointed of God to be wisdom, righteousness, sanctification, and redemption, to all who believe in his name. When ministers themselves are convinced of sin, and feel the necessity of an almighty Saviour, they presently account their former gain but loss, and determine, with the apostle, to know nothing but Jesus Christ, and him crucified. In proportion as they do this, they are sure to be wondered at, laughed at, and railed at, if the providence of God, and the constitution of their country, secure them from severer treatment.—But they have this invaluable compensation, that they no longer speak without effect.

Cardiphonia: Letters to Rev. Mr. Thomas Scott, [1:559]; 1:408

I am sought of them that asked not for me; I am found of them that
sought me not: I said, Behold me, behold me, unto a nation
that was not called by my name.—Isa. 65:1.

THE truths of Scripture are not like mathematical theorems, which present exactly the same ideas to every person who understands the terms. The word of God is compared to a mirror, 2 Cor. 3:18; but it is a mirror in which the longer we look, the more we see: the view will be still growing upon us, and still we shall see but in part while on this side of eternity. When our Lord pronounced Peter blessed, declaring he had learnt that which flesh and blood could not have taught him, yet Peter was at that time much in the dark. The sufferings and death of Jesus, though the only and necessary means of his salvation, were an offence to him. But he lived to glory in what he once could not bear to hear of. Peter had received grace to love the Lord Jesus, to follow him, to venture all and to forsake all for him: these first good dispositions were of God, and they led to further advances. So it is still. By nature, self rules in the heart: when this idol is brought low, and we are truly willing to be the Lord's, and apply to him for strength and direction, that we may serve him, the good work is begun; for it is a truth that holds universally and without exception, a man can receive nothing except it be *given* him from heaven. The Lord first *finds* us when we are thinking of something else (Isa. 65:1), and then we begin to seek him in good earnest, and he has promised to be *found* of us… Here the learned have no real advantage above the ignorant; both see when the eyes of the understanding are enlightened: till then both are equally blind. And the first lesson in the school of Christ is to become a little child, sitting simply at his feet, that we may be made wise unto salvation.

Cardiphonia: Letters to Rev. Mr. Thomas Scott, [1:562]; 1:411

He giveth power to the faint; and to them that have no might he increaseth strength. Even the youths shall faint and be weary, and the young men shall utterly fall: But they that wait upon the LORD shall renew their strength; they shall mount up with wings as eagles; they shall run, and not be weary; and they shall walk, and not faint.—Isa. 40:29-31.

Perseverance.

1. Rejoice, believer, in the Lord,
   Who makes your cause his own;
   The hope that's built upon his word
   Can ne'er be overthrown.

2. Though many foes beset your road,
   And feeble is your arm;
   Your life is hid with Christ in God,[3]
   Beyond the reach of harm.

3. Weak as you are, you shall not faint,
   Or fainting shall not die;
   Jesus, the strength of every saint,
   Will aid you from on high.[4]

4. Though sometimes unperceived by sense,
   Faith sees him always near,
   A Guide, a Glory, a Defence,
   Then what have you to fear?

5. As surely as he overcame,
   And triumphed once for you;
   So surely you, that love his name,
   Shall triumph in him too.

[3] Col. 3:3.
[4] Isa. 40:29.

The Olney Hymns: Book III, No. 84, [3:655]; 2:748

For who maketh thee to differ from another? and what hast thou that
thou didst not receive? now if thou didst receive it, why dost thou
glory, as if thou hadst not received it?—1 Cor. 4:7.

WHATEVER is from God has a sure tendency to ascribe glory to him, to exclude boasting from the creature, to promote the love and practice of holiness, and increase our dependence upon his grace and faithfulness.

Admitting, what I am sure you will admit, the total depravity of human nature, how can we account for the conversion of a soul to God, unless we likewise admit an election of grace? The work must begin somewhere. Either the sinner first seeks the Lord, or the Lord first seeks the sinner. The former is impossible, if by nature we are dead in trespasses and sins; if the god of this world has blinded our eyes, and maintains the possession of our hearts; and if our carnal minds, so far from being disposed to seek God, are enmity against him. Let me appeal to yourself. I think you know yourself too well to say, that you neither sought or loved the Lord first: perhaps you are conscious, that for a season, and so far as in you lay, you even resisted his call; and must have perished, if he had not made you willing in the day of his power and saved you in defiance of yourself. In your own case, you acknowledge that he began with you, and it must be the case universally with all that are called, if the whole race of mankind are by nature enemies to God. Then, further, there must be an election, unless ALL are called. But we are assured that the broad road, which is thronged with the greatest multitudes, leads to destruction. Were not you and I in this road? Were we better than those who continue in it still? What has made us differ from our former selves? *Grace.* What has made us differ from those who are now as we once were? *Grace.* Then this grace, by the very terms, must be differencing, or distinguishing grace; that is, in other words, electing grace.

On the Doctrines of Election and Perseverance, [1:190]; 1:128

But he that shall endure unto the end, the same shall be saved.
—Matt. 24:13.

AS to final perseverance, whatever judgment we form of it in a doctrinal view, unless we ourselves *do so persevere*, our profession of religion will be utterly vain; for only 'they that endure to the end shall be saved'. It should seem, that whoever believes this, and is duly apprised of his own weakness, the number and strength of his spiritual enemies, and the difficulties and dangers arising from his situation in this evil world, will at least be desirous to have (if possible) some security that his labour and expectation shall not be in vain. To be at an uncertainty in a point of so great importance; to have nothing to trust to for our continuance in well-doing, but our own feeble efforts, our partial diligence and short-sighted care, must surely be distressing, if we rightly consider how unable we are in ourselves to withstand the forces of the world, the flesh, and the devil, which are combined against our peace... The Lord claims the honour; and he engages for the accomplishment of a complete salvation, that no power shall pluck his people out of his hand, or separate them from his love. Their perseverance in grace, besides being asserted in many express promises, may be proved with the fullest evidence from the unchangeableness of God, the intercession of Christ, the union which subsists between him and his people, and from the principle of spiritual life he has implanted in their hearts, which in its own nature is connected with everlasting life; for grace is the seed of glory... Upon these grounds ... why may not you, who have fled for refuge to the hope set before you, and committed your soul to Jesus, rejoice in his salvation; and say, 'While Christ is the Foundation, Root, Head, and Husband of his people, while the word of God is Yea and Amen, while the counsels of God are unchangeable, while we have a Mediator and High Priest before the throne, while the Holy Spirit is willing and able to bear witness to the truths of the gospel, while God is wiser than men, and stronger than Satan, so long the believer in Jesus is and shall be safe'?

On the Doctrines of Election and Perseverance, [1:192]; 1:129

Hold thou me up, and I shall be safe.—Psa. 119:117.

A S the doctrines of election and perseverance are comfortable, so they cut off all pretence of boasting and self-dependence when they are truly received in the heart, and therefore tend to exalt the Saviour. Of course they stain the pride of all human glory, and leave us nothing to glory in but the Lord. The more we are convinced of our utter depravity and inability from first to last the more excellent will Jesus appear. The *whole* may give the physician a good word, but the *sick* alone know how to prize him. And here I cannot but remark a difference between those who have *nothing* to trust to but free grace, and those who ascribe a *little* at least to some good disposition and ability in man... If any persons have contributed a mite to their own salvation, it was more than we could do. If any were obedient and faithful to the first calls and impressions of his Spirit, it was not our case. If they were prepared to receive him beforehand, we know that we were in a state of alienation from him. We needed sovereign, irresistible grace to save us, or we had been lost forever. If there are any who have a power of their own, we must confess ourselves poorer than they are. We cannot watch, unless he watches with us; we cannot strive, unless he strives with us; we cannot stand one moment, unless he holds us up; and we believe we must perish after all, unless his faithfulness is engaged to keep us. But this we trust he will do, not for our righteousness, but for his own name's sake, and because, having loved us with an everlasting love, he has been pleased in loving kindness to draw us to himself, and to be found of us when we sought him not.

On the Doctrines of Election and Perseverance, [1:194]; 1:131

The law of the LORD is perfect, converting the soul:
the testimony of the LORD is sure, making wise the simple.—Psa. 19:7.

MY first principle in religion is what the Scripture teaches me of the utter depravity of human nature, in connection with the spirituality and sanction of the law of God. I believe we are by nature sinners, by practice universally transgressors; that we are dead in trespasses and sins; and that the bent of our natural spirit is enmity against the holiness, government, and grace of God. Upon this ground, I see, feel, and acknowledge the necessity of such a salvation as the gospel proposes; which, at the same time that it precludes boasting, and stains the pride of all human glory, affords encouragement to those who may be thought, or who may think of themselves, the weakest or the vilest of mankind. I believe, that whatever notions a person may take up from education or system, no one ever did, or ever will, feel himself and own himself to be such a lost, miserable, hateful sinner, unless he be powerfully and supernaturally convinced by the Spirit of God... Here a change takes place; the person that was spiritually blind begins to see. The sinner's character, as described in the word of God, he finds to be a description of himself; that he is afar off, a stranger, a rebel; that he has hitherto lived in vain. Now he begins to see the necessity of an atonement, an Advocate, a Shepherd, a Comforter: he can no more trust to his own wisdom, strength, and goodness; but, accounting all his former gain but loss, for the excellency of the knowledge of Christ, he renounces every other refuge, and ventures his all upon the person, work, and promise of the Redeemer. In this way, I say, he will find the doctrine of the Trinity not only a proposition, but a principle: that is, from his own wants and situation he will have an abiding conviction that the Son and Holy Spirit are God, and must be possessed of the attributes and powers of Deity, to support the offices the Scriptures assign them, and to deserve the confidence and worship the Scriptures require to be placed in them, and paid to them.

Cardiphonia: Letters to Rev. Mr. Thomas Scott, [1:568]; 1:415

...the excellency of the knowledge of Christ Jesus my Lord...
—Phil. 3:8.

THE gospel, my dear sir, is a salvation appointed for those who are ready to perish, and is not designed to put them in a way to save themselves by their own works. It speaks to us as condemned already, and calls upon us to believe in a crucified Saviour, that we may receive redemption through his blood, even the forgiveness of our sins. And the Spirit of God, by the gospel, first convinces us of unbelief, sin, and misery; and then, by revealing the things of Jesus to our minds, enables us, as helpless sinners, to come to Christ, to receive him, to behold him, or, in other words, to believe in him, and expect pardon, life and grace from him; renouncing every hope and aim in which we once rested, 'and accounting all things loss and dung for the excellency of the knowledge of Christ.'

Our dependence upon him is absolute, our obligations to him infinite. In vain shall men plead their moral discharge of relative duties to each other, if they fail in the unspeakably greater relation under which they stand to God; and therefore, when I see people living without God in the world, as all do till they are converted, I cannot but judge them in a dangerous state; not because I take pleasure in censuring, or think myself authorized to pass sentence upon my fellow creatures, but because the Scripture decides expressly on the case, and I am bound to take my sentiments from thence.

The jailer was certainly a Christian when baptized... He trembled; he cried out, 'What must I do to be saved?' Paul did not bid him amend his life, but, believe in the Lord Jesus. He believed, and rejoiced. But the Lord blessed the apostle's words, to produce in him that saving faith, which filled him with joy and peace. It was ... something more than an assent to the proposition, that Jesus is the Christ; a resting in him for forgiveness and acceptance, and a cleaving to him in love. No other faith will purify the heart, work by love, and overcome the world.

Cardiphonia: Letters to Rev. Mr. Thomas Scott, [1:575, 580]; 1:420

Let no man deceive himself. If any man among you seemeth to be wise in this world, let him become a fool, that he may be wise.—1 Cor. 3:18.

YOU wish me to explain my distinction between faith and rational assent… I believe fallen reason is, of itself, utterly incapable even of assenting to the great truths of revelation; it may assent to the terms in which they are proposed, but it must put its own interpretation upon them, or it would despise them. The natural man can neither receive nor discern the things of God: and if anyone would be wise, the apostle's first advice to him is, 'Let him become a fool, that he may be wise; for the wisdom of the world is foolishness with God.'

Indeed, when the heart is changed, and the mind enlightened; then reason is sanctified, and if I may so say, baptized, renounces its curious disquisitions, and is content humbly to tread in the path of revelation. This is one difference, assent may be the act of our natural reason; faith is the effect of immediate Almighty power. Another difference is, Faith is always efficacious, 'it worketh by love'; whereas assent is often given where it has little or no influence upon the conduct. Thus, for instance, everyone will assent to this truth, All men are mortal: yet the greatest part of mankind, though they readily assent to the proposition, and it would be highly irrational to do otherwise, live as they might do if the reverse were true. But they who have divine faith, feel, as well as say, they are pilgrims and sojourners upon earth. Again, faith gives peace of conscience, access to God and a sure evidence and subsistence of things not seen, Rom. 5:1, 2; Heb. 11:1; whereas a calm, dispassionate reasoner may be compelled to assent to the external arguments in favour of Christianity, yet remain a total stranger to that communion with God, that Spirit of adoption, that foretaste of glory, which is the privilege and portion of believers.

Cardiphonia: Letters to Rev. Mr. Thomas Scott, [1:594]; 1:435

*Unto me, who am less than the least of all saints, is this grace
given, that I should preach among the Gentiles the
unsearchable riches of Christ.*—Eph. 3:8.

FAITH is the effect of a principle of new life implanted in the
soul, that was before dead in trespasses and sins; and it qualifies,
not only for obeying the Saviour's precepts, but chiefly and primarily
for receiving from and rejoicing in his fulness, admiring his love,
his work, his person, his glory, his advocacy. It makes Christ precious; enthrones him in the heart; presents him as the most delightful
object to our meditations,—as our wisdom, righteousness, sanctification, and strength; our root, head, life, shepherd, husband... A most
valued friend of mine, a clergyman now living, had for many years
given a rational assent to the gospel. He laboured with much earnestness ... was very exemplary in his whole conduct; preached almost
incessantly (two or three times every day in the week for years)... He
succeeded likewise with his people so far as to break them off from
outward irregularities; and was mentioned, in a letter to the Society
for Propagating the Gospel ... as the most perfect example of a parish
priest which this nation, or perhaps this age, has produced... One
day, reading Ephesians 3, in his Greek Testament, his thoughts were
stopped... He was struck, and led to think with himself to this purpose: The apostle, when speaking of Christ, uses remarkable expressions; he speaks of heights, and depths, and lengths, and breadths,
and unsearchables, where I seem to find everything plain, easy, and
rational... This led him to a close examination of all his epistles,
and, by the blessing of God, brought on a total change in his views
and preaching. He no longer set his people to keep a law of faith; to
trust in their sincerity and endeavours, upon some general hope that
Christ would help them out where they came short; but he preached
Christ himself, as the end of the law for righteousness to everyone
that believeth. He felt himself, and laboured to convince others, that
there is no hope for a sinner but merely in the blood of Jesus; and no
possibility of his doing any works acceptable to God, till he himself
be first made accepted in the Beloved.

Cardiphonia: Letters to Rev. Mr. Thomas Scott, [1:596]; 1:436

For by grace are ye saved through faith; and that not of yourselves:
it is the gift of God.—Eph. 2:8.

I BELIEVE no sinner is converted without his own hearty will and concurrence. But he is not willing till he is made so. Why does he at all refuse? Because he is insensible of his state; because he knows not the evil of sin, the strictness of the law, the majesty of God whom he has offended, nor the total apostasy of his heart; because he is blind to eternity, and ignorant of the excellency of Christ; because he is comparatively whole, and sees not his need of this great Physician; because he relies upon his own wisdom, power, and supposed righteousness. Now, in this state of things, when God comes with a purpose of mercy, he begins by convincing the person of sin, judgment, and righteousness; causes him to feel and know that he is a lost, condemned, helpless creature; and then discovers to him the necessity, sufficiency, and willingness of Christ to save them that are ready to perish, without money or price, without doings or deservings. Then he sees faith to be very different from a rational assent; finds that nothing but the power of God can produce a well-grounded hope in the heart of a convinced sinner; therefore looks to Jesus, who is the author and finisher of faith, to enable him to believe. For this he waits in what we call the means of grace; he prays, he reads the word, he thirsts for God as the heart pants for the water-brooks; and, though perhaps for a while he is distressed with many doubts and fears, he is encouraged to wait on, because Jesus has said, 'him that cometh unto me, I will in no wise cast out'. The obstinacy of the will remains while the understanding is dark, and ceases when that is enlightened… Sinners are called and warned by the word; but they are wise in their own eyes, and take but little notice, till the Lord gives them light, which he is not bound to give to *any*, and therefore cannot be bound to give to *all*. They who have it, have reason to be thankful, and subscribe to the apostle's words, 'By grace are ye saved, through faith; and that not of yourselves, it is the gift of God.'

Cardiphonia: Letters to Rev. Mr. Thomas Scott, [1:601]; 1:440

Be still, and know that I am God.—Psa. 46:10.

CERTAINLY, if my ability was equal to my inclination, I would remove your tumour with a word or a touch; I would exempt you instantly and constantly from every inconvenience and pain: but you are in the hands of One who could do all this and more, and who loves you infinitely better than I can do, and yet he is pleased to permit you to suffer. What is the plain inference? Certainly, that at the present juncture, he, to whom all the concatenations and consequences of events are present in one view, sees it better for you to have this tumour than to be without it; for I have no more idea of a tumour rising (or any other incidental trial befalling you), without a cause, without a need-be, without a designed advantage to result from it, than I have of a mountain or pyramid rising up of its own accord in the middle of Salisbury Plain. The promise is express, and literally true, that all things, universally and without exception, shall work together for good to them that love God. But they work *together*: the smallest as well as the greatest events have their place and use ... like the movement of a watch, where, though there is an evident subordination of parts, and some pieces have a greater comparative importance than others, yet the smallest pieces have their place and use, and are so far equally important, that the whole design of the machine would be obstructed for want of them. Some dispensations and turns of Divine Providence may be compared to the main spring or capital wheels, which have a more visible, sensible, and determining influence upon the whole tenor of our lives: but the more ordinary occurrences of every day are at least pins and pivots, adjusted, timed, and suited with equal accuracy, by the hand of the same great Artist who planned and executes the whole; and we are sometimes surprised to see how much more depends and turns upon them than we are aware of... Such thoughts as these, when I am enabled to realize them, in some measure reconcile me to what he allots for myself or my friends, and convince me of the propriety of that expostulation, which speaks the language of love as well as authority, 'Be still and know that I am God.'

Cardiphonia: Letters to Rev. Mr. Thomas Scott, [1:619]; 1:452

I can do all things through Christ which strengtheneth me.—Phil. 4:13.

I THINK the greatness of trials is to be estimated rather by the impression they make upon our spirits, than by their outward appearance. The smallest will be too heavy for us if we are left to grapple with it in our own strength, or rather weakness: and if the Lord is pleased to put forth his power in us, he can make the heaviest light. A lively impression of his love, or of his sufferings for us, or of the glories within the veil, accompanied with a due sense of the misery from which we are redeemed; these thoughts will enable us to be not only submissive, but even joyful, in tribulations. When faith is in exercise, though the flesh will have its feelings, the spirit will triumph over them.

But it is needful we should know that we have no sufficiency in ourselves ... and therefore the Lord sometimes withdraws his sensible influence, and then the buzzing of a fly will be an overmatch for our patience: at other times he will show us what he can do in us and for us; then we can adopt the apostle's words, I can do and suffer all things, through Christ strengthening me: he has said, My grace is sufficient for thee. It is observable, that the children of God seldom disappoint our expectations under great trials; if they show a wrongness of spirit, it is usually in such little incidents that we are ready to wonder at them. For which, two reasons may be principally assigned. When great trials are in view, we run simply and immediately to our all-sufficient Friend, feel our dependence, and cry in good earnest for help; but if the occasion seem small, we are too apt secretly to lean to our own wisdom and strength, as if in such slight matters we could make shift without him. Therefore in these we often fail.

Cardiphonia: Letters to Mr. Joseph Foster Barham, [1:621]; 1:454

Every branch in me that beareth not fruit he taketh away:
and every branch that beareth fruit, he purgeth it,
that it may bring forth more fruit.—John 15:2.

I HOPE to be informed ... that the Lord has given you full health and cure. He has preserved me hitherto from the hands of surgeons; but I feel as if my flesh would prove, as you say, a very coward, were it needful to submit to a painful operation. Yet I observe, when such operations are necessary, if people are satisfied of a surgeon's skill and prudence, they will not only yield to be cut at his pleasure, without pretending to direct him where, or how long, he shall make the incision, but will thank and pay him for putting them to pain, because they believe it for their advantage. I wish I could be more like them in my concerns. My body, as I said, is, through mercy, free from considerable ailments, but I have a soul that requires surgeon's work continually: there is some tumour to be discussed or laid open, some dislocation to be reduced, some fracture to be healed, almost daily. It is my great mercy, that One who is infallible in skill, who exercises incessant care and boundless compassion towards all his patients, has undertaken my case; and, complicated as it is, I dare not doubt his making a perfect cure. Yet, alas! I too often discover such impatience, distrust, and complaining, when under his hand; am so apt to find fault with the *instruments* he is pleased to make use of; so ready to think the salutary wounds he makes unnecessary, or too large; in a word, I show such a promptness to control, were I able, or to direct, his operations, that, were not his patience beyond expression, he would before now have given me up. I am persuaded no money would induce Mr **** to attend upon a patient who should act towards him as I have towards my best Physician. Sometimes I indulge a hope that I am growing wiser, and think, Surely, after such innumerable proofs as I have had that he does all things well, I shall now be satisfied to leave myself quietly and without reserve to his disposal. A thousand such surrenders I have made, and a thousand times I have interpretatively retracted them. Yet still is he gracious. Oh, how shall I praise him at last!

Cardiphonia: Letters to Mr. Joseph Foster Barham, [1:623]; 1:456

Behold, I am vile; what shall I answer thee?
I will lay mine hand upon my mouth.—Job 40:4.

I BELIEVE with you, that there is much of the proper and designed efficacy of the gospel mystery which I have not yet experienced; and I suppose they who are advanced far beyond me in the divine life judge the same of their utmost present attainments. Yet I have no idea of any *permanent* state in this life, that shall make my experience cease to be a state of warfare and humiliation. At my first setting out, indeed, I thought to be better, and to feel myself better from year to year... I thought my grain of grace, by much diligence and careful improvement, would, in time, amount to a pound; that pound, in a further space of time, to a talent; and then I hoped to increase from one talent to many; so that, supposing the Lord should spare me a competent number of years, I pleased myself with the thought of dying rich. But, alas! These my golden expectations have been like South-Sea dreams; I have lived hitherto a poor sinner, and I believe I shall die one. Have I then gained nothing by waiting upon the Lord? Yes, I have gained, that which I once would rather have been without, such accumulated proofs of the deceitfulness and desperate wickedness of my heart, as I hope, by the Lord's blessing, has in some measure, taught me to know what I mean, when I say, Behold I am vile! And, in connection with this, I have gained such experience of the wisdom, power, and compassion of my Redeemer, the need, the worth, of his blood, righteousness, attention, and intercession—the glory that he displays in pardoning iniquity and sin and passing by the transgression of the remnant of his heritage, that my soul cannot but cry out, Who is a God like unto thee! Thus, if I have any meaner thoughts of myself, Ezek. 16:63, and any higher thoughts of him than I had twenty years ago, I have reason to be thankful: every grain of this experience is worth mountains of gold.

Cardiphonia: Letters to Mr. Joseph Foster Barham, [1:624]; 1:457

Thy way is in the sea, and thy path in the great waters,
and thy footsteps are not known.—Psalm 77:19.

THE enemy who always fights against the peace of the Lord's children, finds great advantage against them when their spirits are weakened and worn down by long illness, and is often permitted to assault them. The reasons are hidden from us, but they are doubtless worthy of his wisdom and love; and they terminate in victory, to the praise of his glorious grace, which is more signally manifested by his leading them safely through fire and water, than if their path was always smooth. He is sovereign in his dispensations, and appoints some of his people to trials and exercises, to which others, perhaps, are strangers all their days. Believers are soldiers: all soldiers by their profession are engaged to fight, if called upon, but who shall be called to sustain the hottest service, and be most frequently exposed upon the field of battle, depends upon the will of the general or king. Some of our soldiers are now upon hard service in America, while others are stationed round the palace, see the king's face daily, and have no dangers or hardships to encounter. These, however, are as liable to a call as the others; but, if not called upon, they may enjoy with thankfulness the more easy post assigned them. Thus, the Captain of our salvation allots to his soldiers such stations as he thinks proper. He has a right to employ whom he will, and where he will. Some are comparatively at ease; they are not exposed to the fiercest onsets, but live near his presence: others are, to appearance, pressed above measure beyond strength, so that they despair even of life; yet they are supported, and in the end made more than conquerors through him who hath loved them… The Lord's way is in the deep, and his path in the great waters, untraceable by our feeble reasonings; but faith brings in a good report. We need not doubt but he does all things well, and in due time we shall see it. In the mean while he checks our vain inquiries, and calls upon us to be still, and know that he is God.

Cardiphonia: Letters to Mr. Joseph Foster Barham, [1:627]; 1:459

But one thing is needful.—Luke 10:42

HIS favour is the one thing needful, which no outward advantages can compensate the want of; and the right knowledge of him is the one thing needful, which no human teaching can communicate.

As to learning, though it is useful when we know how to make a right use of it, yet, considered as in our own power, and to those who trust to it without seeking a superior guidance, it is usually the source of perplexity, strife, scepticism, and infidelity. It is, indeed, like a sword in a madman's hands, which gives him the more opportunity of hurting himself and others. As to what the world calls pleasure, there is so little in it, that even the philosophers of old, or many of them, though they had little of value to substitute in its room, could despise it. You will perhaps meet with some who will talk another language; who will pretend to be too wise to submit to the Bible, and too happy in worldly things to expect or desire any happiness beside; but I trust you have seen enough to enable you to treat such persons with the pity, and such pretensions with the contempt, they deserve.

Should we set our concerns with an *external world* aside for a moment, it would be easy to demonstrate that religion is necessary, in order to make the most of life, and to enjoy temporal good with the highest relish. In such a world as this, where we are every moment liable to so many unforeseen and unavoidable contingencies, a man without religion may be compared to a ship in a storm, without either rudder, anchor, or pilot. But then, the religion, which *only* deserves the name, must come from above; it must be suited to the state and wants of a sinner; it must be capable of comforting the heart; it must take away the sting and dread of death; and fix our confidence upon One who is always able to help us.

Cardiphonia: Letters to Mr. Joseph Foster Barham, [1:634]; 1:464

Behold, I stand at the door, and knock: if any man hear my voice, and
open the door, I will come in to him, and will sup with him,
and he with me.—Rev. 3:20.

WE are prone, as you observe, to rest too much upon sensible comforts, yet they are very desirable; only, as to the measure and seasons, it is well to be submissive to his will; to be thankful for them when we have them, and humbly waiting for them when we have them not. They are not, however the proper ground of our hope; a good hope springs from such a sense of our wants, and such a persuasion of his power and grace as engages the heart to venture, upon the warrant of his promises, to trust in him for salvation... Ah! had it depended upon myself, upon my wisdom or faithfulness, I should have hindered him to purpose, and ruined myself long ago! How often have I grieved and resisted his Spirit! But hereby I have learned more of his patience and tenderness, than I could otherwise have known. He knows our frame, and what effects our evil nature, fomented by the artifices of Satan, will have; he sees us from first to last. A thousand evils arise in our hearts, a thousand wrongnesses in our conduct, which, as they do arise, are new to ourselves, and perhaps at some times we were ready to think we were incapable of such things; but none of them are new to him, to whom past, present, and future are the same. The foresight of them did not prevent his calling us by his grace. Though he knew we were vile, and should prove ungrateful and unfaithful, yet he would be found of us; he would knock at the door of our hearts, and gain himself an entrance. Nor shall they prevent his accomplishing his gracious purpose. It is our part to be abased before him, and quietly to hope and wait for his salvation in the use of his appointed means. The power, success, and blessing, are wholly from himself.

Cardiphonia: Letters to Miss Mary Barham, [1:636]; 1:466

Being confident of this very thing, that he which hath begun a good work
in you will perform it until the day of Jesus Christ.— Phil. 1:6.

IT is your great and singular mercy, my dear Miss, that he has taught you to seek him so early in life. You are entered in the way of salvation, but you must not expect all at once. The work of grace is compared to the corn, and to a building; the growth of the one, and the carrying forward of the other, are gradual. In a building, for instance, if it be large, there is much to be done in preparing and laying the foundation, before the walls appear above ground; much is doing within, when the work does not seem perhaps to advance without; and when it is considerably forward, yet, being encumbered with scaffolds and rubbish, a by-stander sees it at a great disadvantage, and can form but an imperfect judgment of it. But all the while the architect himself, even from the laying of the first stone, conceives of it according to the plan and design he has formed; he prepares and adjusts the materials, disposing each in its proper time and place, and views it, in idea, as already finished. In due season it is completed, but not in a day. The top-stone is fixed, and then, the scaffolds and rubbish being removed, it appears to others as he intended it should be. Men, indeed, often plan what, for want of skill or ability or from unforeseen disappointments, they are unable to execute: but nothing can disappoint the heavenly Builder; nor will he ever be reproached with forsaking the work of his own hands, or beginning that which he could not or would not accomplish; Phil. 1:6. Let us therefore be thankful for beginnings, and patiently wait the event. His enemies strive to retard the work, as they did when the Jews, by his order, set about rebuilding the temple: yet it was finished, in defiance of them all.

Cardiphonia: Letters to Miss Mary Barham, [1:637]; 1:467

*For as the heavens are higher than the earth, so are my ways higher than
your ways, and my thoughts than your thoughts.*—Isa. 55:9.

THE heart is deep, and, like Ezekiel's vision, presents so many
chambers of imagery, one within another, that it requires time
to get a considerable acquaintance with it, and we shall never know
it thoroughly. It is now more than twenty-eight years since the Lord
began to open mine to my own view; and from that time to this,
almost every day has discovered to me something which till then was
unobserved; and the further I go, the more I seem convinced that
I have entered but a little way. A person that travels in some parts
of Derbyshire may easily be satisfied that the country is cavernous;
but how large, how deep, how numerous the caverns may be, which
are hidden from us by the surface of the ground, and what is contained in them, are questions which our nicest inquirers cannot fully
answer. Thus I judge of my heart: that it is very deep and dark, and
full of evil; but as to particulars, I know not one of a thousand.

And if our own hearts are beyond our comprehension, how
much more incomprehensible is the heart of Jesus! If sin abounds
in us, grace and love superabound in him: his ways and thoughts are
higher than ours, as the heavens are higher than the earth; his love
has a height, and depth, and length, and breadth, that passeth all
knowledge; and his riches of grace are unsearchable riches, Eph. 3:8,
18, 19. All that we have received or can receive from him, or know of
him in this life, compared with what he *is* in himself, or what he *has*
for us, is but as the drop of a bucket compared with the ocean, or a
single ray of light in respect of the sun. The waters of the sanctuary
flow to us at first almost upon a level, ankle deep, so graciously does
the Lord condescend to our weakness; but they rise as we advance,
and constrain us to cry out, with the apostle, O the depth!

Cardiphonia: Letters to Miss Mary Barham, [1:639]; 1:468

And the rain descended, and the floods came, and the winds blew, and
beat upon that house; and it fell not: for it was founded upon a rock.
—Matthew 7:25.

WE saw no danger upon the road homeward; but my judgment tells me we are always upon the brink of danger, though we see it not; and that, without the immediate protection and care of him who preserveth the stars in their courses, there could be no travelling safely a few miles, nor even sitting in safety by the fire-side. But with him we are safe in all places and circumstances, till our race is done, and his gracious purposes concerning us in the present life are completely answered;—then he will call us home, that we may see his face, and be with him for ever; and then it will not much signify what messenger he shall be pleased to send for us.

While he took care of us abroad, he watched over our concerns at home likewise; so that we found all well upon our return, and met with nothing to grieve us. Many go out and return home no more, and many find distressing things have happened in their absence; but we have to set up our Ebenezer, and to say, Hitherto he has helped us. Assist me to praise him. The Lord is leading you in the good old way, in which you may perceive the footsteps of his flock who have gone before you. They had in their day the same difficulties, fears, and complaints as we have, and, through mercy, we partake of the same consolation which supported and refreshed them; and the promises which they trusted and found faithful, are equally sure to us. It is still true, that they who believe shall never be confounded.

If left to ourselves, we should have built upon sand: but he has provided and revealed a sure foundation, removed our natural prejudices against it; and now, though rains, and floods, and storms, assault our building, it cannot fall, for it is founded upon a rock.

Cardiphonia: Letters to Miss Mary Barham, [1:641]; 1:470

*And these are they likewise which are sown on stony ground; who, when
they have heard the word, immediately receive it with gladness; And
have no root in themselves, and so endure but for a time: afterward,
when affliction or persecution ariseth for the word's sake,
immediately they are offended.*—Mark 4:16-17.

THE work of grace is not like Jonah's gourd, which sprang up and flourished in a night, and as quickly withered; but rather like the oak, which, from a little acorn and a tender plant, advances with an almost imperceptible growth from year to year, till it becomes a broad-spreading and deep-rooted tree, and then it stands for ages. The Christian oak shall grow and flourish for ever. When I see any, soon after they appear to be awakened, making a speedy profession of great joy, before they have a due acquaintance with their own hearts, I am in pain for them. I am not sorry to hear them afterwards complain that their joys are gone, and they are almost at their wit's end; for, without some such check, to make them feel their weakness and dependence I seldom find them turn out well; either their fervour insensibly abates, till they become quite cold, and sink into the world again (of which I have seen many instances), or, if they do not give up all, their walk is uneven, and their spirit has not that savour of brokenness and true humility which is a chief ornament of our holy profession. If they do not feel the plague of their hearts at first, they find it out afterwards, and too often manifest it to others. Therefore though I know the Spirit of the Lord is free, and will not be confined to our rules, and there may be excepted cases; yet in general, I believe the old proverb, 'Soft and fair goes far', will hold good in Christian experience. Let us be thankful for the beginnings of grace, and wait upon our Saviour patiently for the increase. And as we have chosen him for our Physician, let us commit ourselves to his management, and not prescribe to him what he shall prescribe for us. He knows us and he loves us better than we do ourselves, and will do all things well.

Cardiphonia: Letters to Miss Mary Barham, [1:642]; 1:471

O taste and see that the LORD is good: blessed is the man that trusteth in him. O fear the LORD, ye his saints: for there is no want to them that fear him.—Psa. 34:8-9.

IT is written, 'Fear not, I am with thee.' It is written again, 'Blessed is the man who feareth always.' There is a perfect harmony in those seemingly different texts. May the wisdom that cometh from above, teach you and me to keep them both united in our view. If the Lord be with us, we have no cause of fear. His eye is upon us, his arm over us, his ear open to our prayer; his grace sufficient, his promise unchangeable. Under his protection, though the path of duty should lie through fire and water, we may cheerfully and confidently pursue it. On the other hand, our hearts are so deceitful, fallible, and frail; our spiritual enemies so subtle, watchful, and powerful; and they derive so many advantages from the occasions of every day, in which we are unavoidably and unexpectedly concerned; there is so much combustible within, and so many temptations arising from without, capable of setting all in a flame; that we cannot be too jealous of ourselves and our circumstances... When we can say, in the psalmist's spirit, *Hold thou me up*, we may warrantably draw his conclusion, *and I shall be safe*; but the moment we lean to our own understanding we are in imminent danger of falling. The enemy who wars against our souls, is a consummate master in his way, fertile in stratagems and equally skillful in carrying on his assaults by sap or by storm. He studies us, if I may so say, all around, to discover our weak sides; and he is a very Proteus for changing his appearances, and can appear as a sly serpent, a roaring lion, or an angel of light, as best suits his purpose. It is a great mercy to be in some measure acquainted with his devices and aware of them. They who wait humbly on the Lord, and consult carefully at his word and throne of grace, are made wiser than the enemy and enabled to escape and withstand his wiles.

Cardiphonia: Letters to Rev. Mr. William Rose, [1:645]; 1:473

But seek ye first the kingdom of God, and his righteousness;
and all these things shall be added unto you.—Matt. 6:33.

THE Lord is all-sufficient. A lively sense of his love, a deep impression of eternity, a heart filled with zeal for his cause, and a thirst for the good of souls, will, I hope, enable you to make a cheerful sacrifice of whatever has no necessary connection with your peace and his service. And you may rest assured, that whenever he, who loves you better than you do yourself, sees it best for you upon the whole to change your condition, he will bring it about; he will point out the person, prepare the means, and secure the success, by his providence, and the power he has over every heart: and you shall see that all previous difficulties were either gracious preventions, which he threw in the way to prevent your taking a wrong step; or temporary bars, which by his removing them afterwards should give you opportunity of more clearly perceiving his care and interposition in your favour.

How does the love of glory stimulate the soldier, make him forget and forego a thousand personal inconveniences, and prompt him to cross oceans, to traverse deserts, to scale mountains, and plunge into the greatest hardships and the thickest dangers! They do it for a cor-ruptible crown, a puff of breath, an empty fame... We are likewise soldiers; we have a Prince and Captain who deserves our all. They who know him, and have hearts to conceive of his excellence, and to feel their obligations to him, cannot, indeed, seek their own glory; but his glory is dearer to them than a thousand lives. They owe him their souls, for he redeemed them with blood, his own blood; and by his grace he subdued and pardoned them when they were rebels, and in arms against him. Therefore they are not their own; they would not be their own... May the Lord make us thus minded; give us a hearty concern for *his* business; and he has engaged to take care of *ours*; and nothing that can conduce to our real comfort and useful-ness shall be withheld.

Cardiphonia: Letters to Rev. Mr. William Rose, [1:647]; 1:475

Who is a God like unto thee?—Mic. 7:18.

I AM willing to hope, that this is but a short season of anxiety, appointed for the exercise of your faith and patience, and to give you, in his good time, a signal proof of his power and goodness in answering prayer. He sometimes brings us into such a situation that the help of creatures is utterly unavailing, that we may afterwards be more clearly sensible of his interposition. Then we experimentally learn the vanity of all things here below, and are brought to a more immediate and absolute dependence upon himself. We have need of having these lessons frequently inculcated upon us; but when his end is answered, how often, after he has caused grief, does he show his great compassions, and save us from our fears by an outstretched arm and such a seasonable and almost unexpected relief, as constrains us to cry out, 'What has God wrought!' and 'Who is a God like unto thee!' Such, I hope will be the issue of your present trial, and that he who gave her to you at first, will restore her to you again. I see you in the furnace; but the Lord is sitting by it as the refiner of silver; to moderate the fire, and manage the process, so that you shall lose nothing but dross, and be brought forth refined as gold, to praise his name. Apparent difficulties, however great, are nothing to him. If he speaks, it is done; for to God the Lord belong the issues from death. Should his pleasure be otherwise, and should he call your dear partner to a state of glory before you, still I know he is able to support you. What he does, however painful to the flesh, must be right, because he does it. Having bought us with his blood, and saved our souls from hell, he has every kind of right to dispose of us and ours as he pleases; and this we are sure of, he will not lay so much upon us as he freely endured for us; and he can make us amends for all we suffer, and for all we lose, by the light of his countenance.

Cardiphonia: Letters to Rev. Mr. William Rose, [1:654]; 1:480

Hold fast the form of sound words, which thou hast heard of me,
in faith and love which is in Christ Jesus.—2 Tim. 1:13.

IF it should be asked, Which are the necessary things? I answer, Those in which the spiritual worshippers of all ages and countries have been agreed. Those, on the contrary, are mere subordinate matters, in which the best men, those who have been the most eminent for faith, prayer, and humility, and nearness to God, always have been, and still are, divided in their judgments. Upon this plan, I should think it no hard matter to draw up a form of sound words (whether dignified with the name of a creed or no, I care not), to which true believers of all sorts and sizes would unanimously subscribe. Suppose it ran something in the following manner:—I believe that sin is the most hateful thing in the world; that I and all men are by nature in a state of wrath and depravity, utterly unable to sustain the penalty or to fulfil the commands of God's holy law; and that we have no sufficiency of ourselves to think a good thought. I believe that Jesus Christ is the chief among ten thousands; that he came into the world to save the chief of sinners, by making a propitiation for sin by his death, by paying a perfect obedience to the law in our behalf; and that he is now exalted on high, to give repentance and remission of sins to all that believe; and that he ever liveth to make intercession for us. I believe that the Holy Spirit (the gift of God through Jesus Christ), is the sure and only guide into all truth, and the common privilege of all believers; and under his influence, I believe the Holy Scriptures are able to make us wise unto salvation, and to furnish us thoroughly for every good work. I believe that love to God, and to man for God's sake, is the essence of religion, and the fulfilling of the law; that without holiness no man shall see the Lord; that those who, by a patient course in well-doing, seek glory, honour, and immortality, shall receive eternal life: and I believe that this reward is not of debt, but of grace, even to the praise and glory of that grace whereby he has made us acceptable in the Beloved. Amen.

Cardiphonia: Letter to Rev. Mr. Francis Okeley, [1:659]; 1:484

If we say that we have no sin, we deceive ourselves,
and the truth is not in us.—1 John 1:8.

YOU say that your experience agrees with mine. It must be so, because our hearts are alike. The heart is deceitful and desperately wicked, destitute of good, and prone to evil. This is the character of mankind universally, and those who are made partakers of grace are renewed but in part; the evil nature still cleaves to them, and the root of sin, though mortified, is far from being dead. While the cause remains, it will have effects; and while we are burdened with the body of this death, we must groan under it. But we need not be swallowed up with over-much sorrow, since we have, in Jesus, a Saviour, a Righteousness, an Advocate, a Shepherd. 'He knows our frame, and remembers that we are but dust.' If sin abounds in us, grace abounds much more in him: nor would he suffer sin to remain in his people, if he did not know how to overrule it, and make it an occasion of endearing his love and grace so much the more to their souls. The Lord forbid that we should plead his goodness as an encouragement to sloth and indifference! Humiliation, godly sorrow, and self-abasement, become us; but, at the same time, we may rejoice in the Lord. Though sin remains, it shall not have dominion over us; though it wars in us, it shall not prevail against us. We have a mercy-seat, sprinkled with blood; we have an Advocate with the Father; we are called to this warfare and we fight under the eye of the Captain of our salvation, who is always near to renew our strength, to heal our wounds, and to cover our heads in the heat of battle. As ministers, we preach to those who have like passions and infirmities with ourselves; and by our own feelings, fears, and changes, we learn to speak a word in season to them that are weary, to warn those who stand, and to stretch out a hand of compassion toward them that are fallen; and to commend it to others, from our own experience, as a faithful saying, 'That Jesus came to save the chief of sinners.'

Cardiphonia: Letters to Rev. Mr. Matthew Powley, [1:664]; 1:488

*O LORD, I know that the way of man is not in himself:
it is not in man that walketh to direct his steps.*—Jer. 10:23.

I MAY learn (only I am a sad dunce) by small and common incidents, as well as by some more striking and important turns in life, that it is not in man that walketh to direct his steps. It is not for me to say, Today or tomorrow I will do this or that. I cannot write a letter to a friend without leave or without help, for neither opportunity nor ability are at my own disposal. It is not needful that the Lord should raise a mountain in my way, to stop my purpose; if he only withdraw a certain kind of imperceptible support, which in general I have, and use it without duly considering whose it is, then, in a moment, I feel myself unstrung and disabled, like a ship that has lost her masts, and cannot proceed till he is pleased to refit me and renew my strength. My pride and propensity to self-dependence render frequent changes of this kind necessary to me, or I should soon forget what I am, and sacrifice to my own drag. Therefore, upon the whole, I am satisfied, and see it best that I should be absolutely poor and penniless in myself, and forced to depend upon the Lord for the smallest things as well as the greatest. And if, by his blessing, my experience should at length tally with my judgment in this point, that without him I can do nothing; then I know I shall find it easy, through him, to do all things; for the door of his mercy is always open, and it is but ask and have. But, alas! a secret persuasion (though contrary to repeated convictions) that I have something at home, too often prevents me going to him for it; and then no wonder I am disappointed. The life of faith seems so simple and easy in theory, that I can point it out to others in few words: but in practice it is very difficult; and my advances are so slow, that I hardly dare say I get forward at all. It is a great thing indeed to have the spirit of a little child, so as to be habitually afraid of taking a single step without leading.

Cardiphonia: Letters to Rev. Mr. Matthew Powley, [1:669]; 1:492

Brethren, pray for us.—1 Thess. 5:25.

WE have much call for thankfulness, and much for humiliation. Some have been removed, some are evidently ripening for glory, and now and then we have a new inquirer. But the progress of wickedness amongst the unconverted here is awful. Convictions repeatedly stifled in many have issued in a hardness and boldness in sinning, which I believe is seldom found but in those places where the light of the gospel has been long resisted and abused. If my eyes suitably affected my heart, I should weep day and night upon this account but, alas! I am too indifferent. I feel a woeful defect in my zeal for God and compassion for souls; and when Satan and conscience charge me with cowardice, treachery, and stupidity, I know not what to reply. I am generally carried through my public work with some liberty; and because I am not put to shame before the people, I seem content and satisfied. I wish to be more thankful for what the Lord is pleased to do amongst us, but, at the same time, to be more earnest with him for a further out-pouring of his Spirit. Assist me herein with your prayers.

As to my own private experience, the enemy is not suffered to touch the foundation of my faith and hope; thus far I have peace: but my conflicts and exercises with the effects of indwelling sin, are very distressing. I cannot doubt of my state and acceptance; and yet it seems no one can have more cause for doubts and fears than myself, if such doubtings were at all encouraged by the gospel: but I see they are not: I see that what I want and hope for, the Lord promises to do, for his own name's sake, and with a *non obstante* [notwithstanding] to all my vileness and perverseness; and I cannot question but he has given me (for how else could I have it?) a thirst for that communion with him in love, and conformity to his image, of which as yet I have experienced but very faint and imperfect beginnings. But if he has begun, I venture, upon his word, that he will not forsake the work of his own hands.

Cardiphonia: Letters to Rev. Mr. Matthew Powley, [1:671]; 1:493

And Jacob awaked out of his sleep, and he said,
Surely the LORD is in this place; and I knew it not.—Gen. 28:16.

THE chief difference between us and the disciples, when our Saviour was upon earth, is in this: they then walked by sight, and we are called to walk by faith. They could see him with their bodily eyes; we cannot, but he said before he left them, 'It is expedient for you that I go away.' How could this be, unless that spiritual communion which he promised to maintain with his people after his ascension, were preferable to the intercourse he allowed them whilst he was visibly with them? But we are sure it is preferable, and they who had tried both were well satisfied he had made good his promise; so that, though they had known him after the flesh, they were content not to know him so any more. Yes, madam, though we cannot see him, he sees us: he is nearer to us than we are to ourselves. In a natural state, we have very dark, and indeed dishonourable, thoughts of God: we conceive of him as at a distance. But when the heart is awakened, we begin to make Jacob's reflection, 'Surely the Lord is in this place, and I knew it not.' And when we receive faith, we begin to know that this ever-present God is in Christ; that the government of heaven and earth, the dispensations of the kingdom of nature, providence, and grace, are in the hands of Jesus; that it is he with whom we have to do, who once suffered agony and death for our redemption, and whose compassion and tenderness are the same, now he reigns over all blessed for ever, as when he conversed amongst men in the days of his humiliation. Thus God is made known to us by the gospel, in the endearing views of a Saviour, a Shepherd, a Husband, a Friend; and a way of access is opened for us through the veil, that is, the human nature of our Redeemer, to enter, with humble confidence, into the holiest of all, and to repose all our cares and concerns upon the strength of that everlasting arm which upholds heaven and earth, and upon that infinite love which submitted to the shame, pain and death of the cross, to redeem sinners from wrath and misery.

Cardiphonia: Letters to Mrs. Gardiner, [1:679]; 1:499

For the grace of God that bringeth salvation hath appeared to all men,
Teaching us that, denying ungodliness and worldly lusts,
we should live soberly, righteously, and godly,
in this present world.—Titus 2:11-12.

THOUGH there is a height, a breadth, a length, and a depth, in this mystery of redeeming love, exceeding the comprehension of all finite minds; yet the great and leading principles which are necessary for the support and comfort of our souls, may be summed up in a very few words. Such a summary we are favoured with in Titus 2:11-14; where the whole of salvation, all that is needful to be known, experienced, practised, and hoped for, is comprised within the compass of four verses. If many books, much study, and great discernment, were necessary in order to be happy, what must the poor and simple do? Yet for them especially is the gospel designed; and few but such as these attain the knowledge and comfort of it. The Bible is a sealed book, till the heart be awakened; and, then, he that runs may read. The propositions are few: I am a sinner, therefore I need a Saviour, one who is able and willing to save to the uttermost; such a one is Jesus; he is all that I want, wisdom, righteousness, sanctification, and redemption. But will he receive me? Can I answer a previous question? Am I willing to receive him? If so, and if his word may be taken, if he meant what he said, and promised no more than he can perform, I may be sure of a welcome: he knew, long before, the doubts, fears, and suspicions which would arise in my mind when I should come to know what I am, what I have done, and what I have deserved; and therefore he declared, before he left the earth, 'Him that cometh to me I will in no wise cast out.' I have no money or price in my hand, no worthiness to recommend me: and I need none, for he saveth freely for his own name's sake. I have only to be thankful for what he has already shown me, and to wait upon him for more. It is my part to commit myself to him as the Physician of sin-sick souls, not to prescribe to him how he shall treat me. To begin, carry on, and perfect the cure, is his part.

Cardiphonia: Letters to Mrs. Gardiner, [1:680]; 1:500

And who is sufficient for these things?—2 Cor. 2:16.

WE are in no worse circumstances than the apostle Paul, who, though eminent and exemplary in the Christian life, found and freely confessed that he had no sufficiency in himself to think a good thought. Nor did he wish it otherwise; he even gloried in his infirmities, that the power of Christ might rest upon him. Unbelief, and a thousand evils, are still in our hearts: though their reign and dominion is at an end, they are not slain nor eradicated; their effects will be felt more or less sensibly, as the Lord is pleased more or less to afford or abate his gracious influence. When they are kept down we are no better in ourselves, for they are not kept down by us; but we are very prone to think better of ourselves at such a time; and therefore he is pleased to permit us at seasons to feel a difference, that we may never forget how weak and how vile we are. We cannot absolutely conquer these evils; but it becomes us to be humbled for them; and we are to fight, and strive, and pray against them. Our great duty is to be at his footstool, and to cry to him who has promised to perform all things for us. Why are we called soldiers, but because we are called to a warfare? And how could we fight, if there were no enemies to resist? The Lord's soldiers are not merely for show, to make an empty parade in a uniform, and to brandish their arms when none but friends and spectators are around them. No, we must stand upon the field of battle; we must face the fiery darts; we must wrestle (which is the closest and most arduous kind of fighting) with our foes; nor can we well expect wholly to escape wounds; but the leaves of the tree of life are provided for their healing. The Captain of our salvation is at hand, and leads us on with an assurance which might make even a coward bold—that, in the end, we shall be more than conquerors through him who has loved us.

Cardiphonia: Letters to Mrs. Gardiner, [1:688]; 1:506

For the flesh lusteth against the Spirit, and the Spirit against the flesh:
and these are contrary the one to the other: so that ye cannot
do the things that ye would.—Gal. 5:17.

WERE I to define a Christian, or rather to describe him at large, I know no text I would choose sooner, as a ground for the subject, than Gal. 5:17. A Christian has noble aims, which distinguish him from the bulk of mankind. His leading principles, motives, and desires, are all supernatural and divine. Could he do as he would, there is not a spirit before the throne should excel him in holiness, love, and obedience. He would tread in the very footsteps of his Saviour, fill up every moment in his service, and employ every breath in his praise. This he would do; but, alas! he cannot. Against this desire of the spirit, there is a contrary desire and working of a corrupt nature, which meets him at every turn. He has a beautiful copy set before him: he is enamoured with it, and though he does not expect to equal it, he writes carefully after it, and longs to attain the nearest possible imitation. But indwelling sin and Satan continually jog his hand, and spoil his strokes. You cannot, madam, form a right judgment of yourself, except you make due allowance for those things which are not peculiar to yourself, but common to all who have spiritual perception, and are indeed the inseparable appendages of this mortal state. If it were not so, why should the most spiritual and gracious people be so ready to confess themselves vile and worthless? One eminent branch of our holiness, is a sense of shame and humiliation or those vile evils which are only known to ourselves, and to him who searches our hearts, joined with an acquaintance in Jesus, who is appointed of God, wisdom, righteousness, sanctification, and redemption. I will venture to assure you, that though you will possess a more stable peace, in proportion as the Lord enables you to live more simply upon the blood, righteousness, and grace of the Mediator, you will never grow into a better opinion of yourself than you have at present.

Cardiphonia: Letters to Mrs. Gardiner, [1:689]; 1:507

Let nothing be done through strife or vainglory; but in lowliness of mind let each esteem other better than themselves.—Phil. 2:3.

ONE great cause of our frequent conflicts is, that we have a secret desire to be rich, and it is the Lord's design to make us poor: we want to gain an ability of doing something; and he suits his dispensations, to convince us that we can do nothing: we want a stock in ourselves, and he would have us absolutely dependent upon him. So far as we are content to be weak, that his power may be magnified in us, so far we shall make our enemies know that we are strong, though we ourselves shall never be directly sensible that we are so; only by comparing what we are, with the opposition we stand against, we may come to a comfortable conclusion, that the Lord worketh mightily in us, Psa. 41:11.

If our views are simple, and our desires towards the Lord, it may be of use to consider some of your faults and mine, not as the faults of you and me in particular, but as the fault of that depraved nature, which is common with us to all the Lord's people, and which made Paul groan as feelingly and as heartily as we can do… As grace resists sin, so sin resists grace; Gal. 5:17. The proper tendency of each is mutually weakened on both sides; and between the two, the poor believer, however blameless and exemplary in the sight of men, appears in his own view the most inconsistent character under the sun. He can hardly think it is so with others, and judging of *them* by what he *sees*, and of *himself* by what he *feels*, in lowliness of heart he esteems others better than himself. This proves him to be right: for it is the will of God concerning him; Phil. 2:3. This is the warfare. But it shall not always be so. Grace shall prevail. The evil nature is already enervated and ere long it shall die the death. Jesus will make us more than conquerors.

Cardiphonia: Letters to Miss Jane Flower, [1:696]; 1:512

And without controversy great is the mystery of godliness:
God was manifest in the flesh.—1 Tim. 3:16.

IT gave me great comfort to find, that what I wrote concerning the divine character of Jesus, as God manifest in the flesh, met with your approbation. This doctrine is, in my view, the great foundation-stone upon which all true religion is built: but, alas! in the present day, it is the stumbling-stone and rock of offence, upon which too many, fondly presuming upon their own wisdom, fall and are broken. I am so far from wondering that any should doubt of it, that I am firmly persuaded none can truly believe it, however plainly set forth in Scripture, unless it be revealed to them from heaven; or, in the apostle's words, that 'no one can call Jesus Christ Lord, but by the Holy Ghost'... Judging by natural light, it seems impossible to believe that the title of the true God and eternal life should properly belong to that despised man who hung dead upon the cross, exposed to the insults of his cruel enemies. I know nothing that can obviate the objections the reasoning mind is ready to form against it, but a real conviction of the sinfulness of sin, and the state of a sinner as exposed to the curse of the holy law, and destitute of every plea and hope in himself. Then the necessity of a Redeemer and the necessity of this Redeemer's being Almighty, is seen and felt, with an evidence which bears down all opposition; for neither the efficacy of his atonement and intercession, nor his sufficiency to guide, save, protect, and feed those who trust in him, can be conceived of without it. When the eyes of the understanding are opened, the soul made acquainted with and attentive to its own state and wants, he that runs may read this truth, not in a few detached texts of a dubious import, and liable to be twisted and tortured by the arts of criticism, but as interwoven in the very frame and texture of the Bible, and written, as with a sunbeam throughout the principal parts both of the Old and New Testament.

Cardiphonia: Letters to Mrs. Lucy Thornton, [2:9]; 1:524

For our gospel came not unto you in word only, but also in power, and in the Holy Ghost, and in much assurance.—1 Thess. 1:5.

THE gospel addresses both head and heart; and where it has its proper effect, where it is received as the word of God, and is closed with the authority and energy of the Holy Spirit, the understanding is enlightened, the affections awakened and engaged, the will brought into subjection, and the whole soul delivered to its impression as wax to the seal. When this is the case, when the affections do not take the lead, and push forward with a blind impulse but arise from the principles of Scripture, and are governed by them, the more warmth the better. Yet in this state of infirmity, nothing is perfect; and our natural temperament and disposition will have more influence upon our religious sensations than we are ordinarily aware. It is well to know how to make proper allowances and abatements upon this head, in the judgment we form both of ourselves and of others. Many good people are distressed and alternately elated by frames and feelings, which perhaps are more constitutional than properly religious experiences. I dare not tell you, madam, what I am; but I can tell you what I wish to be. The love of God, as manifested in Jesus Christ, is what I would wish to be the abiding object of my contemplation; not merely to speculate upon it as a doctrine, but so to feel it, and my own interest in it, as to have my heart filled with its effects, and transformed into its resemblance; that, with this glorious exemplar in my view, I may be animated to a spirit of benevolence, love and compassion, to all around me; that my love may be primarily fixed upon him who has so loved me, and then, for his sake, diffused to all his children, and to all his creatures. Then, knowing that much is forgiven to me, I should be prompted to the ready exercise of forgiveness, if I have aught against any. Then I should be humble, patient, and submissive under all his dispensations; meek, gentle, forbearing, and kind to my fellow worms. Then I should be active and diligent in improving all my talents and powers in his service, and for his glory; and live not to myself, but to him who loved me and gave himself for me.

Cardiphonia: Letters to Mrs. Lucy Thornton, [2:18]; 1:531

Wherefore in all things it behoved him to be made like unto his brethren,
that he might be a merciful and faithful high priest
in things pertaining to God.—Heb. 2:17.

IT is a comfortable consideration, that he with whom we have to do, our great High Priest, who once put away our sins by the sacrifice of himself, and now for ever appears in the presence of God for us, is not only possessed of sovereign authority and infinite power, but wears our very nature... His bowels were moved before his arm was exerted: he condescended to mingle tears with mourners and wept over distresses which he intended to relieve. He is still the same in his exalted state; compassions dwell within his heart... He knows our sorrows, not merely as he knows all things, but as one who has been in our situation, and who, though without sin himself, endured when upon earth inexpressibly more for us than he will ever lay upon us. He has sanctified poverty, pain, disgrace, temptation, and death, by passing through these states; and in whatever states his people are, they may by faith have fellowship with him in their sufferings, and he will by sympathy and love have fellowship and interest with them in theirs. What then shall we fear, or of what shall we complain; when all our concerns are written upon his heart, and their management, to the very hairs of our head, are under his care and providence; when he pities us more than we can do ourselves, and has engaged his almighty power to sustain and relieve us? However, as he is tender, he is wise also: he loves us, but especially with regard to our best interests. If there were not something in our hearts and our situation that required discipline and medicine, he so delights in our prosperity, that we should never be in heaviness... The innumerable comforts and mercies with which he enriches even those we call darker days, are sufficient proofs that he does not willingly grieve us: but when he sees a need-be for chastisement, he will not withhold it because he loves us; on the contrary, that is the very reason why he afflicts.

Cardiphonia: Letters to Mrs. Lucy Thornton, [2:20]; 1:532

It is good for me that I have been afflicted;
that I might learn thy statutes.—Psa. 119:71.

THE advantages of afflictions, when the Lord is pleased to employ them for the good of his people, are many and great. Permit me to mention a few of them; and the Lord grant that we may all find those blessed ends answered to ourselves, by the trials he is pleased to appoint us.

Afflictions quicken us to prayer. It is a pity it should be so; but experience testifies, that a long course of ease and prosperity, without painful changes, has an unhappy tendency to make us cold and formal in our secret worship; but troubles rouse our spirits, and constrain us to call upon the Lord in good earnest, when we feel a need of that help which we only can have from him.

They are useful, and in a degree necessary, to keep alive in us a conviction of the vanity and unsatisfying nature of the present world, and all its enjoyments; to remind us that this is not our rest, and to call our thoughts upwards, where our true treasure is, and where our conversation ought to be. When things go on much to our wish, our hearts are too prone to say, It is good to be here. It is probable, that had Moses, when he came to invite Israel to Canaan, found them in prosperity, as in the days of Joseph, they would have been very unwilling to remove; but the afflictions they were previously brought into made his message welcome. Thus the Lord, by pain, sickness, and disappointments, by breaking our cisterns and withering our gourds, weakens our attachment to this world, and makes the thought of quitting it more familiar and more desirable.

A child of God cannot but greatly desire a more enlarged and experimental acquaintance with his holy word; and this attainment is greatly promoted by our trials. The far greater part of the promises in Scripture are made and suited to a state of affliction; and, though we may believe they are true, we cannot so well know their sweetness, power, and suitableness, unless we ourselves are in a state to which they refer.

Cardiphonia: Letters to Mrs. Lucy Thornton, [2:22]; 1:534

And call upon me in the day of trouble:
I will deliver thee, and thou shalt glorify me.—Psa. 50:15.

THE Lord says, 'Call upon me in the day of trouble, and I will deliver.'—Now, till the day of trouble comes, such a promise is like a city of refuge to an Israelite, who, not having slain a man, was in no danger of the avenger of blood. He had a privilege near him, of which he knew not the use and value, because he was not in the case for which it was provided. But some can say, I not only believe this promise upon the authority of the speaker, but I can set my seal to it: I have been in trouble; I took this course for relief, and I was not disappointed. The Lord verily heard and delivered me. Thus afflictions likewise give occasion of our knowing and noticing more of the Lord's wisdom, power and goodness, in supporting and relieving, than we should otherwise have known.

Afflictions evidence to ourselves and manifest to others, the reality of grace. And when we suffer as Christians, exercise some measure of that patience and submission, and receive some measure of these supports and supplies, which the gospel requires and promises to believers, we are more confirmed that we have not taken up with mere notions; and others may be convinced that we do not follow cunningly devised fables. They likewise strengthen by exercise our graces: as our limbs and natural powers would be feeble if not called to daily exertion; so the graces of the Spirit would languish, without something was provided to draw them out to use. And, to say no more, they are honourable, as they advance our conformity to Jesus our Lord, who was a man of sorrows for our sake. Methinks, if we might go to heaven without suffering, we should be unwilling to desire it. Why should we ever wish to go by any other path than that which he has consecrated and endeared by his own example? Especially as his people's sufferings are not penal; there is no wrath in them: the cup he puts in their hands is very different from that which he drank for their sakes and is only medicinal to promote their chief good.

Cardiphonia: Letters to Mrs. Lucy Thornton, [2:23]; 1:535

Now no chastening for the present seemeth to be joyous, but grievous:
nevertheless afterward it yieldeth the peaceable fruit of righteousness
unto them which are exercised thereby.—Heb. 12:11.

WHAT shall I say? Topics of consolation are at hand in abundance; they are familiar to your mind; and was I to fill the sheet with them, I could suggest nothing but what you already know. Then are they consolatory indeed, when the Lord himself is pleased to apply them to the heart. This he has promised, and therefore we are encouraged to expect it. This is my prayer for you: I sincerely sympathize with you; I cannot comfort you: but he can; and I trust he will. How impertinent would it be to advise you to forget or suspend the feelings which such a stroke must excite! Who can help feeling! Nor is sensibility in itself sinful. Christian resignation is very different from that stoical stubbornness which is most easily practiced by those unamiable characters whose regards centre wholly in self; nor could we in a proper manner exercise submission to the will of God under our trials, if we did not feel them. He who knows our frame is pleased to allow, that afflictions for the present are not joyous, but grievous. But to them that fear him he is near at hand, to support their spirits, to moderate their grief, and in the issue to sanctify it; so that they shall come out of the furnace refined, more humble, and more spiritual. There is, however, a part assigned us: we are to pray for the help in need; and we are not willfully to give way to the impression of overwhelming sorrow. We are to endeavour to turn our thoughts to such considerations as are suited to alleviate it; our deserts as sinners, the many mercies we are still indulged with, the still greater afflictions which many of our fellow creatures endure and, above all, the sufferings of Jesus, that Man of Sorrows, who made himself intimately acquainted with grief for our sakes.

Cardiphonia: Letters to Mrs. Lucy Thornton, [2:24]; 1:536

For whom the Lord loveth he chasteneth.—Heb. 12:6.

WHEN the will of the Lord is manifested to us by the event, we are to look to him for grace and strength, and be still to know that he is God, that he has a right to dispose of us and ours as he pleases, and that in the exercise of this right he is most certainly good and wise. We often complain of losses; but the expression is rather improper. Strictly speaking, we can lose nothing, because we have no real property in anything. Our earthly comforts are lent us; and when recalled, we ought to return and resign them with thankfulness to him who has let them remain so long in our hands... I hope the Lord the only Comforter, will bring such thoughts with warmth and efficacy upon your mind. Your wound, while fresh, is painful; but faith, prayer, and time will, I trust gradually render it tolerable. There is something fascinating in grief: painful as it is, we are prone to indulge it, and to brood over the thoughts and circumstances which are suited (like fuel to fire) to heighten and prolong it. When the Lord afflicts, it is his design that we should grieve: but in this, as in all other things, there is a certain moderation which becomes a Christian, and which only grace can teach; and grace teaches us, not by books or by hearsay, but by experimental lessons; all beyond this should be avoided and guarded against as sinful and hurtful. Grief, when indulged and excessive, preys upon the spirits, injures health, indisposes us for duty, and causes us to shed tears which deserve more tears. This is a weeping world. Sin has filled it with thorns and briars, with crosses and calamities. It is a great hospital, resounding with groans in every quarter. It is a field of battle, where many are falling around us continually; and it is more wonderful that we escape so well, than that we are sometimes wounded. We *must* have some share: it is the unavoidable lot of our nature and state; it is likewise needful in point of discipline... That is a sweet, instructive, and important passage, Heb. 12:5-11. It is so plain, that it needs no comment; so full, that a comment would but weaken it. May the Lord inscribe it upon your heart, my dear madam, and upon mine.

Cardiphonia: Letters to Mrs. Lucy Thornton, [2:25]; 1:537

My brethren, count it all joy when ye fall into divers temptations.
—James 1:2.

WHAT should I do, and how should I behave, were the Lord pleased to take away my desire with a stroke? But we see he can supply their absence, and afford us superior comforts without them. The gospel reveals one thing needful, the pearl of great price; and supposes, that they who possess this are provided for against all events, and have ground of unshaken hope, and a source of never-failing consolation under every change they can meet with during their pilgrimage state. When his people are enabled to set their seal to this, not only in theory, when all things go smooth, but practically, when called upon to pass through the fire and water; then his grace is glorified in them and by them; then it appears, both to themselves and to others, that they have neither followed cunningly devised fables, nor amused themselves with empty notions; then they know in themselves, and it is evidenced to others, that God is with them of a truth. In this view a believer, when in some good measure divested from that narrow selfish disposition which cleaves so close to us by nature, will not only submit to trials, but rejoice in them, notwithstanding the feelings and reluctance of the flesh. For if I am redeemed from misery by the blood of Jesus; and if he is now preparing me a mansion near himself, that I may drink of the rivers of pleasure at his right hand for evermore; the question is not (at least ought not to be), how may I pass through life with the least inconvenience? But, how may my little span of life be made most subservient to the praise and glory of him who loved me, and gave himself for me?

Should we, therefore, not account it an honour and a privilege, when the Captain of our salvation assigns us a difficult post? since he can and does (which no earthly commander can) inspire his soldiers with wisdom, courage and strength, suitable to their situation.

Cardiphonia: Letters to Mrs. Sarah Talbot, [2:34]; 1:544

*In all these things we are more than conquerors through him
that loved us.*—Rom. 8:37.

IT is true that you feel contrary principles, that you are conscious of
defects and defilements; but it is equally true, that you could not
be right, if you did not feel these things... To be conscious of them,
and humbled for them, is one of the surest marks of grace.

Our view of death will not always be alike, but in proportion
to the degree in which the Holy Spirit is pleased to communicate
his sensible influence. We may anticipate the moment of dissolution
with pleasure and desire in the morning, and be ready to shrink from
the thought of it before night. But though our frames and perceptions vary, the report of faith concerning it is the same. The Lord usually reserves dying strength for a dying hour. When Israel was to pass
Jordan, the ark was in the river; and though the rear of the host could
not see it, yet as they successively came forward and approached the
banks, they all beheld the ark, and all went safely over. As you are
not weary of living, if it be the Lord's pleasure so I hope, for the sake
of your friends and the people whom you love, he will spare you
amongst us a little longer; but when the time shall arrive which he
has appointed for your dismission, I make no doubt but he will over-
power all your fears, silence all your enemies, and give you a comfortable, triumphant entrance into his kingdom. You have nothing to
fear from death; for Jesus, by dying, has disarmed it of its stings, has
perfumed the grave, and opened the gates of glory for his believing
people. Satan, so far as he is permitted, will assault our peace, but he
is a vanquished enemy: our Lord holds him in a chain, and sets him
bounds which he cannot pass. He provides for us likewise the whole
armour of God, and has promised to cover our heads himself in the
day of battle, to bring us honourably through every skirmish, and to
make us more than conquerors at last.

Cardiphonia: Letters to Mrs. Sarah Talbot, [2:41]; 1:549

I acknowledged my sin unto thee, and mine iniquity have I not hid.
I said, I will confess my transgressions unto the Lord*; and thou*
forgavest the iniquity of my sin.—Psa. 32:5.

YOU seem sensible where your most observable failing lies, and to take reproof and admonition concerning it in good part; I therefore hope and believe the Lord will give you a growing victory over it. You must not expect habits and tempers will be eradicated instantaneously; but by perseverance in prayer, and observation upon the experiences of every day, much may be done in time. Now and then you will (as is usual in the course of war) lose a battle; but be not discouraged, but rally your forces, and return to the fight. There is a comfortable word, a leaf of the tree of life, for healing the wounds we receive, in 1 John 2:1. If the enemy surprises you, and your heart smites you, do not stand astonished as if there was no help, nor give way to sorrow as if there was no hope, nor attempt to heal yourself; but away immediately to the throne of grace, to the great Physician, to the compassionate High Priest, and tell him all. Satan knows, that if he can keep us from confession, our wounds will rankle; but do you profit by David's experience, Psa. 32:3-5. When we are simple and open-hearted in abasing ourselves before the Lord, though we have acted foolishly and ungratefully, he will seldom let us remain long without affording us a sense of his compassion; for he is gracious; he knows our frame, and how to bear with us, though we can hardly bear with ourselves or with one another.

The main thing is *to have the heart right with God*: this will bring us in the end safely through many mistakes and blunders; but a double mind, a selfish spirit, that would halve things between God and the world, the Lord abhors… If the Lord is pleased to bless you, he will undoubtedly make you humble; for you cannot be either happy or safe, or have any probable hope of abiding usefulness, without it.

Cardiphonia: Letters to Mr. Thomas Jones, [2:48]; 1:554

Take the rod, and gather thou the assembly together, thou, and Aaron thy brother, and speak ye unto the rock before their eyes; and it shall give forth his water, and thou shalt bring forth to them water out of the rock: so thou shalt give the congregation and their beasts drink.—Num. 20:8.

I ADVISE you ... to keep close to the Bible and prayer: bring your difficulties to the Lord, and entreat him to give you and maintain in you a simple spirit. Search the Scripture. How did Peter deal with Simon Magus? We have no right to think worse of any who can hear us, than the apostle did of him. He seemed almost to think his case desperate, and yet he advised him to repentance and prayer... The power is all of God; the means are likewise of his appointment; and he always is pleased to work by such means as may show that the power is his. What was Moses' rod in itself, or the trumpets that threw down Jericho? What influence could the pool of Siloam have, that the eyes of the blind man, by washing in it, should be opened? Or what could Ezekiel's feeble breath contribute to the making dry bones live? All these means were exceedingly disproportionate to the effect; but he who ordered them to be used accompanied them with his power. Yet if Moses had gone without his rod; if Joshua had slighted the rams' horns; if the prophet had thought it foolishness to speak to dry bones, or the blind man refused to wash his eye, nothing could have been done... I do not reason, expostulate, and persuade sinners, because I think I can prevail with them, but because the Lord has commanded it. He directs me to address them as reasonable creatures; to take them by every handle; to speak to their consciences; to tell them of the terrors of the Lord, and of his tender mercies; to argue with them what good they find in sin; whether they do not need a Saviour; to put them in mind of death, judgment, and eternity, &c. When I have done all, I know it is to little purpose, except the Lord speaks to their hearts.

Cardiphonia: Letters to Mr. Thomas Jones, [2:52]; 1:558

For even Christ pleased not himself; but, as it is written, The reproaches of them that reproached thee fell on me.— Rom. 15:3.

I AM persuaded, that love and humility are the highest attainments in the school of Christ, and the brightest evidences that he is indeed our Master... Our Lord has not only taught us to expect persecution from the world, though this alone is a trial too hard for flesh and blood; but we must look for what is much more grievous to a renewed mind, to be in some respects slighted, censured, and misunderstood, even by our Christian brethren; and that, perhaps in cases where we are really striving to promote the glory of God and the good of souls, and cannot, without the reproach of our consciences, alter our conduct, however glad we should be to have their approbation. Therefore we are required, not only to resist the world, the flesh, and the devil, but likewise to bear one another's burdens; which plainly intimates there will be something to be borne with on all hands; and happy indeed is he that is not offended. You may observe what unjust reports and surmises were received, even at Jerusalem, concerning the apostle Paul; and it seems he was condemned unheard, and that by many thousands too, Acts 21:20-21; but we do not find he was at all ruffled, or that he sought to retort anything upon them, though doubtless, had he been so disposed, he might have found something to have charged them with in his turn; but he calmly and willingly complied with everything in his power to soften and convince them. Let us be followers of this pattern, so far as he was a follower of Christ; for even Christ pleased not himself. How did he bear with the mistakes, weakness, intemperate zeal, and imprudent proposals of his disciples while on earth! And how does he bear with the same things from you and me, and every one of his followers now! And do we, can we, think much to bear with each other for his sake? Have we all a full remission of ten thousand talents which we owed him, and were utterly unable to pay; and do we wrangle amongst ourselves for a few pence? God forbid!

Cardiphonia: Letters to Rev. Mr. John Whitford, [2:62]; 1:565

Follow peace with all men, and holiness, without which no
man shall see the Lord.—Heb. 12:14.

THE two great points we are called to pursue in this sinful divided world, are peace and holiness: I hope you are much in the study of them. These are the peculiar characteristics of a disciple of Jesus; they are the richest part of the enjoyments of heaven; and so far as they are received into the heart, they bring down heaven upon earth; and they are more inseparably connected between themselves than some of us are aware of. The longer I live, the more I see of the vanity and the sinfulness of our unchristian disputes: they eat up the very vitals of religion. I grieve to think how often I have lost my time and my temper that way, in presuming to regulate the vineyards of others, when I have neglected my own; when the beam in my own eye has so contracted my sight, that I could discern nothing but the mote in my neighbour's. I am now desirous to choose a better part. Could I speak the publican's words with a proper feeling, I wish not for the tongue of men or angels to fight about notions or sentiments. I allow that every branch of gospel truth is precious, that errors are abounding, and that it is our duty to bear an honest testimony to what the Lord has enabled us to find comfort in, and to instruct with meekness such as are willing to be instructed; but I cannot see it my duty, nay, I believe it would be my sin, to attempt to beat my notions into other people's heads. Too often I have attempted it in time past; but I now judge, that both my zeal and my weapons were carnal. When our dear Lord questioned Peter, after his fall and recovery, he said not, Art thou wise, learned, and eloquent? Nay, he said not, Art thou clear, and sound, and orthodox? But this only, 'Lovest thou me?'

Cardiphonia: Letters to Rev. Mr. John Whitford, [2:65]; 1:567

That in the ages to come he might shew the exceeding riches of his grace
in his kindness toward us through Christ Jesus.—Eph. 2:7.

OH for grace to take warning by the sufferings of others, and set loose to the world, and so number our days as to incline our hearts to the one thing needful! Indeed that one thing includes many things, sufficient to engage the best of our thoughts and the most of our time, if we were duly sensible of their importance; but I may adopt the psalmist's expression, 'My soul cleaveth to the dust.' How is it that the truths of which I have the most undoubted conviction, and which are, of all others, the most weighty, should make so little impression upon me? O I know the cause! It is deeply rooted. An evil nature cleaves to me; so that when I would do good, evil is present with me. It is, however, a mercy to be made sensible of it, and in any measure humbled for it. Ere long it will be dropped in the grave; then all complaints shall cease. That thought gives relief. I shall not always live this poor dying life: I hope one day to be all ear, all heart, all tongue: when I shall see the Redeemer as he is, I shall be like him. This will be a heaven indeed, to behold his glory without a veil, to rejoice in his love without a cloud, and to sing his praises without one jarring or wandering note, for ever. In the mean time, may he enable us to serve him with our best. Oh that every power, faculty, and talent, were devoted to him! He deserves all we have, and ten thousand times more if we had it; for he has loved us, and washed us from our sins in his own blood. He gave himself for us. In one sense we are well suited to answer his purpose; for if we were not vile and worthless beyond expression, the exceeding riches of his grace would not have been so gloriously displayed. His glory shines more in redeeming one sinner, than in preserving a thousand angels.

Cardiphonia: Letters to Mrs. Mary Place, [2:80]; 1:579

> *Righteousness exalteth a nation,*
> *but sin is a reproach to any people.*—PROV. 14:34.

I HOPE the good people at Bristol, and everywhere else, are praying for our sinful, distracted land, in this dark day. The Lord is angry, the sword is drawn, and I am afraid nothing but the spirit of wrestling prayer can prevail for the returning it to the scabbard. Could things have proceeded to these extremities, except the Lord had withdrawn his salutary blessing from both sides? It is a time of prayer. We see the beginning of trouble, but who can foresee the possible consequences? ... I meddle not with the disputes of the party, nor concern myself with any political maxims, but such as are laid down in Scripture. There I read that righteousness exalteth a nation, and that sin is the reproach, and, if persisted in, the ruin of any people. Some people are startled at the enormous sum of our national debt: they who understand spiritual arithmetic may be well startled if they sit down and compute the debt of national sin. *Imprimis* [First and foremost], Infidelity; *Item* [Also], Contempt of the gospel: *Item*, The profligacy of manners: *Item*, Perjury: *Item*, The cry of blood, the blood of thousands, perhaps millions, from the East Indies. It would take sheets, yea quires, to draw out the particulars under each of these heads, and then much would remain untold. What can we answer, when the Lord saith, 'Shall not I visit for these things? Shall not my soul be avenged on such a nation as this?' Since we received the news of the first hostilities in America, we have had an additional prayer-meeting. Could I hear that professors in general, instead of wasting their breath in censuring men and measures, were plying the throne of grace, I should still hope for a respite... There is one political maxim which comforts me: 'The Lord reigns.' His hand guides the storm; and he knows them that are his, how to protect, support, and deliver them. He will take care of his own cause; yea, he will extend his kingdom, even by these formidable methods. Men have one thing in view; he has another, and his counsel shall stand.

Cardiphonia: Letters to Mrs. Mary Place, [2:85]; 1:584

For here have we no continuing city, but we seek one to come.
—Heb. 13:14.

THE time when Mr. and Mrs. C**** removed to Scotland drawing near, Mrs.**** is gone to spend a week or two with them, and take her leave. She feels something at parting with a sister, who is indeed a valuable person; and from children they have always lived in the most tender intimacy and uninterrupted friendship. But all beneath the moon (like the moon itself) is subject to incessant change. Alterations and separations are graciously appointed of the Lord, to remind us that this is not our rest, and to prepare our thoughts for that approaching change which shall fix us for ever in an unchangeable state. O madam! what shall we poor worms render to him who has brought life and immortality to light by the gospel, taken away the sting of death, revealed a glorious prospect beyond the grave, and given us eyes to see it? Now the reflection, that we must, ere long, take a final farewell of what is most capable of pleasing us upon earth, is not only tolerable, but pleasant. For we know we cannot fully possess our best friend, our chief treasure, till we have done with all below: nay, we cannot till then properly see each other. We are cased up in vehicles of clay, and converse together as if we were in different coaches with the blinds close drawn round. We see the carriage, and the voice tells us that we have a friend within; but we shall know each other better, when death shall open the coach doors, and hand out the company successively, and lead them into the glorious apartments which the Lord has appointed to be the common residence of them that love him. What an assembly will there be! What a constellation of glory, when each individual shall shine like the sun in the kingdom of their Father! No sins, sorrows, temptations; no veils, clouds, or prejudices, shall interrupt us then. All names of idle distinction (the fruits of present remaining darkness, the channels of bigotry, and the stumbling-block of the world), will be at an end.

Cardiphonia: Letters to Mrs. Mary Place, [2:88]; 1:586

The Lord reigneth; let the earth rejoice;
let the multitude of isles be glad thereof.—Psa. 97:1.

I WILL tell you then, though you know it, that the Lord reigns. He who once bore our sins, and carried our sorrows, is seated upon a throne of glory, and exercises all power in heaven and on earth. Thrones, principalities, and powers, bow before him. Every event in the kingdoms of providence and of grace are under his rule. His providence pervades and manages the whole, and is as minutely attentive to every part as if there were only that single object in his view. From the tallest archangel to the meanest ant or fly, all depend on him for their being, their preservation, and their powers. He directs the sparrows where to build their nests, and to find their food. He overrules the rise and fall of nations, and bends, with an invincible energy and unerring wisdom, all events; so that while many intend nothing less, in the issue their designs all concur and coincide with the accomplishment of his holy will. He restrains with a mighty hand the still more formidable efforts of the powers of darkness; and Satan with all his hosts cannot exert their malice a hair's-breadth beyond the limits of his permission. This is he who is the head and husband of his believing people. How happy are they whom it is his good pleasure to bless! How safe they are whom he has engaged to protect! How honoured and privileged are they to whom he is pleased to manifest himself, and whom he enables and warrants to claim him as their friend and their portion! Having redeemed them by his own blood, he sets a high value upon them; he esteems them his treasure, his jewels, and keeps them as the pupil of his eye... How should we praise him that he has visited us! For we were once blind to his beauty, and insensible to his love, and should have remained so to the last, had he not prevented us with his goodness, and been found of us when we sought him not.

Cardiphonia: Letters to Mrs. Mary Place, [2:90]; 1:587

What manner of man is this! For he commandeth even the winds and water, and they obey him.—Luke 8:25.

THE ship was safe when Christ was in her, though he was *really* asleep. At present I can tell you good news, though you know it: he is wide awake, and his eyes are in every place. You and I, if we could be pounded together, might perhaps make two tolerable ones. You are too anxious, and I am too easy in some respects. Indeed I cannot be too easy, when I have a right thought that all is safe in his hands; but if your anxiety makes you pray, and my composure makes me careless, you have certainly the best of it. However, the ark is fixed upon an immoveable foundation; and if we think we see it totter, it is owing to a swimming in our heads. Seriously, the times look dark and stormy, and call for much circumspection and prayer; but let us not forget that we have an infallible Pilot, and that the power and wisdom and honour of God are embarked with us. At Venice they have a fine vessel called the *Bucentaur*, in which, on a certain day of the year, the doge and nobles embark, and go a little way to sea, to repeat the foolish ceremony of marriage between the republic and the Adriatic, (in consequence of some lying, antiquated Pope's bull, by which the banns of matrimony between Venice and the Gulf were published in the dark ages,) when, they say, a gold ring is very gravely thrown overboard. Upon this occasion, I have been told, when the honour and government of Venice are shipped on board the *Bucentaur*, the pilot is obliged by his office to take an oath that he will bring the vessel safely back again, *in defiance of winds and weather*. Vain mortals!... But my story will probably remind you, that Jesus has actually entered into such an engagement in behalf of his church. And well he may; for both wind and weather are at his command, and he can turn the storm into a calm in a moment. We may therefore safely and confidently leave the government upon his shoulders. Duty is our part; the care is his.

Cardiphonia: Letters to Rev. Mr. John Ryland Jnr., [2:114]; 1:606

They go from strength to strength, every one of them in Zion appeareth before God.—Psa. 84:7.

YOU must not expect a long letter this morning: we are just going to court, in hopes of seeing the King, for he has promised to meet us. We can say he is mindful of his promise; and yet is it not strange that though we are all in the same place, and the King in the midst of us, it is but here and there one (even of those who love him) can see him at once? However, in our turns we are all favoured with a glimpse of him, and have had cause to say, How great is his goodness! How great is his beauty! We have the advantage of the queen of Sheba; a more glorious object to behold, and not so far to go for the sight of it. If a transient glance exceeds all that the world can afford for a long continuance, what must it be to dwell with him? If a day in his courts be better than a thousand, what will eternity be in his presence? I hope the more you see, the more you drink, the more you thirst; the more you do for him, the more you are ashamed you can do so little; and that the nearer you approach to your journey's end, the more your pace is quickened. Surely, the power of spiritual attraction should increase as the distance lessens. Oh that heavenly loadstone! May it so draw us that we may not creep, but run. In common travelling the strongest become weary if the journey be very long; but in the spiritual journey we are encouraged with a hope of going on from strength to strength. *Instaurabit iter vires* [the journey will renew our strength], as Johnson expresses it. No road but the road to heaven can thus communicate refreshment to those who walk in it, and make them more fresh and lively when they are just finishing their course than when they first set out.

Cardiphonia: Letters to Rev. Mr. John Ryland Jnr., [2:120]; 1:611

*Likewise the Spirit also helpeth our infirmities: for we know not what
we should pray for as we ought: but the Spirit itself maketh intercession
for us with groanings which cannot be uttered.*—Rom. 8:26.

I HOPE your soul prospers. I do not ask you if you are always filled
with sensible comfort: but do you find your spirit more bowed
down to the feet and will of Jesus, so as to be willing to serve him for
the sake of serving him, and to follow him, as we say, through thick
and thin; to be willing to be anything or nothing, so that he may be
glorified? I could give you plenty of good advice upon this head; but
I am ashamed to do it, because I so poorly follow it myself. I want to
live with him by the day, to do all for him, to receive all from him,
to possess all in him, to live all to him, to make him my hiding-place
and my resting-place. I want to deliver up that rebel self to him in
chains; but the rogue, like Proteus, puts on so many forms, that he
slips through my fingers: but I think I know what I would do if I
could fairly catch him.

My soul is like a besieged city: a legion of enemies without the
gates, and a nest of restless traitors within, that hold a correspondence
with them without; so that I am deceived and counteracted continually. It is a mercy that I have not been surprised and overwhelmed
long ago; without help from on high it would soon be over with me.
How often have I been forced to cry out, O God, the heathen are
got into thine inheritance; thy holy temple have they defiled, and
defaced all thy work! Indeed it is a miracle that I still hold out. I trust,
however, I shall be supported to the end, and that my Lord will at
length raise the siege, and cause me to shout deliverance and victory.

Pray for me, that my walls may be strengthened and wounds
healed.

Cardiphonia: Letters to Rev. Mr. John Ryland Jnr., [2:122]; 1:612

*He staggered not at the promise of God through unbelief; but was strong
in faith, giving glory to God; And being fully persuaded that, what he
had promised, he was able also to perform.*—Rom. 4:20, 21.

WE are never more safe, never have more reason to expect the
Lord's help, than when we are most sensible that we can do
nothing without him. This was the lesson Paul learnt, to rejoice in his
own poverty and emptiness, that the power of Christ might rest upon
him. Could Paul have done anything, Jesus would not have had the
honour of doing all. This way of being saved entirely by grace, from
first to last, is contrary to our natural wills: it mortifies self, leaving
it nothing to boast of; and, through the remains of an unbelieving,
legal spirit, it often seems discouraging. When we think ourselves so
utterly helpless and worthless, we are too ready to fear that the Lord
will therefore reject us; whereas, in truth, such a poverty of spirit is
the best mark we can have of an interest in his promises and care.

How often have I longed to be an instrument of establishing
you in the peace and hope of the gospel! and I have but one way of
attempting it, by telling you over and over of the power and grace
of Jesus. You want nothing to make you happy, but to have the eyes
of your understanding more fixed upon the Redeemer and more
enlightened by the Holy Spirit to behold his glory. Oh, he is a suitable Saviour! he has power, authority, and compassion to save to the
uttermost. He has given his word of promise, to engage our confidence, and he is able and faithful to make good the expectations and
desires he has raised in us. Put your trust in him; believe (as we say)
through thick and thin, in defiance of all objections from within and
without. For this, Abraham is recommended as a pattern to us. He
overlooked all difficulties; he ventured and hoped even against hope,
in a case which, to appearance, was desperate; because he knew that
he who had promised was also able to perform.

Cardiphonia: Letters to Sally Johnson, [2:146]; 2:10

...to be spiritually minded is life and peace.—Rom. 8:6.

HIDE yourself under the shadow of his wings; rely upon his care and power; look upon him as a physician who has graciously undertaken to heal your soul of the worst of sicknesses, sin. Yield to his prescriptions, and fight against every thought that would represent it as desirable to be permitted to choose for yourself. When you cannot see your way, be satisfied that he is your Leader. When your spirit is overwhelmed within you, he knows your path: he will not leave you to sink. He has appointed seasons of refreshment, and you shall find he does not forget you. Above all, keep close to the throne of grace.

I pray that you may be enabled more and more to honour the Lord, by believing his promise: for he is not like a man, that should fail or change, or be prevented by anything unforeseen from doing what he has said. And yet we find it easier to trust to worms than to the God of truth. Is it not so with you? And I can assure you it is often so with me. But here is the mercy, that his ways are above ours as the heavens are higher than the earth. Though we are foolish and unbelieving, he remains faithful; he will not deny himself. I recommend to you especially that promise of God, which is so comprehensive that it takes in all our concernments, I mean, that all things shall work together for good. How hard it is to believe, that not only those things which are grievous to the flesh, but even those things which draw forth our corruptions and discover to us what is in our hearts, and fill us with guilt and shame, should in the issue work for our good! Yet the Lord has said it. All your pains and trials, all that befalls you in your own person, or that affects you upon the account of others, shall in the end prove to your advantage. And your peace does not depend upon any change of circumstances which may appear desirable, but in having your will bowed to the Lord's will, and made willing to submit all to his disposal and management.

Cardiphonia: Letters to Sally Johnson, [2:147]; 2:12

But the God of all grace, who hath called us unto his eternal glory by
Christ Jesus, after that ye have suffered a while, make you perfect,
stablish, strengthen, settle you.—1 Pet. 5:10.

I DOUBT not but the Lord whom you love, and on whom you depend, will lead you in a sure way, and establish and strengthen and settle you in his love and grace. Indeed he has done great things for you already. The Lord is your Shepherd; a comprehensive word. The sheep can do nothing for themselves: the Shepherd must guide, guard, feed, heal, recover. Well for us that our Shepherd is the Lord Almighty. If his power, care, compassion, fulness, were not infinite, the poor sheep would be forsaken, starved and worried. But we have a Shepherd full of care, full of kindness, full of power, who has said, I will seek that which was lost, and bind up that which was broken, and bring again that which was driven away, and will strengthen that which was sick. How tender are these expressions, and how well fulfilled! His sheep feed in the midst of wolves, yet are preserved safe; for, though they see him not, his eye and his heart are upon them. Do we wonder that Daniel was preserved in the lion's den? Why, it is a common case. Which of God's children have not cause to say, 'My soul is among lions'? But the angel of the covenant stops their mouths, or only permits them to gape and roar, to show their teeth, and what they would do if they might; but they may not, they shall not, bite and tear us at their own will. Let us trust him, and all shall be well.

As to daily occurrences, it is best to believe that a daily portion of comforts and crosses, each one the most suitable to your case, is adjusted and appointed by the hand which was once nailed to the cross for us; that where the path of duty and prudence leads, there is the best situation we could possibly be in at that juncture.

Cardiphonia: Letters to Mrs. Hannah Wilberforce, [2:177]; 2:34

For the eyes of the LORD run to and fro throughout the whole earth,
to shew himself strong in the behalf of them whose heart
is perfect toward him.—2 Chron. 16:9.

HOW happy is the state of a believer, to have a sure promise that all shall work together for good in the end, and, in the mean time a sure refuge where to find present relief, support, and protection! How comfortable is it, when trouble is near, to know that the Lord is near likewise, and to commit ourselves and all our cares simply to him, believing that his eye is upon us, and his ear open to our prayers. Under the conduct of such a Shepherd we need not fear; though we are called to pass through fire and water, through the valley of the shadow of death, he will be with us, and will show himself mighty on our behalf. It seems almost needless to say, that we were very happy in the company of ****: the only inconvenience was, that it renewed the pain it always gives me to part with them. Though the visit was full as long as I could possibly expect, it seemed very short. This must be the case while we are here: our pleasures are short, interrupted, and mixed with troubles: this is not, cannot be our rest. But it will not be always the case; we are travelling to a better world, where every evil and imperfection shall cease; then we shall be for ever with the Lord, and with each other. May the prospect of this blessed hope set before us revive our fainting spirits, and make us willing to endure hardships as soldiers of Jesus Christ! Here we must often sow in tears, but there we shall reap in joy, and all tears shall be wiped from our eyes for ever.

Let us adore him for his love, that love which has a height, and depth, and length, and breadth, beyond the grasp of our poor conceptions; a love that moved him to empty himself, to take on him the form of a servant, and to be obedient unto death, even the death of the cross.

Cardiphonia: Letters to Mrs. Hannah Wilberforce, [2:178]; 2:35

The name of the LORD is a strong tower:
the righteous runneth into it, and is safe.—Prov. 18:10.

HOW little does the world know of that intercourse which is carried on between heaven and earth; what petitions are daily presented, and what answers are received at a throne of grace! Oh the blessed privilege of prayer! Oh the wonderful love, care, attention, and power of our great Shepherd! His eye is always upon us; when our spirits are almost overwhelmed within us, he knoweth our path. His ear is always open to us; let who will overlook and disappoint us, he will not. When means and hope fail, when everything looks dark upon us, when we seem shut up on every side, when we are brought to the lowest ebb, still our help is in the name of the Lord who made heaven and earth. To him all things are possible; and before the exertion of his power, when he is pleased to arise and work, all hindrances give way and vanish, like a mist before the sun. And he can so manifest himself to the soul, and cause his goodness to pass before it, that the hour of affliction shall be the golden hour of the greatest consolation. He is the fountain of life, strength, grace, and comfort, and of his fulness his children receive according to their occasions: but this is hidden from the world; they have no guide in prosperity, but hurry on as they are instigated by their blinded passions, and are perpetually multiplying mischiefs and miseries to themselves; and in adversity they have no resource, but must feel all the evil of affliction, without inward support, and without deriving any advantage from it. We have therefore cause for continual praise. The Lord has given us to know his name as a resting-place and a hiding-place, a sun and a shield. Circumstances and creatures may change; but he will be an unchangeable friend.

Cardiphonia: Letters to Mrs. Hannah Wilberforce, [2:182]; 2:38

When my spirit was overwhelmed within me,
then thou knewest my path.—Psa. 142:3.

I HOPE I can assure you of a friendly sympathy with you in your trials. I can in some measure guess at what you feel, from what I have seen and felt myself in cases where I have been nearly concerned. But my compassion, though sincere, is ineffectual: if I can pity, I cannot relieve. All I can do is, as the Lord enables me, to remember you both before him. But there is One whose compassion is infinite. The love and tenderness of ten thousand earthly friends, of ten thousand mothers towards their sucklings if compared with his, are less than a drop of water to the ocean; and his power is infinite too. Why then do our sufferings continue, when he is so compassionate, and could remove them with a word? Surely, if we cannot give the particular reasons (which yet he will acquaint us with hereafter, John 13:7), the general reason is at hand; he afflicts not for his own pleasure, but for our profit; to make us partakers of his holiness, and because he loves us.

> Judge not the Lord by feeble sense,
>   But trust him for his grace:
> Behind a frowning providence
>   He hides a smiling face.

I wish you much comfort from David's thought, Psa. 142:3: 'When my spirit was overwhelmed within me, then thou knewest my path.' The Lord is not withdrawn to a great distance, but his eye is upon you, and he sees you not with the indifference of a mere spectator; but he observes with attention, he knows, he considers your path: yea, he appoints it, and every circumstance about it is under his direction. Your trouble began at the hour he saw best: it could not come before, and he has marked the degree of it to a hair's breadth, and the duration to a minute. He knows likewise how your spirit is affected; and such supplies of grace and strength, and in such seasons as he sees needful, he will afford. So that when things appear darkest, you shall still be able to say, Though chastened, not killed. Therefore, hope in God, for you shall yet praise him.

Cardiphonia: Letters to Mrs. Hannah Wilberforce, [2:190]; 2:44

He went away again the second time, and prayed, saying, O my Father,
if this cup may not pass away from me, except I drink it,
thy will be done.—Matt. 26:42.

OUR all-sufficient God can give seasons of refreshment in the darkest hours, and break through the thickest clouds of outward affliction or distress. To you it is given not only to believe in Jesus, but to suffer for his sake: for so we do, not only when we are called to follow him to imprisonment or death, but when he enables us to bear afflictive dispensations with due submission and patience. Then he is glorified: then his grace and power are manifested in us. The world, so far as they know our case, have a proof before them that our religion is not merely notional, but that there is a power and reality in it. And the Lord's people are encouraged by what they see of his faithfulness to ourselves. And there are more eyes upon us still. We are a spectacle to the universe, to angels as well as to men. Cheer up: the Lord has put you in your present trying situation, that you may have the fairer opportunity of adorning your profession of the gospel; and though you suffer much, he is able to make you abundant amends. Nor need I remind you that he has suffered unspeakably more for you: he drank for your sake a cup of unmixed wrath, and only puts into your hand a cup of affliction mixed with many mercies.

We need not look about for long to find others in a worse situation than ourselves. If a fit of the gout or cholic is so grievous and so hard to bear, what do we owe to him who delivered us from that place of unutterable torment, where there is weeping, wailing, and gnashing of teeth forever, without hope or respite?... Oh! if we could always behold him by faith as evidently crucified before our eyes, how would it compose our spirits as to all the sweets and bitters of this poor life!

Cardiphonia: Letters to Mrs. Hannah Wilberforce, [2:191]; 2:45

I was dumb, I opened not my mouth; because thou didst it.—Psa. 39:9.

YOU are bereaved of a valuable friend: but life in her circumstances was burdensome; and who can be sorry to consider her now as freed from all suffering, and possessed of all happiness? But, besides this, I trust the Lord has favoured you with an habitual sense of the wisdom and propriety of all his appointments; so that when his will is manifested by the event, you are enabled to say, 'All is well.' 'I was dumb, and opened not my mouth, because thou didst it.'… Precious in his sight is the death of his saints, and every circumstance under the direction of infinite wisdom. His sovereignty forbids us to say, Why hast thou done this?

I have seen death in a variety of forms, and have had frequent occasion of observing how insignificant many things, which are now capable of giving us pain or pleasure will appear, when the soul is brought near to the borders of eternity. All the concerns which relate solely to this life, will then be found as trivial as the traces of a dream from which we are awakened. Nothing will then comfort us but the knowledge of Jesus and his love; nothing grieve us but the remembrance of our unfaithful carriage to him, and what poor returns we made to his abundant goodness. The Lord forbid that this thought should break our peace! No; faith in his name may forbid our fear, though we shall see and confess we have been unprofitable servants. There shall be no condemnation to them that are in him: but surely shame and humiliation will accompany us to the very threshold of heaven, and ought to do so. I surely shall then be more affected than I am now with the coolness of my love, the faintness of my zeal, the vanity of my heart, and my undue attachment to the things of time. O these clogs, fetters, vales, and mountains, which obstruct my course, darken my views, slacken my pace, and disable me in service! Well it is for me that I am not under the law, but under grace.

Cardiphonia: Letters to Mrs. Hannah Wilberforce, [2:199]; 2:51

For my people have committed two evils; they have forsaken me
the fountain of living waters, and hewed them out cisterns,
broken cisterns, that can hold no water.—Jer. 2:13.

THE two evils charged upon Israel of old, a proneness to forsake the fountain of living waters, and to trust to broke cisterns ... run through the whole of my experience abroad and at home. A few drops of grace in my fellow worms endear them to me exceedingly. If I expect to see any Christian friends, I count the hours till we meet: I promise myself great benefit; but if the Lord withdraws his influence, the best of them prove to me but clouds without water. It was not, however, wholly so with me all the time I stayed with my friends; but I suffer much in learning to depend upon the Lord alone; I have been at this lesson many a long year but am so poor and dull a scholar, that I have not made any tolerable progress in it. I think I received some instruction and advantage where I little expected it: I mean, at Mr. Cox's Museum. The efforts of his ingenuity amazed me, while at the same time I was struck with their insignificance. His fine things were curious beyond all I had any idea of; and yet what are they better than toys and amusements, suited to the taste of children! And notwithstanding the variety of their motions, they were all destitute of life. There is unspeakably more wisdom and contrivance in the mechanism of a butterfly or a bee, that flies unnoticed in the fields, than in all his apparatus put together. But the works of God are disregarded, while the feeble imitations of them which men can produce gain universal applause.

If you and I could make self-moving dragons and elephants, what would it profit us? Blessed be God, that he has given us some glimpses of his wisdom and love! by which our hearts, more hard and lifeless by nature than the stones in the street, are constrained and enabled to move upwards, and to seek after the Lord. He has given us in his word a greater treasure than all that we ever beheld with our eyes, and a hope which shall flourish when the earth and all its works shall be burnt up.

Cardiphonia: Letters to Miss Elizabeth Delafield, [2:203]; 2:54

Thou hast put gladness in my heart, more than in the time that their corn and their wine increased.—Psa. 4:7.

WHAT an important period is a wedding-day! What an entire change of circumstances does it produce! What an influence it has upon every day of future life! How many cares, inquietudes, and trials, does it expose us to, which we might otherwise have avoided! But they who love the Lord, and are guided by his word and providence, have nothing to fear; for in every state, relation, and circumstance in life, he will be with them, and will surely do them good. His grace, which is needful in a single, is sufficient for a married, life. I sincerely wish Mr. **** and you much happiness together; that you may be mutually helps meet, and assist each other in walking as fellow heirs of the hope of eternal life. Your cares and trials I know must be increased; may your comforts be increased proportionally! They will be so, if you are enabled heartily and simply to entreat the Lord to keep your heart fixed near to himself. All the temporal blessings and accommodations he provides to sweeten life, and make our passage through this wilderness more agreeable, will fail and disappoint us, and produce us more thorns than roses, unless we can keep sight of his hand in bestowing them, and hold and use the gifts in some due subserviency to what we owe to the Giver. But, alas! we are poor creatures, prone to wander, prone to admire our gourds, cleave to our cisterns, and think of building tabernacles and taking our rest in this polluted world. Hence the Lord often sees it necessary, in mercy to his children, to embitter their sweets, to break their cisterns, send a worm to their gourds, and draw a dark cloud over their pleasing prospects. His word tells us, that all here is vanity, compared with the light of his countenance; and if we cannot or will not believe it upon the authority of his word, we must learn it by experience. May he enable you to settle it in your hearts, that creature-comforts are precarious, insufficient, and ensnaring; that all good comes from his hand, and that nothing can do us good, but so far as he is pleased to make it the instrument of communicating, as a stream, that goodness which is in him as a fountain.

Cardiphonia: Letters to Miss Elizabeth Delafield, [2:214]; 2:62

When Simon Peter saw it, he fell down at Jesus' knees, saying,
Depart from me; for I am a sinful man, O Lord.—Luke 5:8.

SHOULD we look for light in our own eyes, or in the sun? Is it indwelling sin distresses you? Then I can tell you (though you know it) that Jesus died for sin and sinners. I can tell you, that his blood and righteousness are of infinite value; that his arm is almighty, and his compassions infinite: yea, you yourself read his promises every day and why should you doubt their being fulfilled?… When you read your name on the superscription of this letter, you made no scruple to open it: why then do you hesitate at embracing the promises of the gospel; where you read that they are addressed to those who mourn, who hunger and thirst after righteousness, who are poor in spirit, &c. and cannot but be sensible that a gracious God has begun to work these dispositions in your heart. If you say, that though you do at times mourn, hunger, &c. you are afraid you do it not enough, or not aright; consider, that this sort of reasoning is very far from the spirit and language of the gospel; for it is grounded on a secret supposition, that in the forgiveness of sin, God has a respect to something more than the atonement and mediation of Jesus; namely, to some previous good qualifications in a sinner's heart, which are to share with the blood of Christ in the honour of salvation. The enemy deceives us in this matter the more easily, because a propensity to the covenant of works is part of our natural depravity. Depend upon it, you will never have a suitable and sufficient sense of the evil of sin, and of your share in it, so long as you have any sin remaining in you. We must see Jesus as he is, before our apprehensions of any spiritual truth will be complete. But if we know that we must perish without Christ, and that he is able to save to the uttermost, we know enough to cast our souls upon him, and we dishonour him by fearing that when we do so he will disappoint our hope.

Cardiphonia: Letters to Mrs. Harvey, *[2:221]; 2:68*

I love the Lord, because he hath heard my voice
and my supplications.—Psa. 116:1.

IF I guess right at what passes in your heart, the name of Jesus is precious to you; and this is a sure token of salvation, and that of God. You could not have loved him, if he had not loved you first. He spoke to *you*, and said, 'Seek my face,' before your heart cried to *him*, 'Thy face, O Lord, will I seek.' But you complain, 'Alas! I love him so little.' That very complaint proves that you love him a great deal; for if you loved him but a little, you would think you loved him enough. A mother loves her child a great deal, yet does not complain for not loving it more; nay, perhaps she hardly thinks it possible. But such an infinite object is Jesus, that they who love him better than parents or child, or any earthly relation or comfort, will still think they hardly love him at all; because they see such a vast disproportion between the utmost they can give him, and what in himself he deserves from them. But I can give you good advice and good news: love him as well as you can now, and ere long you shall love him better. O when you see him as he is, then I am sure you will love him indeed! If you want to love him better now while you are here, I believe I can tell you the secret how this is to be attained: *trust him*. The more you trust him, the better you will love him. If you ask further, How shall I trust him? I answer, *Try him*: the more you make trial of him, the more your trust in him will be strengthened. Venture upon his promises; carry them to him, and see if he will not be as good as his word. But, alas! Satan and unbelief work the contrary way. We are unwilling to try him, and therefore unable to trust him; and what wonder, then that our love is faint, for who can love at uncertainties?

If you are in some measure thankful for what you have received, and hungering and thirsting for more, you are in the frame I would wish for myself; and I desire to praise the Lord on your behalf.—Pray for us.

Cardiphonia: Letters to Mrs. Harvey, [2:224]; 2:70

*Surely I have behaved and quieted myself, as a child that is weaned of
his mother: my soul is even as a weaned child.*—Psa. 131:2.

IT is indeed natural to us to wish and to plan, and it is merciful in
the Lord to disappoint our plans, and to cross our wishes. For we
cannot be safe, much less happy, but in proportion as we are weaned
from our own wills, and made simply desirous of being directed by
his guidance. This truth (when we are enlightened by his word) is
sufficiently familiar to the judgment; but we seldom learn to reduce
it into practice, without being trained awhile in the school of disappointment. The schemes we form look so plausible and convenient,
that when they are broken we are ready to say, What a pity! We try
again, and with no better success; we are grieved, and perhaps angry,
and pan out another, and so on: at length, in a course of time, experience and observation begin to convince us, that we are not more able
than we are worthy to choose aright for ourselves. Then the Lord's
invitation to cast our cares upon him, and his promise to take care
of us, appear valuable; and when *we* have done planning, *his* plan in
our favour gradually opens, and he does more and better for us than
we could either ask or think. I can hardly recollect a single plan of
mine, of which I have not since seen reason to be satisfied, that, had
it taken place in season and circumstance just as I proposed, it would,
humanly speaking, have proved my ruin; or, at least, it would have
deprived me of the greater good the Lord had designed for me. We
judge of things by their present appearances, but the Lord sees them
in their consequences: if we could do so likewise, we should be perfectly of his mind; but as we cannot, it is an unspeakable mercy that
he will manage for us, whether we are pleased with his management
or not; and it is spoken of as one of his heaviest judgments, when he
gives any person or people up to the way of their own hearts, and to
walk after their own counsels.

Are not two sparrows sold for a farthing? and one of them shall not fall on the ground without your Father. But the very hairs of your head are all numbered. Fear ye not therefore, ye are of more value than many sparrows.—Matt. 10:29-31.

IF we were blind, and reduced to desire a person to lead us, and should yet pretend to dispute with him, and direct him at every step, we should probably soon weary him, and provoke him to leave us to find the way by ourselves if we could. But our gracious Lord is long-suffering and full of compassion: he bears with our forwardness, yet he will take methods both to shame and to humble us, and to bring us to a confession that he is wiser than we. The great and unexpected benefit he intends us, by all the discipline we meet with, is to tread down our wills, and bring them into subjection to his. So far as we attain to this, we are out of the reach of disappointment: for when the will of God can please us, we shall be pleased every day, and from morning to night; I mean, with respect to his dispensations. O the happiness of such a life! I have an idea of it; I hope I am aiming at it; but surely I have not attained it. Self is active in my heart, if it does not absolutely reign there. I profess to believe that one thing is needful and sufficient, and yet my thoughts are prone to wander after a hundred more. If it be true, that the light of his countenance is better than life, why am I solicitous about anything else? If he be all-sufficient, and gives me liberty to call him *mine*, why do I go a begging to creatures for help? If he be about my path and bed; if the smallest, as well as the greatest, events in which I am concerned are under his immediate direction; if the very hairs of my head are numbered; then my care (any further than a care to walk in the paths of his precepts, and to follow the openings of his providence) must be useless and needless, yea sinful and heathenish, burdensome to myself and dishonourable to my profession.

Cardiphonia: Letters to Miss Perry, [2:227]; 2:72

Lord, what wilt thou have me to do?—Acts 9:6.

LET us cast down the load we are unable to carry; and if the Lord be our Shepherd, refer all, and trust all to him. Let us endeavour to live to him and for him today and be glad that tomorrow, with all that is behind it, is in his hands.

It is storied of Pompey, that when his friends would have dissuaded him from putting to sea in a storm, he answered, It is necessary for me to sail, but it is not necessary for me to live. O pompous speech, in Pompey's sense! He was full of the idea of his own importance, and would rather have died than have taken a step beneath his supposed dignity. But it may be accommodated with propriety to a believer's case. It becomes us to say, It is not necessary for me to be rich, or what the world accounts wise; to be healthy, or admired by my fellow worms; to pass through life in a state of prosperity and outward comfort; these things may be, or they may be otherwise, as the Lord in his wisdom shall appoint: but it is necessary for me to be humble and spiritual, to seek communion with God, to adorn my profession of the gospel, and to yield submissively to his disposal, in whatever way, whether of service or suffering, he shall be pleased to call me to glorify him in the world. It is not necessary for me to live long, but highly expedient that whilst I do live I should live to him. Here then I would bound my desires; and here, having his word both for my rule and my warrant, I am secured from asking amiss. Let me have his presence and his Spirit, wisdom to know my calling, and opportunities and faithfulness to improve them; and as to the rest, Lord, help me to say, What thou wilt, when thou wilt, and how thou wilt.

Cardiphonia: Letters to Miss Perry, [2:228]; 2:72

Casting all your care upon him; for he careth for you.—1 Pet. 5:7.

WHAT a poor, uncertain, dying world is this! What a wilderness in itself! How dark, how desolate, without the light of the gospel and the knowledge of Jesus! It does not appear so to us in a state of nature, because we are then in a state of enchantment, the magical lantern blinding us with a splendid delusion.

It is a great mercy to be undeceived in time; and though our carefree dreams are at an end, and we awake to everything that is disgustful and dismaying, yet we see a highway through the wilderness, a powerful guard, an infallible guide at hand to conduct us through; and we can discern, beyond the limits of the wilderness, a better land, where we shall be at rest and at home. What will the difficulties we met by the way then signify? The remembrance of them will only remain to heighten our sense of the love, care, and power of our Saviour and Leader. O how shall we then admire, adore, and praise him, when he shall condescend to unfold to us the beauty, propriety, and harmony of the whole train of his dispensations towards us, and give us a clear retrospect of all the way and all the turns of our pilgrimage!

In the mean while, the best method of adorning our profession, and of enjoying peace in our souls, is simply to trust him, and absolutely to commit ourselves and our all to his management. By casting our burdens upon him, our spirits become light and cheerful; we are freed from a thousand anxieties and inquietudes, which are wearisome to our minds, and which, with respect to events, are *needless* for us, yea, *useless*. But though it may be easy to speak of this trust, and it appears to our judgment perfectly right and reasonable, the actual attainment is a great thing; and especially so to trust the Lord not by fits and starts ... but to abide by our surrender, and go habitually trusting, through all the changes we meet, knowing that his love, purpose, and promise are unchangeable.

Cardiphonia: Letters to Miss Perry, [2:229]; 2:74

For what the law could not do, in that it was weak through the flesh,
God sending his own Son in the likeness of sinful flesh, and for sin,
condemned sin in the flesh: That the righteousness of the law
might be fulfilled in us, who walk not after the flesh,
but after the Spirit.—Rom. 8:3, 4.

THE Divine law requires perfect, unremitted, unsinning obedience: it denounces a curse upon the least failure. 'Cursed is every one that continueth not in all things which are written in the book of the law to do them,' Gal. 3:10; *every one*, without exception of person or circumstance, *that continueth not*, from the beginning to the end of life, *in all things*, great and small, *to do them* ... to finish them, to do them completely, without any defect either in matter or manner. Most uncomfortable doctrine indeed, were there no remedy provided! For the law of God is as eternal and unchangeable as his nature: it must not, it cannot be attempered or brought down to our capacities; neither can the penalty be evaded: for the God of truth has said, has sworn, that 'the soul that sinneth shall die,' Ezek. 18:4. Here then we must receive 'a sentence of death in ourselves,' 2 Cor. 1:9. Here, 'every mouth must be stopped, and all the world become guilty before God,' Rom. 3:19. Here we must say with the apostle, 'Therefore, by the deeds of the law, there shall be no flesh justified in his sight,' Gal. 2:16; 'for by the law is the knowledge of sin,' Rom. 3:20... Why have I attempted to lay open some of the depths of the heart? But that I might more fully illustrate the wonderful grace and goodness of God, vouchsafed to us in the gospel; and, at the same time, show the utter impossibility, not of being saved at all, but of finding salvation in any other way than that which God has appointed. For, behold! 'God has so loved the world,' John 3, that he sent his Son to accomplish that for us, 'which the law could not do through the weakness of our flesh,' Rom. 8. Jesus Christ performed perfect obedience to the law of God in our behalf: he died, and satisfied the penalty due our sins: he arose from the grave as our representative: he is entered into heaven as our forerunner.

On the Deceitfulness of the Heart, [2:272]; 2:115

*The next day John seeth Jesus coming unto him, and saith, Behold the
Lamb of God, which taketh away the sin of the world.*—John 1:29.

THINK not to satisfy the Divine justice by any poor performances of your own; think not to cleanse or expiate the evil of
your hearts by any of your own inventions; but, 'behold the Lamb
of God, which taketh away the sin of the world;' John 1:29. He died,
that you may live: he lives, that you may live for ever. Put, therefore,
your trust in the Lord; for with him is plenteous redemption. His
sufferings and death are a complete final propitiation for sin. 'He
is able to save to the uttermost;' and he is as willing as he is able. It
was *this* brought him down from heaven; for *this* he emptied himself
of all glory, and submitted to all indignity. His humiliation expiates
our pride; his perfect love atones for our ingratitude; his exquisite
tenderness pleads for our insensibility. Only believe; commit your
cause to him by faith and prayer. As a *Priest*, he shall make atonement
for your sins, and present your persons and your services acceptable
before God. As a *Prophet*, he shall instruct you in the true wisdom,
which maketh wise to salvation: he shall not only cause you to know
his commandments, but to love them too: he shall write them in
your hearts. As a *King*, he shall evermore mightily defend you against
all your enemies. He shall enable you to withstand temptations, to
support difficulties, to break through all opposition. He shall supply
you with everything you need, for this life or a better, out of the
unsearchable riches of his grace. He shall strengthen you to overcome
all things; to endure to the end: and then he shall give you a place in
his kingdom; a seat near his throne; a crown of life; a crown of glory;
incorruptible, undefiled, and that fadeth not away.

On the Deceitfulness of the Heart, [2:275]; 2:116

This is a faithful saying, and worthy of all acceptation, that Christ Jesus came into the world to save sinners; of whom I am chief.—1 Tim. 1:15.

THE apostle well knew the different reception the gospel would meet in the world; that many poor guilty souls, trembling under a sense of sin and unworthiness, would very hardly be persuaded, that such sinners as they could be saved at all. To these he recommends it as 'a faithful saying,' founded upon the immutable counsel, promise, and oath of God, that Jesus Christ came into the world to save *sinners*; sinners in general; 'the chief of sinners;' such as he represents himself to have been. He knew, likewise, that many others, from a mistaken opinion of their own goodness, or a mistaken dependence on something of their own choosing, would be liable to undervalue this faithful saying. For the sake of these, he adds, 'it is worthy of all acceptation.' None are so bad but the gospel affords them a ground of hope: none are so good as to have any just ground of hope without it. There was a time when St. Paul could have made a fair profession of himself likewise: he could say, 'circumcised on the eighth day, of the stock of Israel, of the tribe of Benjamin, an Hebrew of the Hebrews; as to the law, a Pharisee; as to the righteousness which is by the law, blameless;' Phil. 3. But he has been since taught to 'count all things but loss for the excellency of the knowledge of Christ,' and is content to style himself *the chief of sinners*.

Jesus Christ ... came to restore us to the favour of God; to reconcile us to ourselves, and to each other; to give us peace and joy in life, hope and triumph in death, and after death glory, honour, and immortality. For he came, not merely to repair, and to restore, but to exalt; not only, 'that we might have life,' the life we had forfeited, but 'that we might have it more abundantly,' John 10; that our happiness might be more exalted, our title more firm, and our possession more secure, than the state of Adam in paradise could boast.

On the Saviour, and his Salvation, [2:278]; 2:119

For if, when we were enemies, we were reconciled to God
by the death of his Son, much more, being reconciled,
we shall be saved by his life.—Rom. 5:10.

JESUS Christ, the brightness of the Father's glory, and express image of his person, 'so loved the world,' that he assumed our nature, undertook our cause, bore our sins, sustained our deserved punishment; and, having done and suffered all that the case required, he is now gone before, 'to prepare a place,' John 14, for all that believe in him and obey him. Man lay under a double incapacity for happiness; he could neither keep the law of God in future, nor satisfy for his past breach and contempt of it. To obviate the former, Jesus Christ performed a perfect unsinning obedience in our stead. To remove the latter, he became 'the propitiation of our sins;' yielded up his life as a prey into the hands of murderers, and poured forth his precious blood, in drops of sweat in the garden, in streams from his side upon the cross. For this he endured the fiercest temptations of the devil, the scorn, rage, and malice of men, and drank the bitter cup of the wrath of God, when it pleased the Father to bruise him, and make his soul an offering for sin. His love carried him through all; and when he had finally overcome the sharpness of death, he opened the kingdom of heaven to all believers. In few words, he lived and died for us when upon earth: nor is he unmindful of us in heaven, but lives and intercedes on our behalf. He continually executes the offices of Prophet, Priest, and King, to his people; instructing them by his word and Spirit; presenting their persons and prayers, acceptable to God through his merits; defending them, by his power, from all their enemies, ghostly and bodily; and ordering, by his providence, all things to work together for their good, till at length they are brought home, to be with him where he is, and to behold his glory.

On the Saviour, and his Salvation, [2:285]; 2:125

He that spared not his own Son, but delivered him up for us all, how
shall he not with him also freely give us all things?—Rom. 8:32.

FROM the words, 'he spared not his own Son,' we may observe, in one view, the wonderful goodness and inflexible severity of God. So great was his goodness, that, when man was by sin rendered incapable of *any* happiness ... incapable of restoring himself, or of receiving the least assistance from any power in heaven or in earth; God spared not his only begotten Son, but, in his unexampled love to the world, gave him, who alone was able to repair the breach. Every gift of God is good: the bounties of his common providence are very valuable; that he should continue life, and supply that life with food, raiment, and a variety of comforts, to those who by rebellion had forfeited all, was wonderful: but what are all inferior blessings, compared to this unspeakable gift of the Son of his love?

The justice and severity of God is no less conspicuous than his goodness in these words: as he spared not to give his Son for our sakes, so, when Christ appeared in our nature, undertook our cause, and was charged with our sins, though he was the Father's well-beloved Son, 'he was not spared.' he drank the bitter cup of the wrath of God to the very dregs: he bore all the shame, sorrow, and pain, all the distress of body and mind, that must otherwise have fallen upon our heads. His whole life, from the manger to the cross, was one series of humiliation and suffering; John 18... He *gave* his Son; he *gives* all things with him. The gospel allows no place for merit of our own in any respect. There was no moving cause in us, unless our misery may be deemed such. Our deliverance, in its rise, progress, and accomplishment, must be ascribed to grace alone; and he that would glory, must 'glory in the Lord,' 1 Cor. 1.

On All Things Being Given Us with Christ, [2:307]; 2:142

Ye ask, and receive not, because ye ask amiss,
that ye may consume it upon your lusts.—James 4:3.

THE text, having declared that God spared not his Son for our sakes, proceeds to infer, that 'with him he will assuredly give us all things.' Here we may take notice, first, that the words *all things* must be limited to such as are needful and good for us. It may be said of many of our desires, 'Ye know not what ye ask,' Matt. 20: in such cases, the best answer we can receive is a denial. For those blessings which God has promised absolutely to give, such as pardon, grace, and eternal life, we cannot be too earnest or explicit in our prayers; but in temporal things we should be careful to ask nothing but with submission to the Divine will. The promises, it is true, appertain to 'the life that now is, as well as that which is to come,' 1 Tim. 4. 'Whether Paul, or Apollos, or Cephas, or life, or death, or things present, or things to come; all are ours, if we are Christ's,' 1 Cor. 3. But the particular *modus* of these things God has reserved in his own hands, to bestow them as best shall suit our various tempers, abilities, and occasions. And well for us that it is so: for we should soon ruin ourselves if left to our own choice: like children who are fond to meddle with what would hurt them, but refuse the most salutary medicines, if unpalatable; so we often pursue, with earnestness and anxiety, those things which, if we could obtain them, would greatly harm, if not destroy, us. Often, too, with a rash and blind impatience, we struggle to avoid or escape those difficulties which God sees fit to appoint for the most gracious and merciful purposes—to correct our pride and vanity, to exercise and strengthen our faith, to wean us from the world, to teach us a closer dependence upon himself, and to awaken our desires after a better inheritance.

On All Things Being Given Us with Christ, [2:314]; 2:147

> *But godliness with contentment is great gain. For we brought nothing*
> *into this world, and it is certain we can carry nothing out. And having*
> *food and raiment let us be therewith content.*—1 Tim. 6:6-8.

SINCE all we have is the gift of God, let this teach us, 'in what-ever state we are, therewith to be content.' 'Our heavenly Father knoweth what we have need of before we ask him,' Matt. 6. 'The earth is his, and the fulness thereof,' Psa. 24; and his goodness is equal to his power... He has already given us more than ten thousand worlds. Are you poor? Be satisfied with the Lord's appointment. It were as easy to him to give you large estates, as to supply you with the bread you eat, or to continue your breath in your nostrils; but he sees poverty best for you; he sees prosperity might prove your ruin; therefore he has appointed you the honour of being in this respect conformable to your Lord, who, when on earth, 'had not where to lay his head,' Matt. 8. Have any of you lost a dear friend or relative, in whose life you thought your own lives bound up? 'Be still, and know that he is God,' Psa. 46. It was he who gave you that friend; his blessing made your friend a comfort to you; and though the stream is now cut off, the fountain is still full. Be not like a wild bull in a net; the Lord has many ways to turn your mourning into joy. Are any of you sick? Think how the compassionate Jesus healed diseases with a word, in the days of his flesh. Has he not the same power now as then? Has he not the same love? Has he, in his exalted state, *forgot* his poor languishing members here below? No, verily, he still retains his sympathy; 'he is touched with a feeling of our infirmities; he knows our frame; he remembers we are but dust,' Psa. 103. It is because sickness is better for you than health, that he thus visits you. He dealt in the same manner with Lazarus, whom he loved, John 11. Resign yourselves, therefore to his wisdom, and repose in his love. There is a land where the blessed inhabitant shall no more say, 'I am sick,' Isa. 33; and there 'all that love the Lord Jesus' shall shortly be.

On All Things Being Given Us with Christ, [2:318]; 2:150

Let us therefore come boldly unto the throne of grace, that we may obtain mercy, and find grace to help in time of need.—Heb. 4:16.

THE great God is pleased to manifest himself in Christ, as the God of grace. This grace is manifold, pardoning, converting, restoring, persevering grace, bestowed upon the miserable and worthless. Grace finds the sinner in a hopeless, helpless state, sitting in darkness, and in the shadow of death. Grace pardons the guilt, cleanses the pollution, and subdues the power of sin. Grace sustains the bruised reed, binds up the broken heart, and cherishes the smoking flax into a flame. Grace restores the soul when wandering, revives it when fainting, heals it when wounded, upholds it when ready to fall, teaches it to fight, goes before it in the battle, and at last makes it more than conqueror over all opposition, and then bestows a crown of everlasting life. But all this grace is established and displayed by covenant in the man Christ Jesus, and without respect to him as living, dying, rising, reigning, and interceding in the behalf of sinners, would never have been known.

The whole creation proclaims that power belongs unto God. But in nothing will his power be more illustriously displayed than in the wonders of redeeming love! What power is necessary to raise those who are spiritually dead in sin, to soften the heart of stone, to bring light out of darkness, and order out of confusion! Wherever his gospel is faithfully preached, it is always confirmed by this accompanying power. How quickly, how easily, did he change Saul from a persecutor to an apostle! Again, how is his power illustrated by the care he takes of all who believe in his name, affording to every one of them seasonable, suitable, and sufficient supplies in every time of need! So that his weak, helpless, and opposed people, are supported, strengthened, and enabled, to hold on, and hold out, against all the united efforts of the world, sin, and Satan.

The Glory and Grace of God Revealed in Jesus Christ, [2:442]; 2:244

Therefore by the deeds of the law there shall no flesh be justified in his sight: for by the law is the knowledge of sin.—Rom. 3:20.

NONE will prize the Saviour but those who feel their need of him. Two things are necessary to convince man of his lost condition by nature and practice as a sinner, the spirituality of the law, and the sufferings of Christ: the one shows the universality of sin, the other its demerit. But these can be truly discerned only by the light of the Spirit of Christ. While St. Paul (who was never absolutely without the law) was ignorant of the law's spirituality, 'I was (says he) alive.' I had so little knowledge, both of the law and of myself, that I trusted to it for righteousness, and vainly thought that I yielded obedience, and grounded my hopes of salvation thereon. 'But when the commandment came,' when the Spirit explained and enforced it in its full extent, as reaching to the very thoughts of the heart, and requiring an obedience absolutely perfect 'then sin revived, and I died.' All my hopes vanished, I saw every principle, affection, and action polluted, and the corruptions which I supposed were tamed, broke forth with redoubled vigour. Again, though sin is declared to be displeasing to God and destructive to man, by all the evils and miseries with which the world is filled, and all the punishments which the righteous Judge of all the earth has inflicted on the account of it; yet the just demerit of sin is not to be learnt by the destruction of Sodom, or of the old world, but only from the sufferings of Christ, who has borne the curse for sinners. Nor is it sufficient to know historically that he did suffer, and how he suffered. Where these things are not known by the light of the Spirit, they are no more regarded than a worn-out tale. But where the Spirit of Christ reveals by the word, the nature, cause, and end of his sufferings, then sin appears exceedingly sinful. Nothing less than this can make the soul abhor it.

The Glory and Grace of God Revealed in Jesus Christ, [2:444]; 2:246

Come unto me, all ye that labour and are heavy laden,
and I will give you rest.—Matt. 11:28.

WE read that, when David was withdrawn into the wilderness from the rage of Saul, every one that was in distress, or in debt, or discontented, gathered themselves unto him, and he became their captain. This was a small honour in the judgment of Saul and his court, to be the head of a company of fugitives. Those who judge by outward appearances, and are governed by the maxims of worldly wisdom, cannot have much more honourable thoughts of the present state of Christ's mystical kingdom and subjects upon earth. The case of David was looked upon as desperate by those who, like Nabal, lived at their ease. They did not know, or would not believe, the promise of God, that he should be king over Israel; and therefore they preferred the favour of Saul, whom God had rejected. In like manner, though our Lord Jesus Christ was a Divine person, invested with all authority, grace, and blessing, and declared the purpose of God concerning himself, and all who should obey his voice, that he would be their King, and they should be his happy people; yet the most that heard him saw no excellence in him, or need of him; their portion and hearts were in this world, therefore they rejected him, and treated him as a blasphemer and a madman. A few, however, there were, who felt their misery, and desired to venture upon his word. To these he gave the freest invitation. Those who accepted it, found his promise made good, and rejoiced in his light. Thus it is still; he is no longer upon earth to call us; but he has left these gracious words for an encouragement to all who need a Saviour... To these labouring and heavy laden souls, he still says, 'Come unto me, and I will give you rest.'

Labouring and Heavy Laden Sinners Described, [2:448]; 2:248

For with thee is the fountain of life: in thy light shall we see light.
—Psa. 36:9.

WHEN the eyes of the understanding are opened, we begin to see everything around us, to be just as the Scripture has described them. Then, and not till then, we perceive, that what we read in the Bible concerning the horrid evil of sin, the vileness of our fallen nature, the darkness and ignorance of those who know not God, our own emptiness, and the impossibility of finding relief and comfort from creatures, is exactly true. We cannot but apply the words of the woman, and say, Come and see a book that has told me all that I ever did, the ground of all my complaints, the true cause and nature of all the evil I either see, hear, or feel, from day to day. And as we find our disease precisely described, so we perceive a suitableness in the proposed remedy. We need a Saviour, and he must be a mighty one; but though our wants and sins, our fears and enemies, are great and numerous, we are convinced that the character of Christ is sufficient to answer them all. We need a rest, a rest which the world cannot give. Inquire where we will among the creatures, experience brings in the same answer from all, It is not in me. This again confirms the word of God, which has forewarned us that we shall meet nothing but disappointment in such pursuits. But there is a spiritual rest spoken of which we know to be the very thing we want, and all our remaining solicitude is now to attain it. From hence, as I said, we may assuredly conclude, that the book which gives us such just views of everything that passes, must be given by inspiration from him who is the searcher of hearts. This proof is equally plain and conclusive to all capacities that are spiritually enlightened, and such only are able to understand it.

The Present and Future Rest of Believers in Christ, [2:469]; 2:264

Let your light so shine before men, that they may see your good works,
and glorify your Father which is in heaven.—Matt. 5:16.

THE people of the world are not proper judges of spiritual experiences, but they can judge tolerably right of tempers and actions... Pray therefore for wisdom and grace, to make your light so shine before men, that they, seeing your good works, may glorify your Father who is in heaven. This is the great design and proper effect of the gospel, when rightly understood. For as it is the grace of God alone which bringeth salvation, so this grace not only enlightens the understanding, but purifies the heart, regulates the conduct, works by love, and overcomes the world. It effectually teaches and enforces (what the best schemes of morality and philosophy have always failed in) the denial of all ungodliness and worldly lusts; and by the motives it displays, and the strength it communicates, enables the true Christian to adorn his character in every relation, and to fill up the whole circle of duty as it respects himself, his neighbour, and the God with whom he has to do. It teaches to live soberly, righteously, and godly; to avoid whatsoever is contrary to the purity of the gospel; to practise moderation in the use even of lawful things; and to do unto others as we would they should do unto us. It teaches the rich to be humble and bountiful, the poor to be thankful and resigned. It teaches superiors to be kind, inferiors to be faithful. Husbands and wives, parents and children, masters and servants, magistrates and people, all are instructed by this grace to a conduct answerable to their high calling, and to the common relation they stand to him who has loved them and washed them from their sins in his blood. For the morality of the gospel has a nobler spring, and a more extensive scope, than the ties of social life. Their sobriety and righteousness are not substituted in the place of vital goodness, but are the fruits derived from it. The grace of God teaches them to live godly, to delight in him, to obey him, to do everything for his sake, as under his eye, and to be continually governed by a sense of his unspeakable love manifested in his Son.

Believers Cautioned Against Misconduct in Their Profession, [2:513]; 2:295

For as the body without the spirit is dead,
so faith without works is dead also.—James 2:26.

S T. Paul having said, 'That a man is justified by faith without the deeds of the law,' produces the example of Abraham to confirm his assertion. St. James (in the chapter before us), from the example of the same Abraham, draws a conclusion which seems directly to contradict this: 'Ye see then how that by works a man is justified and not by faith only.' Can any two opinions be more opposite in appearance? How then can both be true, or how can we believe both writers infallible in their doctrine, and influenced by the unerring Spirit of God?

We may confidently answer, The apostles are both right; their doctrine is equally from God, and does not clash in any particular.

St. Paul is evidently treating on the great point of a sinner's justification in the sight of God; he shows that it cannot be of the law, because by the law all men were already condemned, and because then boasting could not be excluded; but that it was freely by grace, through the redemption that is by Christ Jesus.

St. James expressly treats of those who rested in a notion which they called faith, and accounted sufficient for their salvation, though it had no influence upon their hearts, tempers, and conduct. He shows that their hope is vain, because such a faith as this the devils have.

The sum is, The one declares that nothing renders us acceptable to God but faith in the Lord Jesus Christ; the other, that such a faith, when true and genuine, is not solitary, but accompanied with every good work. The one speaks of the justification of our persons, this is by faith only; the other of the justification of our profession, this is by faith not alone, but working by love, and producing obedience.

A Living and a Dead Faith, [2:550]; 2:322

Thou shalt also consider in thine heart, that, as a man chasteneth his son, so the LORD thy God chasteneth thee.—Deut. 8:5.

THE history of David is full of instruction. Everything recorded of him affords us either consolation or caution. In his example, we see much of the sovereign power and providence of God. When a youth, though the least of his father's house, he was singled out and called from following sheep, to rule a kingdom. We see him supported through a variety of difficulties, and at length established in his throne, to the amazement and confusion of his enemies. In him likewise we have a striking proof of the evil that is in the heart of man. Who would have thought it, that David, the man highly favoured, so wonderfully preserved, the man after God's own heart, who in the time of his distress could say, 'My soul thirsteth for God, even for the living God;' that he should be in an unguarded hour seduced, surprised, and led captive of the devil! From gazing he proceeds to adultery, from adultery to murder, and at length sinks into such a stupid frame of mind, that an express message from God was needful to convince him of his sin. And in this circumstance we further see the riches of divine grace and mercy; how tenderly the Lord watches over his sheep, how carefully he brings them back when wandering from him, and with what rich goodness he heals their backslidings, and loves them freely. David was fallen but not lost.

However, though the Lord is thus gracious in passing by the iniquity of his children, yet he will let them know, by sorrowful experience, that 'it is an evil and a bitter thing to sin against him.' Though he will not cast off, he will chasten; he will withdraw his presence, and suspend his gracious influences; and this to a sensible heart is a heavy punishment.

Guilt Removed, and Peace Restored, [2:563]; 2:332

And the Lord God said unto the serpent ... I will put enmity between
thee and the woman, and between thy seed and her seed; it shall bruise
thy head, and thou shalt bruise his heel.—Gen. 3:14, 15.

WHEN the first man had fallen from the happiness and perfection of his creation, had rendered himself corrupt and miserable, and was only capable of transmitting depravity and misery to his posterity; the goodness of God immediately revealed a remedy, adequate to his distressed situation. The Lord Jesus was promised under the character *of the seed of the woman*, as the great Deliverer who should repair the breach of sin, and retrieve the ruin of human nature. From that hour, he became the object of faith, and the author of salvation, to every soul that aspired to communion with God, and earnestly sought deliverance from guilt and wrath. This discovery of a Saviour was, in the first ages, veiled under types and shadows; and, like the advancing day, became brighter and brighter, as the time of his manifestation drew near: but it was always sufficient to sustain the hopes, and to purify the hearts, of the true worshippers of God.

At length, in the fulness of time, Gal. 4:4, (as the apostle speaks,) the time marked out by the ancient prophecies, the time to which all the previous dispensations of divine providence had an express reference and subordination, and which was peculiarly suited to place the manifold wisdom of God and the truths of divine revelation in the clearest light; the long-expected Messiah appeared, as the Surety and Saviour of sinners, to accomplish the great work of redemption. For these purposes he was born of a virgin, of the family of David, at the town of Bethlehem as the prophets foretold.

God was not a debtor to sinful men. He might have left them all to perish, (as he left the sinning angels,) without the least impeachment of his goodness. But his mercy interposed, and he spared not his own Son, that sinners might be saved in a way consistent with his perfections.

Ecclesiastical History: The Promise of Messiah, [3:3]; 2:373

Take my yoke upon you, and learn of me; for I am meek and lowly in heart: and ye shall find rest unto your souls.—Matt. 11:29.

WHICH shall we admire most, the majesty, or the grace, conspicuous in this invitation? How soon would the greatest earthly monarch be impoverished, and his treasures utterly exhausted, if all that are poor and miserable had encouragement to apply freely to him, with a promise of relief fully answerable to their wants and wishes! But the riches of Christ are unsearchable and inexhaustible. If millions of millions of distressed sinners seek to *him* for relief, he has a sufficiency for them all. His mercy is infinite to pardon all their sins; his grace is infinite to answer and exceed their utmost desires; his power is infinite to help them in all their difficulties. A number without number have been thus waiting upon him, from age to age; and not one of them has been sent away disappointed and empty. And the streams of his bounty are still flowing, and still full. Thus the sun, his brightest material image, has been the source of light to the earth, and to all its inhabitants, from the creation; and will be equally so to all succeeding generations, till time shall be no more. There is, indeed, an appointed hour when the sun shall cease to shine, and the course of nature shall fail. But the true Sun, the Sun of righteousness, has no variableness nor shadow of turning; and they who depend upon him while in this world, shall rejoice in his light for ever. Can we hesitate to accept of these words, as affording a full proof of the Divine character, the proper Godhead of our Lord and Saviour, supposing only that he meant what he said, and that he is able to make his promise good? Can a creature, however excellent and glorious, use this language? Can a creature discharge the debts, soothe the distresses, and satisfy the desires of every individual who looks to him? Who but the Lord God can raise up all that are bowed down, and comfort all that mourn?

Messiah: Rest for the Weary, [4:163]; 3:129

Great and marvellous are thy works, Lord God Almighty.—Rev. 15:3.

WE live in the midst of them; and the little impression they make upon us, sufficiently proves our depravity. He is great in the very smallest; and there is not a plant, flower, or insect, but bears the signature of infinite wisdom and power. How sensibly then should we be affected by the consideration of the whole, if sin had not blinded our understandings, and hardened our hearts! In the beginning, when all was dark, unformed, and waste, his powerful word produced light, life, beauty, and order. He commanded the sun to shine, and the planets to roll. The immensity of creation is far beyond the reach of our conceptions. The innumerable stars, the worlds, which however large in themselves, are, from their remoteness, but barely visible to us, are of little more immediate and known use, than to enlarge our idea of the greatness of their Author. Small, indeed, is the knowledge we have of our own system; but we know enough to render our indifference inexcusable. The glory of the sun must strike every eye; and in this enlightened age, there are few persons but have some ideas of the magnitude of the planets, and the rapidity and regularity of their motions. Further, the rich variety which adorns this lower creation, the dependence and relation of the several parts, and their general subserviency to the accommodation of man, the principal inhabitant, together with the preservation of individuals, and the continuance of every species of animals, are subjects not above the reach of common capacities, and which afford almost endless and infinite scope for reflection and admiration. But the bulk of mankind regard them not... Thus men 'live without God in the world,' though they 'live, and move, and have their being in him,' and are incessantly surrounded by the most striking proofs of his presence and energy.

Messiah: The Lamb of God, the Great Atonement [4:184]; 3:145

But he was wounded for our transgressions.—Isa. 53:5.

IN the person and sufferings of Christ there is at once a discovery of the misery of fallen man, and the means of his complete recovery... Isaiah had foretold, that the Lord would lay upon him the iniquities of us all; that he was to be wounded for our transgressions, and by his stripes we should be healed. Here then we see the manifold wisdom of God. His inexpressible love to us commended; his mercy exalted in the salvation of sinners; his truth and justice vindicated, in the full satisfaction for our sin exacted from the Surety; his glorious holiness and opposition to all evil, and his invariable faithfulness to his threatenings and his promises.

Would we learn the depth of the fall of man, let us consider the depth of the humiliation of Jesus to restore him. Behold the Beloved of God, perfectly spotless and holy, yet made an example of the severest vengeance ... suspended, naked, wounded, and bleeding upon the cross, and there heavily complaining, that God had for a season forsaken him. Sin was the cause of all his anguish. He stood in the place of sinners, and therefore was not spared. Not any, or all, the evils which the world has known, afford such proof of the dreadful effects and detestable nature of sin, as the knowledge of Christ crucified. Sin had rendered the case of mankind so utterly desperate, that nothing less than the blood and death of Jesus could retrieve it. If any other expedient could have sufficed, his prayer, that the bitter cup might pass from him, would have been answered. But what his enemies intended as the keenest reproach, his redeemed people will for ever repeat as the expression of his highest praise, 'he saved others, himself he cannot save.' Justice would admit no inferior atonement, love would not give up the cause of fallen, ruined man. Being therefore determined to save others, he could not, consistently with this gracious design and undertaking, deliver himself.

> *Whom God hath set forth to be a propitiation through faith in his blood,*
> *… To declare, I say, at this time his righteousness: that he might be just,*
> *and the justifier of him which believeth in Jesus.*—Rom. 3:25, 26

WE may now be assured, that the forgiveness of one sinner, and, indeed, of one sin, by an act of mere mercy, and without any interposing consideration, was incompatible with the inflexibility of the law, and the truth and justice of the Lawgiver. But mercy designed the forgiveness of innumerable sinners, each of them chargeable with innumerable sins; and the declaration that God is thus merciful, was to be recorded and publicly known, through a long succession of ages, and to extend to sins not yet committed. An act of grace so general and unreserved, might lead men (not to speak of superior intelligences) to disparaging thoughts of the holiness of God, and might even encourage them to sin with hope of impunity, if not connected with some provision, which might show that the exercise of his mercy was in full harmony with the honour of all his perfections. How God could 'be just, and yet justify those' whom his own righteous constitution condemned, was a difficulty too great for finite understandings to solve. But herein is God glorious. His wisdom propounded, and his love afforded, the adequate, the only possible expedient. He revealed to our first parents his purpose, which in the fulness of time he accomplished, of sending 'forth his Son, made of a woman, made under the law, to redeem sinners from the curse of the law,' by sustaining it for them. Considering the dignity of his person and the perfection of his obedience, his sufferings and death for sins not his own, displayed the heinousness of sin, and the severe displeasure of God against it, in a much stronger light than the execution of the sentence upon the offenders could possibly do. It displays likewise the justice of this sentence, since neither the dignity nor the holiness of the Surety could exempt him from suffering; and that, though he was the Beloved of God, he was not spared. This is what I understand by atonement and satisfaction for sin.

Messiah: The Lamb of God, the Great Atonement [4:188]; 3:148

Elect according to the foreknowledge of God the Father,
through sanctification of the Spirit, unto obedience and sprinkling
of the blood of Jesus Christ.—1 Pet. 1:2.

THE efficacy of this atonement is complete. 'The Lamb of God,' thus slain, 'taketh away sin,' both with respect to its guilt and its defilement. The Israelites, by looking to the brazen serpent, were saved from death, and healed of their wounds. 'The Lamb of God' is an object proposed, not to our bodily sight, but to the eye of the mind, which indeed, in fallen man, is naturally blind; but the gospel message, enlivened by the powerful agency of the Holy Spirit, is appointed to open it. He who thus 'seeth the Son, and believeth on him,' is delivered from guilt and condemnation, is justified from all sin. He is warranted to plead the sufferings of the 'Lamb of God' in bar of his own; the whole of the Saviour's obedience unto death, as the ground and title of his acceptance unto life. Guilt or obnoxiousness to punishment being removed, the soul has an open way of access to God, and is prepared to receive blessings from him. For as the sun, the fountain of light, fills the eye that was before blind, the instant it receives sight; so God, who is the fountain of goodness, enlightens all his intelligent creatures according to their capacity, unless they are by sin blinded, and rendered incapable of communion with him. The Saviour is now received and enthroned in the heart and from his fulness the life of grace is derived and maintained. Thus not only the guilt, but the love of sin, and its dominion, are taken away, subdued by grace, and cordially renounced by the believing pardoned sinner. The blood which frees him from distress, preserves a remembrance of the great danger and misery from which he has been delivered warm upon his heart, inspires him with gratitude to his Deliverer, and furnishes him with an abiding and constraining motive for cheerful and universal obedience.

Messiah: The Lamb of God, the Great Atonement [4:189]; 3:148

Rivers of waters run down mine eyes,
because they keep not thy law.—Psa. 119:136.

WHOEVER has a measure of the mind that was in Christ, must be proportionally burdened and grieved, like righteous Lot in Sodom, with the wickedness around him, if he lives in society. Who that has any regard for the honour of God, or the souls of men, can hear and see what passes every hour; how the authority of God is affronted, his goodness abused, and his mercy despised, without emotions of grief and compassion? If we are spiritually-minded, we must be thus affected; and we should be more so, if we were more spiritual. But the holiness of MESSIAH, and, consequently his hatred of sin, was absolutely perfect. His view of the guilt and misery of sinners, was likewise comprehensive and clear. How must he be therefore grieved by the wickedness and insensibility of those with whom he daily conversed! Especially as he not only observed the outward conduct of men, but had an intimate knowledge of the evil heart, which is hidden from us. In this sense his sufferings and sorrows began with his early years, and continued throughout the whole of his life. He undoubtedly could say, with an emphasis peculiar to himself, 'I beheld the transgressors, and was grieved;' 'rivers of waters ran down my eyes, because men keep not thy law.'

We call ourselves the followers and servants of him who was despised of men, and encompassed with sorrows. And shall we then 'seek great things for ourselves,' as if we belonged to the present world, and expected no portion beyond it? Or shall we be tremblingly alive to the opinion of our fellow creatures, and think it a great hardship, if it be our lot to suffer shame for his sake, who endured the cross, and despised the shame for us? Rather may we account such disgrace our glory, and every loss and suffering, that we may endure for him, a gain; while, on the other hand, we learn with the apostle Paul, to esteem every gain and honour this world can afford, 'to be but loss and dung in comparison of the excellency of the knowledge of Christ Jesus our Lord.'

Messiah: Despised and Rejected of Men, [4:207]; 3:162

Who, being in the form of God, thought it not robbery to be equal with
God: But made himself of no reputation, and took upon him the form
of a servant, and was made in the likeness of men.—Phil. 2:6, 7.

THEY expected a Messiah to come in pomp and power, to deliver them from the Roman yoke. For a person truly Divine, who made himself equal with God, to be encompassed with poverty and distress, seemed such profane contradiction as might justify every mark of indignity they could offer him. And this difficulty must equally affect every unenlightened mind. If *man* had been left to devise in what manner the Lord of the universe would probably descend to dwell a while with poor mortals in a visible form, they would undoubtedly have imagined such a scene (if their thoughts could have reached it) as described by the prophets on other occasions. The heavens bowing, the earth shaking, the mountains ready to start from their places, and all nature labouring to do homage to her Creator. Or, if he came in a milder way, they would, at least, have contrived an assemblage of all that we conceive magnificent; a pomp and splendour surpassing all the world ever saw. Expecting nations, crowding to welcome his arrival, and thrones of gold, and palaces of ivory, would have been judged too mean to accommodate so glorious a guest. But the Lord's thoughts and ways are different from man's. The beloved Son of God, by whom all things were made, was born in a stable, and grew up in an obscure and mean condition. He came to suffer and to die for sin, to sanctify poverty and affliction to his people, to set a perfect example of patience and submission; therefore he made himself of no reputation, but took on him the form and offices of a servant. This was the appointment of divine wisdom; but so incredible in the judgment of blinded mortals, that the apostle assures us 'no man can say that Jesus is the Lord;' can perceive and acknowledge his inherent excellence and authority, through the disgraceful circumstances of his humiliation, 'but by the Holy Ghost.'

Ecclesiastical History: The Reception Christ Received, [3:42]; 2:402

For consider him that endured such contradiction of sinners against himself, lest ye be wearied and faint in your minds.—Heb. 12:3.

WHEN the apostle would dispose believers by an argument or motive (which, if we fully understood it, would render all other arguments unnecessary) to endure sufferings and crosses patiently; he says, 'Consider him'—he uses a word which is properly a mathematical term, denoting the ratio or proportion between different numbers, or figures... Compare yourselves with him, and his sufferings with your own. Consider who he is, no less than what he endured.

In the apprehensions of men, insults are aggravated in proportion to the disparity between the person who receives and who offers them. A blow from an equal is an offence, but would be still more deeply resented from an inferior. But if a subject, a servant, a slave, should presume to strike a king, it would justly be deemed an enormous crime. But Jesus, the King of kings, and Lord of lords, whom all the angels of God worship, made himself so entirely of no reputation, that the basest of the people, the servants, the common soldiers, were not afraid to make him the object of their derision, and to express their hatred in the most sarcastic and contemptuous manner. It is said, that he endured the contradiction of 'sinners.' So, perhaps, do we; but we are sinners likewise, and deserve much more than we suffer, if not immediately from the instruments of our grief, yet from the Lord, who has a right to employ what instruments he pleases to afflict us for our sins. This thought quieted the spirit of David, when his own son rose up against his life, and his own servant cursed him to his face. But Jesus was holy, harmless, and undefiled, he had done nothing amiss; yet the usage he met with was such as has seldom been offered to the vilest malefactor... He was engaged to make a full atonement for sin, by his sufferings; and as he had power over his own life, he would not dismiss his spirit, till he could say, 'It is finished.'

Messiah: Voluntary Suffering, [4:214]; 3:167

And, behold, there talked with him two men, which were Moses and
Elias: Who appeared in glory, and spake of his decease which
he should accomplish at Jerusalem.—Luke 9:30, 31.

WHEN our Lord was transfigured, Moses and Elijah appeared in glory and conversed with him. Had we been informed of the interview only, we should probably have desired to know the subject of their conversation, as we might reasonably suppose it turned upon very interesting and important topics. The Scripture makes little provision for the indulgence of our curiosity, but omits nothing that is necessary for our instruction; and we learn thus much from it, that they discoursed, not upon the trifling things which the world accounts great, such as the rise and fall of empires; but they spoke of the sufferings of Jesus, and of the decease which he should accomplish at Jerusalem. They spake of his Exodus, (as the word is,) his departure out of life, the issue and completion of his engagement for sinners, that is, his crucifixion and death. This is the grand theme of heaven and heaven-born souls... The cross of Christ displays the Divine perfections with peculiar glory. Here the name of God is revealed, as a just God and a Saviour. Here the believer contemplates, in one view, the unspeakable evil of sin, and the unsearchable riches of mercy. This gives him the most affecting sense of the misery which he has deserved, while at the same time he receives the fullest assurance that there is forgiveness with God, and discovers a sure foundation whereon he may build his hope of eternal life, without fear of disappointment. From the moment the apostle Paul was enlightened to understand this mystery of redeeming love, he accounted his former gain but loss; his former supposed wisdom no better than folly, and became determined to know nothing, to depend upon nothing, to glory in nothing, but Jesus Christ, and him crucified.

Messiah: Suffering and Wounded for Us, [4:219]; 3:171

...the living God, who giveth us richly all things to enjoy.— 1 Tim. 6:17.

THEY who are delivered by grace from the spirit and power of this evil world, and who live by his death, and likewise they who see they must perish unless saved by him, are authorized to consider him as mindful of them, and making provision for them in the day of his trouble. They who were actually healed by looking at the brazen serpent according to God's appointment, had a sufficient proof in themselves, that it was erected and placed in view of the camp on their account, Num. 21:9. 'He bore our griefs.'—It does not follow that sinners must have been crucified, if the Saviour had not been crucified on their behalf. But as this was a painful and terrible punishment, it may teach us, that without his interposition we were justly liable to extremity of misery in the present life. That we who have offended God should enjoy health, peace, or satisfaction for a single hour; that we do not draw every breath in the most excruciating pain; that we derive any comfort from creatures; that we are not a burden and a terror to ourselves, and mutually to each other; that our state while upon earth is, in any respect, better than an image of hell,—must wholly be ascribed to him. A sinner as such, is under the curse of the law; and this curse includes every species of misery that can affect us, either in mind, body, or estate. But *he* was appointed, from the beginning, to sustain and exhaust the curse for us. And therefore the earth, though so long inhabited by wretches in a state of bold rebellion against their Maker, is filled with the fruits and evidences of his long-suffering patience and mercy. Therefore he still affords 'us rain and fruitful seasons,' indulges us with a variety of temporal blessings, and gives us power to take comfort in them. This consideration greatly enhances the value of temporal good things to his people. They receive them as from his hand, as tokens of his love and pledges of his favour, sanctified to their use by his blood and promise. Cheered by such thoughts as these, his poor people often enjoy their plain fare with a pleasure, of which the expensive and dissipated sensualist has no conception.

Messiah: Suffering and Wounded for Us, [4:221]; 3:172

But I said, Not so, Lord.—Acts 11:8.

I T is a sufficient proof of our depravity, that we prefer our own ways to the Lord's; nor can he inflict a heavier judgment upon us in this life, than to give us up entirely to the way of our own hearts. He made us to be happy; but as he made us for himself, and gave us a capacity, and a vastness of desire, which only he himself can satisfy, the very constitution and frame of our nature render happiness impossible to us, unless in a way of dependence upon him, and obedience to his laws. The lamb that grazes in the meadow, and the fish that swims in the stream, are each in their proper element. If you suppose them to change places they must both perish. But the brute creation have no propensity to such changes as would destroy them. The instincts implanted in them by their great Creator are conducive to their welfare; and to these instincts they are uniformly faithful. If you can conceive of beasts impatient to leave the shore, and improve their situation by rushing into the ocean; and the fishes equally earnest to forsake the waters, in quest of new and greater advantages upon the dry land; it may illustrate the folly of fallen man, who, turned aside by a deceived heart, refuses life, and seeks death in the error of his ways. For the will of God (if I may so speak) is our proper element; and if we depart from it, our sin unavoidably involves our punishment. We naturally indulge hard thoughts of God, and think the rule he has enjoined us too strict and severe, intended to restrain us from real good, and propose to ourselves some unknown advantages by transgressing it. Thus Satan persuaded Eve, and we derive from her: and though we know that she only gained misery by the experiment, we rashly repeat it for ourselves. The Scripture assures us that the ways of God are pleasant, but we will not be persuaded. Experience proves that the way of transgressors is hard, but we resist the conviction, and hurry on in a round of continual disappointment. Are the proud, the covetous, the voluptuous, or the ambitious, happy? I appeal to conscience.

Messiah: Sin Charged Upon the Surety, [4:232]; 3:180

But where sin abounded, grace did much more abound.—Rom. 5:20.

WHERE sin abounded, grace has much more abounded. Man sinned, and MESSIAH suffered. 'The Lord hath laid,' or caused to meet upon him, 'the iniquity of us all,' that is, the punishment due to them. The evils we have deserved were in pursuit of us; but Jesus interposed, and they all seized upon him; and he endured them, that we might be spared. Do we ask upon what grounds? It was on the ground of his voluntary substitution for sinners, as their covenant Head and Representative.

So much, correspondent to this appointment, obtains amongst men, as may show that the idea accords with our notion of justice. If a man be unable to pay a debt, and the creditor should exact the payment from a third person who was no way concerned, it would, with reason, be deemed a very oppressive action. But if it be known that this person became freely bound and responsible for the debtor, he is allowed to be justly liable. But in the present case I make no appeal to human customs. It is a divine appointment, and therefore is and must be right. It was a great design, the triumph of infinite wisdom, the highest effect of the love of God. It is revealed, not to be submitted to our discussion, or that we may sit in judgment upon the propriety of the measure, but it demands our highest admiration and praise; and, like the sun, brings with it that light by which the whole system of our knowledge is illuminated. For till we know this great truth, and are able to see its influence upon everything we are related to, whatever attainments we may boast, we are, in fact, encompassed with thick darkness, with darkness which may be felt. For the accomplishment of this design, the Son of God was so manifested in the nature of man, that he, and they who believe in him, participate in a real, though mystical union, and are considered as one: he their living Head; they his body, consisting of many members: each of them represented by him, accepted in him, and deriving from his fulness their life, their light, their strength, and their joy.

Messiah: Sin Charged Upon the Surety, [4:234]; 3:182

...our Lord Jesus, that great shepherd of the sheep.—Heb. 13:20.

AFTER man had sinned, this glorious Head and Surety made known the certainty and benefit of his mediation and engagement on the behalf of sinners, according to the good pleasure of his wisdom, and as the case required; otherwise, upon the entrance of sin, the full execution of the sentence of the law denounced against the offenders, might perhaps have immediately followed: but he revealed himself. He showed mercy to Adam, covenanted with Noah, walked with Abraham, conversed with Moses, dwelt with his church in the wilderness, and was known by the name of the 'Holy One of Israel.' David ascribes to the Shepherd of Israel the name of Jehovah, and Isaiah declares, that the Lord of Hosts is the Husband of the church. These characters of Shepherd, and Bridegroom, and Husband, are appropriated to MESSIAH in the New Testament. He therefore is Jehovah, the Lord of hosts, whom Abraham, David, and Isaiah, worshipped; or his appearance upon earth would be evidently to the disadvantage of those who believe in him. If he were not God, he would be a creature, for there is no medium; and consequently our Shepherd would be infinitely inferior to the Almighty Shepherd, who was the refuge, the trust, and the salvation of his people, before MESSIAH was manifested in the flesh.

In the fulness of time he veiled his glory. He 'who was in the form of God, and thought it not robbery to be equal with God, took upon him the form of a servant, and was made of a woman, made under the law.' Then the union between him and the people whom he came into the world to save was completed; because 'the children were partakers of flesh and blood, he likewise took part of the same.' 'The Word, who in the beginning was God, and was with God, was made flesh.' And in our nature, though he knew no sin, he was treated as a sinner for us, to declare the righteousness of God, in his forbearance and goodness to all who had been saved in former ages, and in the forgiveness and salvation of all who should trust in him to the end of time. He suffered 'once,' once for all, 'the just for the unjust, to bring us to God.'

Messiah: Sin Charged Upon the Surety, [4:236]; 3:183

O my Father, if it be possible, let this cup pass from me.—Matt. 26:39.

AND now God is revealed, not only as merciful, but as just, 'in justifying him which believeth in Jesus.' God is well pleased in him, and for his sake, with all who accept him. Their sins are expiated by his sufferings, and his perfect righteousness, the whole of his obedience unto death, is the consideration or ground on which they are accounted righteous.

By virtue of this union likewise he is their life. They receive of his fulness, as the branches derive their life and fruitfulness from the tree whereon they grow; therefore the apostle said, 'I live, yet not I, but Christ liveth in me.'

From this subject, the substitution of MESSIAH for sinners, we may learn,

How to estimate the evil of sin. That sin is a great evil, is evident by its effects. It deprived Adam of the life and presence of God, and brought death and all natural evil into the world. It caused the destruction of the old world by water. It is the source of all the misery with which the earth is now filled; it will kindle the last great conflagration; yea, it has already kindled that fire which shall never be quenched. But in no view does the sinfulness of sin appear so striking as in this wonderful effect,—the suffering and death of MESSIAH: that notwithstanding the dignity of his person, and the perfection of his obedience to the law, and that though he prayed in his agonies, 'that if it were possible the cup might pass from him,' yet, if sinners were to be saved, it was indispensably necessary that he should drink it. This shows the evil of sin in the strongest light; and in this light it is viewed by all who derive life from his death, and healing from his wounds. We may be afraid of the consequences of sin from other considerations; but it is only by looking to him who was pierced for our transgressions, that we can learn to hate it, Zech. 12:10.

How great are his signs! and how mighty are his wonders!—Dan. 4:3.

GREAT and marvellous is this Lord God omnipotent in his king-dom of universal providence. His mighty arm sustains the vast fabric of the universe. He upholds the stars in their courses. If we attentively consider their multitude, their magnitudes, their distances from us and from each other, and the amazing swiftness, variety, and regularity of their motions, our minds are overwhelmed, our thoughts confounded, by the vastness and the wonders of the scene. But he spoke them into being, and they are preserved in their stations and revolutions by his power and agency. If we fix our thoughts upon the earth, though in comparison of the immensity of his creation it is but as a point or a grain of sand, it is the object of his incessant care. All its various inhabitants derive their existence and their support from him. He provides for the young ravens when unable to fly, and for the young lions that traverse the woods. The instinct of animals, whereby they are unerringly instructed in whatever concerns the wel-fare and preservation of their species, so vastly exceeding the boasted wisdom of man, that he can neither imitate nor comprehend it, is communicated by him. He teaches the birds to build their nests, the spider to weave his web, and instructs the communities of bees, and insignificant emmets, to form their admirable policies and govern-ment among themselves. If we speak of intelligent beings, 'he does what he pleases in the armies of heaven and among the inhabitants of earth.' He directs and overrules the counsels and purposes of men, so that, though they act freely, the event of all their different interfering schemes is only the accomplishment of his purposes... Thus they who dwell under his shadow are safe; for all things are in his power, and he always careth for them, and keepeth them, as the pupil of his eye; and therefore, though they are exercised with trials, and suffer many things for their good, his eye being always upon them, and his ear open to their prayer, they are supported, supplied, relieved, delivered, and, at last, made more than conquerors.

Messiah: The Lord Reigneth, [4:403]; 3:306

Now I Nebuchadnezzar praise and extol and honour the King of heaven, all whose works are truth, and his ways judgment: and those that walk in pride he is able to abase.—Dan. 4:37.

WE are by nature at variance with him. We are too proud to be indebted to his grace, too wise in our own conceits to desire his instruction, too obstinately attached to the love and practice of sin, to be capable of relishing the beauty and spirituality of his commandments. And our love of the world, and the things of it, is too strong and grasping, to permit us to be satisfied with the lot and with the dispensations he appoints for us. We wish, if possible, and as far as possible we attempt, to be our own carvers. We are unthankful when he bestows, impatient if he withholds, and if he sees fit to resume the gifts of which we are unworthy, we repine and rebel against his will. This enmity must be subdued, before we can be pleased with his government: in other words, we must be made new creatures. To produce this change, this new creation, the gospel is the only expedient; and when revealed and applied to the heart by the power of the Holy Spirit, the miracle is wrought. The sinner who is first convinced of his guilt and misery, and then reconciled to God by faith in the great atonement, willingly yields to his administration. He owns and feels the propriety of his proceedings, is ready to acknowledge, in his sharpest afflictions, that the Lord is gracious, and has not dealt with him according to the desert of his iniquities. He considers himself as no longer his own, but bought with a price, and brought under the strongest obligations, 'to live no longer to himself, but to him who loved him, and gave himself for him.' And what was before his dread and dislike, becomes now the joy of his heart, the thought that the Lord reigneth, and that all his concerns are in the hands of him who doeth all things well.

The kingdoms of this world are become the kingdoms of our Lord, and of his Christ; and he shall reign for ever and ever.—Rev. 11:15.

HIS kingdom, founded upon the Rock of ages, is building, advancing, and the gates of hell shall not be able to withstand its progress. Only detached and inconsiderable parts of the plan are as yet visible, and the beauties are everywhere obscured by attendant blemishes; but his counsel shall stand, and he will do all his pleasure. Princes and statesmen seldom think of him, are seldom aware that in prosecuting their own schemes, they are eventually fulfilling his purposes, and preparing the way to promote the cause which they despise, and often endeavour to suppress. But thus it is. Sometimes he employs them, more directly, as his instruments; and when they are thus engaged in his work, their success is secured. So Cyrus, whom Isaiah mentioned by name, long before his birth, as the appointed deliverer of Israel from their captivity, prospered in his enterprises being guided and girded by him whom he knew not, and established his own power upon the ruins of the Assyrian monarchy. The Roman Empire likewise increased and prospered from small beginnings, that a way might be opened, in the proper season, for the destruction of the Jewish economy, and for facilitating the preaching of the gospel. And posterity will see, that the principal events of the present age in Asia and America, have all a tendency to bring forward the accomplishment of my text; and are leading to one grand point, the spreading and establishment of the church and the kingdom of our Lord. His plan is unalterably fixed. He has said it, and it shall be done. Things will not always remain in their present disordered state; and though this desirable period may be yet at a distance, and appearances very dark and unpromising, the word of the Lord shall prevail over all discouragements and opposition.

Messiah: The Extent of his Spiritual Kingdom, [4:412]; 3:313

No weapon that is formed against thee shall prosper; and every tongue
that shall rise against thee in judgment thou shalt condemn.—Isa. 54:17.

THE wrath of man, like the waves of the sea, has bounds prescribed to it which it cannot pass. So far as he is pleased to overrule it to his own praise, he will permit it to operate; but the remainder, that is not subservient to the accomplishment of his purpose, he will restrain.

If the Lord of hosts, the Lord of lords, be for us, what weapon or counsel can prosper against us? However dark and threatening appearances may be, we need not tremble for the ark of God. The concernments of his church are in safe hands. The cause so dear to us, is still more dear to him. He has power to support it when it is opposed, and grace to revive it when it is dropping. It has often been brought low, but never has been, never shall be forsaken. When he will work, none can hinder. Nor need you fear for yourself, if you have committed yourself and your all to him. 'The very hairs of your heard are numbered.' There is a hedge of protection around you, which none can break through without his permission; nor will he permit you to be touched, except when he designs to make a temporary and seeming evil conducive to your real and permanent advantage.

It should affect us with an admiring and thankful sense of his condescension. 'Lord, what is man that thou shouldest be so mindful of him?' 'He humbles himself to behold the things that are in heaven,' Psa. 113:6. But he stoops still lower. He affords his attention and favour to sinful men. His eye is always upon his people, his ear open to their prayers. Not a sigh or falling tear escapes his notice. He pities them, as a father pities his children; he proportions their trials to their strength, or their strength to their trials, and so adjusts his dispensations to their state, that they never suffer unnecessarily, nor in vain.

Messiah: King of Kings and Lord of Lords, [4:430]; 3:326

What shall be done unto the man whom the king
delighteth to honour?—Est. 6:6.

HOW great is the dignity and privilege of true believers! Is the man congratulated or envied whom the king delighteth to honour? Believers are more frequently despised than envied in this world. But they may congratulate one another. The King of kings is their friend. They have honours and pleasures which the world knows nothing of. Their titles are high, they are the 'sons and the daughters of the Lord Almighty.' Their possessions are great, for 'all things are theirs.' They are assured of what is best for them in this life, and of life eternal hereafter. They are now nearly related to the King of kings, and shall ere long be acknowledged and owned by him, before assembled worlds. They who now account the proud happy, will be astonished and confounded when they shall see the righteous, who they once undervalued, 'shine forth like the sun in the kingdom of God.'

We may ... infer the extreme folly and danger of those who persist in their rebellion and opposition against this King of kings, and Lord of lords. Though he exercises much patience and long suffering towards them for a season, the hour is approaching when his wrath will burn like fire. It is written and must be fulfilled, 'the wicked shall be turned into hell, and all the nations that forget God,' Psa. 9:17. Oh the solemnities of that great day, when the frame of nature shall be dissolved, when the Judge shall appear, the books be opened, and all mankind shall be summoned to his tribunal! Will not you yet tremble and bow before him, ye careless ones, while he is seated upon a throne of grace, and while the door of mercy stands open?... Are you prepared for the summons? If not, seize the present opportunity. Attend to the 'one thing needful.' Seek his face, that your soul may live.

Messiah: King of Kings and Lord of Lords, [4:433]; 3:328

…but now once in the end of the world hath he appeared to put away
sin by the sacrifice of himself.—Heb. 9:26.

WHEN Adam by transgression had violated the order and law of his creation, his religion, that is, the right disposition of his heart towards God, was at an end. Sin deprived him at once of faith and hope, of love and joy. He no longer desired, he no longer could bear, the presence of his offended Maker. He vainly sought to avoid it; and when compelled to answer, though he could not deny his guilt, instead of making an ingenuous confession, he attempted to fix the blame upon the woman, or rather indeed upon the Lord himself, who had provided her for him. But mercy, undeserved, and undesired, relieved him from a state in which he was already become obdurate and desperate. A promise was given him of 'the seed of the woman,' which virtually contained, as the seed contains the future plant, the substance of all the subsequent promises which were fulfilled by the incarnation of the Son of God and by all that he did, or suffered, or obtained for sinners, in the character of Mediator. For a sinner can have no comfortable intercourse with the holy God but through a Mediator. Therefore the apostle observes of the patriarchs and servants of God, under the Old Testament, 'these all died in faith.' We can say nothing higher than this of the apostles and martyrs under the New Testament. They died, not trusting in themselves that they were righteous, not rejoicing in the works of their own hands; but they died, like the thief upon the cross, in faith, resting all their hope upon him who, by his obedience unto death, 'is the end of the law for righteousness unto every one that believeth.' We have greater advantages, in point of light and liberty, than those of old. The prophecies concerning MESSIAH, which, at the time of delivery, were obscure, are to us infallibly interpreted by their accomplishment. And we know that the great atonement, typically pointed out by their sacrifices, has actually been made; that the Lamb of God has, by the one offering of himself, put away sin.

Messiah: Job's Faith and Expectation, [4:435]; 3:329

As for our redeemer, the LORD *of hosts is his name,*
the Holy One of Israel.—Isa. 47:4.

THERE is no name of MESSIAH more significant, comprehensive or endearing, than the name REDEEMER. The name of *Saviour* expresses what he does for sinners. He saves them with an everlasting salvation. But the word 'Redeemer' intimates likewise the manner in which he saves them. For it is not merely by the word of his power, as he saved his disciples when in jeopardy upon the lake, by saying to the winds and the seas, 'Peace, be still: and there was a great calm;' but by price, by paying a ransom for them, and pouring out the blood of his heart, as an atonement for their sins. The Hebrew word for Redeemer, *Goel*, primarily signifies, a near kinsman, or the next of kin. He with whom the right of redemption lay, and who, by virtue of his nearness of relation, was the legal avenger of blood. Thus MESSIAH took upon him our nature, and, by assuming our flesh and blood, became nearly related to us, that he might redeem our forfeited inheritance, restore us to liberty, and avenge our cause against Satan, the enemy and murderer of our souls. But thus he made himself also responsible for us, to pay our debts, and to answer the demands of justice and law of God on our behalf. He fulfilled his engagement. He suffered, and he died on this account. But our Redeemer, 'who was once dead is now alive, and liveth forevermore, and has the keys of death and of hades.'... He is the living One, having life in himself, 'the same yesterday, today, and for ever.' Such was his own language to the Jews, 'Before Abraham was, I am.' Therefore the Redeemer is mighty, and his redemption is sure. He is able to save to the uttermost. His power is unlimited, and his official authority, as Mediator, is founded in a covenant, ratified by his own blood, and by the oath of the unchangeable God, Psa. 110:4.

Messiah: Job's Faith and Expectation, [4:438]; 3:331

The Lord thy God will raise up unto thee a Prophet from
the midst of thee, of thy brethren, like unto me;
unto him ye shall hearken.—Deut. 18:15.

HOW shall I know that he is my Redeemer? I may use the prophet's words, 'Then shall ye know, if ye follow on to know the Lord.' Our names are not actually inserted in the Bible, but our characters are described there. He is the Redeemer of all who put their trust in him. You *will* not trust in him, unless you feel your need of him; you *cannot*, unless you know him as he is revealed in the word; you *do not*, unless you love him and are devoted to his cause and services. If you know yourself to be a sinner deserving to perish, if that you see there is no help or hope for you but in Jesus, and venture yourself upon his gracious invitation, believing that he is able to save to the uttermost; and if you include holiness and a deliverance from sin, in the idea of the salvation which you long for, then he is your Redeemer. If, among us, an act of grace was published, inviting all criminals to surrender themselves, with a promise of mercy to those who did; though no one was mentioned by name in the act, yet everyone who complied with it, and pleaded it, would be entitled to the benefit. Such an act of grace is the gospel. The Lord says, 'This is my beloved Son, hear him.' If you approve him, he is yours. If you are still perplexed with doubts, they are owing to the weakness of your faith. But there are means appointed for the growth of faith. Wait patiently upon the Lord in the use of those means, and you shall find he has not bid you seek his face in vain... Allowances must be made for the effects of constitution and temperament. Some sincere persons are beset and followed, through life, with distressing temptations. But, in general, simplicity and obedience lead to assurance.

Messiah: Job's Faith and Expectation, [4:443]; 3:335

And though after my skin worms destroy this body,
yet in my flesh shall I see God.—Job 19:26.

FROM the Redeemer's appearance upon earth, Job infers the res-
toration and resurrection of his own body. His trials had been
great—bereaved of his children and substance, afflicted with grievous boils, harassed with temptations, reproached by his friends: out
of all these troubles the Lord his Redeemer delivered him, and his
latter days were more prosperous than his beginning. But he knew
that he must go the way of all the earth, that his body must lie in
the grave, and return to dust. But he expected a future time after his
dissolution, when in the flesh, for himself, and with his own eyes, he
should see God. The expressions are strong and repeated. He does
not speak the language of hesitation and doubt, but of confidence
and certainty. It likewise appears that he placed his ultimate happiness in seeing God. His words are not very different from those of
the apostle, 'When he shall appear, we shall be like him, for we shall
see him as he is.' To behold the glory of God, as our Redeemer, to be
in a state of favour and communion with him, and according to the
utmost capacity of our nature, to be conformed to him in holiness
and love, is that felicity which God has promised, and to which all
his servants aspire. Some foretastes of it they enjoy in the present life,
which cheer them under their trials, and raise them above the grovelling pursuits of those who have their portion only in this world. But
their chief possession is hope. They look forward to a brighter period,
when they shall awaken from the sleep of death, 'to behold his face
in righteousness,' Psa. 17:15. Then, and not till then, they shall be
completely satisfied.

Messiah: Job's Faith and Expectation, [4:446]; 3:337

He that believeth on the Son of God hath the witness in himself.
—1 John 5:10.

BUT the proof of the resurrection of Christ, which is the most important and satisfactory of any, does not depend upon arguments and historical evidence, with which multitudes of true Christians are unacquainted, but is, in its own nature equally convincing in all ages, and equally level to all capacities. They who have found the gospel to be the power of God to the salvation of their souls, have the witness in themselves; and are very sure that the doctrine, which enlightened their understandings, awakened their consciences, delivered them from the guilt and dominion of sin, brought them into a state of peace and communion with God, and inspired them with a bright and glorious hope of eternal life, must be true. They know that the Lord is risen indeed, because they are made partakers of the power of his resurrection, and have experienced a change in themselves, which could only be wrought by the influence of that Holy Spirit which Jesus is exalted to bestow. And many believers, though not qualified to dispute with philosophers and sceptics upon their own learned ground, can put them to shame and to silence, by the integrity and purity of their conduct, by their patience and cheerfulness under afflictions; and would especially silence them, if they were eye-witnesses of the composure and elevation of spirit with which true believers in a risen Saviour welcome the approach of death.

What a train of weighty consequences depend on his resurrection! If he rose from the dead, then he is the Lord of the dead and of the living—then he has the keys of Death and Hades—then he will return to judge the world, and you must see him for yourself, and appear at his tribunal—then it is he with whom you have to do—and then, finally, unless you really love, trust and serve him, unless he is the Beloved and the Lord of your heart, your present state is awfully dangerous and miserable. But let those who love his name be joyful in him. Your Lord who was dead, is alive, and 'because he liveth ye shall live also.'

Messiah: The Lord is Risen Indeed, [4:456]; 3:344

Wherefore, as by one man sin entered into the world, and death by sin; and so death passed upon all men, for that all have sinned.—Rom. 5:12.

B Y one man came death. 'By one man sin entered into the world, and death by sin.' Sin opened the door to death. The creation, at the beginning, was full of order and beauty. 'God saw everything that he had made, and behold all was very good.' Adam, happy in the image and favour of his Maker, breathed the air of immortality in Paradise. While moral evil was unknown, natural evils, such as sickness, pain, and death had no place. How different has the state of things been since! Would you account for the change? Charge it upon man. He sinned against his Creator, Lawgiver, and Benefactor; and thus, by him, came death. The fact is sure; and therefore our reasonings upon it, in order to account for it, further than we are enlightened and taught by Scripture, are unnecessary and vain. God is infinitely wise, and therefore this change was foreseen by him. He doubtless could have prevented it, for to Omnipotence everything that does not imply a contradiction is possible, is easy. But he permitted it, and therefore it must have been agreeable to his wisdom, holiness, and goodness, to permit it. He can overrule it to the purposes of his own glory, and to ends worthy of himself, and he has assured us that he will do so. Thus far I can go, nor do I wish to go further. An endeavour to vindicate the ways of God to man, to fallen man, upon the grounds of what he proudly calls his reason, would be an impracticable, and in my view, a presumptuous attempt. In proportion as his grace enlightens our minds, convinces us of our ignorance, and humbles our pride, we shall be satisfied, that, in whatever he appoints or permits, he acts in a manner becoming his own perfections. Nor can we be satisfied in any other way.

Messiah: Death by Adam, Life by Christ, [4:458]; 3:346

*For since by man came death, by man came also the resurrection
of the dead. For as in Adam all die, even so in Christ
shall all be made alive.*—1 Cor. 15:21-22.

WE see, we feel, that evil is in the world. Death reigns. It has pleased God to afford us a revelation, to visit us with the light of his gospel. If, instead of reasoning, we believe and obey, a way is set before us, by which we may finally overcome every evil, and obtain a happiness and honour, superior to what belonged to man in his original state. They who refuse this gospel must be left to their cavils and perplexities, until the day in which the great Judge and Governor of all shall arise to plead his own cause, and to vindicate his proceedings from their arrogant exceptions. Then 'every mouth will be stopped.' Let us look to the heavens, which are higher than we; and attend to what we may learn from sure principles, that the earth, with all its inhabitants, is but as dust upon the balance, if compared with the immensity of God's creation. Unless we could know the whole, and the relation which this very small part bears to the rest of his government, we must be utterly incompetent to judge how it becomes the great God to act. We are infected with the sin, and we are subject to the death, with all its concomitant evils, which came into the world by the first man. But we are likewise invited to a participation of all the blessings which the Second Man has procured, by his atonement for sin, and by his victory over death. 'For as by man came death, so by man came also the resurrection of the dead.'

MESSIAH has made an end of sin, and destroyed the power of death. They who 'believe in him, though they were dead, shall live,' John 11:25. For he is the Resurrection of the dead, and the Life of the living.

Messiah: Death by Adam, Life by Christ [4:459]; 3:347

O wretched man that I am! who shall deliver me from
the body of this death?—Rom. 7:24.

HE raises the soul from the death of sin unto a life of righteousness. By his blood he procures a right and liberty, and by his Spirit he communicates a power, that those who were afar off may draw nigh to God. Thus, even at present, believers are said to be 'risen with him.' Their spiritual life is renewed, and their happiness is already commenced, though it be as yet subject to abatements.

Though when they are made partakers of his grace, and thereby delivered from the condemning power of the law, sin, has no longer dominion over them, as formerly; yet it still wars and strives within them, and their life is a state of continual warfare. They now approve the law of God 'as holy, just, and good, and delight in it after the inward man,' yet they are renewed but in part. They 'feel a law in their members warring against the law of their minds. They cannot do the things that they would, nor as they would: for when they would do good, evil is present with them.' They are conscious of a defect and a defilement attending their best services. Their attainments are unspeakably short of the desires which love to the Redeemer has raised in their hearts. They are ashamed, and sometimes almost discouraged. They adopt the apostle's language, 'Oh wretched man that I am, who shall deliver me from the body of this death?' But with him they can likewise say, 'I thank God through Jesus Christ our Lord.' They know he is on their side, and expect that he will at last 'make them more than conquerors:' yet, while the conflict lasts, they have much to suffer, and much to lament.

I have only further to observe upon this subject at present, that as Adam is the root and head of all mankind, from whence they all derive a sinful and mortal nature; so Jesus, the Second Adam, is the root of a people who are united to him, planted and engrafted in him by faith.

Messiah: Death by Adam, Life by Christ, [4:464]; 3:350

...the mystery of the gospel.—Eph. 6:19.

A *MYSTERY*, according to the notation of the Greek word, signi-fies a secret. And all the peculiar truths of the gospel may justly be styled mysteries or secrets for two reasons.

1. Because the discovery of them is beyond the reach of fallen man, and they neither would nor could have been known without a revelation from God. This is eminently true of the resurrection. The light of nature, which we often hear so highly commended, may afford some faint glimmerings of a future state, but gives no intim-ation of a resurrection. The men of wisdom at Athens, the Stoic and Epicurean philosophers, who differed widely in most parts of their respective schemes, united in deriding this sentiment, and contemp-tuously styled the apostle Paul a babbler for preaching it. But this secret is to us made known. And we are assured, not only that the Lord will receive to himself the departing spirits of his people, but that he will give commandment concerning their dust, and, in due time, raise their vile bodies to a conformity with his own glorious body.

2. Because, though they are revealed expressly in the Scripture, such is the grossness of our conceptions, and the strength of our prejudices, that the truths of revelation are still unintelligible to us, without a further revelation of their true sense to the mind, by the influence of his Holy Spirit. Otherwise, how can the secret of the Lord be restrained to those who fear him, when the book which con-tains it is open to all, and the literal and grammatical meaning of the words is in the possession of many who fear him not?

Divine truths lie thus far equally open to all, that though none can learn them unless they are taught of God, yet all who are sensible of their own weakness may expect his teaching, if they humbly seek it in prayer... He can give not only light, but sight; not only lessons, but the capacity necessary for their reception. And, while his myster-ies are hidden from the wise and prudent, who are too proud to wait upon him for instruction, he reveals them unto babes.

Messiah: The General Resurrection, [4:472]; 3:355

Kiss the Son, lest he be angry, and ye perish from the way, when his
wrath is kindled but a little. Blessed are all they
that put their trust in him.—Psa. 2:12.

S O large a part of divine prophecy remains yet to be fulfilled, that I apprehend it is not probable that any of us shall be alive when this great and terrible day of the Lord shall be revealed. But are not some of us exposed to a similar dreadful surprise? If you die in your sins, the consequences will be no less deplorable to you, than if you saw the whole frame of nature perishing with you. Alas! what will you do, whither will you flee for help, or where will you leave your glory, if, while you are engrossed by the cares or pleasures of this world, death should arrest you, and summon you to judgment? The rich man in the gospel is not charged with any crimes of peculiar enormity. It is not said that he ground the faces of the poor, or that he, by fraud or oppression, kept back the hire of the labourers who had reaped his harvest; he only rejoiced in his wealth, and in having much goods laid up for many years, and that therefore he might securely eat, drink, and be merry. But God said unto him, 'Thou fool, this night shall thy soul be required of thee.' Awful disappointment! Thus will it be, sooner or later, with all whose hearts and portions are in this world, but are not rich towards God! Consider this, you that are like-minded with him. Tremble at the thought of being found in the number of those who have all their consolation here, and who, when they die, must leave their all behind them. Now is the acceptable time, the day of salvation. Now, if you will seek the Lord, he will be found of you. Now, if you pray for grace and truth, he will answer you. But 'when once the Master of the house shall arise, and' with his own sovereign authoritative hand 'shall shut the door' of his mercy, it will then be in vain, and too late, to say, 'Lord, Lord, open unto us!'

Messiah: The General Resurrection, [4:475]; 3:358

For the Lord himself shall descend from heaven with a shout, with the voice of the archangel, and with the trump of God.—1 Thess. 4:16.

THE great scene will be introduced by a signal: 'At the last trump; for the trumpet shall sound.' Thus the approach of a king or a judge is usually announced; and the Scripture frequently borrows images from our little affairs and customs, and, in condescension to our weakness, illustrates things in themselves too great for our conceptions, by comparing them with those which are more familiar to us.

When the Lord shall come, attended by his holy angels, his redeemed people will reassume their bodies, refined and freed from all that was corruptible; and those of them who shall be then living will be changed, and caught up to meet him in the air. He will then own them, approve and crown them before assembled worlds. Every charge that can be brought against them will be overruled, and their plea, that they trusted in him for salvation, be admitted and ratified. They will be accepted and justified. They will shine like the sun in his train, and attend, as assessors with him, when he shall pass final judgment upon his and their enemies.

He who will then be seated upon the throne of judgment, is to us made known as seated upon a throne of grace. It is time, it is high time, and blessed be God it is not yet too late, to seek his mercy. Still the gospel invites us to hear his voice, and to humble ourselves before him. Once more you are invited, some of you, perhaps, for the last time; how know you but sickness or death may be at the very door? Consider, Are you prepared? Examine the foundation of your hope—and do it quickly, impartially, and earnestly, lest you should be cut off in an hour when you are not aware, and perish with a lie in your right hand.

Messiah: The General Resurrection, [4:476]; 3:359

*...our Saviour Jesus Christ, who hath abolished death, and hath
brought life and immortality to light through the gospel.—2 Tim. 1:10.*

DEATH, simply considered, is no more than a privative idea,
signifying a cessation of life; or, that what was once living, lives
no longer. But it has been the general, perhaps the universal custom
of mankind to personify it. Imagination gives death a formidable
appearance, arms it with a dart, sting, or scythe, and represents it as
an active, inexorable, and invincible reality. In this view death is a
great devourer; with his iron tongue he calls for thousands at a meal.
He has already swallowed up all the preceding generations of men;
all who are now living are marked as his inevitable prey; he is still
unsatisfied, and will go on devouring until the Lord shall come. Then
this destroyer shall be destroyed; he shall swallow no more, but be
swallowed up himself in victory. Thus the Scripture accommodates
itself to the language and apprehensions of mortals. Further, the meta-
phorical usage of the word 'swallow' still enlarges and aggrandizes the
idea. Thus the earth is said to 'have opened her mouth and swallowed
up Korah' and his accomplices, Num. 16:32. And thus a pebble, a
millstone, or a mountain, if cast into the ocean, would be swallowed
up, irrecoverably lost and gone, as though they had never been. Such
shall be the triumphant victory of MESSIAH in the great day of the
consummation of all things. Death, in its cause and in its effects
shall be utterly destroyed. Man was created upright, and lived in a
paradise, till, by sin, he brought death into the world. From that time
death has reigned by sin, and evils abound. But MESSIAH came to
make an end of sin, to destroy death, and him that hath the power of
it, to repair every disorder, and to remove every misery; and he will so
fully, so gloriously accomplish his great undertaking in the final issue,
that everything contrary to holiness and happiness shall be swallowed
up and buried beyond the possibility of a return, as a stone, that is
sunk in the depths of the sea. Thus 'where sin has abounded, grace
will much more abound.'

Messiah: Death Swallowed Up in Victory, [4:479]; 3:361

Death is swallowed up in victory.—1 Cor. 15:54

THE 'all,' who 'in Christ shall be made alive,' are those who, by faith in him, are delivered from the sting of death, which is sin, and are made partakers of a new nature. There is a 'second death,' which, though it shall not hurt the believers in Jesus, will finally swallow up the impenitent and ungodly. We live in an age when there is, if I may so speak, a resurrection of many old and exploded errors, which, though they have been often refuted and forgotten, are admired and embraced by some persons as new and wonderful discoveries. Of this stamp, is the conceit of a universal restitution to a state of happiness of all intelligent creatures, whether angels or men, who have rebelled against the will and government of God. This sentiment contradicts the current doctrine of Scripture, which asserts the everlasting misery of the finally impenitent, in as strong terms, in the very same terms, as the eternal happiness of the righteous, and sometimes in the very same verse. Nor can it possibly be true, if our Lord spake the truth concerning Judas, when he said, 'It had been good for that man if he had never been born.' If I could consider this notion as harmless, though useless, and no worse than any mistakes which men of upright minds have made, through inattention and weakness of judgment, I should not have mentioned it. But I judge it to be little less pernicious and poisonous, than false. It directly tends to abate that sense of the evil of sin, of the inflexible justice of God, and the truth of his threatenings, which is but too weak in the best of men. Let us abide by the plain declarations of his word, which assures us, that 'there remaineth no other sacrifice for sin,' no future relief against it, for those who now refuse the gospel; and that they who cordially receive it shall be saved with an everlasting salvation, and shall one day sing, 'Death is swallowed up in victory.'

Messiah: Death Swallowed Up in Victory, [4:480]; 3:362

And one of the elders answered, saying unto me, What are these which are arrayed in white robes? and whence came they?—Rev. 7:13.

LET us ask the question which the elder proposed to John, 'Who are these clothed with white robes, and whence came they?' 'They came out of great tribulation;' they were once under the power of death, but now death, as to them, is swallowed up in victory.

They were once dead in law. They had revolted from their Maker. They had violated the holy order of his government, and stood exposed to his righteous displeasure, and to the heavy penalty annexed to the transgression of his commandments. But mercy interposed. 'God so loved them, that he gave his only begotten Son' to make an atonement for their sins, and to be their 'wisdom, righteousness, sanctification, and redemption.' They received grace to believe in this Saviour, and now they are delivered from condemnation. They are 'accepted in the Beloved.' They are considered as one with him, and interested in all that he did, and in all that he suffered. Now they are the children of God, and heirs of his kingdom. 'Though they were afar off, they are brought nigh' admitted into a nearer relation than the holy angels to him who sitteth upon the throne. For he took upon him, and still is pleased to wear, not the nature of angels, but the human nature. Their former guilt is cancelled, blotted out, and swallowed up. All their sins are covered, sunk in his precious blood as in a deep sea, so that, even if sought for, they can no more be found. That they have sinned, will always be a truth; and probably they will never lose a consciousness of what they were by nature and practice while in this world. But this so far from abating their joy, will heighten their gratitude and praise 'to him who loved them, and washed them from their sins in his own blood.'

Messiah: Death Swallowed Up in Victory, [4:482]; 3:363

But thanks be to God, which giveth us the victory through our Lord Jesus Christ.—1 Cor. 15:57.

ONE branch of the death due to sin is the tyranny and power of Satan. For a time he ruled in their hearts, as in his own strong hold; and while they were blinded by his influence, they were little affected with their bondage. Hard as his service was, they did not often complain of it. They were led by him according to his will, for the most part without resistance, or, if they attempted to resist, they found it was in vain. But in his own hour their Lord, who had bought them, dispossessed their strong enemy, and claimed their hearts for himself. Yet, after they were thus set free from his ruling power, this adversary was always plotting and fighting against them. How much have some of them suffered from his subtle wiles and his fiery darts! From his rage as a roaring lion, from his cunning as a serpent lying in their path, and from his attempts to deceive them under the semblance of an angel of light! But now they are placed out of his reach. Death and Satan are swallowed up. The victory is complete. The wicked one shall never have access to touch or disturb them any more. Now he is shut up in his own place, and the door sealed, no more to open. While he was permitted to vex and worry them, he acted under a limited commission, which he could not exceed; all was directed and overruled by the wisdom and love of their Lord for their advantage. Such exercises were necessary then, to discover to them more of the weakness and vileness of their own hearts, to make them more sensible of their dependence upon their Saviour, and to afford them affecting proofs of his power and care engaged in their behalf. But they are necessary no longer. Their warfare is finished. They are now where the wicked cease from troubling, and where the weary are at rest.

Messiah: Death Swallowed Up in Victory, [4:484]; 3:365

The Lord shall laugh at him: for he seeth that his day is coming.
—Psa. 37:13.

WHILE they were in the world, they had a share, many of them a very large share, of the woes and sufferings incident to this mortal state; which, as they are the fruits and effects of sin, and greatly contribute to shorten the life of man, and hasten his return to dust, are ... properly included in the comprehensive meaning of the original sentence, 'death.' They belong to its train, and are harbingers of its approach. None of the race of Adam are exempted from these; but especially the servants of God have no exemption. Their gracious Lord, who frees them from condemnation, and gives them peace in himself, assures them that in this world they shall have tribulation. This is so inseparable from their calling, that it is mentioned as one special mark of their adoption and sonship. If the prosperity of the wicked sometimes continues for a season without interruption, 'their day is coming;' but the righteous may expect chastisement and discipline daily. Thus their graces are refined, strengthened, and displayed, to the praise of their heavenly Father. There is no promise in the Bible that secures the most eminent and exemplary believer from participating in the heaviest calamities in common with others, and they have many trials peculiar to themselves. Thus, while upon earth, they endure hardship for his sake... But they were supported under these exercises, brought safely through them, and now their sorrows are swallowed up in victory. 'Now the days of their mourning are ended.' They now confess, that their longest afflictions were momentary, and their heaviest burdens were light, in comparison of that far more exceeding and eternal weight of glory which they have entered upon. Sorrow and sighing have taken their everlasting flight, and joy and gladness have come forth to meet them, and to dwell with them for ever.

Messiah: Death Swallowed Up in Victory, [4:486]; 3:366

This charge I commit unto thee, son Timothy, according to the prophecies which went before on thee, that thou by them mightest war a good warfare.—1 Tim. 1:18.

THE Christian soldier may, with the greatest propriety, be said 'to war a good warfare.' He is engaged in a good cause; he fights under the eye of the Captain of his salvation. Though he be weak in himself, and though his enemies are many and mighty, he may do that which in other soldiers would be presumption, and has often been the cause of a defeat; he may triumph while he is in the heat of battle, and assure himself of victory before the conflict is actually decided; for the Lord, his great Commander, fights for him, goes before him, and treads his enemies under his feet. Such a persuasion, when solidly grounded upon the promises and engagement of a faithful unchangeable God, is sufficient, it should seem, to make a coward bold. True Christians are not cowards; yet, when they compare themselves with their adversaries, they see much reason for fear and suspicion on their own parts; but when they look to their Saviour, they are enlightened, strengthened, and comforted. They consider who he is, what he has done; that the battle is not so much theirs as his; that he is their strength and their shield, and that his honour is concerned in the event of the war. Thus out of weakness they are made strong; and however pressed and opposed, they can say, 'Nay, in all these things we are more than conquerors through him that loved us!' The whole power of the opposition against them is summed up in the words 'sin,' and 'death;' but these enemies are already weakened and disarmed. It is sin that furnished death with his sting; a sting sharpened and strengthened by the law. But Jesus, by his obedience unto death, has made an end of sin, and has so fulfilled and satisfied the law on their behalf, that death is deprived of its sting, and can no longer hurt them. They may therefore meet it with confidence, and say, 'Blessed be God, who giveth us the victory through our Lord Jesus Christ.'

Messiah: Triumph Over Death and the Grave, [4:490]; 3:369

And lo a voice from heaven, saying, This is my beloved Son,
in whom I am well pleased.—Matt. 3:17.

WHEN he entered upon his office, a voice from heaven commended him to sinners, 'This is my beloved Son in whom I am well pleased.' And they who are enlightened to behold the glory of God in his person and engagement, accept him as the beloved Saviour, in whom and with whom they are well pleased. Without this acceptance of the Mediator there can be no agreement. Jesus is the only door, the only way of a sinner's access to the knowledge and favour of God. This is the precious and sure foundation which he has laid in Zion; and to presume to build our hope upon any other, is to build upon a quicksand. In this point, reason, in its present distempered state, would lead us, if followed, directly contrary to the simplicity of faith. Reason suggests, that if we have acted wrong we must repent and amend, and what can we do more? But the law against which we have sinned makes no provision for repentance. Nor is such a repentance as includes a change of heart (and nothing short of this deserves the name) in our power. 'Repentance unto life' is the gift of God; and Jesus, who is exalted 'to be a Prince and a Saviour,' bestows it upon those who acknowledge him, and implore it of him. But God will only treat with us as those who are condemned already, who have nothing but sin, and deserve nothing but misery. When we feel this to be our proper state, we are referred to Jesus, in whom God is well pleased, and for whose sake sins are pardoned, and sinners accepted and justified, without condition and without exception. And then likewise we begin to see the necessity, propriety, and sufficiency of this appointment. Herein all who are taught of God are of one mind. However they may differ in some respects, they agree in cordially 'receiving Christ Jesus the Lord,' as he is made of God for us, 'wisdom, righteousness, and salvation.'

Messiah: Divine Support and Protection, [4:506]; 3:380

What shall we then say to these things? If God be for us,
who can be against us?—Rom. 8:31.

NO opposition can prevail against us, if God be for us. It is impossible to deny, or even to doubt, this truth, upon the principles of reason; for who, or what, can injure those who are under the protection of Omnipotence? And yet it is not always easy to maintain the persuasion of it in the mind, and to abide in the exercise of faith, when, to an eye of sense, all things seem against us. But, though we believe not, he continueth faithful, and will not forsake those whom he once enables to put their trust in him. Job was a faithful and approved servant of God, yet for a season his trials were great, and his confidence was sometimes shaken. But he was supported, and at length delivered. There are many instances recorded in Scripture to confirm our faith, and to teach us that God manifests himself to be for his people, and in different ways renders them superior to all their difficulties and enemies.

At one time he prevents the threatened danger. They only see it, or expect it; for he is better to them than their apprehensions and fears. Thus when Sennacherib was furious against Jerusalem, and supposed he could easily prevail, he was not suffered to come near it. When he thought to destroy it, he felt a hook and a bridle which he could not resist, and was compelled to retire disappointed and ashamed.

At another time the enemies go a step farther. His people are brought into trouble, but God is with them, and they escape unhurt. So Daniel, though he was cast into a den of lions, received no more harm from them, than if he had been among a flock of sheep.

The most that opposers can do is to kill the body. If God permits his people to be thus treated, still they are not forsaken. Their death is precious in his sight. They who die in the Lord are blessed. They are highly honoured who are called and enabled to die for him. If he is pleased to comfort them with his presence, and then to take them home to himself, they can desire no more.

Messiah: Divine Support and Protection, [4:511]; 3:384

Who shall lay any thing to the charge of God's elect?
It is God that justifieth. —Rom. 8:33.

THE persons who will be finally justified by God are here styled his 'elect.' Very near and strong is the connexion between peace and truth. Yet a mistaken zeal for truth has produced many controversies, which have hurt the peace of the people of God among themselves; and at the same time have exposed them to the scorn and derision of the world. On the other hand, a pretended or improper regard for peace has often been prejudicial to the truth. But that peace which is procured at the expense of truth, is too dearly purchased. Every branch of doctrine, belonging to the faith once delivered to the saints, is not equally plain to every believer. Some of these doctrines the apostle compares to milk, the proper and necessary food for babes; others to strong meat, adapted to a more advanced state in the spiritual life, when experience is more enlarged, and the judgment more established. The Lord, the great teacher, leads his children on gradually, from the plainer to the more difficult truths, as they are able to bear them. But human teachers are often too hasty; they do not attend sufficiently to the weakness of young converts, but expect them to learn and receive everything at once; they are not even content with offering strong meat prematurely to babes, but force upon them the *bones* of subtleties, distinctions, and disputations. But, though a judicious minister will endeavour to accommodate himself to the state of his hearers, no gospel truth is to be tamely and voluntarily suppressed from a fear of displeasing men... They who professedly hold and avow the doctrine of an election of grace, are now called Calvinists; and the name is used by some persons as a term of reproach. They would insinuate that Calvin invented the doctrine; or, at least, that he borrowed it from Augustine, who, according to them, was the first of the fathers that held it. It is enough for me that I find it in the New Testament.

Messiah: Accusers Challenged, [4:516]; 3:388

And such were some of you: but ye are washed, but ye are sanctified,
but ye are justified in the name of the Lord Jesus,
and by the Spirit of our God.—1 Cor. 6:11

AS all mankind spring from one stock, there are not two different sorts of men by nature; consequently they who receive the gospel, are no better in themselves than they who reject it. The apostle, writing to the believers at Corinth, having enumerated a catalogue, in which he comprises some of the most flagitious and infamous characters, and allowed to be so by the common consent of mankind, adds, 'Such were some of you.' Surely it cannot be said, that they who had degraded themselves, below the brutes, by their abominable practices, were better disposed than others to receive that gospel which is not more distinguished by the sublimity of its doctrine, than by the purity and holiness of conversation which it enjoins!

It seems, therefore, at least highly probable, that all men universally, if left to themselves, would act as the majority do to whom the word of salvation is sent; that is, they would reject and despise it. And it is undeniable, that some, who in the day of God's power have cordially received the gospel, did for a season oppose it with no less pertinacity, than any of those who have continued to hate and resist it to the end of life. Saul of Tarsus was an eminent instance. He did not merely slight the doctrine of a crucified Saviour; but, according to his mistaken views, thought himself bound in conscience to suppress those who embraced it. He breathed out threatenings and slaughter, and, as he expresses it himself, 'was exceedingly mad against them,' and made havoc of them. His mind was filled with this bitter and insatiable rage, at the moment when the Lord Jesus appeared to him in his way to Damascus. Is it possible that a man thus disposed should suddenly become a preacher of the faith which he had long laboured to destroy, if his heart and views had not been changed by a supernatural agency? Or that the like prejudices in other persons can be removed in any other manner?

Messiah: Accusers Challenged, [4:519]; 3:390

Blessed be the God and Father of our Lord Jesus Christ.—Eph. 1:3.

HOW can I begin better than with the apostle's words; 'Blessed be the God and Father of our Lord Jesus Christ, the Father of mercies, and God of all consolation, who, according to his abundant mercy, hath begotten us again to a lively hope, by the resurrection of Jesus Christ from the dead?' What a fountain of life, and joy, and praise is here! that the God and Father of our Lord Jesus Christ should vouchsafe to be our Father, our God; that he who is the source of all mercy and consolation, should direct the streams of his fulness to flow into our souls; that, when we were dead in sins, he should look upon us and bid us live; that, when we were sunk into the depth of despair, he should send his word and raise us to a lively hope; that he should give us such a bright prospect, and such a sweet foretaste of the exceeding riches of his glory.—Oh! who can say which is the most wonderful part of this wonderful subject? that he should provide such a happiness for such hell-deserving wretches, and that he should commend his great and undeserved love to us in such a wonderful way, as to give his own and his only Son to be born, to be buffeted, to be crucified for us.—Alas! alas! for our stupidity, that we can write, or hear, or speak of these things, with so little feeling, affection, and fruitfulness. Oh! that the power of God would set my heart and pen at liberty while writing, and fill your hearts while reading, that we may rejoice with joy unspeakable and full of glory. Oh, this unbelief! Why can we not pierce through the veil of flesh and blood, and by faith behold the humble worship of heaven? What countless multitudes have gone before us in the path that leads to that kingdom! They were, in their time, followers of an unseen Saviour, as we are now; but now they see him as he is, face to face, in all his glory, and in all his love; with them are joined the innumerable hosts of angels. Angels and saints, however distinguished, are joined in one happiness, and one employment. Even now, while I write, and while you read, they are praising the Lamb that was slain, and casting their crowns at his feet. And perhaps this scene is not so far distant as we imagine.

Sequel to Cardiphonia: Letters to Several Ladies, [6:17]; 4:286

… him that justifieth the ungodly.—Rom. 4:5.

BELIEVERS plead guilty to the charge of the law; but they can likewise plead, that they renounce all hope and righteousness in themselves, and, upon the warrant of the word of promise, put their whole trust in Jesus, 'as the end of the law for righteousness to every one that believeth', Rom. 10:4: and this plea is accepted. 'To him that worketh not, but believeth on him who justifieth the ungodly, his faith is counted for righteousness,' Rom. 4:5, and his sins are no more remembered against him.

This justification, in its own nature, is authoritative, complete, and final. It is an act of God's mercy, which, because founded upon the mediation of Jesus, may, with no less truth, be styled an act of his justice, whereby the believing sinner is delivered from the curse of the law, from the guilt and power of sin, and is 'translated into the kingdom of his dear Son,' Col. 1:13. It includes the pardon of all sin, and admission to the state of a child of God.—It is a 'passing from death unto life,' John 5:24. By faith of the operation of God, the sinner, once afar off, is brought nigh, is accepted in the Beloved, and becomes one with him, as the branch is united to the vine, and the members with the head, John 15:5. The sanctification of a believer is imperfect and gradual; but his justification, in this sense, from the moment when he begins to live a life of faith in the Son of God, is perfect, and incapable of increase.

The right knowledge of this doctrine is a source of abiding joy; it likewise animates love, zeal, gratitude, and all the noblest powers of the soul, and produces a habit of cheerful and successful obedience to the whole will of God. But it may be, and too often is, misunderstood and abused. If you receive it by divine teaching, it will fill you 'with those fruits of righteousness, which are by Jesus Christ to the glory and praise of God,' Phil. 1:11.

Wherefore in all things it behoved him to be made like unto his brethren,
that he might be a merciful and faithful high priest in things pertaining
to God, to make reconciliation for the sins of the people.—Heb. 2:17.

IF we compare our best performances with the demands of the law, the majesty of God, and the unspeakable obligations we are under; if we consider our innumerable sins of omission, and that the little we can do, is polluted and defiled by the mixture of evil thoughts, and the working of selfish principles, aims, and motives, which, though we disapprove, we are unable to suppress; we have great reason to confess, 'To us belong shame and confusion of face.' But we are relieved by the thought, that Jesus, the High Priest, bears the iniquity of our holy things, perfumes our prayers with the incense of his mediation, and washes our tears in his own blood. This inspires a confidence, that though we are unworthy of the least of his mercies, we may humbly hope for a share in the greatest blessings he bestows, because we are heard and accepted, not on the account of our own prayers and services, but in the beloved Son of God, who maketh intercession for us. Thus the wisdom and love of God have provided a wonderful expedient, which, so far as it is rightly understood, and cordially embraced, while it lays the sinner low as the dust in point of humiliation and self-abasement, fills him at the same time with a hope full of glory, which, with respect to its object, can be satisfied with nothing less than all the fulness of God. There are favoured seasons in which the believer, having a lively impression of the authority and love of the Intercessor, can address the great Jehovah as his Father, with no less confidence than if he was holy and spotless as the angels before the throne, at the very moment that he has abundant cause to say, 'Behold, I am vile! I abhor myself, and repent in dust and ashes!'

Messiah: The Intercession of Christ, [4:531]; 3:399

*For every high priest taken from among men is ordained for men in things
pertaining to God, that he may offer both gifts and sacrifices for sins:
Who can have compassion on the ignorant, and on them that are out of the
way; for that he himself also is compassed with infirmity.*—Heb. 5:1, 2.

EXPERIENCE confirms what the Scripture declares of our insufficiency to order our own cause before the Lord, to specify our
various wants, and to fill our mouths with such arguments, as may
engage the attention, and enliven the affections of our hearts: 'We
know not how to pray as we ought.' And though the Holy Spirit
teaches believers to form petitions, which, in the main, are agreeable
to the will of God, yet we often mistake and ask amiss; we often
forget what we ought to ask, and we are too often cold, negligent,
weary, distracted, and formal in prayer. How prone are we to enter
by prayer into the Lord's presence, as the thoughtless 'horse rushes
into the battle!' to speak to God as if we were only speaking into the
air, and to have our thoughts dissipated and wandering to the ends of
the earth, while his holy name is upon our polluted lips! It is well for
us, that God is both able and gracious to do more than we can ask
or think; but that he actually does so, for such unworthy creatures,
is owing to our Intercessor. He knows all our wants, and pleads and
provides accordingly. He is not negligent, though we too frequently
are. He prayed for Peter's safety, before Peter himself was aware of
his danger. Have we not sometimes been, as it were, surprised and
shamed by the Lord's goodness, when he has condescended to bestow
special and needful mercies upon us, before we thought of asking for
them? These are affecting proofs of our Intercessor's attention and
care, and that he is always mindful of us.

Jesus the High Priest is upon a throne. He is a King, 'King of
saints, and King of nations.' he is not only a righteous Advocate, but
he possesses all authority and power. And it belongs to his office as
King, effectually to manage for those in whose behalf he intercedes.

Messiah: The Intercession of Christ, [4:532]; 3:400

For the LORD God is a sun and shield: the LORD will give grace and glory: no good thing will he withhold from them that walk uprightly.—Psa. 84:11.

ON [Jesus] the eyes of all who know him, wait from age to age, and are not disappointed. 'He opens his hand, and satisfies them with good.' Nor is the store of his bounty diminished by all that he has distributed, for it is unsearchable and inexhaustible; like the light of the sun, which gladdens the eyes of millions at once, has done so from the beginning, and will continue to do so to the end of time.

He appoints and adjusts their various dispensations, with an unerring suitableness to their several states, capacities, and circumstances. If a skilful gardener had the command of the weather, he would not treat all his plants, nor the same plant at all times, exactly alike. Continual rain, or continual sunshine, would be equally unfavourable to their growth and fruitfulness. In his kingdom of providence, he so proportions the rain and the sunshine to each other, that the corn is usually brought forward from the seed to the blade, the ear, and the full ripe ear. And I believe it would be always so, were it not for the prevalence of sin, which sometimes makes the 'heavens over our head brass, the earth under our feet iron,' and turns a fruitful land into barrenness. So, in his kingdom of grace, he trains his people up by various exercises. He delights in their prosperity, and does not willingly grieve them. But afflictions in their present state are necessary; and his blessing makes them salutary. But this is their great privilege, that their comforts and their crosses are equally from his hand, are equally tokens of his love, and alike directed to work together for their good. He appoints the bounds of their habitations, numbers the hairs of their heads, and is their Guide and Guard, their Sun and Shield, even unto death. Here they meet with many changes, but none that are unnoticed by him, none that can separate them from his love; and they all concur in leading them on to a state of unchangeable and endless joy.

Messiah: The Intercession of Christ, [4:533]; 3:401

O our God, wilt thou not judge them? for we have no might against this great company that cometh against us; neither know we what to do: but our eyes are upon thee.—2 Chron. 20:12.

ISRAEL of old were to muster their forces, to range themselves for the fight, to use every precaution and endeavour, as though success depended entirely upon themselves. Yet they obtained not the victory by their own sword, but it was the Lord who fought for them, and trod down their enemies before them; and they had little more to do than to pursue the vanquished, and to divide the spoil. And thus it is in the warfare which true Christians maintain, 'not against flesh and blood only, but against principalities and powers;' against the spirit of the world, and against Satan and his legions. They fight in his cause, but he upholds them and conquers for them. Their enemies are too many and too mighty for them to grapple with in their own strength; but he rebukes them, and pleads the cause of his people. His gracious interposition in their favour, is beautifully set forth, together with its effects, in the vision which the prophet saw, when he was sent to encourage the rulers and people of the Jews, against the difficulties they met with when rebuilding the temple. He 'saw Joshua the high priest,' who, in that character, represented the collective body of the people, 'standing before the Lord, clothed in filthy garments, and Satan standing at his right hand to resist him.' Such is our attire as sinners, all our righteousness are as filthy rags; and such are the attempts of our enemy, to deter us from approaching to him who alone can relieve us, or to distress us when we appear before him. But when Joshua could not speak for himself, the Lord spake for him, claimed him for his own, as a brand plucked out of the fire, silenced his adversary, clothed him with a change of raiment, and set a fair mitre upon his head.

Messiah: The Intercession of Christ, [4:535]; 3:402

...your life is hid with Christ in God.—Col. 3:3.

HOW precious is this Saviour! How justly is he entitled to the chief place in the hearts of those who know him! In the work of salvation, from the first step to the last, he is all in all. If he had not died and risen again, we must have died forever. If he had not ascended into heaven, there to appear in the presence of God for us, we must have been thrust down into the lowest hell. If he did not plead for us, we could not, we durst not, offer a word in our own behalf. If he was not on our part, engaged to keep us night and day, our enemies would soon be too hard for us. May we, therefore, give him the glory due to his name, and cleave to him, and trust in him alone.

How safe are the people of whom he undertakes the care! While his eye is upon them, his ear open to their prayer, and his arm of power stretched out for their protection; while he remembers that word of promise, upon which he himself has caused them to hope; while he retains that faithfulness which encouraged them to commit their souls to him, it is impossible that any weapon or stratagem formed against them can prevail. There are many, it is true, who will rise up against them, but God is for them, and with them, a very present help in trouble. They are full of wants and fears, and in themselves liable to many changes; but since Jesus is their Head, their Security, their Intercessor, no needful good shall be withheld from them, no charge admitted against them, none shall condemn them, for it is God himself who justifies the believer in Jesus.

If these things be so, how much are they to be pitied, who hear of them without being affected or influenced by them!... As yet, there is room. Strive to enter while the gate of mercy remains open.

Messiah: The Intercession of Christ, [4:536]; 3:403

...for thou wast slain, and hast redeemed us to God by thy blood out of every kindred, and tongue, and people, and nation.—Rev. 5:9.

THE extent, variety, and order of the creation, proclaim the glory of God. He is likewise *Maximus in minimis*. The smallest of his works that we are capable of examining, such, for instance, as the eye or the wing of a little insect, the creature of a day, are stamped with an inimitable impression of his wisdom and power. Thus in his written word, there is a greatness, considering it as a *whole*, and a beauty and accuracy in the smaller parts, analogous to what we observe in the visible creation, and answerable to what an enlightened and humble mind may expect in a book which bears the character of a divine revelation. A single verse, a single clause, when viewed (if I may so speak) in the microscope of close meditation, is often found to contain a fulness, a world of wonders. And though a connected and comprehensive acquaintance with the whole Scripture be desirable and useful, and is no less the privilege, than the duty, of those who have capacity and time at their own disposal to acquire it; yet there is a gracious accommodation to the weakness of some persons, and the circumstances of others. So that in many parts of Scripture, whatever is immediately necessary to confirm our faith, to animate or regulate our practice, is condensed into a small compass, and comprised into a few verses; yea, sometimes a single sentence, when unfolded and examined, will be found to contain all the great principles of duty and comfort.

The redemption spoken of, is suited to the various cases of sinners of every nation, people, and language. And many sinners of divers descriptions, and from distant situations, scattered abroad into all lands, through a long succession of ages, will, by the efficacy of this redemption, be gathered together into one.

Messiah: The Song of the Redeemed, [4:539]; 3:405

He brought them out of darkness and the shadow of death,
and brake their bands in sunder.—Psa. 107:14.

'THOU hast redeemed us to God.' Redemption or ransom is applicable to a state of imprisonment for debt, and to a state of bondage or slavery. From these ideas, taken together, we may form some estimate of the misery of our fallen state; a theme which, if I cannot insist upon at large in every discourse, I would never wholly omit. For we can neither understand the grace, nor enjoy the comfort of the gospel, but in proportion as we have a heart-felt and abiding conviction of our wretched condition as sinners without it. They who think themselves whole, know not their need of a physician; but to the sick he is welcome.

If a man, shut up in prison for a heavy debt, which he is utterly incapable of discharging, should obtain his liberty, in consideration of payment made for him by another, he might be properly said to be redeemed from imprisonment. This supposition will apply to our subject. The law and justice of God have demands upon us, which we cannot answer. We are therefore shut up, under the law, in unbelief, helpless and hopeless, till we know and can plead the engagement of a surety for us. For a time, like Peter, we are sleeping in our prison, regardless of danger. The first sensible effect of the grace of God is, to awaken us from this insensibility. Then we begin to feel the horrors of our dungeon, and the strength of our chains, and to tremble under the apprehension of an impending doom. But grace proceeds to reveal the Saviour and Friend of sinners, and to encourage our application to him. In a good hour the chains fall off, the bars of iron and brass are broken asunder, and the prison-doors fly open. The prisoner understands that all his great debt is forgiven, blesses his Deliverer, obtains his liberty, and departs in peace.

Messiah: The Song of the Redeemed, [4:541]; 3:407

Deliver him from going down to the pit: I have found a ransom.
—Job 33:24.

SATAN, though not by right, yet by a righteous permission, tyrannizes over us, till Jesus makes us free. The way of transgressors is hard. Though the solicitations and commands of that enemy who worketh in the children of disobedience, are, in some respects, suited to our depraved inclinations; yet the consequences are grievous. A burdened conscience, a wasted constitution, a ruined fortune and character, swiftly and closely follow the habits of intemperance and lewdness; and they who seem to walk in a smoother path, are deceived, mortified, and disappointed daily. If persons who live openly and habitually in a course that is contrary to the rule of God's word, 'speak swelling words of vanity,' and boast of their liberty, believe them not. We are sure they carry that in their bosom, which hourly contradicts their assertions. Yea, sometimes their slavery is so galling, that they attempt to escape, but in vain. They are soon retaken, and their bonds made stronger. The issue of their short-lived reformations, which they defer as long as possible, and at last set about with reluctance, usually is, that their latter end proves worse than their beginning. At most, they only exchange one sinful habit for another, sensuality for avarice, or prodigality for pride. The strong one armed will maintain his dominion, till the stronger than he interposes and says, 'Loose him and let him go, for I have found a ransom.' Then by the virtue of the redemption price, 'the prey is taken from the mighty, and the captive is delivered.' Then, the enslaved sinner, like the man out of whom the legion was cast, sits at the feet of Jesus, in peace, 'and in his right mind.' He becomes the Lord's freedman.

For, he is not only delivered from guilt and thrall, he 'is redeemed to God.' He is now restored to his original state, as an obedient and dependent creature, devoted to his Creator, conformed to his will and image, and admitted to communion with him in love. These are blessings which alone can satisfy the soul, and without which it is impossible for man to be happy.

Messiah: The Song of the Redeemed, [4:542]; 3:407

And ye know that he was manifested to take away our sins;
and in him is no sin.—1 John 3:5.

THE sentence denounced by the law against transgressors, was death. And therefore when MESSIAH became our Surety to satisfy the law for us, he must die. The expression of 'his blood,' is often used figuratively for his death, perhaps to remind us how he died. His was a bloody death. When he was in his agony in Gethsemane, his 'sweat was as great drops of blood, falling down to the ground.' His blood flowed when he gave his back to the smiters, under the painful strokes of the scourging he endured previous to his crucifixion. It flowed from his head, when the soldiers, having mocked his character of King, by crowning him with thorns, by their rude blows forced the thorns into his temples. His blood streamed from the wounds made by the spikes, which pierced his hands and his feet, when they fastened him to the cross. When he hung upon the cross, his body was full of wounds, and covered with blood. And, after his death, another large wound was made in his side, from which issued blood and water. Such was the redemption-price he paid for sinners, his blood, the blood of his heart. Without shedding of blood there could be no remission. Nor could any blood answer the great design but his. Not any; not all the bloody sacrifices appointed by the law of Moses could take away sin, as it respects the conscience, nor afford a plea with which a sinner could venture to come before the High God. But the blood of MESSIAH, in whom were united the perfections of the divine nature and the real properties of humanity, and which the apostle therefore styles 'the blood of God,' this precious blood cleanses from all sin. It is exhibited as a propitiation of perpetual efficacy, 'by which God declares his righteousness,' no less than his mercy, 'in forgiving iniquities,' and shows himself just to the demands of his holiness, and the honour of his government, when he accepts and justifies the sinner who believes in Jesus.

Messiah: The Song of the Redeemed, [4:544]; 3:409

*No man hath seen God at any time; the only begotten Son, which is in
the bosom of the Father, he hath declared him.*—John 1:18.

HE is 'the only wise God, and our Saviour.' His knowledge is perfect, his plan is perfect. In himself he is essentially the wisdom of God, and he is our wisdom. It is 'life eternal to know the only true God,' and therefore it is life eternal to 'know Jesus Christ whom he hath sent.' For he is the only way, and the only door, to this knowledge; no one can come unto God, or attain to any just conceptions of him, but in and by the Son of his love, who so perfectly represents God to us, is so completely the brightness of his glory, and the express image of his person, that whoso hath seen him, 'hath seen the Father.' By him is opened to us the unsearchable wisdom of the Divine counsels, particularly in the great work of redemption. 'No one hath seen God at any time; the only begotten Son, who is in the bosom of the Father, he hath revealed him.' It is by wisdom communicated from him, that his people are made wise unto salvation. Though there are few scholars and philosophers among them, and many of them are despised for their ignorance and weakness, yet, in truth, they have all a good understanding, for they know the Lord and his will; they know wherein their proper happiness consists, and how it is to be obtained. They are instructed, how to walk and to please God, how to bear afflictions with patience, and to meet death with composure. This wisdom is far superior to that of the schools. But he bestows and maintains it. The eyes of their mind are opened, and they see by his light; but they have no light of their own, or in themselves. They wait upon him for direction in every difficulty, for the solution of every hard question which perplexes their spirits; and he makes the crooked straight, teaches them to avoid the snares that are laid for them, or extricates them when entangled. Therefore in time, and to eternity, they will admire and adore his wisdom.

Messiah: The Chorus of Angels, [4:561]; 3:421

He is wise in heart, and mighty in strength: who hath hardened himself
against him, and hath prospered?—Job 9:4.

'STRENGTH:' that energy and efficacy of his power, by which he accomplishes his holy purposes. Who can conceive of this? How just is the psalmist's reasoning, 'He that formed the eye, shall not he see? he that planted the ear, shall not he hear?' So we may say, How strong is he from whom all created strength is derived, and before whom the strength of all creatures, if collected into one effort, would be as chaff before the whirlwind? The Lord of all power and might speaks, and it is done; he commandeth, and it standeth fast. Though the waves of the stormy sea toss themselves, they cannot prevail; he checks them in the height of their rage, setting bounds to their violence which they cannot pass, saying, 'Hitherto shalt thou come and no further, and here shall thy proud billows be stayed.' With equal sovereignty, certainty, and ease, he rules over moral agents. He formed the heart of man, and he can fill it with terror or with comfort in a moment, in any assignable circumstances. He can make it happy in a dungeon, or impress it with dismay and despair upon a throne. All hearts are thus incessantly under his influence. And the hedge of his promise and protection surrounds those who trust in him, as with mountains and walls of brass and fire, impenetrable to the assaults of the powers of darkness, unless so far as he, for wise and holy ends, is pleased to give permission. With the arm of his strength he 'upholdeth them that are falling, and raiseth up them that are bowed down;' and is, in one and the same instant, a present and immediate help in trouble to all who call upon him. Therefore they that abide under his shadow are safe; they pass unhurt through floods and flames, because their Redeemer is strong. And when, in defiance of all their enemies, he has brought them together in his heavenly kingdom, they will, with one consent, ascribe unto the Lord glory and strength.

Messiah: The Chorus of Angels, [4:563]; 3:422

Blessed is the nation whose God is the LORD; and the people whom he hath chosen for his own inheritance.—Psa. 33:12.

HE is the author of all blessings, of all the happiness and good which his people receive, and he is the deserved object of their universal praise. The different senses in which we use the word 'blessing,' taken together, may express that intercourse or communion which is between the Head and the mystical members of his body. He blesses them effectually with the light of his countenance, with liberty, grace, and peace. He blesses them daily. His mercies are renewed to them every morning. He will bless them eternally. 'Blessed are the people who have this Lord for their God.' They can make him no suitable returns, yet in their way they bless him. They admire, adore, and praise him. They call upon all the powers of their souls to bless him. They proclaim his goodness, and that he is worthy to receive the ascription of power, and riches, and wisdom, and strength, and honour, and glory, and blessing. In proportion to their attainments in this delightful exercise of worship, love, and gratitude, they enjoy a heaven upon earth; and to stand before him continually, to behold his glory, to live under the unclouded beams of his favour, and to be able to bless and praise him as they ought, without weariness, abatement, interruption, or end, is what they mean when they speak of the heaven they hope for hereafter. Such is the blessedness of those who have already died in the Lord. They see his face, they drink of the rivers of pleasure which are at his right hand, they cast down their crowns before him, and say, Thou art worthy,—'Let us not be slothful, but followers of them who, through faith and patience,' have finished their course, and are entered into the joy of their Lord.

Of this glory and honour the Scripture declares the Lamb that was slain to be worthy.

Messiah: The Chorus of Angels, [4:565]; 3:424

Because that, when they knew God, they glorified him not as God,
neither were thankful; but became vain in their imaginations,
and their foolish heart was darkened.—Rom. 1:21.

MEN have generally agreed to dignify their presumptuous and arrogant disquisitions on the works and ways of God with the name of wisdom; though the principles upon which they proceed, and the conclusions which they draw from them, are, for the most part, evident proofs of their depravity and folly. Instead of admiring the effects of his wisdom and power in the creation, they have rashly endeavoured to investigate the manner of its production. A variety of hypotheses have been invented to account for the formation of the world, and to state the laws by which the frame of nature is governed; and these different and inconsistent accounts have been defended with a magisterial tone of certainty, and an air of demonstration, by their respective authors, as though they had been by-standers and spectators, when God spoke all things into being, and produced order out of confusion by the word of his power. They have, however, been much more successful in showing the absurdity of the schemes proposed by others, than in reconciling their own to the sober dictates of plain common sense.

But if, by indulging their speculations on the creation of the world, the causes of the deluge, and similar subjects, their employment has been no better than 'weaving spiders' webs;' the result of their reasoning on morals has been much worse ... their labours have been not only fallacious, but mischievous. Their metaphysical researches, while they refuse the guidance of revelation, if pursued to their just consequences, will always lead into the labyrinths of scepticism, weaken the sense of moral obligation, rob the mind of the most powerful motives of right conduct, and of the only consolations which can afford it solid support in the hour of trouble... The more they reason, the more they involve themselves in uncertainty and error, till at last they make lies their refuge, and adopt, with implicit credulity, as so many undoubted axioms, opinions which are equally dishonourable to God, and contradictory to truth and experience.

Messiah: The Universal Chorus, [4:569]; 3:427

Shall I not visit for these things? saith the LORD;
shall not my soul be avenged on such a nation as this?—Jer. 5:29.

THREE times the Lord God repeats, by his prophet, this alarming question. Their ingratitude and obstinacy were so notorious, their sins so enormous and aggravated, the sentence denounced against them, however severe, was so undeniably just, that partial as they were to themselves, God is pleased to appeal to their own consciences, and to make them judges in their own cause; inviting, or rather challenging, them, to offer any plea why his forbearance and patience, which they had so long despised, should be still afforded them.

But the form of the question will not permit us to continue the application to Israel or Judah. The words are not *On this nation* particularly, but 'On such a nation as this.' The Lord, the Governor of the earth, has provided, in the history of one nation, a lesson of instruction and warning to every nation under the sun; and the nearer the state and spirit of any people resemble the state and character of Judah when Jeremiah prophesied among them, the more reason they have to tremble under the apprehension of the same or similar judgments.

God brought Israel out of Egypt with an outstretched arm, divided the Red Sea before them, led them in the wilderness by a cloud and pillar of fire, fed them with manna, and gave them water from the rock. He planted them in a good land; and though they often sinned, and were often punished, they were distinguished by many tokens of his presence, and effects of his goodness, above any other nation.

We likewise are a highly favoured people, and have long enjoyed privileges which excite the admiration and envy of surrounding nations: and we are a sinful, ungrateful people; so that, when we compare the blessings and mercies we have received from the Lord, with our conduct towards him, it is to be feared we are no less concerned with the question in my text than Israel of old.

The Guilt and Danger of Such a Nation as This, [5:139]; 3:549

Shall a trumpet be blown in the city, and the people not be afraid? shall
there be evil in a city, and the LORD hath not done it?—Amos 3:6.

THOUGH the occasion will require me to take some notice of
our public affairs, I mean not to amuse you with what is usually
called a political discourse. The Bible is my system of politics. There I
read, that the Lord reigns; that he doth what he pleaseth in the armies
of heaven, and among the inhabitants of the earth; that no wisdom,
understanding, counsel, or power, can prevail without his blessing;
that as righteousness exalteth a nation, so sin is the reproach, and will
even totally be the ruin of any people. From these, and other maxims
of a like import, I am learning to be still, and to know that he is
God. My part, as a minister of the gospel of peace, is not to inflame,
but, if possible, to soothe and sweeten the spirits of my hearers; to
withdraw their attention from the instrumental and apparent causes
of the calamities we feel or fear, and to fix it upon sin, as the original
and proper cause of every other evil. As a peaceful and a loyal subject,
I profess and inculcate obedience to the laws of my country, to which
I conceive myself bound by the authority of God's command, and
by gratitude for the civil and religious liberty I possess. For the rest,
political disquisitions, except immediately connected with scriptural
principles, appear to me improper for the pulpit at all times, and
more especially unseasonable and indecent on a day of public humiliation. I hope we are now met, not to accuse others, but to confess
our sins; not to justify ourselves, but to plead for mercy.

In order to estimate the state of the nation, we must attend to
two views, which, when contrasted, illustrate each other, and, in
their combination, constitute our national character, and discrimi-
nate it not only from that of every nation around us, but from all the
kingdoms recorded in the history of past ages. I mean our national
privileges, and our national sins.

The Guilt and Danger of Such a Nation as This, [5:140]; 3:550

Woe unto them that call evil good, and good evil;
that put darkness for light, and light for darkness.—Isa. 5:20.

A WOE is denounced against those who call evil good, and good evil; but this dreadful abuse of language, sentiment, and conduct can only be avoided by making the inspired writings the standard of judgment. In a land that bears the name of Christian, adultery is deemed gallantry; murder, in some cases, is a point of honour; avarice is prudence; profuseness wears the mask of generosity, and dissipation is considered an innocent amusement. On the other hand, meekness is accounted meanness of spirit, and grace is branded with the opprobrious names of melancholy and enthusiasm. Habituated from our infancy to the effects of these prepossessions, and more or less under their influence, very few of us are duly sensible how utterly repugnant the spirit and temper of the world around us is to the genius and spirit of the Christianity we profess. It would, I think, appear in a much more striking light to an intelligent and unbiassed observer, who, upon hearing that Great Britain was favoured with the knowledge of true religion, should visit us from some very remote country, with a view of sharing in our advantage. If I could make the tour of the kingdom with such a stranger, and show him what is transacting in the busy and in the carefree world, in city, court, and country; if I could describe to him the persons he would see at our theatres and public places, at Newmarket, at contested elections; and explain the motives and aims which bring them together; if I could introduce him into the families of the great, the reputed wise, and the wealthy; from these data, together with the ignorance and licentiousness of the populace, which must unavoidably engage his notice wherever he went, I apprehend he would not be long at a loss to form a tolerable judgment of our national character. And if, after this survey, he were attentively to read the New Testament, I think he must allow, that, admitting it was a revelation from God, our national character was neither more nor less than the union and combination of our national sins.

The Guilt and Danger of Such a Nation as This, [5:146]; 3:554

And even as they did not like to retain God in their knowledge,
God gave them over to a reprobate mind, to do those things
which are not convenient.—Rom. 1:28.

WHEN God is exceedingly displeased with a people, it is not necessary, in order to their punishment, that he should bury them alive by an earthquake, or destroy them by lightning. If he only leave them to themselves, withdraw his blessing from their counsels, and his restraint from their passions, their ruin follows of course, according to the necessary order and connexion of causes and effects. The destruction of Jerusalem affords a striking proof and illustration of this remark. Our Saviour foretold that the calamities of that siege would be greater and more aggravated than had ever been known from the creation; and infidels must confess that the relation of Josephus, who was an eye-witness of that catastrophe, exhibits such scenes of distress as cannot be paralleled in any other history. Yet the Roman armies, which were led on by an invisible hand to accomplish the prediction, were not headed by a Nero, or a Caligula, whose savage disposition and thirst of blood might have prompted them to unrelenting slaughter; but by Titus, who, for his singular moderation and clemency, obtained the title of *Delicae humani generis*, the friend and delight of mankind. He desired not their destruction, he entreated them to have pity on themselves, but in vain; they were judicially infatuated, and devoted to ruin. If God gives up a people to the way of their own hearts, they will, they must, perish. When a general corruption of morals takes place, when private interest extinguishes all sense of public virtue, when a profligate and venal spirit has infected every rank and order of the state, when presumptuous security and dissipation increase in proportion as danger approaches, when, after repeated disappointments, contempt of God, and vain confidence in imagined resources of their own, grow bolder and stronger, then there is reason to fear that the sentence is already gone forth, and that the execution of it is at hand.

The Guilt and Danger of Such a Nation as This, [5:155]; 3:561

For he hath looked down from the height of his sanctuary; from heaven did the LORD behold the earth; To hear the groaning of the prisoner; to loose those that are appointed to death.—Psa. 102:19, 20.

IF the Lord be graciously pleased to succeed the professed design of this day's service, and to put forth that power which accompanied his message by Jonah to Nineveh, so that a general spirit of repentance and humiliation may spread throughout the land—if he bow the hearts of both rulers and people, to confess and forsake those sins which have awakened his displeasure—if the laws which concern his honour, will, and worship, be speedily and impartially enforced; and profaneness and immorality discountenanced and suppressed—if, instead of trusting in fleets and armies, we acknowledge the Lord of hosts, and look up to him for a blessing—if men, 'fearing God and hating covetousness,' are raised up to assist in our councils, and to stand forth in their country's cause; men, who will rely on his guidance and protection, and disdain the little arts and intrigues on which alone short-sighted politicians depend for the success of their measures. Should I live to see such a happy internal change, I should hope, that notwithstanding our great provocations, the Lord, whose mercies are infinite, would be yet entreated for us; that he would turn from the fierceness of his anger, maintain our tranquility at home, and, by his wisdom, and his influence over the hearts of men, put an honourable and satisfactory end to the unhappy war in which we are engaged.

However the bulk of the nation may determine, if the remnant who know his name, and have tasted of his love, should be deeply impressed with a concern for his glory and, forsaking their little animosities and party interests, should unite in application to the throne of grace, and be found in those duties and practices which their profession of the gospel, and the state of things around them require, there is yet hope. For the prayers of God's people have a powerful efficacy.

The Guilt and Danger of Such a Nation as This, [5:158]; 3:563

Except the LORD build the house, they labour in vain that build it: except the LORD keep the city, the watchman waketh but in vain.—Psa. 127:1.

WHEN Sennacherib invaded Judea, had overrun the greatest part of the country, and thought Jerusalem would be an easy conquest, Hezekiah, though he took such precautions as prudence suggested, did not defeat him by arms, but by prayer. In the prayers of true believers is our best visible resource. These are the chariots and horsemen of Israel. United prayer, humiliation of heart, a mourning for sin in secret, and a faithful testimony against it in public, will more essentially contribute to the safety and welfare of the nation, than all our military preparations without them. We boast of our navy and it has often proved, by the blessing of God, our bulwark; but how easily can he who walketh upon the wings of the wind, dash the best appointed fleet to pieces against the rocks, or sink it like lead in the mighty waters! We boast of our troops; but he can easily cut them off with sickness, give them up to a spirit of discord, or impress them with a sudden terror, so that the stoutest hearts shall tremble, and the mighty warriors turn pale and drop their weapons! A thousand unforeseen events and contingencies are always at his disposal, to blast and disappoint the best concerted enterprises; for that the race is not necessarily sure to the swift, nor the battle to the strong, is not only asserted in Scripture, but confirmed by the experience and observation of all ages. But his people are precious in his sight, and their prayers he will hear. Unknown and unnoticed as they are in the world, he highly values them. He has redeemed them by his blood; he inhabits them by his Spirit; he has prepared heaven for them; and the earth itself is continued for their sakes, and shall be destroyed when they are removed from it. They are the light, the salt, the strength, and the safety of the nations among whom they are dispersed. Except the Lord of hosts had left a small remnant of these among us, we should long ago have been as Sodom, and made like unto Gomorrah, Isa. 1:9.

The Guilt and Danger of Such a Nation as This, [5:159]; 3:563

Let not your heart be troubled: ye believe in God, believe also in me.
—John 14:1.

WE are commissioned to say to the righteous, 'It shall be well with him,' Isa. 3:10. The Saviour to whom you have fled for refuge, has all power in heaven and earth. He will keep you as the apple of his eye, and hide you under the shadow of his wings. He can screen you from evil, though thousands and ten thousands should suffer and fall around you. Or, if he appoints you a share in suffering, he will be with you to support and comfort you, and to sanctify all your troubles. His word to you is, 'When you hear of wars and rumours of wars, see that ye be not troubled,' Matt. 24:6. Fear not them who, at the most, can but kill the body. The light of his countenance is sufficient to cheer you in the darkest hour, and your best interest, your everlasting inheritance, is safe beyond the reach of enemies, in a kingdom (how unlike the kingdoms of the earth!) which cannot be shaken. Your life is hid with Christ in God; and, 'when Christ, who is your life, shall appear, then shall ye also appear with him in glory,' Col. 3:3, 4. Thither neither sin nor sorrow shall be able to follow you. Then your sun shall go down no more, and the days of your mourning shall be ended. In patience, therefore, possess your souls. Be not moved by appearances, but remember all your concerns are in the hands of him who loved you, and gave himself for you. Let those who know him not, tremble when he ariseth to judgment and to shake terribly the earth; but do you sanctify the Lord God in your hearts, make him your fear and your dread, and he shall be to you for a sanctuary; and in a little time he will come to receive you to himself, and to wipe all tears from your eyes.

The Guilt and Danger of Such a Nation as This, [5:162]; 3:565

Howbeit for this cause I obtained mercy, that in me first Jesus Christ might shew forth all longsuffering, for a pattern to them which should hereafter believe on him to life everlasting.—1 Tim. 1:16.

ONLY he who redeemed the soul by his blood, is able effectually to win it to himself. The work is his, and they who know him will render the praise to him alone. But in this respect, as in many others, there is an analogy between the natural and the moral world. In both, he displays his power, and executes his purposes, by an instituted course of means and instruments. In both, he often so conceals his operations under the veil of second causes, that, to a common and inattentive eye, he seems to do nothing, when in reality, he does all. The manna with which he fed Israel in the wilderness, though more immediately and visibly, was not more certainly, the effect and proof of his providence and goodness, than the bread by which we live. It is he who giveth the earth virtue to produce corn; the discretion of the husbandman who prepareth the ground and soweth the seed is from him; and the influence of the sun and the rain, so necessary to ripen the grain, and to clothe the fields with plenty in the season of harvest, is the influence of him who worketh all in all. In this process, the blessing which secures the desired event is wholly from the Lord, though the labour of man and the use of means are indispensable, because his appointment has made them so.

The Lord God usually employs those whom he has already won and subdued by his grace, as instruments of winning others; and there are none of his people, however weak their capacities, or however low their situations in life, but may hope for a share in this honour, if they are faithful to the light he has given them, and live according to the rule of his word.

The Best Wisdom, [5:193]; 3:589

...the glorious gospel of the blessed God.—1 Tim. 1:11.

THE experience of ages has demonstrated all endeavours to win souls, to free them from prejudice, to reclaim them from the love and practice of sin, by the mere force of human arguments and moral suasion, to be equally chimerical and unsuccessful... Virtue is defined, described, recommended, and praised, but wickedness and folly rapidly increase... The gospel of Christ, the glorious gospel of the blessed God, is the only effectual mean for reforming mankind. To the man who possesses and knows the use of this grand, this wonderful machine, if I may be allowed the comparison, what is otherwise impracticable becomes easy. The gospel removes difficulties insuperable to human power. It causes the blind to see, the deaf to hear; it softens the heart of stone, and raises the dead in trespasses and sins to a life of righteousness. No force but that of the gospel is sufficient to remove the mountainous load of guilt from an awakened conscience, to calm the violence of tumultuous passions, to raise an earthly soul, from grovelling in the mire of sensuality or avarice, to a spiritual and divine life, a life of communion with God. No system but the gospel can communicate motives, encouragements, and prospects, sufficient to withstand and counteract all the snares and temptations with which the spirit of this world, by its frowns or its smiles, will endeavour either to intimidate or to bribe us from the path of duty. But the gospel, rightly understood and cordially embraced, will inspire the slothful with energy and the fearful with courage. It will make the miser generous, melt the churl into kindness, tame the raging tiger in the breast, and, in a word, expand the narrow selfish heart, and fill it with a spirit of love to God, cheerful and unreserved obedience to his will, and benevolence to mankind.

The Best Wisdom, [5:197]; 3:592

God was manifest in the flesh—1 Tim. 3:16.

THAT [Jesus the Saviour] is very God, and very man, 'God manifest in the flesh:' that 'in the beginning was the Word, the Word was with God, and the Word was God:' that this divine Word assumed our nature into a personal union with himself, lived and died in behalf of sinners, and now reigns upon the throne of glory, over all, God blessed for ever: that he is the proper object of our worship, supreme love, trust, and adoration: that it is he on whom the eyes and expectation of sinners, sensible of their wants and miseries, are fixed; and out of whose fulness they all receive life, strength, comfort, and grace, to help in time of need. This doctrine is the pillar and ground of truth. They who have a right sense of the guilt and power of sin, of the holiness and majesty of God, and of the hosts of enemies combined against their peace, must sin into despair, unless supported by the knowledge of an Almighty Omnipresent Saviour; who is always near, a very present help in trouble, and who can discern the thoughts of the heart; for often their most trying and dangerous exigencies are beyond the reach of a creature's eye. Whatever they thought of him before, when they know themselves, they cannot entrust their souls to the power, or care, or compassion of a creature; and, therefore, rejoice that they are warranted and encouraged to commend themselves to him, as to a faithful Creator.

That Christ, in his state of humiliation, by his 'obedience unto death, even the death of the cross,' made a full, proper, and perfect satisfaction for sin; that is, his sufferings unto death, the torments which he endured in his body, and the agonies of his soul, inconceivable to us but by their effects, (his bloody sweat in the garden, and his astonishing complaint upon the cross, that God had forsaken him,) exhibited a striking and solemn proof to the world, to the universe no less to angels than to men, that God, in affording mercy to sinners, still shows his inflexible displeasure against sin, and makes no relaxation in the awful demands of his holiness, justice, and truth.

The Best Wisdom, [5:199]; 3:593

Hold fast the form of sound words, which thou hast heard of me, in faith and love which is in Christ Jesus.—2 Tim. 1:13.

WHEREVER and whenever the doctrines of free grace and justification by faith have prevailed in the Christian church, and according to the degree of clearness with which they have been enforced, the practical duties of Christianity have flourished in the same proportion. Wherever they have declined, or been tempered with the reasonings and expedients of men, either from a well meant though mistaken fear lest they should be abused, or from a desire to accommodate the gospel, and render it more palatable to the depraved taste of the world, the consequence has always been an equal declension in practice. So long as the gospel of Christ is maintained without adulteration, it is found sufficient for every valuable purpose; but when the wisdom of man is permitted to add to the perfect work of God, a wide door is opened for innumerable mischiefs—the Divine commands are made void, new inventions are continually taking place, zeal is diverted into a wrong channel, and the greatest stress laid upon things, either unnecessary or unwarrantable. Hence, perpetual occasion is given for strife, debates, and divisions, till at length the spirit of Christianity is forgot, and the power of godliness lost, amidst fierce contentions for the form.

The gospel is a wise and gracious dispensation, equally suited to the necessities of man and to the perfections of God. It proclaims relief to the miserable, and excludes none but those who exclude themselves. It convinces a sinner that he is unworthy of the smallest mercy, at the same time that it gives him a confidence to expect the greatest. It cuts off all pretence of glorying in the flesh, but it enables a guilty sinner to glory in God. To them that have no might, it increases strength; it gives eyes to the blind, and feet to the lame; subdues the enmity of the heart, shows the nature of sin, the spirituality and sanction of the law with the fullest evidence; and, by exhibiting Jesus as made of God, wisdom, righteousness, sanctification, and redemption to all who believe, it makes obedience practicable, easy, and delightful.

A Review of Ecclesiastical History, [3:33]; 2:395

...the gospel of God.—Rom. 1:1.

THE gospel, then, is a message from God. It stains the pride of human glory, and, without regarding the petty distinctions which obtain among men, with respect to character or ranks, it treats them all as sinners in the sight of God, and under the power of depravity strengthened by habit. As such, it points them to a Saviour; it invites and enjoins them to apply to him, to submit to him, and to put their whole trust in him; to renounce all pleas of their own, and to plead his name and his atonement for their pardon and acceptance; and promises to all who thus plead, that the Holy Spirit of God will visit them, dwell in them, and abide with them, to enable them, by his gracious influence, both to will and to do according to his pleasure.

Let us appeal to facts. The apostle Paul was eminently successful in winning souls. He planted churches in many different and distant parts of the Roman empire; wherever he went, power from on high accompanied his word, and made it effectual, according to the commission he had received from the Lord... Would we know the subject matter of that preaching which produced such extensive and salutary effects? He gives us full information. He preached Christ crucified; Christ the wisdom and power of God; the unsearchable riches of Christ; Christ the Man who shall judge the quick and dead; Christ as God, who purchased the church with his own blood. As a wise master-builder, he laid this foundation, and declared that 'other foundation can no man lay.' He preached the atonement, that Christ made peace by the blood of his cross, died for us while sinners, and that we are justified by his blood. He preached the agency of the Holy Spirit, as absolutely necessary and powerfully efficacious, and ascribes that operation, by which Christ in his true character is revealed to the heart, to the same power which commanded light to shine out of darkness, in the beginning. These truths were the weapons of his warfare.

The Best Wisdom, [5:201]; 3:595

> *Whether therefore ye eat, or drink, or whatsoever ye do,*
> *do all to the glory of God.*—1 Cor. 10:31.

BUT if we speak strictly, the most important employments and discoveries of which mankind are capable, if directed no higher than to the concerns of the present life, are trivial and worthless as the sports of children... The desire of pleasing God and of doing all to his glory, which should be the ultimate end of a rational creature, and will be, if he feels his dependence and his obligations; this, like the fabled philosopher's stone, turns everything into gold, sanctifies the most common actions of life which belong to the situation in which Divine Providence has placed us, and gives them a sublimity and dignity. Consecrated by this intention, they become acts of devotion. They have a very low idea of religion who confine it to what we usually mean by devotional exercises. The truly religious man does, indeed, bow his knees in secret before the Most High God; he carefully consults his holy word; he waits upon him in his public ordinances. In these ways he derives fresh supplies from the fountain of wisdom and grace, and his strength is renewed. But he does not leave his religion in the closet or the church; it abideth in him, is the governing spring of his whole conduct, and according to the degree of his attainment in faith and love, and allowing for the unavoidable abstractions incidental to our frames, (which are too weak and limited to be able to fix our attention closely upon many things at once,) whether he be upon the throne or the bench, upon the parade or the exchange, whether he be called to serve God in a public capacity or in a private life, whether he be in a state of affluence, or earns his honest bread by sweeping the streets—in every station and situation he is a servant of God from morning to night; and these very different services are all equally acceptable to him, who seeth not as man seeth, and estimates them, not by their comparative importance in our view, but according to the principle of love by which they are performed, and the sublime end to which they are directed.

The Best Wisdom, [5:207]; 3:599

Having a form of godliness, but denying the power thereof.—2 Tim. 3:5.

A GREAT stress has, indeed, been often laid upon uniformity of sentiment and modes of worship; but this, in the present state of human nature, can no more be effected either by force or persuasion, than men can be forced or persuaded to a uniformity of stature or complexion; and, if it were practicable, it might prove of little value. The form of religion may be strenuously contended for by those who are strangers to the power of it; but the best form we can conceive, if destitute of power, is lifeless, like the body without the soul. The true unity of spirit is derived from the things in which those who are taught and born of God agree, and should not be affected by those in which they differ. The church of Christ, collectively considered, is an army; they serve under one Prince, have one common interest, and are opposed by the same enemies. This army is kept up, and the places of those who are daily removed to the church triumphant, supplied entirely by those who are rescued and won from the power of the enemy, which is chiefly affected by the gospel ministry. This consideration should remind ministers, that it is highly improper (I might use a stronger expression) to waste much of their time and talents, which ought to be employed against the common foe, in opposing those who, though they cannot exactly agree with them in every smaller point, are perfectly agreed, and ready to concur with them, in promoting their principal design... When I see ministers of acknowledged piety and respectable abilities very busy in defending or confuting the smaller differences which already too much separate those who ought to be of one heart and one mind, though while they are all fallible, they cannot be exactly of one judgment; though I give them credit for their good intention, I cannot but lament the misapplication of their zeal which, if directed into another channel, would, probably, make them much more successful in winning souls. Let us sound an alarm in the enemy's camp, but not in our own!

The Best Wisdom, [5:214]; 3:604

For the Lord himself shall descend from heaven with a shout, with
the voice of the archangel, and with the trump of God: and the dead
in Christ shall rise first: then we which are alive and remain, shall be
caught up together with them in the clouds, to meet the Lord in the air:
and so shall we ever be with the Lord. Wherefore comfort one another
with these words.—1 Thess. 4:16–18.

THE immediate design of the apostle in these words, is to comfort believers under a trial, which some of you perhaps feel at this hour, and to which any of us may be called sooner than we are aware, the removal of our Christian friends or relatives, with whom we have often taken sweet counsel, to a better world. Such a stroke, whenever it takes place, will awaken painful sensations, which he who knows our frame does not condemn. The tendency of the gospel is to moderate and regulate, but not to stifle or eradicate, the feelings of humanity. We may sorrow, but provision is made that we should not sorrow like those who have no hope: 'Blessed are the dead who die in the Lord.' It is but a temporary separation; we shall see them again to unspeakable advantage; 'for, if we believe that Jesus died and rose again, even so them that sleep in Jesus shall God bring with him.' The change of expression here is observable; 'Jesus died.' Death, to him, was death indeed; death in all its horrors; but he died for his people, to disarm death of its sting, to throw a light upon the dark passage to the grave and to open the kingdom of heaven to all believers. For now they 'that believe in him shall never die.' He so dispels their fears, and enlivens their hopes, that to them death is no more than a sleep; they sleep in Jesus, and are blessed. And when he, 'who is their life shall appear,' as he certainly will, and every eye shall see him, 'they also shall appear with him in glory.'

The Great Advent, [5:228]; 3:615

I am the good shepherd:
the good shepherd giveth his life for the sheep.—John 10:11.

FOR similar reasons, but vastly superior in importance, even as the heavens are higher than the earth, we rejoice in the assurance and prospect, that the Lord himself will descend. He is 'the good Shepherd, who laid down his life for the sheep;' and, therefore, they who know his name, and trust in him for salvation, are bound to him by the strongest ties of attachment and gratitude. They admire his condescension and his love. To his mediation and care they are indebted for their life and hopes. They remember what they were doing and how carelessly they were sporting in the path that leadeth to destruction, when he first stopped them, turned them, and led them into his fold. He is, even now, their sun and shield, their wisdom and strength; on him they cast their cares, from him they receive their supplies; therefore they love him, though unseen, and rejoice in the hope of his appearance.

They know that he who will descend to receive them was once a man of sorrows and companion of grief. And, though this too little affected them in the time of their ignorance, it has been otherwise since they have derived life from his death, and healing from his wounds. They have sympathized with him in the agonies which he endured, in Gethsemane, and upon Mount Golgotha. They remember that his face was defiled with spitting, his head crowned with thorns, his back torn by scourges, his hands and feet pierced with spikes; that he made his soul an offering for their sins, and was crucified for their sakes. Thus 'he loved them, and gave himself for them.' Thus he delivered them from approaching wrath; and this love has won their hearts. And they are waiting his return from heaven; that, when they shall see him as he is, with all his angels, and with all his saints, they may join in nobler strains than they can at present reach, in songs of praise to him who redeemed them to God by his own blood.

The Great Advent, [5:233]; 3:620

Whom having not seen, ye love.—1 Pet. 1:8.

WHEN Peter saw his Saviour transfigured upon the mount, a glance of his glory instantly fixed and filled his mind. He forgot all inferior attachments, and said, 'It is good to be here.' He would have been glad to build tabernacles upon the mount, and to return to the world no more. He knew not, indeed, what he said; there was much for him yet to do and to suffer for his Master; but he well knew why he said it: and all who are partakers of the grace of God are like-minded with Peter. And though, at present, they walk by faith, and not by sight, they are sometimes favoured with seasons of refreshment, with golden hours, when, according to his gracious promise, he manifests himself unto them, as he does not unto the world, and causes his goodness to pass before them: then, for the time, they are raised above both the cares and the comforts of this world, and could be glad to remain with him. But, like Peter, they must return to fill up the duties of their situation in life, till his appointed hour of dismission. However, these foretastes convince them, that they cannot be properly happy till they are with him in his kingdom, where nothing will conceal him for a moment from their view.

Their nearest approaches to him now are likewise subject to abatements. Something from within or from without still occurs to interrupt, and too often to suspend their joys. Their communion with him is indistinct, through the medium of ordinances, and a veil of flesh and blood. This veil hinders them, not only as it is polluted, but as it is weak, and subject to many infirmities. We cannot see him, as yet, and live. If he did not accommodate the discoveries of himself to the frailty of our nature, we should be overpowered. The beloved disciple had often conversed familiarly with his Lord, and reclined on his bosom during his state of humiliation; but, when he appeared in the isle of Patmos, though his majesty was attempered with mildness and love, and his design was to honour and comfort him, he says, 'When I saw him, I fell at his feet as dead.'

The Great Advent, [5:241]; 3:625

The king's heart is in the hand of the LORD, as the rivers of water:
he turneth it whithersoever he will.—Prov. 21:1.

HOW great is the power of God over the hearts of men! Nineveh was the capital of a powerful empire. The inhabitants were heathens. The many prophets who, during a long series of years, had spoken in the name of the Lord to his professed people of Judah and Israel, had spoken almost in vain. The messengers were often mocked, and their message despised. The inhabitants of Nineveh, it is probable, had never seen a true prophet till Jonah was sent to them. If they had reasoned on his prediction, they might have thought it very improbable, that a great city, the head of a great kingdom, and in a time of peace, could be in danger of an overthrow within forty days. But it is said, 'they believed God.' The awful denunciation made a general, a universal impression. The king arose from his throne, laid aside his robes, covered himself with sackcloth, and sat in ashes. A sudden cessation of business and of pleasure took place; he proclaimed a strict fast, the rigour of which was extended even to the cattle. His subjects readily complied, and unanimously concurred in crying for mercy: though they had no encouragement but a peradventure, 'Who can tell if God will turn and repent, and turn from the fierceness of his anger, that we perish not?'

It appears from this, and other passages of Scripture, that the most express declarations of God's displeasure against sinners, still afford ground and room for repentance... The Lord God speaks to us by his word, in plain and popular language. He condescends to our feeble apprehensions. God cannot repent, he is of one mind, who can turn him? Yet, when afflictive providences lead men to a sense of their sins, to an acknowledgement of their demerits, and excite a spirit of humiliation, repentance, and prayer, he often mercifully changes his dispensations, and averts from them the impending evil. Such was the effect of Jonah's message to the Ninevites. The people humbled themselves, and repented of their wickedness; and God suspended the execution of the sentence which he had pronounced against them.

The Danger and Resource of this Nation, [5:251]; 3:633

The men of Nineveh shall rise in judgment with this generation, and
shall condemn it: because they repented at the preaching of Jonas;
and, behold, a greater than Jonas is here.—Matt. 12:41.

MY brethren, may we not fear, that the men of Nineveh will rise up in judgment against us, and condemn us, if we do not imitate their example, and humble ourselves before God? They repented at the preaching of Jonah, and immediately, on their first hearing him; and they sought for mercy upon a peradventure, when they could say no more, than, Who can tell, whether there may be the least room to hope for it, after what the prophet has so solemnly declared?

God does not speak to us by the audible voice of an inspired prophet; nor is it necessary. We know, or may know, from his written word, that it shall be well with the righteous, and ill with the wicked. The appearance of an angel from heaven could add nothing to the certainty of the declarations he has already put into our hands. He has likewise raised up, and perpetuated a succession of his ministers, to enforce the warnings he has given us in the Scripture; to remind us of our sins, and the sure and dreadful consequences, if we persist in them. Nor are we left at an uncertainty as to the event, if we humbly confess them, and implore forgiveness, in the way which he has prescribed. The gospel, the glorious gospel of the blessed God, is preached unto us. Jesus Christ, as crucified, is set forth among us. His blood cleanseth from all sin; and they who believe in him are freed from condemnation, and completely justified. They have also free access to a throne of grace, and, like Israel, they have power, by prayer, to prevail with God and with man. And shall it be said of any of us, that the Lord gave us space to repent, and invited us to repentance, and we repented not? May his mercy forbid it!

*And Jonathan said to the young man that bare his armour, Come, and
let us go over unto the garrison of these uncircumcised: it may be that the
Lord will work for us: for there is no restraint to the Lord
to save by many or by few.*—1 Sam. 14:6.

THE great God has a controversy with the potsherds of the earth.
The point to be decided between him and many abroad, and, I
fear, too many at home, is, whether he be the Governor of the earth
or not? His own people, to whom his name and glory are dear, will
hold all inferior concernments in subordination to this. If there be
no other alternative, misery and havoc must spread, men must perish
by millions, yea, the frame of nature must be dissolved, rather than
God be dishonoured and defied with impunity. But he will surely
plead and gain his own cause, and either in a way of judgment or of
mercy, all men shall know that he is the Lord. I believe there is no
expression in the Old Testament so frequently repeated as this, 'Ye,'
or they, 'shall know that I am the Lord! Hath he said it, and shall he
not make it good?'

The rivers of human blood, and all the calamities and horrors
which overspread a great part of the Continent, the distant report
of which is sufficient to make our ears tingle, are all to be ascribed
to this cause. God is not acknowledged; yea, in some places, he has
been formally disowned and renounced. Therefore men are left to
themselves, their furious passions are unchained, and they are given
up, without restraint, to the way of their own hearts. A more dreadful
judgment than this cannot be inflicted on this side of hell.

And, though we are still favoured with peace at home, the dreadful storm is at no great distance; it seems moving our way, and we
have reason to fear it may burst upon us. But I would be thankful
for the appointment of this day; for I should think the prospect dark
indeed, if I did not rely on the Lord's gracious attention to the united
prayers of those who fear and trust him, and who know it is equally
easy to him either to save or to destroy, by many or by few.

The Danger and Resource of this Nation, [5:254]; 3:635

If thou, LORD, shouldest mark iniquities, O Lord, who shall stand? But
there is forgiveness with thee, that thou mayest be feared.—Psa. 130:3, 4.

L ET us first look at home. I am a man of unclean lips. I am a
sinner. This confession suits us all, and is readily made by all
who know themselves. A person approaching London from the
neighbouring hills, usually sees it obscured by a cloud of smoke. This
cloud is the aggregate of the smoke, to which every house furnishes
its respective quota. It is no unfit emblem of the sin and the misery
which abound in this great metropolis. The Lord said of the Amor-
ites, at a certain period, 'Their iniquity is not yet full.' I hope the
measure of our iniquity is not yet full; but it is filling every day, and
we are all daily contributing to fill it. True believers, though, by grace,
delivered from the reigning power of sin, are still sinners. In many
things we offend all in thought, word, and deed. We are now called
upon to humble ourselves before God, for the sins of our ignorance,
and for the more aggravated sins we have committed against light
and experience; for those personal sins, the record of which is known
only to God and our consciences; for the defects and defilements of
our best services; for our great and manifold failures in the discharge
of our relative duties, as parents, children, husbands, wives, masters,
or servants, and as members of the community. Our dullness in the
ways of God, our alertness in the pursuit of our own will and way; our
indifference to what concerns his glory, compared with the quickness
of our apprehensions, when our own temporal interests are affected,
are so many proofs of our ingratitude and depravity. The sins of the
Lord's own people are so many, and so heightened by the consideration of his known goodness, that, if he was to enter into judgment
with them only, they could offer no other plea than that which he
has so mercifully provided for them,—'If thou, Lord, shouldst mark
iniquity, who could stand? But there is forgiveness with thee, that
thou mayest be feared.'

The Danger and Resource of this Nation, [5:258]; 3:638

*Blessed be the L*ORD *God, the God of Israel, who only doeth wondrous things. And blessed be his glorious name for ever: and let the whole earth be filled with his glory; Amen, and Amen.*—Psa. 72:18, 19.

HE who loved you and died for your sins, is the Lord of glory. All power in heaven and earth is committed unto him. The Lord reigneth, let the earth be never so unquiet. All creatures are instruments of his will. The wrath of man, so far as it is permitted to act, shall praise him, shall be made subservient to the accomplishment of his great designs; and the remainder of that wrath, of all their projected violence, which does not coincide with his wise and comprehensive plan, he will restrain. In vain they rage, and fret, and threaten. They act under a secret commission, and can do no more than he permits them. If they attempt it, he has a hook and a bridle in their mouths. When the enemies would come in like a flood, he can lift up a standard against them. As he has set bounds and bars to the tempestuous sea, beyond which it cannot pass, saying, Hitherto, shalt thou come and no further, and there shall thy proud waves be stayed; so, with equal ease, he can still the madness of the people.

You do well to mourn for the sins and miseries of those who know him not. But if you make him your fear and your dread, he will be a sanctuary to you, and keep your hearts in peace, though the earth be removed, and the mountains cast into the midst of the sea.

Your part and mine is to watch and pray. Let us pray for ourselves, that we may be found waiting, with our loins girded up, and our lamps burning, that we may be prepared to meet his will in every event. Let us pray for the peace of Jerusalem, for his church, which is dear to him, as the pupil of his eye, for the spread of his gospel, and the extension of his kingdom, till his great name be known and adored from the rising to the setting of the sun, and the whole earth shall be filled with his glory.

The Danger and Resource of this Nation, [5:267]; 3:644

O Lord, according to all thy righteousness, I beseech thee, let thine anger and thy fury be turned away from thy city Jerusalem, thy holy mountain: because for our sins, and for the iniquities of our fathers, Jerusalem and thy people are become a reproach to all that are about us.—Dan. 9:16.

MAY the Lord soften our hearts for our own sins, the sins of professors of the gospel, and those national sins which strongly mark our character as a people!

The true Christian sees much cause of humiliation in himself. Though he cannot but take sorrowful notice of what passes around him, he is more ready to scrutinize and blame his own misconduct, than that of other men. He confesses that his best is defective and defiled. Though he exercises himself to maintain a conscience void of offence, and dares appeal to the Lord for the sincerity of his aims, he owns that in everything he comes short. His obligations to the Redeemer are immense, and his sensations of gratitude, and exertions in service, are vastly disproportionate to them: yet, having accepted the atonement, and resting his hope of salvation upon Jesus, though his imperfections humble him, they do not discourage him. But he acknowledges that, if justice were strict to mark what is amiss, his own sins are so many and so great, that he could have no right to complain, though he had a large share of the heaviest calamities incident to this mortal life. They who are thus minded, are the chariots and horsemen of the land in which they live. They sigh and mourn for their own sins, and the evils which they cannot prevent. They have little thanks from the blind, careless, ungodly many around them. They are rather scorned and despised for their singularity, and unfashionable preciseness; but, if this nation be spared from destruction, it will be for their sakes, and for the attention with which God regards their prayers. If we had no such persons among us, our fleets and armies would prove but a poor and precarious defence. But I trust their number is not small. They are dispersed up and down throughout the kingdom, and are the salt of the earth, which preserves us from total putrefaction.

The Danger and Resource of this Nation, [5:281]; 3:655

And Abraham drew near, and said,
Wilt thou also destroy the righteous with the wicked?—Gen. 18:23.

'I AM the Holy One in the midst of thee.' Next to the consideration of his infinite mercy, this is our strongest ground for consolation. The Holy One is still in the midst of us! Degenerate and wicked
as we are, God has a people, a remnant among us. I have spoken of
these already. Their number is small if compared with the bulk of
the nation; but, if they could be collected together, they would form
a considerable body, (I trust it is an increasing body), who, though
distinguished by different names, and dispersed far and wide into different parts of the land, are united, by a faith of divine operation, to
one Head, and in one common interest and design. They belong to
that kingdom which is not of this world, and which (unlike all other
kingdoms) cannot be shaken. But their principles lead them to seek
the welfare of the communities in which they live. These, are, under
God ... the glory and the defence of Great Britain. They are lights
shining in a dark place. They are believers, and their faith worketh
by love. But as they follow the example of their Lord and Master, the
world knows not them, because it knows not him... But their record
is on high. They have access to God and communion with him, by
the Son of his love. They have the spirit of prayer, and their prayers
are heard. The ship in which Paul sailed to Italy, was preserved from
sinking, though apparently in the utmost danger, because the apostle
was on board her. The state ship of this nation is now in jeopardy, she
is brought into deep waters, tossed with tempests, and her rowers are
almost at their wits' end; but there is a precious *depositum* on board.
A people dear to the Lord are embarked in the same bottom with the
rest, and we hope their prayers will prevail for the safety of the whole.

Motives to Humiliation and Praise, [5:297]; 3:667

*The angel of the LORD encampeth round about them that fear him,
and delivereth them.*—Psa. 34:7.

REJOICE, believers, in the Lord. You may be assured, upon the warrant of his faithful promise, either that he will preserve you from the evils which our sins give us such cause to apprehend; or, if he should appoint you to share in a common calamity, he will make your strength equal to your day, and will prepare you shoes of iron and brass, when any part of the road, on which you travel through this wilderness towards your heavenly home, shall prove very difficult and rugged. Pray for grace to sit loose to the world, and you will have nothing to fear. The first Christians rejoiced in the spoiling of their goods; and so shall you, if the Lord calls you to the trial. You have the same Saviour to support you, and you likewise have treasures, far better and more enduring, out of the reach of violence. The Lord teaches us to consider even the loss of life as comparatively of small importance, when he says, 'Fear not them that can kill the body, but can do no more.' They cannot do that without his permission. The very hairs of your head are numbered. And most of those who have suffered death for him who died upon the cross for them, have thought the honour of dying in his cause more to be valued than a thousand lives.

The Lord reigns, *your* Lord reigns. He who loved you, and gave himself for you, possesses and exercises all power in heaven and earth. Though clouds and darkness are about his throne and his paths are untraceable by us, we are sure that he is carrying on his great designs, for the glory of his great name, and for the extension and establishment of his church, in a way worthy of himself—worthy of infinite wisdom and goodness. Make his name your tower of refuge. Hold out faith and patience.

Motives to Humiliation and Praise, [5:299]; 3:669

Though an host should encamp against me, my heart shall not fear: though war should rise against me, in this will I be confident.—Psa. 27:3.

THE Christian calling, like many others, is easy and clear in theory, but not without much care and difficulty to be reduced to practice. Things appear quite otherwise, when felt experimentally, to what they do when only read in a book. Many learn the art of navigation (as it is called) by the fire-side at home, but when they come to sea, with their heads full of rules, and without experience, they find that the art is only to be thoroughly learned upon the spot. So, to renounce self, to live upon Jesus, to walk with God, to overcome the world, to hope against hope, to trust the Lord when we cannot trace him, and to know that our duty and privilege consist in these things, may be readily acknowledged or quickly learned; but, upon repeated trial, we find, that saying and doing are two things. We think at setting out that we sit down and count the cost; but, alas! our views are so superficial at first, that we have occasion to correct our estimate daily. For every day shows us some new thing in the heart, or some new turn in the management of the war against us which we were not aware of; and upon these accounts, discouragements may arise so high as to bring us (I speak for myself) to the very point of throwing down our arms, and making either a tame surrender or a shameful flight. Thus it would be with us at last, if the Lord of hosts were not on our side. But though our enemies thrust sore at us that we might fall, he has been our stay. And if he is the Captain of our salvation; if his eye is upon us, his arm stretched out around us, and his ear open to our cry, and if he has engaged to teach our hands to war, and our fingers to fight, and to cover our heads in the day of battle, then we need not fear, though a host rise up against us; but, lifting up our banner in his name, let us go forth conquering and to conquer, Rom. 16:20.

Sequel to Cardiphonia, Letters to Mr. William Cowper [6:122]; 4:386

Therefore being justified by faith, we have peace with God through our Lord Jesus Christ: By whom also we have access by faith into this grace wherein we stand, and rejoice in hope of the glory of God.—Rom. 5:1-2.

HAPPY state! to have peace with God, by Jesus Christ; liberty of access at a throne of grace; an interest in all the promises; a sure guide by the way; and a sure inheritance at our journey's end! These things were once hidden from us. We were so blinded by the god of this world, that we could look no further than the present life. But, even then, the Lord looked upon us with an eye of mercy. He led us on, gradually, by a way which we knew not, to bring us into the paths of peace. How wonderful has our history been, not mine only, but also yours! How often has he made himself known as your Deliverer and Physician, in raising you up from the gates of the grave! May we always remember his goodness in your last affliction! How did he sweeten the bitter cup; strengthen you with strength in your soul; enable you to pray for yourself; engage the hearts of many in prayer for you, and then speedily answer our prayers! Let us then excite each other to praise him! I hope this little interval of absence will be useful, to make me more sensible of his goodness in still sparing you to me. I make but a poor shift without you now from day to day; but I am comforted by the hope of seeing you again shortly. Had you been removed by your late fever, I should not have had this relief! May we then live to him, and may every day be a preparation for the parting hour! Dark as this hour seems in the prospect, if we are established in the faith and hope of our Lord, we shall find it supportable; and the separation will be short. We shall soon meet again, happy meeting! to part no more! to be forever with the Lord; to join in an eternal song to him who loved us, and washed us from our sins in his own blood! Then all tears shall be wiped from our eyes, and we shall weep no more forever.

Letters to a Wife, [5:548]; 4:191

I therefore, the prisoner of the Lord, beseech you that ye walk worthy of the vocation wherewith ye are called.—Eph. 4:1.

TO love and trust the Lord Jesus, is the great lesson we have to learn. We are slow scholars but he can teach us effectually. Without him, the very *best* of this life is insipid, and his presence can make the *worst* supportable.

Your health is restored, and mine is preserved. May we devote our whole selves to him. He has great things to bestow; and, if we feel our need of his mercy, we are properly qualified to receive it. We are not called to buy, but to beg; to receive, without money and without price. By believing, all becomes freely and surely our own; not on the account of our prayers, but of his promise, blood, and mediation. And all he requires of us is to be humble and thankful; and the more he gives us, to desire still more.

May the Lord open your ears and your heart, that you may receive profit where you are. Do not give place to unbelief. Jesus is both an able and a willing Saviour. Pray for a tender conscience, and a dependent spirit. Watch against the motions of self; they are subtle and various. Let no engagements prevent you from reserving seasons of retirement for prayer, and reading the Scriptures. The best company, the best public ordinances, will not compensate for neglect of these. At the same time, guard against a spirit of bondage; nor fetter your mind by too many rules and resolves. It is our privilege to serve the Lord with cheerfulness; not considering him as a hard Master, but as a tender Father, who knows and pities our weakness; who is ready to pardon our mistakes, and to teach us to do better. He accepts us, freely and graciously, when we present ourselves before him, in the name of Jesus, his beloved Son.

Letters to a Wife, [5:549]; 4:192

Behold, God is my salvation; I will trust, and not be afraid:
for the LORD JEHOVAH *is my strength and my song; he also is become my*
salvation. Therefore with joy shall ye draw water out of
the wells of salvation.—Isa. 12:2, 3.

I WROTE yesterday to Mr. A****, and, in my evening walk, my thoughts and prayers turned much upon the affecting stroke he has received. Indeed, it has been seldom out of my mind since I came home. Besides my concern for his loss and my own, (there is no cause to mourn for *her*,) I consider it as a loud speaking lesson to me and to you. How often has she been raised up from the brink of the grave, in answer to prayer; and yet, now, suddenly and unexpectedly removed! We likewise have been long preserved, and often restored to each other. But a time will come when every gourd will wither, every cistern be broken. Let us pray for a waiting, resigned, and dependent frame of spirit; for ability to commit ourselves, and our all, into the merciful hands of him who careth for us; and that, while we are spared, we may walk together, as help-meets and fellow heirs of eternal life. We shall not be parted a moment sooner, for living in daily expectation of our appointed change; but the thought may be a happy mean of composing our minds, and of preventing us from being too much engrossed, either by the sweets or the bitters of this transitory life. Many occasions of care and perplexity, that are apt to waste our time and wound our peace, would be avoided, could we duly consider how soon we shall have done with all these things. May you, may I, be more rooted and grounded in the truth, more humbled and comforted, more filled with that love, joy, and unspeakable peace, which the gospel reveals, and for which the promises of God warrant us to pray. Be not discouraged, because you have nothing of your own. The bucket is put into the well empty, and, because it is empty, the Lord has opened wells of salvation for us, and has promised that we shall not seek his face in vain.

Letters to a Wife, [5:554]; 4:196

All that the Father giveth me shall come to me;
and him that cometh to me I will in no wise cast out.—John 6:37.

BUT I am sure my love has suffered no abatement; yea, I am sure it has increased, from year to year, though I endeavour to hold you more in subordination to him to whom I owe you, and by whose blessing alone it is that we have found comfort in each other.

If youth, and health, and life could be prolonged for a thousand years, and every moment of that space be filled up with the greatest satisfaction we can conceive, this seemingly long period must at last terminate; and, then once past, it would appear short and inconsiderable, as the eighteen years we have already spent together do at present. But, if we are united in the faith and hope of the gospel, we shall never part. Even that separation which must take place, (so painful at times to think of,) will not deserve the name of parting. It will be but like the one coming down first from London, and the other safely following in a few days. And, however flesh and blood may start at the apprehension, the case of Mr. A****, and many others, sufficiently prove the Lord's faithfulness to his promise, and that he can support those who trust him in the most trying circumstances. Let it, therefore, be our chief concern to attain a good hope that we are his, and he is ours, and then we may cheerfully commit the rest to him. He can forgive sin, impart grace, subdue corruption, silence unbelief, make us strong out of weakness, and do more than we can either ask or think. And what he does, he does freely, without money and without price. He does not require us to help ourselves, before we apply to him, but to come to him for help, and we shall not come in vain. Fight, therefore, my dearest, against unbelief, and the Lord will give you the victory. Tell him, what I am sure you are convinced of, that you have nothing, deserve nothing, can do nothing; but that you have heard he is mighty to save, and has promised, that none who apply to him shall be in any wise cast out. None ever did miscarry in this way.

Letters to a Wife, [5:556]; 4:197

But he answered and said, It is not meet to take the children's bread,
and to cast it to dogs. And she said, Truth, Lord: yet the dogs eat of the
crumbs which fall from their masters' table.—Matt. 15:26-27.

DO you not see, and say, He has done great things? How often
has he raised you from the gates of death! With what mercies
and gentleness has he followed you! What a great advantage has he
afforded you, in so large an acquaintance and intimacy with those
who fear and love him! Shall the enemy urge you to draw discouragements from these multiplied instances of the Lord's goodness? I
hope not. Do not give way to unbelief. Do not indulge perplexing
thoughts of the secret counsels of God. What is revealed in the Scripture calls for our attention; and there it is written, as with a sun-beam,
'They that seek shall find.' It is true, when we are seeking, he often
exercises our patience; but he has told us beforehand to expect it, and
has given us encouragement, by parables, examples, and promises, to
continue praying, and not to faint. Though he tarry, wait for him.
Though he may seem to treat you like the woman of Canaan for a
time, yet he is full of compassion and mercy. The humble spirit, the
principle of faith, the heart-felt repentance, and every other gracious
disposition to which the promises are made, are all his gifts, which he
bestows freely on the unworthy.

Since you know that you are a sinner, and that he is the only
Saviour, what should prevent your comfort? Had he bid you do some
great thing, you would, at least, have attempted it. If a pilgrimage to
some distant place was the appointed mean of salvation, would you
be content to sit at home and perish? How much rather then should
you keep close to the throne of grace, when he has only said, 'Ask,
and you shall receive!'

Continue to pray, and watch over your spirit. Keep always in
mind that you are a sinner, and Jesus is a Saviour of sinners. Such
thoughts frequently recurred to, are means by which the Lord com-
poses and sanctifies the frame of our tempers, and the strain of our
conversation.

Letters to a Wife, [5:558]; 4:199

*Every good gift and every perfect gift is from above, and cometh down
from the Father of lights, with whom is no variableness,
neither shadow of turning.*—James 1:17.

IF we are happy in a mutual affection when we set out, we are too
apt to think that nothing more is wanting; and to suppose our
own prudence, and good judgment, sufficient to carry us on to the
end.

It is an undoubted truth, that the Most High God, who is ever
present with and over his creatures, is the author and giver of all that
is agreeable or comfortable to us in this world. We cannot be either
easy in ourselves, or acceptable to others, but by his favour; and,
therefore, when we presume to use his creature-comforts without
consulting and acknowledging him in them, his honour is concerned
to disappoint us. Dreaming of sure satisfaction, in the prosecution,
or enjoyment, of our own desires, we do but imitate the builders of
Babel, who said, Go to, let us build a tower, to get ourselves a name.
So we, too often, when circumstances smile upon us, vainly think of
securing happiness upon earth; a sensual happiness, and on an earth
that stands accursed and subject to vanity for our sins. In every state
and scene of life there are instances of this folly; but, perhaps, it is in
no one more insinuating and plausible than in the commencement
of marriage between those whose hearts are united. But, alas! God
looks down upon such short-sighted projectors as he did upon those
of old. He pours contempt upon their designs; he divides their language; he permits separate views and interests to rise in their minds;
their fair scheme of happiness degenerates into confusion; and they
are left under the reproach of having begun to build what they will
never be able to finish. This is the true cause of half the unhappiness
complained of, and observed among those who come together by
their own consent. Not for want of good-will at first, nor for want of
any necessary qualification in themselves; but because, neglecting to
own and seek God in their concerns, he has refused them that blessing without which no union can subsist.

Letters to a Wife, [5:470]; 4:130

He hath not dealt with us after our sins;
nor rewarded us according to our iniquities.—Psa. 103:10.

B Y his grace he brought me from a state of apostasy, to the knowledge of his gospel; and, by his good providence, he has no less
distinguished me in temporals. He brought me, as I may say, out of
the land of Egypt, out of the house of bondage; from slavery and
famine on the coast of Africa, into my present easy situation. And
he brought me from the most abandoned scenes of profligacy, when
I was sunk into a complacency with the vilest wretches, to make me
happy in the possession of your heart and person. And thus he has
continued to me, in your love and its endearing consequences, all
that I hold valuable in life for so many years; though I have not
endeavoured, in the manner I ought, to deserve you for one whole
day. Often the consciousness of my disingenuous behaviour has made
my heart tremble upon your account. I have feared lest you should
be snatched away, for my punishment. But the Lord is God, and not
man. As in a thousand instances, so particularly in this, I may well
say, he has not dealt with me according to my sins, nor rewarded
me after my iniquities. He has neither separated us by death, nor
involved us in heavy afflictions, nor suffered our affections to fail. Let
us praise him for these three articles, for there is scarcely one couple
in a thousand that is favoured with them all for an equal space of
time.

Philosophy and reasoning have their use; but religion alone can
teach us, how to use the good things of this world without abusing
them; and to make our earthly comforts blessings indeed, by improving them to a further view; by tracing them, as streams to their fountain; by extending our views, from time to eternity; and making our
mutual affection a mean of raising our desires to the great Lord of all.

Letters to a Wife, [5:472]; 4:131

...be thankful unto him, and bless his name.
For the LORD is good.—Psa. 100:4, 5.

I LAID me down in peace, and awoke in safety; for the Lord sustained me. He is about our path by day, and our bed by night, and preserves us from innumerable evils, which would come upon us every hour if his watchful providence did not protect us. He is our sure, though invisible, shield; therefore we are unhurt, though, in ourselves, we are weak and defenceless, like a city without walls or gates, and open to excursions from every quarter. Could we but live more sensible of his goodness, and maintain that feeling of gratitude towards him which we do to some of our fellow creatures, we should be happy. For what is the great design of the gospel? Is it not to introduce us into a state of the most honourable and interesting friendship, and to perpetuate to us the pleasure which we find in pleasing those who are dearest to us? The Lord Jesus is our best Friend: his character is supremely excellent, our obligations to him are inexpressible, our dependence upon him is absolute, and our happiness, in every sense, is in his hands. May our love therefore be fixed upon him, and we shall do well. He will guide us with his eye, guard us with his power, and his fulness and bounty will supply all our wants.

As to dear Eliza, I hope I have made up my mind about her. If her recovery could be purchased, I think I would bid as high for it as my ability would reach, provided it was the Lord's will. But I am so short-sighted, that I dare not ask for the continuance of her life, (nor even of yours), but with a reserve of submission to his wisdom. I know not what might be the possible consequences, if I could have my own will. I know he can restore her, and I believe he will, if it be for the best. If not, I desire to submit, or rather, to acquiesce, to be satisfied. I shall feel for myself if she be removed; and probably my feeling will be doubled and accented upon your account. But he can support us, and sanctify the painful dispensation to us both. I pray to be enabled to entrust and resign everything to him.

Letters to a Wife, [5:610]; 4:239

...the LORD gave, and the LORD hath taken away;
blessed be the name of the LORD.—Job 1:21.

I WAS not supported [when my wife died] by lively sensible consolations, but by being enabled to realize to my mind some great and
leading truths of the word of God. I saw, what indeed I knew before,
but never till then so strongly and so clearly perceived, that as a sinner,
I had no right, and as a believer, I could have no reason, to complain.
I considered her as a loan, which he who lent her to me had a right
to resume whenever he pleased; and that as I had deserved to forfeit
her every day from the first, it became me rather to be thankful that
she was spared to me so long, than to resign her with reluctance when
called for. Further, that his sovereignty was connected with infinite
wisdom and goodness; and that consequently, if it were possible for
me to alter any part of his plan, I could only spoil it,—that such a
short-sighted creature as I, so blind to the possible consequences of
my own wishes, was not only unworthy, but unable, to choose well
for myself; and that it was therefore my great mercy and privilege that
the Lord condescended to choose for me. May such considerations
powerfully affect the hearts of my readers under their troubles, and
then I shall not regret having submitted to the view of the public, a
detail which may seem more proper for the subject of a private letter
to a friend.

When my wife died, the world seemed to die with her, (I hope
to revive no more). The Bank of England is too poor to compensate for such a loss as mine. But the Lord, the all-sufficient God,
speaks, and it is done. Let those who know him, and trust him, be
of good courage. The power and faithfulness on which the successive
changes of day and night, and of the seasons of the year, depend, and
which uphold the stars in their orbits, is equally engaged to support
his people, and to lead them safely and unhurt (if their path be so
appointed) through floods and flames.

On the Death of Mrs. Mary Newton, [5:623]; 4:251

And Hezekiah received the letter of the hand of the messengers, and read it: and Hezekiah went up into the house of the Lord, and spread it before the Lord.—2 Kings 19:14.

LET us remember what great things the Lord has done in answer to prayer. When sin had given Sennacherib rapid success in his invasion of Judah, he did not know that he was no more than an axe, or a saw in the hand of God. He ascribed his victories to his own prowess, and thought himself equally sure of Jerusalem. But Hezekiah defeated him upon his knees. He spread his blasphemous letter before the Lord in the temple and prayed; and the Assyrian army melted away like snow. When Peter was shut up, and chained in prison, the chains fell from his hands, the locks and bolts gave way, and the iron gate opened, while the church was united in earnest prayer for his deliverance.

The present likewise is a very important crisis. All that is dear to us, as men, as Britons, as Christians, is threatened. Our enemies are inveterate and enraged. Our sins testify against us. But if we humble ourselves before God, forsake our sins, and unite in supplications for mercy, who can tell, but he may be entreated to give us that help which it would be in vain to expect from man? Yea, we have encouragement to hope, that 'he will be for us,' and then none can prevail against us. But without his blessing, our most powerful efforts, and best concerted undertakings, cannot succeed.

You, who have access to the throne of grace, whose hearts are concerned for the glory of God, and who lament not only the temporal calamities attendant upon war, but the many thousands of souls who are yearly precipitated by it into an eternal, unchangeable state—you, I trust, will show yourselves true friends to your country, by bearing your testimony, and exerting your influence against sin, the procuring cause of all our sorrows; and by standing in the breach, and pleading with God for mercy, in behalf of yourselves, and of the nation. If ten persons, thus disposed, had been found even in Sodom, it would have escaped destruction.

The Danger and Resource of this Nation, [5:269]; 3:646

Looking unto Jesus the author and finisher of our faith.—Heb. 12:2.

THE best advice I can send, or the best wish I can form for you, is, that you may have an abiding and experimental sense of those words of the apostle, which are just now upon my mind,—'Look-ing unto Jesus.' The duty, the privilege, the safety, the unspeakable happiness, of a believer, are all comprised in that one sentence. Let us first pray that the eyes of our faith and understanding may be opened and strengthened; and then let us fix our whole regard upon him. But how are we to behold him? I answer, in the glass of his written word; there he is represented to us in a variety of views; the wicked world can see no form nor comeliness in the portraiture he has given of himself; yet, blessed be God, there are those who can 'behold his glory as the glory of the only begotten Son of God, full of grace and truth;' and while they behold it, they find themselves, 'changed into the same image, from glory to glory,' by the transforming influence of his Spirit. In vain we oppose reasonings, and arguments, and resolutions, to beat down our corruptions, and to silence our fears; but a believing view of Jesus does the business. When heavy trials in life are appointed us, and we are called to give up, or perhaps to pluck out, a right eye, it is an easy matter for a stander-by to say, 'Be comforted;' and it is as useless as easy—but a view of Jesus by faith comes home to the point. When we can fix our thoughts upon him, as laying aside all his honours, and submitting, for our sakes, to drink of the bitter cup of the wrath of God to the very dregs; and when we further consider, that he who thus suffered in our nature, who knows and sympathizes with all our weakness, is now the supreme Disposer of all that concerns us, that he numbers the very hairs of our heads, appoints every trial we meet with in number, weight, and measure, and will suffer nothing to befall us but what shall contribute to our good—this view, I say, is a medicine suited to the disease, and power-fully reconciles us unto every cross.

Sequel to Cardiphonia: Letters to Several Ladies, [6:4]; 4:276

But he, being full of the Holy Ghost, looked up stedfastly into heaven,
and saw the glory of God, and Jesus standing on the right hand of God.
—Acts 7:55.

SO when a sense of sin prevails, and the tempter is permitted to assault us with dark and dreadful suggestions, it is easy for us to say, 'Be not afraid;' but those who have tried, well know that looking to Jesus is the only and sure remedy in this case—if we can get a sight of him by faith, as he once hung between the two thieves, and as he now pleads within the veil, then we can defy sin and Satan, and give our challenge in the apostle's words, 'Who is he that condemneth? It is Christ that died, yea, rather, that is risen again; who also maketh intercession for us,' Rom. 8:34. Again, are we almost afraid of being swallowed up by our many restless enemies? Or, are we almost weary of our long pilgrimage through such a thorny, tedious, barren wilderness? A sight of Jesus, as Stephen saw him, crowned with glory, yet noticing all the sufferings of his poor servants, and just ready to receive them to himself, and make them partakers of his everlasting joy, this will raise the spirits, and restore strength; this will animate us to hold on, and to hold out; this will do it, and nothing but this can. So, if obedience be the thing in question, looking unto Jesus is the object that melts the soul into love and gratitude, and those who greatly love, and are greatly obliged, find obedience easy. When Jesus is upon our thoughts, either in his humbled or his exalted state, either as bleeding on the cross, or as our nature by all the host of heaven, then we can ask the apostle's question with a becoming disdain, 'Shall we continue in sin that grace may abound?' God forbid. What! Shall I sin against my Lord, my Love, my Friend, who once died for my sins, and now lives and reigns on my behalf; who supports, and leads, and guides, and feeds me every day? God forbid. No; rather I would wish for a thousand hands and eyes, and feet, and tongues, for ten thousand lives, that I might devote them all to his service: he should have all then; and surely he shall have all now!

Sequel to Cardiphonia: Letters to Several Ladies, [6:5]; 4:277

> *And the king commanded Joab and Abishai and Ittai, saying,*
> *Deal gently for my sake with the young man.*—2 Sam. 18:5.

AS you are likely to be engaged in controversy, and your love of truth is joined with a natural warmth of temper, my friendship makes me solicitous on your behalf.

As to your opponent, I wish, that, before you set pen to paper against him, and during the whole time you are preparing your answer, you may commend him by earnest prayer to the Lord's teaching and blessing. This practice will have a direct tendency to conciliate your heart to love and pity him; and such a disposition will have a good influence upon every page you write. If you account him a believer, though greatly mistaken in the subject of debate between you, the words of David to Joab, concerning Absalom, are very applicable: 'Deal gently with him for my sake.' The Lord loves him and bears with him; therefore you must not despise him, or treat him harshly. The Lord bears with you likewise, and expects that you should show tenderness to others, from a sense of the much forgiveness you need yourself. In a little while you will meet in heaven; he will then be dearer to you than the nearest friend you have upon earth is to you now. Anticipate that period in your thoughts; and though you may find it necessary to oppose his errors, view him personally as a kindred soul, with whom you are to be happy in Christ for ever. But if you look upon him as an unconverted person, in a state of enmity against God and his grace, (a supposition which, without good evidence, you should be very unwilling to admit,) he is a more proper object of your compassion than of your anger. Alas! 'he knows not what he does.' But you know who has made you to differ. If God, in his sovereign pleasure, had so appointed, you might have been as he is now; and he, instead of you, might have been set for the defence of the gospel. You were both equally blind by nature. If you attend to this, you will not reproach or hate him, because the Lord has been pleased to open your eyes, and not his.

On Controversy, [1:268]; 1:186

And the servant of the Lord must not strive; but be gentle unto all men,
apt to teach, patient, In meekness instructing those that oppose themselves;
if God peradventure will give them repentance to the
acknowledging of the truth.—2 Tim. 2:24, 25.

WHATEVER it be that makes us trust in ourselves that we are comparatively wise or good, so as to treat those with contempt who do not subscribe to our doctrines, or follow our party, is a proof and fruit of a self-righteous spirit. Self-righteousness can feed upon doctrines, as well as upon works; and a man may have the heart of a Pharisee, while his head is stored with orthodox notions of the unworthiness of the creature and the riches of free grace. Yea, I would add, the best of men are not wholly free from this leaven; and therefore are too apt to be pleased with such representations as hold up our adversaries to ridicule, and by consequence flatter our own superior judgments. Controversies, for the most part, are so managed as to indulge rather than to repress this wrong disposition; and therefore, generally speaking, they are productive of little good. They provoke those whom they should convince, and puff up those whom they should edify. I hope your performance will savour of a spirit of true humility, and be a means of promoting it in others.

This leads me, in the last place, to consider your own concern in your present undertaking. It seems a laudable service to defend the faith once delivered to the saints; we are commanded to contend earnestly for it, and to convince gainsayers. If ever such defences were seasonable and expedient, they appear to be so in our day, when errors abound on all sides, and every truth of the gospel is either directly denied, or grossly misrepresented. And yet we find but very few writers of controversy who have not been manifestly hurt by it. Either they grow in a sense of their own importance, or imbibe an angry contentious spirit, or they insensibly withdraw their attention from those things which are the food and immediate support of the life of faith, and spend their time and strength upon matters which at most are but of a secondary value.

On Controversy, [1:272]; 1:189

...when he was reviled, reviled not again; when he suffered,
he threatened not; but committed himself to him
that judgeth righteously.—1 Peter 2:23.

WHAT will it profit a man if he gains his cause, and silences his adversary, if at the same time he loses that humble, tender frame of spirit in which the Lord delights, and to which the promise of his presence is made! Your aim, I doubt not, is good; but you have need to watch and pray, for you will find Satan at your right hand to resist you: he will try to debase your views; and though you set out in defence of the cause of God, if you are not continually looking to the Lord to keep you, it may become your own cause, and awaken in you those tempers which are inconsistent with true peace of mind, and will surely obstruct communion with God. Be upon your guard against admitting anything personal into the debate. If you think you have been ill treated, you will have an opportunity of showing that you are a disciple of Jesus, who, 'when he was reviled, reviled not again; when he suffered, he threatened not.' This is our pattern, thus we are to speak and write for God, 'not rendering railing for railing, but, contrariwise, blessing; knowing that hereunto we are called.' The wisdom that is from above is not only pure, but peaceable and gentle; and the want of these qualifications, like the dead fly in the pot of ointment, will spoil the savour and efficacy of our labours. If we act in a wrong spirit, we shall bring little glory to God, do little good to our fellow creatures and procure neither honour nor comfort to ourselves. If you can be content with showing your wit, and gaining the laugh on your side, you have an easy task; but I hope you have a far nobler aim, and that, sensible of the solemn importance of gospel truths, and the compassion due to the souls of men, you would rather be a means of removing prejudices in a single instance, than obtain the empty applause of thousands. Go forth, therefore, in the name and strength of the Lord of hosts, speaking the truth in love; and may he give you a witness in many hearts, that you are taught of God, and favoured with the unction of his Holy Spirit.

On Controversy, [1:273]; 1:190

For whom he did foreknow, he also did predestinate to be conformed
to the image of his Son.—Rom. 8:29.

THE leading desires of every person under the influence of gospel principles, will be, to maintain an habitual communion with God in his own soul, and to manifest the power of his grace in the sight of men. So far as a Christian is infected by a conformity to the spirit, maxims, and sinful customs of the world, these desires will be disappointed. Fire and water are not more opposite, than that peace of God which passeth all understanding, and that poor precarious pleasure which is sought in a compliance with the world; a pleasure (if worthy the name) which grieves the Spirit of God, and stupefies the heart. Whoever, after having tasted that the Lord is gracious, has been prevailed on to make the experiment, and to mingle with the world's vanities, has certainly thereby brought a damp upon his experience, and indisposed himself for the exercise of prayer, and the contemplation of divine truths. And if any are not sensible of a difference in this respect, it is because the poison has taken a still deeper effect, so as to benumb their spiritual senses. Conformity to the world is the bane of many professors in this day. They have found a way, as they think, to serve both God and mammon. But because they are double-minded, they are unstable; they make no progress; and, notwithstanding their frequent attendance upon ordinances, they are lean from day to day; a form of godliness, a scheme of orthodox notions, they may attain to, but they will remain destitute of the life power, and comfort of religion, so long as they cleave to those things which are incompatible with it.

Conformity to the world is equally an obstruction in the way of those who profess a desire of glorifying God in the sight of men. Such professors do rather dishonour him... May the Lord enable you and me to lay this subject to heart, and to pray that we may, on the one hand, rightly understand and prize our Christian liberty; and, on the other hand, be preserved from that growing evil, a conformity to the world!

On Conformity to the World, [1:280]; 1:195

> *For God, who commanded the light to shine out of darkness, hath shined*
> *in our hearts, to give the light of the knowledge of the glory of God*
> *in the face of Jesus Christ.*—2 Cor. 4:6.

THE reason why men in a natural state are utterly ignorant of spiritual truths is, that they are wholly destitute of a faculty suited to their perception. A remarkable instance we have in the absurd construction which Nicodemus put upon what our Lord had spoken to him concerning the new birth. Those passages of Scripture wherein the gospel truth is compared to light, lead to a familiar illustration of my meaning. Men by nature are stark blind with respect to this light; by grace the eyes of the understanding are opened. Among a number of blind men, some may be more ingenious and of better capacity than others. They may be better qualified for such studies and employments which do not require eyesight than many who can see, and may attain to considerable skill in them; but with respect to the true nature of light and colours, they are all exactly upon a level. A blind man, if ingenious and inquisitive, may learn to talk about the light, the sun, or the rainbow, in terms borrowed from those who have seen them; but it is impossible that he can have (I mean a man born blind) a just idea of either; and whatever hearsay knowledge he may have acquired, he can hardly talk much upon these subjects without betraying his real ignorance... Nor can all the learning or study in the world enable any person to form a suitable judgment of divine truth, till the eyes of his mind are opened, and then he will perceive it at once.

Neither education, endeavours, nor arguments can open the eyes of the blind. It is God alone, who at first caused light to shine out of darkness, who can shine into our hearts, 'to give us the light of the knowledge of the glory of God in the face of Jesus Christ.'

On Blindness, [1:282]; 1:197

Behold, I stand at the door, and knock: if any man hear my voice, and
open the door, I will come in to him, and will sup with him,
and he with me.—Rev. 3:20.

A S the incarnation of that mighty One, on whom our help is
laid, was necessary, that a perfect obedience to the law, and a
complete and proper atonement for sin, might be accomplished in
the human nature that had sinned and fallen short of the glory of
God; so, in another view, it affords us unspeakable advantage for our
comfortable and intimate communion with God by him. The adorable and awful perfections of Deity are softened, if I may so speak, and
rendered more familiar and engaging to our apprehensions, when
we consider them as resident in him, who is very bone of our bone,
and flesh of our flesh; and who, having by himself purged our sins, is
now seated on the right hand of the Majesty on high, and reigns, in
the nature of man, over all, God blessed for ever. Thus he who knows
our frame, by becoming man like ourselves, is the supreme and ultimate object of that philanthropy, that human affection, which he
originally implanted in us. He has made us susceptive of the endear-
ments of friendship and relative life; and he admits us to communion
with himself under the most engaging characters and relations, as our
Friend, our Brother, and our Husband.

They who, by that faith which is of the operation of God, are
thus united to him in Christ, are brought thereby into a state of
real habitual communion with him. The degree of its exercise and
sensible perception on our parts, is various in different persons, and
in the same person at different times; for it depends upon the communications we receive from the Lord, the Spirit, who distributes to
every man severally according to his will, adjusting his dispensations
with a wise and merciful respect to our present state of discipline. If
we were wholly freed from the effects of a depraved nature, the snares
of an evil world, and the subtle temptations of Satan, our actual communion with God would be always lively, sensible, and fervent. It
will be thus in heaven; there its exercise will be without obstruction,
abatement, or interruption.

On Communion with God, [1:307]; 1:215

...the love of God is shed abroad in our hearts by the Holy Ghost
which is given unto us.—Rom. 5:5.

THE Lord, by his Spirit, manifests and confirms his love to his people. For this purpose he meets them at his throne of grace, and in his ordinances. There he makes himself known unto them, as he does not unto the world; causes his goodness to pass before them; opens, applies, and seals to them, his exceeding great and precious promises; and gives them the Spirit of adoption whereby, unworthy as they are, they are enabled to cry 'Abba, Father.' He causes them to understand that great love wherewith he has loved them, in redeeming them by price and by power, washing them from their sins in the blood of the Lamb, recovering them from the dominion of Satan and preparing for them an everlasting kingdom, where they shall see his face, and rejoice in his glory. The knowledge of this his love to them, produces a return of love from them to him. They adore him, and admire him; they make an unreserved surrender of their hearts to him. They view him and delight in him, as their God, their Saviour, and their portion. They account his favour better than life. He is the Sun of their souls: if he is pleased to shine upon them, all is well, and they are not greatly careful about other things; but if he hides his face, the smiles of the whole creation can afford them no solid comfort. They esteem one day or hour spent in the delightful contemplation of his glorious excellencies, and in the expression of their desires towards him, better than a thousand; and when their love is most fervent, they are ashamed that it is so faint, and chide and bemoan themselves that they can love him no more. This often makes them long to depart, willing to leave their dearest earthly comforts, that they may see him as he is, without a veil or cloud; for they know that then, and not till then, they shall love him as they ought.

On Communion with God, [1:309]; 1:217

The secret of the Lord is with them that fear him;
and he will shew them his covenant.—Psa. 25:14.

THE secret of the Lord is with them that fear him. He deals familiarly with them. He calls them not servants only, but friends; and he treats them as friends. He affords them more than promises; for he opens to them the plan of his great designs from everlasting to everlasting; shows them the strong foundations and inviolable securities of his favour towards them, the height, and depth, and length, and breadth of his love, which passeth knowledge and the unsearchable riches of his grace. He instructs them in the mysterious conduct of his providence, the reasons and ends of all his dispensations in which they are concerned; and solves a thousand hard questions to their satisfaction, which are inexplicable to the natural wisdom of man. He teaches them likewise the beauty of his precepts, the path of their duty, and the nature of their warfare. He acquaints them with the plots of their enemies, and snares and dangers they are exposed to, and the best methods of avoiding them. And he permits and enables them to acquaint him with all their cares, fears, wants, and troubles, with more freedom than they can unbosom themselves to their nearest earthly friends. His ear is always open to them; he is never weary of hearing their complaints, and answering their petitions. The men of the world would account it a high honour and privilege to have an unrestrained liberty of access to an earthly king; but what words can express the privilege and honour of believers, who, whenever they please, have audience of the King of kings, whose compassion, mercy, and power are, like his majesty, infinite? The world wonders at their indifference to the vain pursuits and amusements by which others are engrossed... They have obtained the pearl of great price; they have communion with God; they derive their wisdom, strength, and comfort from on high; and cast all their cares upon him, who, they assuredly know, vouchsafes to take care of them.

On Communion with God, [1:310]; 1:218

> *And ye became followers of us, and of the Lord, having received the word*
> *in much affliction, with joy of the Holy Ghost: So that ye were*
> *ensamples to all that believe.*—I Thess. 1:6, 7.

THE Lord claims [his people] for his portion; he accounts them his jewels; and their happiness in time and eternity is the great end which, next to his own glory, and in inseparable connection with it, he has immediately and invariably in view. In this point all his dispensations of grace and providence shall finally terminate. He himself is their guide and their guard; he keeps them as the apple of his eye; the hairs of their head are numbered; and not an event in their lives takes place but in an appointed subserviency to their final good. And as he is pleased to espouse *their* interest, they, through grace, are devoted to *his*. They are no longer their own; they *would not* be their own; it is their desire, their joy, their glory, to live to him who died for them. He has won their hearts by his love, and made them a willing people in the day of his power. The glory of his name, the success of his cause, the prosperity of his people, the accomplishment of his will—these are the great and leading objects which are engraven upon their hearts, and to which all their prayers, desires, and endeavours are directed. They would count nothing dear, not even their lives, if set in competition with these. In the midst of their afflictions, if the Lord is glorified, if sinners are converted, if the church flourishes, they can rejoice. But when iniquity abounds, when love waxes cold, when professors depart from the doctrines of truth and the power of godliness, then they are grieved and pained to the heart; then they are touched in what they account their nearest interest, because it is their Lord's.

This is the spirit of a true Christian. May the Lord increase it in us, and in all who love his name!

On Communion with God, [1:312]; 1:219

And the apostles said unto the Lord, Increase our faith.—Luke 17:5.

THE first object of solicitude to an awakened soul, is *safety*. The law speaks, the sinner hears and fears: a holy God is revealed, the sinner sees and trembles; every false hope is swept away; and an earnest inquiry takes place, 'What shall I do to be saved?' In proportion as faith is given, Jesus is discovered as the only Saviour, and the question is answered; and as faith increases, fear subsides, and a comfortable hope of life and immortality succeeds.

When we have thus 'a good hope through grace' that heaven shall be our home, I think the next inquiry is, or should be, How we may possess as much of heaven by the way as is possible? in other words, How a life of communion with our Lord and Saviour may be maintained in the greatest power, and with the least interruption that is consistent with the present imperfect state of things?

In the first place, it is plain, from Scripture and experience, that all our abatements, declensions, and langours arise from a defect of faith; from the imperfect manner in which we take up the revelation of our Lord Jesus Christ in the Scripture. If our apprehensions of him were nearly suitable to the characters he bears in the word of God; if we had a strong and abiding sense of his power and grace always upon our hearts; doubts and complaints would cease. This would make hard things easy, and bitter things sweet, and dispose our hearts with cheerfulness to do and suffer the whole will of God; living upon and to him, as our wisdom, righteousness, sanctification, joy, and supreme end, we should live a heaven upon earth.

I apprehend, that the growth of faith, no less than of all other graces, of which faith is the root, is gradual, and ordinarily affected in the use of appointed means; yet not altogether arbitrary, but appointed by him who knows our frame; and therefore works in us, in a way suited to those capacities he has endued us with.

On Faith, and the Communion of Saints, [1:313]; 1:220

Like as a father pitieth his children,
so the LORD pitieth them that fear him.—Psa. 103:13.

THE experience of past years has taught me to distinguish between ignorance and disobedience. The Lord is gracious to the weakness of his people; many involuntary mistakes will not interrupt their communion with him; he pities their infirmity, and teaches them to do better. But if they dispute his known will, and act against the dictates of conscience, they will surely suffer for it. This will weaken their hands, and bring distress into their hearts. Wilful sin sadly perplexes and retards our progress. May the Lord keep us from it! It raises a dark cloud, and hides the Sun of righteousness from our view; and till he is pleased freely to shine forth again, we can do nothing; and for this perhaps he will make us wait, and cry out often, 'How long, O Lord! how long?'

Thus, by reading the word of God, by frequent prayer, by a simple attention to the Lord's will, together with the use of public ordinances, and the observations we are able to make upon what passes within us and without us, which is what we call *experience*, the Lord watering and blessing with the influence of his Holy Spirit, may we grow in grace, and the knowledge of our Lord and Saviour; be more humble in our own eyes, more weaned from self, more fixed on him as our all in all, till at last we shall meet before his throne.

> Then all the chosen race
>   Shall meet before the throne,
> Shall bless the conduct of his grace,
>   And make his wonders known.

Let us then, dear Sir, be of good courage; all the saints on earth, all the saints in heaven, the angels of the Lord, yea, the Lord of angels himself, all are on our side. Though the company is large, yet there is room;—many mansions;—a place for you;—a place, I trust, for worthless me.

On Faith, and the Communion of Saints, [1:316]; 1:222

For thou wilt light my candle:
the LORD my God will enlighten my darkness.—Psa. 18:28.

THE day is now breaking; how beautiful its appearance! how welcome the expectation of the approaching sun! It is this thought makes the dawn agreeable, that it is the presage of a brighter light; otherwise, if we expect no more day than it is this minute, we should rather complain of darkness, than rejoice in the early beauties of the morning. Thus the life of grace is the dawn of immortality: beautiful beyond expression, if compared with the night and thick darkness which formerly covered us; yet faint, indistinct, and unsatisfying, in comparison of the glory which shall be revealed.

It is, however, a sure earnest; so surely as we now see the light of the Sun of righteousness, so surely shall we see the Sun himself, Jesus the Lord, in all his glory and lustre. In the mean time, we have reason to be thankful for a measure of light to walk and work by, and sufficient to show us the pits and snares by which we might be endangered: and we have a promise, that our present light shall grow stronger and stronger, if we are diligent in the use of the appointed means, till the messenger of Jesus shall lead us within the veil, and then farewell shades and obscurity forever.

I can now almost see to write, and shall soon put the extinguisher over my candle: I do this without the least reluctance, when I enjoy a better light; but I should have been unwilling half an hour ago. Just thus, methinks, when the light of the glorious gospel shines into the heart, all our former feeble lights, our apprehensions, and our contrivances, become at once unnecessary and unnoticed. How cheerfully did the apostle put out the candle of his own righteousness, attainments, and diligence, when the true Sun arose upon him!... Adored be the grace that has given us to be like-minded, even to 'account all things but loss for the excellency of the knowledge of Christ Jesus our Lord.'

On the Gradual Increase of Gospel Illumination [1:319]; 1:224

*Then shall we know, if we follow on to know the Lord: his going forth is
prepared as the morning; and he shall come unto us as the rain,
as the latter and former rain unto the earth.*—Hos. 6:3.

T HUS some are called by grace earlier in life, and some later; but
the seeming difference will be lost and vanish when the great
day of eternity comes on. There is a time, the Lord's best appointed
time, when he will arise and shine upon many a soul that now sits 'in
darkness, and in the region of the shadow of death.'

I have been thinking of the Lord's conference with Nicodemus;
it is a copious subject, and affords room, in one part or other, for the
whole round of doctrinal and experimental topics. Nicodemus is an
encouraging example to those who are seeking the Lord's salvation:
he had received some favourable impressions of Jesus; but he was very
ignorant, and much under the fear of man. He durst only come by
night, and at first, though he heard, he understood not; but he, who
opens the eyes of the blind, brought him surely, though gently, forward. The next time we hear of him, he durst put in a word in behalf
of Christ, even in the midst of his enemies, John 7; and at last, he
had the courage openly and publicly to assist in preparing the body
of his Master for its funeral, at a time when our Lord's more avowed
followers had all forsook him and fled. So true is *that*, 'Then ye shall
know, if ye follow on to know the Lord;' and again, 'He giveth power
to the faint; and to them that have no might, he increaseth strength.'

Hope then, my soul, against hope; though thy graces are faint
and languid, he who planted them will water his own work, and
not suffer them wholly to die. He can make a little one as a thousand; at his presence mountains sink into plains, streams gush out of
the flinty rock, and the wilderness blossoms as the rose. He can pull
down what sin builds up, and build up what sin pulls down; that
which was impossible to us, is easy to him; and he has bid us expect
seasons of refreshment from his presence. Even so, come, Lord Jesus.

On the Gradual Increase of Gospel Illumination [1:320]; 1:225

But of him are ye in Christ Jesus, who of God is made unto us wisdom,
and righteousness, and sanctification, and redemption.—1 Cor. 1:30.

THE union of a believer with Christ is so intimate, so unalterable, so rich in privilege, so powerful in influence, that it cannot be fully represented by any description or similitude taken from earthly things. The mind, like the sight, is incapable of apprehending a great object, without viewing it on different sides.

In our natural state, we are driven and tossed about, by the changing winds of opinion, and the waves of trouble, which hourly disturb and threaten us upon the uncertain sea of human life. But faith, uniting us to Christ, fixes us upon a sure foundation, the Rock of ages, where we stand immovable, though storms and floods unite their force against us.

By nature we are separated from the Divine life, as branches broken off, withered and fruitless. But grace, through faith, unites us to Christ the living Vine, from whom, as the root of all fulness, a constant supply of sap and influence is derived into each of his mystical branches, enabling them to bring forth fruit unto God, and to persevere and abound therein.

By nature we are hateful and abominable in the sight of a holy God and full of enmity and hatred towards each other. By faith, uniting us to Christ, we have fellowship with the Father and the Son, and joint communion among ourselves.

In our natural estate, we were cast out and naked and destitute, without pity, and without help, Ezek. 16; but faith, uniting us to Christ, interests us in his righteousness, his riches, and his honours. Our Redeemer is our Husband; our debts are paid, our settlements secured, and our names changed.

Thus the Lord Jesus, in declaring himself the Foundation, Root, Head, and Husband, of his people, takes in all the ideas we can frame of an intimate, vital, and inseparable union.

On Union with Christ, [1:322]; 1:226

Let the word of Christ dwell in you richly in all wisdom.—Col. 3:16.

IN general, [God] guides and directs his people, by affording them, in answer to prayer, the light of his Holy Spirit, which enables them to understand and to love the Scriptures. The word of God is not to be used as a lottery; nor is it designed to instruct us by shreds and scraps, which, detached from their proper places, have no determinate import; but it is to furnish us with just principles, right apprehensions, to regulate our judgments and affections, and thereby to influence and direct our conduct. They who study the Scriptures, in an humble dependence upon Divine teaching, are convinced of their own weakness, are taught to make a true estimate of everything around them, are gradually formed into a spirit of submission to the will of God, discover the nature and duties of their several situations and relations in life, and the snares and temptations to which they are exposed. The word of God dwells richly in them, as a preservative from error, a light to their feet, and a spring of strength and consolation. By treasuring up the doctrines, precepts, promises, examples, and exhortations of Scripture, in their minds, and daily comparing themselves with the rule by which they walk, they grow into an habitual frame of spiritual wisdom, and acquire a gracious taste, which enables them to judge of right and wrong with a degree of readiness and certainty, as a musical ear judges of sounds. And they are seldom mistaken, because they are influenced by the love of Christ, which rules in their hearts, and a regard to the glory of God, which is the great object they have in view.

In particular cases, the Lord opens and shuts doors for them, breaks down walls of difficulty which obstruct their path, or hedges up their way with thorns, when they are in danger of going wrong, by the dispensations of his providence. They know that their concernments are in his hands. He leads them by a right way, preserves them from a thousand snares, and satisfies them that he is and will be their guide even unto death.

Of the Divine Guidance, [1:330]; 1:232

But we know that the law is good, if a man use it lawfully.—1 Tim. 1:8.

THE law of God, then, in the largest sense, is that rule, or pre-scribed course, which he has appointed for his creatures accord-ing to their several natures and capacities, that they may answer the end for which he has created them. Thus it comprehends the inan-imate creation. The wind or storm fulfils his word or law. He hath appointed the moon for its seasons; and the sun knoweth his going down, or going forth, and performs all its revolutions according to its Maker's pleasure. The law of God in this sense, or what many choose to call the law of nature, is no other than the impression of God's power, whereby all things continue and act according to his will from the beginning: for 'he spake, and it was done; he commanded, and it stood fast.'

The animals destitute of reason are likewise under a law; that is, God has given them instincts according to their several kinds, for their support and preservation, to which they invariably conform. A wisdom unspeakably superior to all the contrivance of man disposes their concernments, and is visible in the structure of a bird's nest, or the economy of a bee-hive. But this wisdom is restrained within narrow limits; they act without any remote design, and are incapable either of good or evil in a moral sense.

When God created man, he taught him more than the beasts of the earth, and made him wiser than the fowls of heaven. He formed him for himself, breathed into him a spirit immortal and incapable of dissolution, gave him a capacity not to be satisfied with any crea-ture good, endured him with an understanding, will, and affections, which qualified him for the knowledge and service of his Maker, and a life of communion with him. The law of God, therefore, concern-ing man, is that rule of disposition and conduct to which a crea-ture so constituted ought to conform; so that the end of his creation might be answered, and the wisdom of God be manifested in him and by him.

On the Right Use of the Law, [1:340]; 1:240

For the LORD is our judge, the LORD is our lawgiver,
the LORD is our king; he will save us.—Isa. 33:22.

AS man was capable of continuing in the state in which he was created, so he was capable of forsaking it. He did so, and sinned by eating the forbidden fruit. We are not to suppose that this prohibition was the whole of the law of Adam, so that if he had abstained from the tree of knowledge, he might in other respects have done (as we say) what he pleased. This injunction was the test of his obedience, and while he regarded it, he could have no desire contrary to holiness, because his nature was holy. But when he broke through it, he broke through the whole law, and stood guilty of idolatry, blasphemy, rebellion, and murder. The divine light in his soul was extinguished; the image of God defaced; he became like Satan, whom he had obeyed and lost his power to keep that law which was connected with his happiness. Yet still the law remained in force: the blessed God could not lose his right to that reverence, love, and obedience, which must always be due to him from his intelligent creatures. Thus Adam became a transgressor, and incurred the penalty, death. But God, who is rich in mercy, according to his eternal purpose, revealed the promise of the Seed of the woman, and instituted sacrifices as types of that atonement for sin, which he in the fulness of time should accomplish by the sacrifice of himself.

Adam, after his fall, was no longer a public person; he was saved by grace, through faith; but the depravity he had brought upon human nature remained. His children, and so all his posterity, were born in his sinful likeness, without either ability or inclination to keep the law. The earth was soon filled with violence. But a few in every successive age were preserved by grace, and faith in the promise. Abraham was favoured with a more full and distinct revelation of the covenant of grace; he saw the day of Christ and rejoiced. In the time of Moses, God was pleased to set apart a peculiar people to himself, and to them he published his law with great solemnity at Sinai.

On the Right Use of the Law, [1:342]; 1:241

Christ hath redeemed us from the curse of the law, being made a curse
for us: for it is written, Cursed is every one that hangeth on a tree.
—Gal. 3:13.

CHRIST, and he alone, delivers us, by faith in his name, from the curse of the law, having been made a curse for us.

We cannot be at enmity with God, and at the same time approve of his law; rather, this is the ground of our dislike to him, that we conceive the law by which we are to be judged is too strict in its precepts, and too severe in its threatenings; and therefore men, so far as in them lies, are for altering the law. They think it would be better if it required no more than we can perform, if it allowed us more liberty, and especially if it was not armed against transgressors with the penalty of everlasting punishment... In short, the spirituality and strictness of the law, its severity, and its levelling effect, confounding all seeming differences in human characters, and stopping every mouth without distinction, are three properties of the law, which the natural man cannot allow to be good.

These prejudices against the law can only be removed by the Holy Spirit. It is his office to enlighten and convince the conscience; to communicate an impression of the majesty, holiness, justice, and authority of the God with whom we have to do, whereby the evil and desert of sin is apprehended: the sinner is then stripped of all his vain pretences, is compelled to plead guilty, and must justify his Judge, even though he should condemn him. It is *his* office likewise to discover the grace and glory of the Saviour, as having fulfilled the law for us, and as engaged by promise to enable those who believe in him to honour it with a due obedience in their own persons. Then a change of judgment takes place, and the sinner consents to the law, that it is holy, just, and good.

On the Right Use of the Law, [1:344]; 1:243

I kept back nothing that was profitable unto you, but have shewed you,
and have taught you publickly, and from house to house, Testifying both
to the Jews, and also to the Greeks, repentance toward God, and faith
toward our Lord Jesus Christ.—Acts 20:20, 21.

THOUGH the Bible is to be found in almost every house; yet we see, in fact, it is a sealed book; little read, little understood, and therefore but little regarded, except in those places which the Lord is pleased to favour with ministers who can confirm [its truths] from their own experience; and who, by a sense of his constraining love, and the worth of souls, are animated to make the faithful discharge of their ministry the one great business of their lives.

When the gospel, in this sense of the word, first comes to a place, though the people are going on in sin, they may be said to sin ignorantly; they have not yet been warned of their danger. Some are drinking down iniquity like water; others more soberly burying themselves alive in the cares and business of the world: others find a little time for what they call religious duties, which they persevere in, though they are utter strangers to the nature or the pleasure of spiritual worship; partly, as thereby they think to bargain with God, and to make amends for such sins as they do not choose to relinquish; and partly because it gratifies their pride, and affords them (as they think) some ground for saying, 'God, I thank thee I am not as other men.' The preached gospel declares the vanity and danger of these several ways which sinners choose to walk in. It declares, and demonstrates, that, different as they appear from each other, they are equally remote from the path of safety and peace, and all tend to the same point, the destruction of those who persist in them. At the same time it provides against that despair into which men would be otherwise plunged, when convinced of their sins, by revealing the immense love of God, the glory and grace of Christ, and inviting all to come to him, that they may obtain pardon, life, and happiness. In a word, it shows the pit of hell under men's feet, and opens the gate and points out the way to heaven.

On Man in his Fallen Estate, [1:372]; 1:264

Who is a God like unto thee, that pardoneth iniquity, and passeth by the transgression of the remnant of his heritage?—Micah 7:18.

THE apostle Paul's recollection of his course while in a natural state, and the singular manner of his conversion, were evidently suited to make him a humble Christian, and he was so. By an especial favour of the Lord, he was afterwards taken up into the third heaven; what he saw or heard there he has not told us, but surely he met with nothing that could have a tendency to make him proud ... but Paul, though an eminent saint, was still liable to the effects of indwelling sin; he was in danger of being exalted through the abundance of revelations, and the Lord, his wise and gracious Keeper, saw fit, in order to prevent it, that a messenger from Satan should be given him to buffet him. Pride is so subtle, that it can gather strength even from these gracious manifestations which seem directly calculated to mortify it; so dangerous, that a messenger from Satan himself may be esteemed a mercy, if overruled and sanctified by the Lord to make or keep us more humble: therefore, though we can never be too earnest in striving against sin, too watchful in abstaining from all appearance of evil, and though they who wait upon the Lord may comfortably hope that he will preserve them from such things as would dishonour their profession in the sight of men; yet I apprehend they who appear most to adorn the gospel in their outward conversation, are conscious of many things between the Lord and their own souls which covers them with shame, and that his tenderness and mercy to them, notwithstanding their perverseness, constrains them with admiration to adopt the language of Micah, 'Who is a God like unto thee, that pardoneth iniquity, and passeth by the transgression of the remnant of his heritage?' And I believe, likewise, that, without such striking and repeated proofs of what is in their hearts, they would not so feelingly enter into the spirit of Job's confession, 'Behold, I am vile!' nor would they have such a lively sense of their obligations to the merciful care and faithfulness of their great Shepherd, or of their entire and absolute dependence upon him, for wisdom, righteousness, sanctification, and redemption.

On Some Points of Christian Experience, [1:396]; 1:282

What fruit had ye then in those things whereof ye are now ashamed?
for the end of those things is death.—Rom. 6:21.

IF you were to send me an inventory of your pleasures, how charmingly your time runs on, and how dexterously it is divided between the coffee-house, play-house, the card-table, and tavern, with intervals of balls, concerts, &c.; I could answer, that most of these I have tried and tried again, and know the utmost they can yield, and have seen enough of the rest, most heartily to despise them all... I am sure, while I lived in these things I found them unsatisfying and empty to the last degree; and the only advantage they afforded (miserable are they who are forced to *deem* it an advantage) was, that they often relieved me from the trouble and burden of thinking... Thus far we stand upon even ground. You know all that a life of pleasure can give, and I know it likewise.

On the other hand, if I should attempt to explain to you the source and streams of *my* best pleasures, such as a comfortable assurance of the pardon of my sins, an habitual communion with the God who made heaven and earth, a calm reliance on the Divine Providence, the cheering prospect of a better life in a better world, with the pleasing foretastes of heaven in my own soul; should I, or could I, tell you the pleasure I often find in reading the Scripture, in the exercise of prayer, and in that sort of preaching and conversation which you despise; I doubt not but you would think as meanly of my happiness as I do of yours. But here lies the difference, my dear friend, you condemn that which you have never tried.

But I need not tell you, that the present life is not made up of pleasurable incidents only. Pain, sickness, losses, disappointments, injuries, and affronts with men, will, more or less, at one time or other, be our lot... You cannot view these trials as appointed by a wise and heavenly Father in subservience to your good; you cannot taste the sweetness of his promises, nor feel the secret supports of his strength, in an hour of affliction; you cannot so cast your burden and care upon him, as to find a sensible relief to your spirit thereby; nor can you see his hand engaged and employed in effecting your deliverance.

On Religion as Necessary to the Enjoyments of Life, [1:399]; 1:285

Are they not all ministering spirits, sent forth to minister for them who shall be heirs of salvation?—Heb. 1:14.

T HE great God works all in all in both worlds. It is he who filleth the earth with good things, causes the grass to grow for the cattle, and provides corn for the food of man. But in thus spreading a table for us, he makes use of *instruments*. He commands his sun to shine, and his rain to descend. So he is the life, strength, and comfort, of the renewed soul. All the streams of grace flow from Christ, the fountain. But, from the analogy observable in his works, we might reasonably suppose, that, on many occasions, he is pleased to use means and instruments, and particularly the ministry of his angels, to communicate good to his children. Scripture expressly confirms this inference, and leaves it no longer a point of mere conjecture. He *gives his angels charge* over them, and they *encamp* around them that fear him. In this way honour is given to Jesus, as the Lord both of angels and men; and a sweet intercourse is kept up between the different parts of the household of God. That angels have been thus employed in fact, is plain from the history both of the Old and New Testament. They have often made themselves *visible*, when sent to declare the will of God, as to Jacob, Elijah, and David. Gabriel appeared to Zacharias and Mary; and a multitude joined in ascribing 'glory to God in the highest,' when they brought to the shepherds the joyful news of a Saviour's birth. An angel delivered Peter from prison, and comforted Paul when tossed by a tempest upon the seas. How far the *sensible* ministration of angels is continued in these days, is not easy to determine... The apostle, pressing believers to exercise hospitality, uses this argument, that 'thereby some have entertained angels unawares;' which would hardly seem to be a pertinent motive, if it were absolutely certain that angels would never offer themselves as visitants to the servants of God in future times, as they had formerly done. But, waving speculation as to their visible appearance, it is sufficient to know, that they are *really*, though invisibly, near us, and mindful of us.

On the Ministry of Angels, [1:417]; 1:298

For he shall give his angels charge over thee,
to keep thee in all thy ways.—Psa. 91:11.

THE ministry of angels preserves us from innumerable dangers and alarms which await us in our daily path. This is expressly taught in Psalm 91. When we receive little or no harm from a fall, or when a sudden motion of our minds leads us to avoid a danger which we were not aware of, perhaps the angels of God have been the means of our preservation; nay, it may be owing to their good offices that we ever perform a journey in safety, or are preserved from the evils we are liable to when sleeping upon our beds, and incapable of taking any care of ourselves.

We are often cast down to think how few there are who worship God in spirit and in truth; and are ready to complain, with Elijah, that we are almost left to serve him alone. But Jesus is not slighted and despised in yonder world as he is in this. If, like the servant of Elisha, our eyes were supernaturally opened, to take a glance within the veil, what a glorious and astonishing prospect would the innumerable host of angels afford us! Then we should be convinced, that, far from being alone, there are unspeakably more for us than against us. Faith supplies the want of sight; is the evidence of things not seen, and, upon the authority of the word of God, is as well satisfied of their existence and employment, as if they were actually in our view.

May we take a pattern from the angels! Their whole desire is, to fulfil the will of God; and they account no service mean in which he is pleased to employ them; otherwise, great and holy as they are, they might disdain to wait upon sinful worms. Our vanity prompts us to aim at something great, and to wish for such services as might make us known, talked of, and regarded. But a child of God, if in the way of duty, and in the place which the Lord's providence has allotted him, is well employed ... provided he does it humbly, thankfully, and heartily, as to the Lord. An angel so placed could do no more.

On the Ministry of Angels, [1:420]; 1:300

*And to you who are troubled rest with us, when the Lord Jesus shall be
revealed from heaven with his mighty angels, In flaming fire taking
vengeance on them that know not God, and that obey not
the gospel of our Lord Jesus Christ.*—2 Thess. 1:7, 8.

THE hour is coming, when all impediments shall be removed.—
All distinctions shall cease that are founded upon sublunary
things, and the earth and all its works shall be burnt up. Glorious
day! May our souls be filled with the thought, and learn to estimate
all things around us *now*, by the view in which they will appear to
us *then*. Then it will be of small moment who was the prince, and
who was the beggar, in this life;—but who in their several situations
sought, and loved, and feared, and honoured the Lord. Alas! how
many of the kings of the earth, and the rich men, and the chief cap-
tains, and the mighty men, will then say (in vain) to the mountains
and the rocks, Fall on us and hide us! In this world they are for the
most part too busy to regard the commands of God, or too happy to
seek his favour; they have their good things here; they please themselves for a while, and in a moment they go down to the grave: in that
moment their thoughts perish, their schemes are left unfinished, they
are torn from their possessions, and enter upon a new, and untried,
and unchangeable, a never-ending state of existence. Alas, is this all
the world can afford!... I doubt not but you are often affected with
a sense of ... distinguishing mercy. But though we know that we are
debtors, great debtors to the grace of God, which alone has made
us to differ, we know it but imperfectly at present. It doth not yet
appear what we shall be; nor can we form a just conception of the
misery from which we are redeemed, much less of the price paid for
our redemption. How little do we know of the Redeemer's dignity,
and of the unutterable distress he endured when his soul was made
an offering for sin, and it pleased the Father to bruise him, that by
his stripes we might be healed! These things will strike us quite in
another manner, when we view them in the light of eternity.

Cardiphonia: Letters to a Nobleman, [1:470]; 1:340

*For we have not an high priest which cannot be touched with the feeling
of our infirmities; but was in all points tempted like as we are,
yet without sin.*—Heb. 4:15.

METHINKS I could never venture to open my heart freely to [an angel], and unfold to him my numberless complaints and infirmities; for, as he could have no experience of the like things himself, I should suppose he would not know how fully to pity me, indeed, hardly how to bear with me, if I told him all. Alas! what a preposterous, strange, vile creature should I appear to an angel, if he knew me as I am! It is well for me that Jesus was made lower than the angels, and that the human nature he assumed was not distinct from the common nature of mankind, though secured from the common depravity; and because he submitted to be under the law in our name and stead, though he was free from sin himself, yet, sin and its consequences being (for our sakes) charged upon him, he acquired, in the days of his humiliation, an experimental sympathy with his poor people. He knows the effects of sin and temptation upon us, by that knowledge whereby he knows all things; but he knows them likewise in a way more suitable for our comfort and relief, by the sufferings and exercises he passed through for us. Hence arises encouragement. We have not an High Priest who cannot be touched with a feeling of our infirmities, but was in all points tempted even as we are. When I add to this, the consideration of his power, promises, and grace, and that he is exalted on purpose to pity, relieve, and save, I gather courage. With him I dare be free; and am not sorry, but glad, that he knows me perfectly, that not a thought of my heart is hidden from him; for, without this infinite and exact knowledge of my disease, how could he effectually administer to my cure?

Cardiphonia: Letters to a Nobleman, [1:511]; 1:372

Blessed be the God and Father of our Lord Jesus Christ, who hath blessed
us with all spiritual blessings in heavenly places in Christ.—Eph. 1:3.

THE state of true believers, compared with that of others, is
always *blessed*. If they are born from above, and united to Jesus,
they are delivered from condemnation, and are heirs of eternal life,
and may therefore well be accounted happy.

In the first place, a clear, well-grounded, habitual persuasion of
our acceptance in the Beloved, is attainable; and though we may be
safe, we cannot be said to enjoy blessedness without it. To be in a
state of suspense and uncertainty in a point of so great importance,
is painful; and the Lord has accordingly provided that his people
may have strong consolation on this head. They are blessed, therefore, who have such views of the power, grace, and suitableness of
Jesus, and the certainty and security of redemption in him, together
with such a consciousness that they have anchored their hopes, and
ventured their all, upon his person, work, and promise, as furnishes
them with a ready answer to all the cavils of unbelief and Satan, in
the apostle's manner, Rom. 8:31-37. That Paul could thus challenge
and triumph over all charges and enemies, was not an appendage of
his office as an apostle, but a part of his experience as a believer; and
it lies equally open to us: for we have the same gospel and the same
promises as he had; nor is the efficacy of the Holy Spirit's teaching a
whit weakened by length of time. But many stop short of this. They
have a hope, but it rather springs from their frames and feelings,
than from a spiritual apprehension of the Redeemer's engagements
and fulness, and therefore fluctuates and changes like the weather.
Could they be persuaded to pray with earnestness and importunity,
as the apostle prays for them, Eph. 1:17-18, and 3:16-19, they would
find a blessedness which they have not yet known; for it is said, 'Ask,
and ye shall receive;' and it is said likewise, 'Ye receive not, because
ye ask not.'

Cardiphonia: Letters to a Nobleman, [1:519]; 1:378

*Thus saith the Lord G*OD *unto these bones; Behold, I will cause breath
to enter into you, and ye shall live.*—Ezek. 37:5.

B UT he is the potter, we are the clay: his ways and thoughts are
above ours, as the heavens are higher than the earth. The Judge
of all the earth *will* do right. He has appointed a day, when he will
manifest, to the conviction of *all*, that *he has done right*. Till then,
I hold it best to take things upon his word, and not too harshly
determine what it becomes Jehovah to do. Instead of saying what
I think, let it suffice to remind you of what St. Paul thought, Rom.
9:15-21. But, further, I say, that unless mercy were afforded to those
who perish, I believe no one soul could be saved. For I believe fallen
man, universally, considered *as* such, is as incapable of doing the least
thing towards his salvation till prevented by the grace of God, ... as a
dead body is of restoring itself to life. Whatever difference takes place
between men in this respect, it is *of grace*, that is, of God, undeserved.
Yea, his first approaches to our hearts are undesired too; for, till he
seeks us, we cannot, we will not seek him, Psa. 110:3. It is in the day of
his power, and not before, his people are made willing. But I believe,
where the gospel is preached, they who do perish do wilfully resist the
light, and choose and cleave to darkness, and stifle the convictions
which the truths of God, *when his true gospel is indeed preached*, will,
in one degree or other, force upon their minds. The cares of this
world, the deceitfulness of riches, the love of other things, the violence of sinful appetites, their prejudices, pride, and self-righteousness either prevent the reception, or choke the growth of the good
seed: thus their own sin and obstinacy is the proper cause of their
destruction; they *will* not come to Christ that they might have life.
At the same time, it is true that they cannot, unless they are supernaturally drawn of God; John 5:40; 6:44... [Man] is so blinded by
Satan, so alienated from God by nature and wicked works, so given
up to sin, so averse from that way of salvation which is contrary to his
pride and natural wisdom, that he will not embrace it or seek after it;
and therefore he cannot, till the grace of God powerfully enlightens
his mind, and overcomes his obstacles.

Cardiphonia: Letters to Rev. Mr. Thomas Scott [1:600]; 1:438

At that time Jesus answered and said, I thank thee, O Father, Lord of heaven and earth, because thou hast hid these things from the wise and prudent, and hast revealed them unto babes. Even so, Father: for so it seemed good in thy sight.—Matt. 11:25, 26.

I HAVE seen [dying believers] rejoicing in the prospect of death, free from fears, breathing the air of immortality; heartily disclaiming their duties and performances; acknowledging that their best actions were attended with evil sufficient to condemn them; renouncing every shadow of hope, but what they derived from the blood of Christ, as the sole cause of their acceptance; yet triumphing in him over every enemy and fear, and as sure of heaven as if they were already there. And such were the apostle's hopes, wholly founded on knowing whom he had believed, and his persuasion of his ability to keep that which he had committed unto him. This is faith, a renouncing of everything we are apt to call our own, and relying wholly upon the blood, righteousness, and intercession of Jesus.

True faith, my dear sir, unites the soul to Christ, and thereby gives access to God, and fills it with a peace passing understanding, a hope, a joy unspeakable and full of glory; teaches us that we are weak in ourselves, but enables us to be strong in the Lord, and in the power of his might. To those who thus believe, Christ is precious, their Beloved; they hear and know his voice; the very sound of his name gladdens their hearts, and *he manifests himself to them as he does not to the world.* Thus the Scriptures speak, thus the first Christians experienced; and this is precisely the language which in our days is despised as enthusiasm and folly. For it is now as it was then, though *these things are revealed to babes*, and they are as sure of them as that they see the noon-day sun, they are hidden from the wise and prudent, till the Lord makes them willing to renounce their own wisdom, and to become fools, that they may be truly wise, 1 Cor. 1:18-19; 3:8; 8:2.

Cardiphonia: Letters to Rev. Mr. Thomas Scott, [1:609, 612]; 1:445

*Then Jesus beholding him loved him, and said unto him, One thing thou
lackest: go thy way, sell whatsoever thou hast, and give to the poor, and
thou shalt have treasure in heaven: and come, take up the cross,
and follow me.*—Mark 10:21.

YOU say a death-bed repentance is what you would be sorry to give any hope of. My dear friend, it is well for poor sinners that God's thoughts and ways are as much above men's, as the heavens are higher than the earth. We agreed to communicate our sentiments freely, and promised not to be offended with each other's freedom, if we could help it. I am afraid of offending you by a thought just now upon my mind, and yet I dare not in conscience suppress it: I must therefore venture to say, that I hope they who depend upon such a repentance as your scheme points out, will repent of their repentance itself upon their death-bed at least, if not sooner. You and I, perhaps, should have encouraged the fair-spoken young man, who said he had kept all the commandments from his youth, and rather have left the thief upon the cross to perish like a villain, as he lived. But Jesus thought differently. I do not encourage sinners to defer their repentance to their death-beds; I press the necessity of a repentance this moment. But then I take care to tell them, that repentance is the gift of God; that Jesus is exalted to bestow it; and that all their endeavours that way, unless they seek to him for grace, will be vain… I know the evil heart will abuse the grace of God; the apostle knew this likewise, Rom. 3:8, and 6:3. But this did not tempt him to suppress the glorious grace of the gospel, the power of Jesus to save to the uttermost, and his merciful promise, that whosoever cometh unto him, he will in no wise cast out… But that gracious change of heart, views, and dispositions, which always takes place when Jesus is made known to the soul as having died that the sinner might live, and been wounded that he might be healed; this, at whatever period God is pleased to afford and effect it by his Spirit, brings a sure and everlasting salvation with it.

Cardiphonia: Letters to Rev. Mr. Thomas Scott, [1:615]; 1:450

But God hath revealed them unto us by his Spirit.—1 Cor. 2:10.

THE gospel … is a divine revelation, a discovery of truths which, though of the highest moment, could have been known no other way. That God will forgive sin, is beyond the power of unassisted reason to prove.

And as the subject-matter of the gospel contained in the New Testament is a revelation from God, so it is only by a divine revelation, that what is there read or heard can be truly understood. This is an offensive assertion, but must not be omitted, when the question is concerning the marks and characters of Christ's doctrine. Thus when Peter made that noble confession, 'Thou art Christ the Son of the living God,' our Lord answers, 'Blessed art thou, Simon, for flesh and blood hath not revealed this to thee, but my Father which is in heaven.' If Peter could read, and had the Scriptures to peruse, these were advantages derived from flesh and blood, from his birth, parents, and teachers; advantages which the scribes and Pharisees, our Lord's most inveterate enemies, enjoyed in common with him. The difference lay in a revelation of the truth to his heart. As it is said in another place, 'Thou hast hid these things from the wise and prudent, and revealed them unto babes.'

It is a revelation, in the person of Jesus Christ. As a revelation, it stands distinguished from all false religions; and as revealed in the person of Jesus, it is distinguished from all former dispensations of the true God, who, in time past, had spoken by the prophets, but was pleased, in those last days, to speak unto us by his Son. The law was given by Moses, both to enforce the necessity of a universal sinless obedience, and to point out the *efficacy* of a better mediator; but grace and truth, grace *answerable to the sinner's guilt and misery*, and the truth and full accomplishment of all typical services, came by Jesus Christ. All the grand peculiarities of the gospel centre in this point, the constitution of the person of Christ. In the knowledge of him standeth our eternal life.

Ecclesiastical History: The Character and Genius of the Gospel, [3:18]; 2:384

For I am in a strait betwixt two, having a desire to depart, and to be with Christ; which is far better.—Phil. 1:23.

YOU have heard of the trial with which the Lord has been pleased to visit us; it still continues, though considerably alleviated. It is tempered with many mercies, and I hope he disposes us in a measure to submission. I trust it will be for good. My dear friend, you are coming into my school, where you will learn, as occasions offer, to feel more in the person of another than in your own. But be not discouraged; the Lord only afflicts for good. It is necessary that our sharpest trials should sometimes spring from our dearest comforts, else we should be in danger of forgetting ourselves, and setting up our rest here. In such a world, and with such hearts as we have, we shall often need something to prevent our cleaving to the dust, to quicken us to prayer and to make us feel that our dependence for one hour's peace is upon the Lord alone. I am ready to think I have known as much of the good and happiness which this world can afford, as most people who live in it. I never saw the person with whom I wished to exchange in temporals. And for many years past I have thought my trials have been light and few, compared with what many, or most, of the Lord's people have endured. And yet, though in the main possessed of my own wishes, when I look back upon the twenty-seven years past, I am ready to style them, with Jacob, 'few and evil'… If I take these years to pieces, I see a great part of them was filled up with sins, sorrows, and inquietudes. The pleasures, too, are gone, and have no more real existence than the baseless fabric of a dream. The shadows of the evening will soon begin to come over us; and if our lives are prolonged, a thousand pains and infirmities, from which the Lord has in a remarkable measure exempted us hitherto, will probably overtake us; and at last we must feel the parting pang. *Sic transit gloria mundi.* [So the world's glory vansihes.] Sin has so envenomed the soil of this earth, that the amaranth will not grow upon it. But we are hasting to a better world, and bright unclouded skies, where our sun will go down no more, and all tears shall be wiped from our eyes.

Cardiphonia: Letters to Rev. Mr. John Ryland, Jnr., [1:651]; 1:478

Be kindly affectioned one to another with brotherly love; in honour preferring one another; Not slothful in business; fervent in spirit; serving the Lord.—Rom. 12:10-11.

TO combine zeal with prudence is indeed difficult. There is often too much self in our zeal, and too much of the fear of man in our prudence. However, what we cannot *attain* by any skill or resolution of our own, we may hope in measure to *receive* from him who giveth liberally to those who seek him, and desire to serve him. Prudence is a word much abused; but there is a heavenly wisdom, which the Lord has promised to give to those who humbly wait upon him for it. It does not consist in forming a bundle of rules and maxims, but in a spiritual taste and discernment, derived from an experimental knowledge of the truth, and of the heart of man, as described in the word of God; and its exercise consists much in simple dependence upon the Lord, to guide and prompt us in every action. We seldom act wrong, when we truly depend upon him, and can cease from leaning to our own understanding. When the heart is thus in a right tune and frame, and his word dwells richly in us, there is a kind of immediate perception of what is proper for us to do in present circumstances, without much painful inquiry; a light shines before us upon the path of duty; and if he permits us in such a spirit to make some mistakes, he will likewise teach us to profit by them; and our reflections upon what was wrong one day, will make us to act more wisely the next. At the best, we must always expect to meet with new proofs of our own weakness and insufficiency; otherwise, how should we be kept humble, or know how to prize the liberty he allows us of coming to the throne of grace, for fresh forgiveness and direction every day? But if he enables us to walk before him with a single eye, he will graciously accept our desire of serving him better if we could; and his blessing will make our feeble endeavours in some degree successful, at the same time that we see defects and evils attending our best services sufficient to make us ashamed of them.

Cardiphonia: Letters to Rev. Mr. Matthew Powley, [1:673]; 1:495

O my God, my soul is cast down within me:
therefore will I remember thee.—Psa. 42:6.

IF, as you observe, the Song of Solomon describes the experience of his church, it shows the dark as well as the bright side. No one part of it is the experience of every individual at any particular time. Some are in his banqueting-house, others upon their beds. Some sit under his banner, supported by his arm; have a faint perception of him at a distance, with many a hill and mountain between. In one thing, however, they all agree, that he is the leading object of their desires, and that they have had such a discovery of his person, work, and love, as makes him precious to their hearts. Their judgment of him is always the same, but their sensibility varies. The love they bear him, though rooted and grounded in their hearts, is not always equally in exercise; nor can it be so… Were we always alike, could we always believe, love, and rejoice, we should think the power inherent, and our own; but it is more for the Lord's glory, and more suited to form us to a temper becoming the gospel, that we should be made deeply sensible of our own inability and dependence, than that we should be always in a lively frame. I am persuaded a broken and contrite spirit, a conviction of our vileness and nothingness, connected with a cordial acceptance of Jesus as revealed in the gospel, is the highest attainment we can reach in this life. Sensible comforts are desirable, and we must be sadly declined when they do not appear so to us; but I believe there may be a real exercise of faith and growth in grace, when our sensible feelings are faint and low. A soul may be in as thriving a state when thirsting, seeking, and mourning after the Lord, as when actually rejoicing in him; as much in earnest when fighting in the valley, as when singing upon the mount; nay, dark seasons afford the surest and strongest manifestations of the power of faith. To hold fast the word of promise, to maintain a hatred of sin, to go on steadfastly in the path of duty, in defiance both of the frowns and the smiles of the world, when we have but little comfort, is a more certain evidence of grace, than a thousand things which we may do or forbear when our spirits are warm and lively.

Cardiphonia: Letters to Rev. Mr. Matthew Powley, [1:675]; 1:497

A man can receive nothing, except it be given him from heaven.
—John 3:27.

OBSERVATION and experience contribute, by the grace of God, gradually to soften and sweeten our spirits; but then there will always be ground for mutual forbearance and mutual forgiveness on this head. However, so far as I may judge of myself, I think this hastiness is not my most easily besetting sin. I am not indeed an advocate for that indifference and lukewarmness to the truths of God, which seem to constitute the candour many plead for in the present day. But while I desire to hold fast the sound doctrines of the gospel towards the persons of my fellow creatures, I wish to exercise all moderation and benevolence: Protestants or Papists, Socinians or Deists, Jews, Samaritans, or Mohammedans, all are my neighbours; they have all a claim upon me for the common offices of humanity. As to religion, they cannot all be right; nor may I compliment them by allowing the differences between us are but trivial, when I believe and know they are important; but I am not to expect them to see with my eyes. I am deeply convinced of the truth of John Baptist's aphorism, John 3:27, 'A man can receive nothing, except it be given him from heaven.' I well know, that the little measure of knowledge I have obtained in the things of God has not been owing to my wisdom or docility, but to his goodness. Nor did I get it all at once; he has been pleased to exercise much patience and long-suffering towards me, for about twenty-seven years past, since he first gave me a desire of learning from himself. He has graciously accommodated himself to my weakness, borne with my mistakes, and helped me through innumerable prejudices, which, but for his mercy, would have been insuperable hindrances; I have therefore no right to be angry, impatient, or censorious, especially as I have still much to learn, and am so poorly influenced by what I seem to know.

Cardiphonia: Letters to Mrs. Lucy Thornton, [2:1]; 1:519

Yet the LORD will command his lovingkindness in the daytime,
and in the night his song shall be with me, and my prayer
unto the God of my life.—Psa. 42:8.

REPEATED trying occasions have made me well acquainted with the anxious inquiries with which the busy poring mind is apt to pursue departed friends: it can hardly be otherwise under some circumstances. I have found prayer the best relief. I have thought it very allowable to avail myself to the utmost of every favourable consideration; but I have had the most comfort, when I have been enabled to resign the whole concern into his hands, whose thoughts and ways, whose power and goodness, are infinitely superior to our conceptions. I consider, in such cases, that the great Redeemer can save to the uttermost, and the great Teacher can communicate light, and impress truth, when and how he pleases. I trust the power of his grace and compassion will hereafter triumphantly appear, in many instances, of persons, who, on their dying beds, and in their last moments, have been, by his mercy, constrained to feel the importance and reality of truths which they did not properly understand and attend to in the hour of health and prosperity. Such a salutary change I have frequently, or at least more than once, twice, or thrice, been an eye-witness to, accompanied with such evidence as, I think, has been quite satisfactory. And who can say such a change may not often take place, when the person who is the subject of it is too much enfeebled to give an account to by-standers of what is transacting in his mind! Thus I have encouraged my hope. But the best satisfaction of all is, to be duly impressed with the voice that says, 'Be still, and know that I am God.' These words direct us, not only to his sovereignty, his undoubted right to do what he will with his own, but to all his adorable and amiable perfections, by which he has manifested himself to us in the Son of his love.

Cardiphonia: Letters to Mrs. Lucy Thornton, [2:27]; 1:538

Now the king spake and said unto Daniel, Thy God whom thou servest
continually, he will deliver thee.—Dan. 6:16.

I WRITE not to remind you of what you have lost, but of what you
have, which you cannot lose. May the Lord put a word into my
heart that may be acceptable; and may his good Spirit accompany
the perusal, and enable you to say with the apostle, that, as sufferings
abound, consolations also abound by Jesus Christ. Indeed I can sympathize with you. I remember too the delicacy of your frame, and the
tenderness of your natural spirits; so that were you not interested in
the exceeding great and precious promises of the gospel, I should be
ready to fear you must sink under your trial. But I have some faint
conceptions of the all-sufficiency and faithfulness of the Lord, and
may address you in the king's words to Daniel, 'Thy God whom
thou servest continually, he will deliver thee.' Motives for resignation
to his will abound in his word; but it is an additional and crowning
mercy, that he has promised to apply and enforce them in time of
need. He has said, 'My grace is sufficient for thee; and as thy day is,
so shall thy strength be.' This I trust you have already experienced.
The Lord is so rich, and so good, that he can by a glance of thought
compensate his children for whatever his wisdom sees fit to deprive
them of. If he gives them a lively sense of what he has delivered them
from, and prepared for them, or of what he himself submitted to
endure for their sakes, they find at once light springing up out of
darkness, hard things become easy, and bitter sweet... Yes, madam,
though every stream must fail, the fountain is still full and still flowing. All the comfort you ever received in your dear friend was from
the Lord, who is abundantly able to comfort still; and he is gone but
a little before you. May your faith anticipate the joyful and glorious
meeting you will shortly have in a better world.

Cardiphonia: Letters to Mrs. Sarah Talbot, [2:31]; 1:541

> *And I thank Christ Jesus our Lord, who hath enabled me, for that he*
> *counted me faithful, putting me into the ministry. Who was before a*
> *blasphemer ... but I obtained mercy.*—1 Tim. 1:12-13.

WHAT a privilege is it to be a believer! They are comparatively few, and we by nature were no nearer than others: it
was grace, free grace, that made the difference. What an honour to
be a minister of the everlasting gospel! These upon comparison are
perhaps fewer still. How wonderful that one of these few should be
sought for among the wilds of Africa, reclaimed from the lowest state
of impiety and misery, and brought to assure other sinners, from his
own experience, that 'there is, there is forgiveness with him, that he
may be feared.'

We are called to an honourable service, but it is arduous. What
wisdom does it require to keep the middle path in doctrines, avoiding the equally dangerous errors on the right hand and the left! What
steadiness, to speak the truth boldly and faithfully in the midst of a
gainsaying world! What humility, to stand against the tide of popu-
larity! What meekness, to endure all things for the elect's sake, that
they may be saved! 'Who is sufficient for these things?' We are not in
ourselves, but there is an all-sufficiency in Jesus. Our enemy watches
us close; he challenges and desires to have us, that he may sift us as
wheat; he knows he can easily shake us if we are left to ourselves;
but we have a Shepherd, a Keeper, who never slumbers nor sleeps...
When we are prone to wander, he calls us back; when we say, my feet
slip, his mercy holds us up; when we are wounded, he heals; when
we are ready to faint, he revives. The people of God are sure to meet
with enemies, but especially the ministers: Satan bears them a double
grudge: the world watches for their halting, and the Lord will suffer
them to be afflicted, that they may be kept humble, that they may
acquire a sympathy with the sufferings of others, that they may be
experimentally qualified to advise and help them, and to comfort
them with the comforts with which they themselves have been comforted of God.

Cardiphonia: Letters to Rev. Mr. William Bull, [2:94]; 1:590

Not unto us, O Lord, not unto us, but unto thy name give glory,
for thy mercy, and for thy truth's sake.—Psa. 115:1.

THE enemy assaults me more by sap than storm; and I am ready to think I suffer more by languor than some of my friends do by the sharper conflicts to which they are called. So likewise, in those seasons which comparatively I call my best hours, my sensible comforts are far from lively. But I am in general enabled to hold fast my confidence, and to venture myself upon the power, faithfulness, and compassion of that adorable Saviour to whom my soul has been directed and encouraged to flee for refuge. I am a poor, changeable, inconsistent creature; but he deals graciously with me; he does not leave me wholly to myself; but I have such daily proofs of the malignity and efficacy of the sin that dwelleth in me, as ought to cover me with shame and confusion of face, and make me thankful if I am permitted to rank with the meanest of those who sit at his feet. That I was ever called to the knowledge of his salvation, was a singular instance of his sovereign grace; and that I am still preserved in the way, in defiance of all that has arisen from within and from without to turn me aside, must be wholly ascribed to the same sovereignty: and if, as I trust, he shall be pleased to make me a conqueror at last, I shall have peculiar reason to say, Not unto me, not unto me, but unto thy name, O Lord, be the glory and the praise!

The Lord leads me, in the course of my preaching to insist much on a life of communion with himself, and of the great design of the gospel to render us conformable to him in love… Could I be myself what I recommend to them, I should be happy indeed. Pray for me, my dear friend, that, now the Lord is bringing forward the pleasing spring, he may favour me with a spring season in my soul; for indeed I mourn under a long winter.

Cardiphonia: Letters to Rev. Mr. William Bull, [2:107]; 1:601

For by grace are ye saved through faith; and that not of yourselves: it is the gift of God: Not of works, lest any man should boast.—Eph. 2:8-9.

I HOPE the Lord has contracted my desires and aims almost to the one point of study, the knowledge of his truth. All other acquisitions are transient and comparatively vain. And yet, alas! I am a slow scholar; nor can I see in what respect I get forward, unless that every day I am more confirmed in the conviction of my own emptiness and inability to all spiritual good. And as, notwithstanding this, I am still enabled to stand my ground, I would hope, since no effect can be without an adequate cause, that I have made some advance, though in a manner imperceptible to myself, towards a more simple dependence upon Jesus as my all in all. It is given me to thirst and to taste, if it is not given me to drink abundantly; and I would be thankful for the desire. I see and approve the wisdom, grace, suitableness, and sufficiency of gospel salvation; and since it is for sinners, and I am a sinner, and the promises are open, I do not hesitate to call it mine. I am a weary, laden soul; Jesus has invited me to come, and has enabled me to put my trust in him. I seldom have an uneasy doubt, at least not of any continuance, respecting my pardon, acceptance, and interest in all the blessings of the New Testament. And, amidst a thousand infirmities and evils under which I groan, I have the testimony of my conscience, when under the trial of his word, that my desire is sincerely towards him, that I choose no other portion, that I allowedly serve no other master… O what a mystery is the heart of man! What a warfare is the life of faith (at least in the path the Lord is pleased to lead me)! What reason have I to lie in the dust as the chief of sinners, and what cause for thankfulness that salvation is wholly of grace! Notwithstanding all my complaints, it is still true that Jesus died and rose again; that he ever liveth to make intercession, and is able to save to the uttermost.

Cardiphonia: Letters to Rev. Mr. William Bull, [2:109]; 1:602

Delight thyself also in the LORD;
and he shall give thee the desires of thine heart.—Psa. 37:4.

WORLDLY people expect their schemes to run upon all-fours, as we say, and the objects of their wishes to drop into their mouths without difficulty; and if they succeed, they of course burn incense to their own drag, and say, This was my doing: but believers meet with rubs and disappointments, which convince them, that if they obtain anything, it is the Lord must do it for them. For this reason I observe, that he usually brings a death upon our prospects, even when it is his purpose to give us success in the issue. Thus we become more assured that we did not act in our own spirits, and have a more satisfactory view that his providence has been concerned in filling up the rivers and removing the mountains that were in our way. Then when he has given us our desire, how pleasant it is to look at it and say, This I got, not by my own sword, and my own bow; but I wrestled for it in prayer, I waited for it in faith, I put it into the Lord's hand, and from his hand I received it.

You have met with the story of one of our kings (if I mistake not) who wanted to send a nobleman abroad as his ambassador, and he desired to be excused on account of some affairs which required his presence at home: the king answered, 'Do you take care of my business, and I will take care of yours.' I would have you think the Lord says thus to you. You were sent into the world for a nobler end than to be pinned to a girl's apron-string; and yet if the Lord sees it not good for you to be alone, he will provide you a help-mate. I say, if he sees the marriage state best for you, he has the proper person *already* in his eye; and though she were in Peru or Nova Zembla, he knows how to bring you together... Believe, likewise, that as the Lord has the appointment of the person, so he fixes the time. His time is like the time of the tide; all the art and power of man can neither hasten nor retard it a moment; it must be waited for; nothing can be done without it, and, when it comes, nothing can resist it.

Cardiphonia: Letters to Rev. Mr. John Ryland, Jnr., [2:124]; 1:613

Good and upright is the Lord: *therefore will he teach sinners in the way.*
The meek will he guide in judgment: and the meek
will he teach his way.—Psa. 25:8, 9.

IT is unbelief that talks of delays: faith knows that, properly, there can be no such thing. The only reason why the Lord seems to delay what he afterwards grants is, that the best hour is not yet come. I know you have been enabled to commit and resign your all to his disposal. You did well. May he help you to stand to the surrender. Sometimes he will put us to the trial, whether we mean what we say. He takes his course in a way we did not expect; and then, alas! how often does the trial put us to shame! Presently there is an outcry raised in the soul against his management; this is wrong, that unnecessary, the other has spoiled the whole plan; in short, all these things are against us. And then we go into the pulpit, and gravely tell the people how wise and how good he is; and preach submission to his will, not only as a duty, but a privilege! Alas, how deceitful is the heart! Yet since it is and will be so, it is necessary we should know it by experience. We have reason, however, to say, he is good and wise; for he bears with our perverseness, and in the event shows us that if he had listened to our murmurings, and taken the methods we would have prescribed to him, we should have been ruined indeed, and that he has been all the while doing us good in spite of ourselves.

If I judge right, you will find your way providentially opened more and more; and yet it is possible, that when you begin to think yourself sure, something may happen to put you in a panic again. But a believer, like a sailor, is not to be surprised if the wind changes, but to learn the art of suiting himself to all winds for the time; and though many a poor sailor is shipwrecked, the poor believer shall gain his port. O it is good sailing with an infallible Pilot at the helm, who has the wind and weather at his command.

Cardiphonia: Letters to Rev. Mr. John Ryland, Jnr., [2:125]; 1:614

And … the LORD God … brought her unto the man.—Gen. 2:22.

SURELY when he crosses our wishes it is always in mercy, and because we short-sighted creatures often know not what we ask, nor what would be the consequences if our desires were granted.

Your pride it seems has received a fall by meeting a repulse. I know self does not like to be mortified in these affairs; but if you are made successful in wooing souls for Christ, I hope that will console you for meeting a rebuff when only wooing for yourself… Perhaps all your difficulties have arisen from this, that you have not yet seen the right person; if so, you have reason to be thankful that the Lord would not let you take the wrong, though you unwittingly would have done it if you could. Where the right one lies hid, I know not, but upon a supposition that it will be good for you to marry, I may venture to say, *Ubi ubi est, diu celari non potest.* [Wherever she is, she cannot lie hidden for long.] The Lord in his providence will disclose her, put her in your way, and give you to understand, This is she. Then you will find your business go forward with wheels and wings, and have cause to say, his choice and time were better than your own.

Did I not tell you formerly, that if you would take care of his business he will take care of yours? I am of the same mind still. He will not suffer them who fear him and depend upon him to want any thing that is truly good for them. In the mean while, I advise you to take a lodging as near as you can to Gethsemane, and to walk daily to Mount Golgotha, and borrow (which may be had for asking) that telescope which gives a prospect into the unseen world. A view of what is passing within the veil has a marvellous effect to compose our spirits, with regard to the little things that are daily passing here. Praise the Lord, who has enabled you to fix your supreme affection upon him who is alone the proper and suitable object of it, and from whom you cannot meet a denial or fear a change.

Cardiphonia: Letters to Rev. Mr. John Ryland, Jnr., [2:127]; 1:616

Thou therefore ... be strong in the grace that is in Christ Jesus.—2 Tim. 2:1.

I HAVE rejoiced to see the beginning of a good and gracious work in you; and I have confidence in the Lord Jesus, that he will carry it on and complete it; and that you will be amongst the number of those who shall sing redeeming love to eternity. Therefore fear none of the things appointed for you to suffer by the way; but gird up the loins of your mind, and hope to the end. Be not impatient, but wait humbly upon the Lord. You have one hard lesson to learn, that is, the evil of your own heart: you know something of it, but it is needful that you should know more; for the more we know of ourselves, the more we shall prize and love Jesus and his salvation. I hope what you find in yourself by daily experience will humble you, but not discourage you; humble you it should, and I believe it does. Are not you amazed sometimes that you should have so much as a hope that, poor and needy as you are, the Lord thinketh of you? But let not all you feel discourage you; for if our Physician is almighty, our disease cannot be desperate; and if he casts none out that come to him, why should you fear? Our sins are many, but his mercies are more: our sins are great, but his righteousness is greater: we are weak, but he is power. Most of our complaints are owing to unbelief, and the remainder of a legal spirit; and these evils are not removed in a day. Wait on the Lord and he will enable you to see more and more of the power and grace of our High Priest. The more you know him, the better you will trust him; the more you trust him, the better you will love him; the more you love him, the better you will serve him. This is God's way: you are not called to buy, but to beg; not to be strong in yourself, but in the grace that is in Christ Jesus.

Cardiphonia: Letters to Sally Johnson, [2:140]; 2:6

Now ... Daniel ... went into his house; and his windows being open in
his chamber toward Jerusalem, he kneeled upon his knees three times a
day, and prayed, and gave thanks before his God, as he did aforetime.
—Dan. 6:10.

I WAS far from well on the Tuesday, but supposed it owing to the fatigue of riding, and the heat of the weather; but the next day I was taken with a shivering, to which a fever succeeded. I was then near sixty miles from home. The Lord gave me much peace in my soul, and I was enabled to hope he would bring me safe home, in which I was not disappointed... I have reason to speak much of his goodness, and to kiss the rod, for it was sweetened with abundant mercies... Thus he fulfils his promise in making our strength equal to our day; and every new trial gives us a new proof how happy it is to be enabled to put our trust in him.

I hope, in the midst of all your engagements, you find a little time to read his good word, and to wait at his mercy-seat. It is good for us to draw nigh to him. It is an honour that he permits us to pray; and we shall surely find he is a God hearing prayer. Endeavour to be diligent in the means; yet watch and strive against a legal spirit, which is always aiming to represent him as a hard master, watching, as it were, to take advantage of us. But it is far otherwise. His name is Love: he looks upon us with compassion; he knows our frame, and remembers that we are but dust; and when our infirmities prevail, he does not bid us despond, but reminds us that we have an Advocate with the Father, who is able to pity, to pardon, and to save to the uttermost. Think of the names and relations he bears. Does he not call himself a Saviour, a Shepherd, a Friend, and a Husband? Has he not made known unto us his love, his blood, his righteousness, his promises, his power, and his grace, and all for our encouragement? Away with all doubting, unbelieving thoughts; they will not only distress your heart, but weaken your hands... Be strong, therefore, not in yourself, but in the grace that is in Christ Jesus.

Cardiphonia: Letters to Sally Johnson, [2:142]; 2:8

Thou therefore endure hardness, as a good soldier of Jesus Christ.
—2 Tim. 2:3.

I CAN sympathize with you in your troubles; yet, knowing the nature of our calling, that by an unalterable appointment, the way to the kingdom lies through many tribulations, I ought to rejoice, rather than otherwise, that to you it is given, not only to believe, but also to suffer. If you escaped these things, whereof all the Lord's children are partakers, might not you question your adoption into his family? How could the power of grace be manifest, either to you, in you, or by you, without afflictions? How could the corruptions and devastations of the heart be checked without a cross? How could you acquire a tenderness and skill in speaking to them that are weary, without a taste of such trials as they also meet with?… But the Lord will take better care of those whom he loves and designs to honour. He will try, and permit them to be tried, in various ways. He will make them feel much in themselves, that they may know how to feel much for others.

The root of pride lies deep in our fallen nature, and, where the Lord has given natural and acquired abilities, it would grow apace, if he did not mercifully watch over us, and suit his dispensations to keep it down. Therefore I trust he will make you willing to endure hardships, as a good soldier of Jesus Christ. May he enable you to behold him with faith holding out the prize, and saying to you, Fear none of those things that thou shalt suffer; be thou faithful unto death, and I will give thee a crown of life.

We sail upon a turbulent and tumultuous sea; but we are embarked on a good bottom, and in a good cause, and we have an infallible and almighty Pilot, who has the winds and weather at his command, and can silence the storm into a calm with a word whenever he pleases.

Cardiphonia: Letters to Mr. Bryan Collins, [2:153]; 2:16

Humble yourselves therefore under the mighty hand of God,
that he may exalt you in due time.—1 Pet. 5:6.

THE complaints you make are inseparable from a spiritual acquaintance with our own hearts: I would not wish you to be less affected with a sense of indwelling sin. It becomes us to be humbled into the dust: yet our grief, though it cannot be too great, may be under a wrong direction; and if it leads us to impatience or distrust, it certainly is so.

Sin is the sickness of the soul, in itself mortal and incurable, as to any power in heaven or earth but that of the Lord Jesus only. But he is the great, the infallible Physician. Have we the privilege to know his name? Have we been enabled to put ourselves into his hand? We have then no more to do but to attend his prescriptions, to be satisfied with his methods, and to wait his time. It is lawful to wish we were well; it is natural to groan, being burdened; but still he must and will take his own course with us; and, however dissatisfied with ourselves, we ought still to be thankful that he has begun his work in us, and to believe that he will also make an end. Therefore while we mourn, we should likewise rejoice; we should encourage ourselves to expect all that he has promised; and we should limit our expectations by his promises... He has appointed that sanctification should be effected, and sin mortified, not at once completely, but by little and little; and doubtless he has wise reasons for it. Therefore, though we are to desire a growth in grace, we should, at the same time, acquiesce in his appointment, and not be discouraged or despond, because we feel that conflict which his word informs us will only terminate with our lives.

It is by the experience of these evils within ourselves, and by feeling our utter insufficiency, either to perform duty or to withstand our enemies, that the Lord takes occasion to show us the suitableness, the sufficiency, the freeness, the unchangeableness of his power and grace.

Cardiphonia: Letters to Mrs. Hannah Wilberforce, [2:169]; 2:28

My soul, wait thou only upon God; for my expectation is from him.
—Psa. 62:5.

I HOPE the Lord will give me an humble sense of what I am, and that broken and contrite frame of heart in which he delights. This is to me the chief thing. I had rather have more of the mind that was in Christ, more of a meek, quiet, resigned, peaceful, and loving disposition, than to enjoy the greatest measure of sensible comforts, if the consequence should be (as perhaps it would) spiritual pride, self-sufficiency, and a want of that tenderness to others which becomes one who has reason to style himself the chief of sinners.

What reason have we to charge our souls in David's words! 'My soul, wait thou *only* upon God.' A great stress should be laid upon that word *only*. We dare not entirely shut him out of our regards, but we are too apt to suffer something to share with him. This evil disposition is deeply fixed in our hearts; and the Lord orders all his dispensations towards us with a view to rooting it out; that, being wearied with repeated disappointments, we may at length be compelled to betake ourselves to him alone. Why else do we experience so many changes and crosses? why are we so often in heaviness? We know that he delights in the pleasure and prosperity of his servant; that he does not willingly afflict or grieve his children; but there is a necessity on our parts, in order to teach us that we have no stability in ourselves, and that no creature can do us good but by his appointment. While the people of Israel depended upon him for food, they gathered up the manna every morning in the field; but when they would hoard it up in their houses, that they might have a stock within themselves, they had it without his blessing, and it proved good for nothing; it soon bred worms, and grew offensive. We may often observe something like this occurs, both in our temporal and spiritual concerns.

Cardiphonia: Letters to Mrs. Hannah Wilberforce, [2:186]; 2:41

...him with whom we have to do.—Heb. 4:13.

CEASE from man, cease from creatures, for wherein are they to be accounted of? My soul, wait thou *only, only* upon the Lord, who is (according to the expressive phrase, Heb. 4:13), he with whom we have to do for soul and body, for time and eternity. What thanks do we owe, that though we have not yet attained perfectly this great lesson, yet we are admitted into that school where alone it can be learnt; and though we are poor, slow scholars, the great and effectual Teacher to whom we have been encouraged and enabled to apply, can and will bring us forward! He communicates not only instructions, but capacities and powers. There is none like him; he can make the blind to see, the deaf to hear, and the dumb to speak: and how great is his condescension and patience! how does he accommodate himself to our weakness, and teach us as we are able to bear!... O that we may set him always before us, and consider every dispensation, person, thing, we meet in the course of every day, as messengers from him, each bringing us some *line of instruction* for us to copy into that day's experience! Whatever passes within us or around us may be improved (when he teaches us how) as a perpetual commentary upon his good word. If we converse and observe with this view, we may learn something every moment, wherever the path of duty leads us, in the streets as well as in the closet, and from the conversation of those who know not God, (when we cannot avoid being present at it,) as well as from those who do.

Therefore I can for the most part rejoice, that all things are in the hand and under the direction of him who knows our frame, and has himself borne our griefs, and carried our sorrows, in his own body. A time of weeping must come, but the morning of joy will make amends for all.

Cardiphonia: Letters to Mrs. Hannah Wilberforce, [2:188]; 2:42

Now no chastening for the present seemeth to be joyous, but grievous:
nevertheless afterward it yieldeth the peaceable fruit of righteousness
unto them which are exercised thereby.—Heb. 12:11.

MUCH we read and much we hear concerning the emptiness, vanity, and uncertainty of the present state. When our minds are enlightened by his Holy Spirit, we receive and acknowledge what his word declares to be truth: yet if we remain long without changes, and our path is very smooth, we are for the most part but faintly affected with what we profess to believe. But when some of our dearest friends are taken from us, the lives of others threatened, and we ourselves are brought low with pain and sickness, then we not only *say* but *feel* that this must not, cannot be our rest. You have had several exercises of this kind of late in your family, and I trust you will be able to set your seal to that gracious word, That though afflictions in themselves are not joyous, but grievous, yet in due season they yield the peaceful fruits of righteousness. Various and blessed are the fruits they produce. By affliction prayer is quickened, for our prayers are very apt to grow languid and formal in a time of ease. Affliction greatly helps us to understand the Scriptures, especially the promises; most of which being made to times of trouble, we cannot so well know their fulness, sweetness, and certainty, as when we have been in the situation to which they are suited, have been enabled to trust and plead them, and found them fulfilled in our own case. We are usually indebted to affliction as the means or occasion of the most signal discoveries we are favoured with of the wisdom, power, and faithfulness of the Lord. These are best observed by the evident proofs we have that he is near to support us under trouble, and that he can and does deliver us out of it... Afflictions do us good likewise, as they make us more acquainted with what is in our own hearts, and thereby promote humiliation and self-abasement... But I must write a sermon rather than a letter, if I would enumerate all the good fruits which, by the power of sanctifying grace, are produced from this bitter tree.

Cardiphonia: Letters to Mrs. Hannah Wilberforce, [2:197]; 2:49

The disciple is not above his master, nor the servant above his lord.
—Matt. 10:24.

WHAT! The Master *always* a man of sorrow and acquainted with grief, and the servant *always* happy and full of comfort! Jesus despised, reproached, neglected, opposed, and betrayed; and his people admired and caressed: *he* living in the want of all things, and *they* filled with abundance: *he* sweating blood for anguish, and *they* strangers to distress: how unsuitable would these things be! How much better to be called to the honour of filling up the measure of his sufferings! A cup was put into his hand on our account, and his love engaged him to drink it for us. The wrath which it contained he drank wholly himself; but he left us a little affliction to taste, that we might pledge him and remember how he loved us, and how much more he endured for us than he will ever call us to endure for him. Again, how could we without sufferings manifest the nature and truth of gospel grace? What place should we then have for patience, submission, meekness, forbearance, and a readiness to forgive, if we had nothing to try us either from the hand of the Lord or from the hand of men? A Christian without trials would be like a mill without wind or water... Nor would our graces grow, unless they were called out to exercise: the difficulties we meet with not only prove but strengthen the graces of the Spirit. If a person was always to sit still, without making use of legs or arms, he would probably wholly lose the power of moving his limbs at last; but by walking and working he becomes strong and active. So, in a long course of ease, the powers of the new man would certainly languish; the soul would grow soft, indolent, cowardly, and faint; and therefore the Lord appoints his children such dispensations as make them strive, and struggle, and pant; they must press through a crowd, swim against a stream, endure hardships, run, wrestle, and fight, and thus their strength grows in the using.

Cardiphonia: Letters to Mrs. Harvey, [2:218]; 2:65

> *But I have trusted in thy mercy;*
> *my heart shall rejoice in thy salvation.*—Psa. 13:5.

AT present it is January with me, both within and without. The outward sun shines and looks pleasant; but his beams are faint, and too feeble to dissolve the frost. So is it in my heart; I have many bright and pleasant beams of truth in my view, but cold predominates in my frost-bound spirit, and they have but little power to warm me. I could tell a stranger something about Jesus that would perhaps astonish him: such a glorious person! Such wonderful love! Such humiliation! Such a death! And then what he is now in himself, and what he is to his people! What a sun! What a Shield! What a Root! What a Life! What a Friend! My tongue can run on upon these subjects sometimes; and could my heart keep pace with it, I should be the happiest fellow in the country. Stupid creature! to know these things so well, and yet be no more affected with them! Indeed I have reason to be upon ill terms with myself! It is strange that pride should ever find anything in my experience to feed upon; but this completes my character for folly, vileness, and inconsistence, that I am not only poor, but proud; and though I am convinced I am a very wretch, and nothing before the Lord, I am prone to go forth among my fellow creatures as though I were wise and good.

I dare not say I am absolutely idle, or that I wilfully waste much of my time. I have seldom one hour free from interruption. Letters come that must be answered, visitants that must be received, business that must be attended to. I have a good many sheep and lambs to look after, sick and afflicted souls, dear to the Lord... Amongst these various avocations, night comes before I am ready for noon... O precious, irrecoverable time! O that I had more wisdom in redeeming and improving thee! Pray for me, that the Lord may teach me to serve him better.

Cardiphonia: Letters to Rev. Mr. William Bull, [2:232]; 2:76

*The LORD is good, a strong hold in the day of trouble;
and he knoweth them that trust in him.*—Nah. 1:7.

ONE thing is needful: to have our hearts united to the Lord in humble faith; to set him always before us; to rejoice in him as our Shepherd and our portion; to submit to all his appointments, not of necessity, because he is stronger than we, but with a cheerful acquiescence, because he is wise and good, and loves us better than we do ourselves; to feed upon his truth; to have our understandings, wills, affections, imaginations, memory, all filled and impressed with the great mysteries of redeeming love; to do all for him, to receive all from him, to find all in him. I have mentioned many things, but they are all comprised in one, a life of faith in the Son of God. We are empty vessels in ourselves, but we cannot remain empty. Except Jesus dwells in our hearts, and fills them with his power and presence, they will be filled with folly, vanity, and vexation.

I rejoice on your account, to see you supported and comforted, and enabled to say, he has done all things well. I rejoice on my own account. Such instances of his faithfulness and all-sufficiency are very encouraging. We must all expect hours of trouble in our turn. We must all feel in our concernments the vanity and uncertainty of creature comforts. What a mercy is it to know from our own past experience, and to have it confirmed to us by the experience of others, that the Lord is good, a strong hold in the day of trouble, and that he knoweth them that trust in him. Creatures are like candles; they waste while they afford us a little light, and we see them extinguished in their sockets one after another. But the light of the sun makes amends for them all. The Lord is so rich that he easily can, so good that he certainly will, give his children more than he ever will take away. When his gracious voice reaches the heart, It is I, be not afraid; Be still, and know that I am God; when he gives us an impression of his wisdom, power, love, and care, then the storm which attempts to rise in our natural passions is hushed into a calm; the flesh continues to feel, but the spirit is made willing.

Cardiphonia: Letters to Rev. Mr. William Bull, [2:253]; 2:94

Open thou mine eyes, that I may behold wondrous things
out of thy law.—Psa. 119:18.

DAVID says, 'Open thou mine eyes, that I may behold wondrous things out of thy law,' Psa. 119. He knew there were wonderful things contained in the law, but confesses himself incapable of discerning them till the Lord should interpose. This he has promised to do in behalf of all who call upon him. But those who seek not assistance from God can find it nowhere else: for 'every good and perfect gift is from above, and cometh down from the Father of lights,' James 1, who hath said, 'If any man lack wisdom, let him ask of God.' A critical knowledge of the original languages, a skill in the customs and manners of the ancients, an acquaintance with the Greek and Roman classics, a perusal of councils, fathers, scholiasts, and commentators, a readiness in the subtleties of logical disputation; these, in their proper place and subserviency, may be of considerable use to clear, illustrate, or enforce the doctrines of Scripture: but unless they are governed by a temper of humility and prayer; unless the man that possess them accounts them altogether as nothing, without that assistance of the Spirit of God which is promised to guide believers into all truth; unless he seeks and prays for this guidance no less earnestly than those who understand nothing but their mother-tongue; I make no scruple to affirm, that all his *apparatus* of knowledge only tends to lead him so much the further astray; and that a plain honest ploughman, who reads no book but his Bible, and has no teacher but the God to whom he prays in secret, stands abundantly fairer for the attainment of true skill in divinity. But happy he, who, by faith and prayer, can realize the Divine presence always with him! who is sincere in his intentions, diligent in the use of means, diffident of himself, yet full of trust and hope, that God, whom he desires to serve, will lead and guide him in the paths of peace and righteousness for his mercy's sake, Psa. 31.

On Searching the Scriptures, [2:328]; 2:158

...that it might be fulfilled which was spoken by the prophets.
—Matt. 2:23.

THE first glimmering of light which dawned upon a lost world was that promise ... which God (who in the midst of 'judgment, remembers mercy') made to the woman, that 'her seed should bruise the serpent's head,' Gen. 3... In the time of Noah, the Hope and Desire of all nations was restrained to the line of Shem, Gen. 9, and afterwards more expressly to the family of Abraham... Jacob had twelve sons, which made a still more explicit restriction necessary: accordingly, the patriarch, before his death, declared this high privilege of perpetuating the line of Messiah was fixed in the tribe of Judah, Gen. 49, and the time of his advent was obscurely marked out, by the promise, 'that the sceptre should not depart from Judah till the Shiloh come.' The last personal limitation was to David, 1 Chron. 17, that of *his* family God would raise up the King, who should reign for ever, and over all. Succeeding prophets gradually foretold the time, place, and circumstances of his birth, the actions of his life, the tenor of his doctrine, the success he met with, and the cause, design, and manner of his sufferings and death; in short, to almost everything that we read in the gospel, we may annex the observation that the evangelists have made upon a few instances, (in order, as it may be presumed, to direct us in searching out the rest,) 'then was fulfilled that which was spoken by the prophets.' From them we learn, that the Messiah should be born of a virgin, in Bethlehem of Judah, four hundred and ninety years after the commandment given to rebuild Jerusalem; that he should begin his ministry in Galilee; that he should be despised and rejected of men, betrayed by one of his disciples, sold for thirty pieces of silver, with which money the Potter's field should be afterwards purchased; 'that he should be cut off, but not for himself;' and that his death should be followed by the sudden and total ruin of the Jewish government. To compare these promises and prophecies among themselves ... would afford us the most convincing proofs of their Divine original and excellence.

On Searching the Scriptures, [2:330]; 2:159

...the figure of him that was to come.—Rom. 5:14.

THE types of Christ in the Old Testament may be considered as two-fold, personal and relative: the former describing, under the veil of history, his character and offices as considered in himself; the latter teaching, under a variety of metaphors, the advantages those who believe in him should receive from him. Thus Adam, Enoch, Melchizedek, Isaac, Joseph, Moses, Aaron, Joshua, Samson, David, Solomon, and others, were, in different respects, types of figures of Christ. Some more immediately represented his person; others prefigured his humiliation; others referred to his exaltation, dominion, and glory. So, in the latter sense, the ark of Noah, the rainbow, the manna, the brazen serpent, the cities of refuge, were so many emblems pointing out the nature, necessity, means, and security of that salvation which the Messiah was to establish for his people.

The like may be said of the Levitical ceremonies. The law of Moses is, in this sense, a happy schoolmaster to lead us unto Christ, Gal. 3: and it may be proved beyond contradiction, that in these the gospel was preached of old to all those *Israelites indeed*, whose hearts were right with God, and whose understandings were enlightened by his Spirit. The ark of the covenant, the mercy-seat, the tabernacle, the incense, the altar, the offerings, the high priest with his ornaments and garments, the laws relating to the leprosy, the Nazarite, and the redemption of lands;—all these ... had a deep and important meaning beyond their outward appearance; each, in their place, pointed to 'the Lamb of God who was to take away the sins of the world,' John 1, derived their efficacy *from him*, and received their full accomplishment *in him*.

Thus the Old and New Testament do mutually illustrate each other; nor can either be well understood singly. The Old Testament, in histories, types, prophecies, and ceremonies, strongly delineate him who, in the fulness of time, was to come into the world to effect a reconciliation between God and man. The New Testament shows, that all these characters and circumstances were actually fulfilled in Jesus of Nazareth; that it was he of whom 'Moses in the law and the prophets did write;' and that we are not to look for another.

On Searching the Scriptures, [2:332]; 2:160

...him that justifieth the ungodly.—Rom. 4:5.

MAN having departed from God, 'became vain in his imaginations; and his foolish heart was darkened,' Rom. 1, so that he totally lost the knowledge of his Creator, and how entirely his happiness depended thereon. He forgot God and himself, and sunk so low as to worship the work of his own hands. His life became vain and miserable; in prosperity, without security or satisfaction; in adversity, without support or resource; his death dark and hopeless; no pleasing reflection on the past, no ray of light on the future. Such was the unhappy case when Christ undertook the office of a Prophet; in which character, under various dispensations, first by his servants inspired of old, and afterwards more clearly in his own person, and by his apostles, he has instructed us in the things pertaining to our peace; not only renewing in us the knowledge of the true God, which, where revelation prevailed not, was universally lost out of the world, but disclosing to us the counsels of Divine love and wisdom in our favour, those great things 'which eye hath not seen, nor ear heard,' and which never could have entered 'into the heart of man to conceive,' had not he who dwelt in the bosom of the Father declared them to us. We can now give a sufficient answer to that question, which must have for ever overwhelmed every serious awakened mind, 'Wherewithal shall I appear before the Most High God,' Mic. 6. We have now learnt how God can declare and illustrate his righteousness and truth, by that very act which, without respect to satisfaction given, would seem the highest impeachment of both; I mean, his justifying the ungodly. We have now a *glass* by which we can discover the presence of the Creator in every part of his creation, and a *clue* to lead us through the mysterious mazes of Divine Providence.

On Searching the Scriptures, [2:344]; 2:170

For the law made nothing perfect, but the bringing in of a better hope did; by the which we draw nigh unto God.—Heb. 7:19.

THE principal parts of the priest's office were, to sacrifice in behalf of the people, to make atonement, to pray for them, and to bless them in the name of the Lord. No sacrifices could be offered or accepted, no blessings expected, but through the hands of the priests whom God had appointed. Thus Christ, the High Priest of our profession, offered himself a sacrifice without either spot or blemish: he entered with his own blood within the veil, to the immediate presence of our offended God; and through him peace and good-will is proclaimed to sinful men. He continues still to exercise the other part of his appointment; he makes continual intercession for his people; he presents their prayers and imperfect services acceptable before the throne; he gives them confidence and access to draw nigh to God; and he bestows upon them those gifts and blessings which are the fruits of his sufferings and obedience. The Levitical priests were, like their people, sinners; and were therefore constrained first to make atonement for themselves; they were mortal, therefore their service passed from hand to hand; their sacrifices were imperfect, therefore needed continual repetition, and had at last only a typical and ceremonial efficacy; 'for it was not possible that the blood of bulls and goats,' Heb. 9 and 10, could remove either the guilt or pollution of sin. 'The law made nothing perfect.' But Jesus, the 'Mediator of the New Covenant,' is 'such a High Priest as became us; holy, harmless, undefiled, separate from sinners; who needeth not (as those of old) to offer sacrifice first for his own sins, and then for the people; for this he did once, when he offered up himself,' Heb. 7. The great inference from this doctrine, several times repeated by the apostle in a variety of phrase, is, that we may now have boldness to appear before God, that our prayers and services are pleasing in his sight, and all the blessings of grace and glory ready to be bestowed on us, if we faithfully apply for them, through the merits of his Son.

On Searching the Scriptures, [2:347]; 2:171

Surely he shall deliver thee from the snare of the fowler,
and from the noisome pestilence.—Psa. 91:3.

MAN is not only ignorant of God and himself, and too full of guilt to plead in his own name, but he is likewise weak and defenceless; unable to make his way through the opposition that withstands his progress to eternal life, or to secure him from the many enemies 'that rise up against him,' Psa.3... [The] soul that is desirous to submit to Jesus Christ, immediately finds itself in the midst of war: the world, the flesh, and the devil, unite their forces, either to recall such a one to the practice and service of sin, or to distress him to the uttermost for forsaking it. And none could support this conflict, if not themselves supported by a higher hand. But Jesus, the antitype of Joshua, the true Captain of the Lord's hosts, reveals himself in his word as the King of his church. He can inspire the fainting soul with unseen supplies: he, 'when the enemy comes in like a flood,' Isa. 59, can by his Spirit lift up a standard against him; he can take the prey even out of the hand of the mighty. He has said it of his church in general, and he will make it good to every individual that trusts in him, that the gates of hell shall never prevail against them. What though a sense of the guilt and remaining power of sin often fills the humble soul with inexpressible distress? He that stills the raging of the sea, and the violence of the winds, with a word, can, with equal ease, calm all the unruly motions of the mind. What though the world opposes in every quarter, and presents snares or terrors all around? what though rage or contempt, threats or allurements, are by turns, or all together, employed to ruin us? Behold, 'greater is he that is in us, than he that is in the world', 1 John 4, and has promised to make us conquerors, yea more than conquerors, in our turn. What though 'the devil goes about like a roaring lion, seeking whom he may devour?' 1 Pet. 5. It is an argument of the strongest kind for watchfulness and prayer; but we need not fear him: the 'beloved of the Lord shall dwell in safety,' Deut. 33; 'the Lord shall cover him all the day long; he shall deliver him from the snare of the fowler,' Psa. 91.

On Searching the Scriptures, [2:348]; 2:172

...they received the word with all readiness of mind, and searched the scriptures daily, whether those things were so.—Acts 17:11.

SOME of us, I hope, do already make conscience of frequent reading the Scriptures; but let us remember the force of the word *search*. It is not a careless superficial reading, or dispatching such a number of chapters in a day, as a task, that will answer the end. I have already reminded you, that it is a business will need your best application; a serious, impartial, humble, persevering inquiry, accompanied with earnest prayer for the light and assistance of God's Holy Spirit. When we set about it in this method, we shall soon find happy effects; pleasure and instruction will go hand in hand, and our knowledge advance as the growing light. The precepts shall inspire us with true wisdom; teach us how to order all our affairs respecting both worlds, to fill up our several stations in life with propriety, usefulness, and comfort; and to avoid the numerous evils and distresses which those who live by no rule, or by any other rule than God's word, are perpetually running into. The *promises* shall be a support in every trouble, a medicine in every sickness, a supply in every need. Above all, the Scriptures will repay our trouble, as they testify of Christ. The more we read of his person, offices, power, love, doctrine, life, and death, the more our hearts will cleave to him: we shall, by insensible degrees, be transformed into his spirit. We shall, with the apostle, say, 'I know in whom I have believed,' 2 Tim. 1. Everything we see shall be at once a *memorial* to remind us of our Redeemer, and a *motive* to animate us in his service. And at length we shall be removed to see him as he is, without a cloud, and without a veil; to be for ever with him; to behold, and to share the glories of that heavenly kingdom 'which (Matt. 25) he has prepared (for his followers) from before the foundation of the world.' Amen.

On Searching the Scriptures, [2:353]; 2:176

Hath not the potter power over the clay, of the same lump to make one vessel unto honour, and another unto dishonour?—Rom. 9:21.

THE best relief against those discouragements we meet with from men, is to raise our thoughts to God and heaven. For this the Lord Jesus is our precedent here. He said, 'I thank thee, O Father.'

The Divine Sovereignty is the best thought we can retreat to for composing and strengthening our minds under the difficulties, discouragements, and disappointments, which attend the publication of the gospel. The more we give way to reasonings and curious inquiries, the more we shall be perplexed and baffled. When Jeremiah had been complaining of some things which were too hard for him, the Lord sent him to the potter's house, and taught him to infer, from the potter's power over the clay, the just right which the Lord of all hath to do what he will with his own. It is only the pride of our own hearts that prevents this consideration from being perfectly conclusive and satisfactory. How many schemes derogatory from the free grace of God, tending to darken the glory of the gospel, and to depreciate the righteousness of the Redeemer, have taken their rise from vain unnecessary attempts to vindicate the ways of God; or rather to limit the actings of Infinite Wisdom to the bounds of our narrow understandings, to sound the depths of the Divine counsels with our feeble plummets, and to say to Omnipotence, 'Hitherto shalt thou go, and no further.' But upon the ground of the Divine Sovereignty we may rest satisfied and stable: for if God appoints and overrules all, according to the purpose of his own will, we have sufficient security, both for the present and for the future.

The Small Success of the Gospel Ministry Considered, [2:362]; 2:185

Shall not the Judge of all the earth do right?—Gen. 18:25.

WE may firmly expect, what Scripture and reason concur to assure us, that 'the Judge of all the earth will do right.' Whatever to us appears otherwise in his proceedings, should be charged to the darkness and weakness of our minds. We know, that in every point of science difficulties and objections occur to young beginners, which at first view may seem almost unanswerable; but as knowledge increases, the difficulties gradually subside, and at last we perceive they were *chiefly* owing to the defects of our apprehension. In divinity it is wholly so: 'God is light, and in him is no darkness at all:' his revealed will is, like himself, just, holy, pure in the whole, and perfectly consistent in every part. We may safely rest upon this general maxim, that 'the Judge of all the earth shall do right.' Though he does not give us a particular account of his dealings, and we are not fully able to comprehend them; yet we ought, against all appearances and proud reasonings, to settle it firmly in our minds, that everything is conducted worthy the views which God has given us of himself in his holy word, as being of infinite justice, wisdom, goodness, and truth.

He has appointed a day when he will make it appear that he *has done* right. Though clouds and darkness are now upon his proceedings, they shall ere long be removed. When all his designs in providence and grace are completed; when the present imperfect state of things shall be finished; when the dead, small and great, are summoned to stand before him; then the great Judge will condescend to unfold the whole train of his dispensations, and will justify his proceedings before angels and men; then every presumptuous cavil shall be silenced, every difficulty solved. His people shall admire his wisdom, his enemies shall confess his justice. The destruction of those who perish shall be acknowledged deserved, and of themselves; and the redeemed of the Lord shall ascribe all the glory of their salvation to him alone. What we shall then see, it is now our duty and our comfort assuredly to believe.

The Small Success of the Gospel Ministry Considered, [2:365]; 2:187

*Take heed therefore how ye hear: for whosoever hath, to him shall be
given; and whosoever hath not, from him shall be taken
even that which he seemeth to have.*—Luke 8:18

TAKE heed how you hear. The gospel of salvation, which is
sent to you, will be either a 'savour of life unto life, or of death
unto death,' to every soul of you. There is no *medium*. Though, in a
common and familiar way of speaking, we sometimes complain, that
the gospel is preached without effect, there is in reality no possibility
that it can be without effect. An effect it must and will have upon
all who hear it. Happy they who receive and embrace it as a joyful
sound, the unspeakable gift of God's love. To these it will be 'a savour
of life unto life.' It will communicate life to the soul at first, and
maintain that life, in defiance of all opposition, till it terminates in
glory. But woe, woe to those who receive it not! It will be to them 'a
savour of death unto death.' It will leave them under the sentence of
death, already denounced against them by the law which they have
transgressed; and it will consign them to eternal death, under the
heaviest aggravations of guilt and misery.

The gospel is not proposed to you to ask your opinion of it, that
it may stand or fall according to your decision; but it peremptorily
demands your submission. If you think yourselves qualified to judge
and examine it by that imperfect and depraved light which you call
your reason, you will probably find reasons enough to refuse your
assent. Reason is properly exercised in the ordinary concerns of life,
and has so far a place in religious inquiries, that none can or do
believe the gospel, without having sufficient reasons for it. But you
need a higher light, the light of God's Spirit, without which the most
glorious displays of his wisdom will appear foolishness to you. If you
come simple, dependent, and teachable; if you pray from your heart,
with David, 'Open thou mine eyes, that I may see wondrous things
in thy law,' you will be heard and answered; you will grow in the
knowledge and grace of our Lord Jesus Christ.

The Small Success of the Gospel Ministry Considered, [2:366]; 2:188

But the path of the just is as the shining light, that shineth more
and more unto the perfect day.—Prov. 4:18.

I F the Lord has taught you the secret of them that fear him, if he has
shown you the way of salvation, if he has directed your feet in the
paths of his commandments, then you have the true wisdom which
shall be your light through life, and in death your glory. Therefore,

Be not grieved that ye are strangers to human wisdom and glory.
These things, which others so highly prize, you may resign content-
edly, and say, 'Lord, it is enough if thou art mine.' Nay, you have
good reason to praise his wisdom and goodness for preserving you
from those temptations which have ensnared and endangered so
many.

Do you desire more of this true wisdom? Seek it in the same
way in which you have received the first beginnings. Be frequent and
earnest in secret prayer. Study the word of God, and study it not to
reconcile and make it bend to your sentiments, but to draw all your
sentiments from it to copy it in your heart, and express it in your
conduct. Be cautious of paying too great a regard to persons and
parties. One is your Master, even Christ. Stand fast in the liberty
with which he has made you free; and, while you humbly endeavour
to profit by all, do not resign your understanding to any, but to him
who is the only wise God, the only effectual and infallible Teacher.
Compare the experience of what passes within your own breast, with
the observations you make of what daily occurs around you; and
bring all your remarks and experiences to the touchstone of God's
holy word. Thus shall you grow in knowledge and in grace; and,
amidst the various discouragements which may arise from remaining
ignorance in yourselves or others, take comfort in reflecting, that you
are drawing near to the land of light, where there will be no darkness
at all. Then you shall know as you are known; your love and your
joy shall likewise be perfect, and you shall be satisfied with the rivers
of pleasure which are before the throne of God, world without end.

Of Those from Whom the Gospel Doctrines are Hid, [2:390]; 2:206

And we know that the Son of God is come, and hath given us an under-standing, that we may know him that is true.—1 John 5:20.

B Y nature the will is perverse and rebellious, and the affections alienated from God: the primary cause of these disorders lies in the darkness of the understanding. Here then the change begins. The Spirit of God enlightens the understanding, by which the sinner perceives things to be as they are represented in the word of God; that he is a transgressor against the Divine law, and on this account obnoxious to wrath; that he is not only guilty, but depraved and unclean, and utterly unable either to repair past evil or to amend his own heart and life. He sees that the great God might justly refuse him mercy; and that he has no plea to offer in arrest of judgment. This discovery would sink him into despair, if it went no further; but by the same light which discovers him to himself, he begins to see a suitableness, wisdom, and glory, in the method of salvation revealed in the gospel. He reads and hears concerning the person, sufferings, and offices of Christ, in a very different manner to what he did before; and as, by attending to the word and ministry, his apprehensions of Jesus, and his understanding, become more clear and distinct, a spiritual hope takes place, and increases, in his soul; and the sure effect of this is, he feels his love drawn forth to him who so loved him as to die for his sins. Beholding, by faith, the Lord Jesus Christ, as bleeding and dying upon the cross; and knowing for whom, and on what account, he suffered, he learns to hate, with a bitter hatred, those sins which nailed him there. The amazing love of Christ constrains him to account all things which he formerly valued as dross and dung, for the excellency of the knowledge of his Saviour. Nor does his faith stop here; he views him who once suffered and died, rising triumphant from the tomb, and ascending into heaven in the character of the Representative, Friend, and Forerunner of his people. Having such a High Priest, he is encouraged to draw near to God, to claim an interest in the promises respecting the life that now is, and that which is to come.

The Nature of Spiritual Revelation, [2:395]; 2:210

That the God of our Lord Jesus Christ, the Father of glory, may give unto you
the spirit of wisdom and revelation in the knowledge of him.—Eph. 1:17.

SET a high value upon the word of God. All that is necessary to make you wise to salvation is there, and there only. In this precious book you may find direction for every doubt, a solution of every difficulty, a promise suited to every circumstance you can be in. There you may be informed of your disease by sin, and the remedy provided by grace. You may be instructed to know yourselves, to know God and Jesus Christ, in the knowledge of whom standeth eternal life. The wonders of redeeming love, the glories of the Redeemer's person, the happiness of the redeemed people, the power of faith, and the beauty of holiness, are here represented to the life. Nothing is wanting to make life useful and comfortable, death safe and desirable, and to bring down something of heaven upon earth. But this true wisdom can be found nowhere else. If you wander from the Scripture, in pursuit either of present peace or future hope, your search will end in disappointment. This is the fountain of living waters; if you forsake it, and give the preference to broken cisterns of your own devising, they will fail you when you most need them. Rejoice, therefore, that such a treasure is put into your hand; but rejoice with trembling. Remember this is not all you want; unless God likewise gives you a heart to use it aright, your privilege will only aggravate your guilt and misery. Therefore remember, the necessity of prayer.

For though the things of nearest consequence to you are in the Bible, and you should read it over and over, till you commit the whole book to your memory; yet you will not understand, or discern the truth as it is in Jesus, unless the Lord the Spirit shows it to you. The dispensation of truth is in his hand; and without him all the fancied advantages of superior capacity, learning, criticism, and books, will prove as useless as spectacles to the blind. The great encouragement is, that this infallible Spirit, so necessary to guide us into the way of peace, is promised to all who sincerely ask it. This Spirit, Jesus is exalted to bestow... Therefore water your reading with frequent prayer.

The Nature of Spiritual Revelation, [2:398]; 2:212

*Where is boasting then? It is excluded. By what law? of works? Nay: but
by the law of faith. Therefore we conclude that a man is justified by faith
without the deeds of the law.*—Rom. 3:27, 28.

IF men were saved either in whole, or in part, by their own wisdom
and prudence, they might, in the same degree, ascribe the glory
and praise to themselves. They might say, My own power and wisdom
gave me this; and thus God would be robbed of the honour due to
his name. But now this is prevented. The word of the Lord is, 'Let
not the wise man glory in his wisdom, neither let the mighty man
glory in his might; let not the rich man glory in his riches; but let
him that glorieth glory in this, that he understandeth and knoweth
me, that I am the Lord.' For whatever outward advantages some may
seem to possess, as to the things of God they stand altogether upon
a level with the meanest. These things cannot be understood by any
sagacity on our parts, but must be revealed by the Father of lights.
What could be done in this way, you may collect from St. Paul's rep-
resentation in the first chapter of his Epistle to the Romans. Many of
the heathens were eminent for wisdom and abilities, and made great
proficiency in science; but with regard to the knowledge of God,
the result of all their researches was error, superstition, and idolatry;
professing themselves to be wise, they became fools, and their disquisitions had no other effect than to leave them without excuse. Their
practice (as will always be the case) was correspondent to their principles; and, in the midst of a thousand refinements in theory, they were
abandoned to the grossest and most detestable vices... When there
is a difference, it is owing to grace, and grace is acknowledged. Such
will readily say, 'Not unto us, O Lord, Not unto us, but unto thy
name be praise.' Thus all pretence to boasting is effectually excluded;
and he that can glory upon good grounds, must glory only in the
Lord.

Therefore it is of faith, that it might be by grace; to the end the promise might be sure to all the seed; not to that only which is of the law, but to that also which is of the faith of Abraham.—Rom. 4:16.

LET not any be cast down on account of any peculiar incapacity or difficulty in their case. If none but the wise and the learned, the rich, and those who are esteemed well-behaved and virtuous, could be saved, or if these stood in a fairer way for it than others, the greatest part of mankind might give up hope, and sit down in despair at once. But the case is exactly the reverse. It is true, the persons I am speaking of are not the worse for these distinctions, whenever they are sensible how vain and insufficient they are, and betake themselves, as poor, helpless, miserable, blind, and naked, to flee for refuge to the mercy of God in Christ. But, alas! their supposed qualifications too often harden them to reject the counsel of God against themselves. They think themselves whole, and therefore see not the necessity or value of the Physician. You who are sensible you have nothing of your own to trust to, take encouragement; the Lord has suited his gospel to your circumstances.

In this way the salvation of believers is sure. If it depended on anything in man, it might miscarry. Man's boasted wisdom is soon changed. A few hours of a fever, a small blow on the head, may change a wise man into a fool. 'But it is of grace, to the end that the promise might be sure to all the seed.' Adam had a stock of wisdom; yet when he was trusted with his own happiness, he could not preserve it. But the Second Adam is all-sufficient. Our dependence is upon him. To those who are babes, he is wisdom, righteousness, sanctification, and all that they want. If this concern had been left to the wisdom of man, it is most probable that Christ would have lived and died in vain, without a single real disciple. But now the dispensation of grace is in his hands, we are sure that some will believe in him; and we are likewise sure, that those who truly do so shall never be ashamed of their hope.

The Sovereignty of Grace Asserted and Illustrated, [2:410]; 2:221

He shall feed his flock like a shepherd: he shall gather the lambs with his
arm, and carry them in his bosom, and shall gently lead those
that are with young.—Isa. 40:11.

CHRIST's works of office can be performed by none but God. This might be proved concerning each of the offices he exercises in consequence of his high character as Mediator between God and man.

It is his office to his believing people in this present evil world, to act the part of a Shepherd towards them, to supply their wants of every kind, to direct their steps, to control their enemies, to overrule all things for their good, and to be a very present help in every time of trouble. To execute this important charge, it is necessary that his knowledge, his compassion, his power, and his patience, must be boundless. His eye must be every moment upon all their cases at once; his ear must be incessantly open to receive the prayers of all people, nations, and languages; his arm must be continually stretched out to support so many that stand, to raise up so many that fall, to afford seasonable and suitable supplies, at the same instant, to the distresses and temptations of millions. If this is the office he has undertaken, and if he is acknowledged sufficient and faithful in the discharge of it, what more undeniable evidence can be given, that he has all the attributes we can conceive as essential and peculiar to the Godhead? The provocations, defects, and backslidings of his people, are likewise so numerous, so often repeated, and attended with such black aggravations, that if he was not God, invincible in goodness, unchangeable in purpose, if his mercy was not, as his majesty, infinite, he would be wearied out, and provoked to cast them off for ever. The great reason why he bore with his people of old holds equally strong with respect to us: 'I am the Lord, I change not; therefore ye sons of Jacob are not consumed.'

Of the Person of Christ, [2:421]; 2:229

I will seek that which was lost, and bring again that which was driven away, and will bind up that which was broken, and will strengthen that which was sick.—Ezek. 34:16.

HEALING. This is often necessary; for the spiritual warfare is not to be maintained long without wounds. Our great enemy is so subtle, so watchful, so well provided with temptations adapted to every temper and circumstance; and we are so weak, unpractised, and so often remiss and off our guard, that he will at times prevail to bring us into a dark, barren, backsliding state, despoiled of comfort, and oppressed with fears. But see what a good and gracious Shepherd we have: hear his comfortable words: 'I will seek that which was lost, and bring again that which was driven away, and will bind up that which was broken, and will strengthen that which was sick.'

He has engaged to lead his people safely, through fire and through water. He gives them leave to cast all their care upon him, with an assurance that he careth for them. He has said, 'all things shall work together for their good; that his grace shall be sufficient for them; and that in good time he will bruise Satan under their feet, make them more than conquerors,' and place them out of the reach of sin and sorrow for ever. Besides the habitual peace which arises from the believing consideration of these truths, he has likewise peculiar seasons of refreshment, when he manifests himself to the soul in a way that the world knows not of, and often makes the hour of their sharpest trials the time of their sweetest and highest consolations: 'As the sufferings of Christ abound in us, so our consolation aboundeth by Christ.'

All dispensations are under his direction. He is Lord of all, and does according to his pleasure among the armies of heaven and the inhabitants of the earth.

Those who are thus stayed upon the Lord Jesus, as overruling and managing all their concerns, are not terrified with every shaking leaf; 'their hearts are fixed, trusting in the Lord.'

Of the Authority of Christ, [2:430]; 2:235

*I went out full, and the LORD hath brought me home again empty: why
then call ye me Naomi, seeing the LORD hath testified against me,
and the Almighty hath afflicted me?*—Ruth 1:21.

AFFLICTIVE dispensations are likewise of his sending. And the
consideration of his hand in them, the good he designs us by
them, the assurance we have of being supported under them, and
brought through them; according to the degrees in which these
things are apprehended by faith, and accompanied with a humbling
sense of their own demerits, his people submit to his appointment
with patience and thankfulness, and say, after the pattern which he
has left them, The cup which my Saviour puts into my hand, shall I
not drink it?

In brief, it is he who appointed the time and place of our birth,
and all the successive connections of our lives. Our civil and our religious liberties are both owing to his favour; and in these he has been
peculiarly favourable to *us*. 'He has not dealt so with every nation.'

Our times are in his hands. He claims it as his own prerogative, that he keeps the key of death and the invisible state. None can
remove us sooner, none can detain us a moment longer, than his
call. In this likewise he is little observed. We charge death to fevers,
frights, and falls; but these are only the messengers which he sends.
Sin has brought us all under a sentence of death; but the moment
and the manner of the execution befall us according to his good
pleasure. Till then, though his providence leads us through fire and
water, though we walk upon the brink of a thousand apparent, and a
million of unseen, dangers, we are in reality in perfect safety. Having
appointed St. Paul to stand before Caesar, though the tempest greatly
assaulted, and seemingly overpowered the ship he was in, St. Paul was
as safe on the stormy sea, when all probable hope of being saved was
taken away, as Caesar himself upon his throne. But when his time is
come, in vain are all the assistance of friends, or the healing arts of
medicines, to procure the smallest respite.

Of the Authority of Christ, [2:432]; 2:237

As the hart panteth after the water brooks,
so panteth my soul after thee, O God.—Psa. 42:1.

THE grace of God enabled you both to walk honourably in a single life; I trust the same grace will enable you to adorn your profession in the married state... I take it for granted that you are very happy, that you are united to your husband, not only by marriage, but by mutual affection, and, what is better still, by mutual faith; and that, as you sought the Lord's direction before the connexion was formed, so you came together evidently by his blessing. What then shall I say to you? Only, or chiefly this,—Beware of being too happy—beware of idolatry. Husbands, children, possessions, everything by which the Lord is pleased to afford us content or pleasure, are full of snares. How hard is it to love a creature just as we ought; and so to possess our temporal blessings as neither to overvalue nor undervalue them! How rare is it to see a believer go on steadily, and in a lively, thriving spirit, if remarkably favoured with prosperous circumstances! It is hard, but it is not impossible: impossible, indeed, it is to us; but it is easy to him who has said, 'My grace is sufficient for you.' My desire is, that you may be both witnesses of the Lord's faithfulness to this his good promise. I wish you health, peace, and prosperity; but, above all, that your souls may prosper; that you may still prefer the light of God's countenance to your chief joy; that you may still delight yourselves in the Lord; be daily hungering and thirsting after him, and daily receiving from his fulness, even grace for grace; that you may rejoice in his all-sufficiency, may taste his love in every dispensation; that every blessing of his common providence may come to you as a fruit and token of his covenant love; that the frame of your spirits may be heaven-ward, your conduct exemplary, and your whole conversation may breathe the meekness, simplicity, and spirituality, which become the gospel of Christ.

Sequel to Cardiphonia: Letters to Several Ladies, [6:46]; 4:308

And as it is appointed unto men once to die,
but after this the judgment.—Heb. 9:27.

I F you believe the Scriptures, you acknowledge, that after death there is an appointed judgment, and an unchangeable, everlasting state. If so, should you not carefully examine the ground of your hope, and fear even the possibility of a mistake, which, if not rectified before death, will then be fatal and without remedy? If you would not sign a lease or a contract without examining it for yourselves, why will you venture your eternal concernments implicitly upon the prevailing opinions of those around you? Especially, when our Lord himself has told us, that whoever may be right, the *many* are undoubtedly wrong. For 'wide is the gate, and broad is the way that leadeth to destruction, and *many* there be that go in thereat; because straight is the gate, and narrow is the way that leadeth unto life, and *few* there be that find it.' If for the present you seem confirmed in your manner of thinking and living, by the numbers, names, and examples, of those with whom you agree; yet consider, you must soon be separated from them all. Not one of them will be able to comfort you in a dying hour, to answer for you to God. You may live in a throng, but you must die alone. Religious subjects are seldom the chosen topics of conversation, in what is usually called good company; if occasionally introduced, how superficially are they treated, yet how peremptorily are they decided upon, and then how readily dismissed! But sooner or later their importance will be known. The Scripture is the rule by which we must all be judged at last; it is therefore our wisdom to judge ourselves by it now. Would you be persuaded to do this, praying to God for that assistance which you need to direct your inquiries, and which he has promised he will afford to them that ask him, it would have a happy effect upon your principles and your peace. Search and read for yourselves.

A Token of Affection and Respect, [6:578]; 4:725

Nevertheless I am continually with thee.—Psa. 73:23.

MY dear child, when you look at the sun, I wish it may lead your thoughts to him who made it, and who placed it in the firmament, not only to give us light, but to be the brightest, noblest emblem of himself: there is but one sun, and there needs not another; so there is but one Saviour; but he is complete and all-sufficient, the Sun of Righteousness, the Fountain of life and comfort; his beams, wherever they reach, bring healing, strength, peace, and joy to the soul. Pray to him, my dear, to shine forth, and reveal himself to you. Oh, how different is he from all that you have ever seen with your bodily eyes! he is the Sun of the soul, and he can make you as sensible of his presence as you are of the sunshine at noon-day; and, when once you obtain a clear sight of him, a thousand little things, which have hitherto engaged your attention, will in a manner disappear.

I entreat, I charge you, to ask him every day to show himself to you. Think of him as being always with you; about your path by day, about your bed by night, nearer to you than any object you can see, though you see him not; whether you are sitting or walking, in company or alone. People often consider God as if he saw them from a great distance: but this is wrong; for, though he be in heaven, the heaven of heavens cannot contain him; he is as much with us as with the angels; in him we live, and move, and have our being; as we live in the air which surrounds us, and is within us, so that it cannot be separated from us a moment. And whatever thoughts you can obtain of God from the Scripture, as great, holy, wise, and good, endeavour to apply them all to Jesus Christ, who once died upon the cross, for he is the true God, and eternal life, with whom you have to do; and, though he be the King of kings, and Lord of lords, and rules over all, he is so condescending and compassionate, that he will hear and answer the prayer of a child. Seek him, and you shall find him; whatever else you seek, you may be disappointed, but he is never sought in vain.

Sequel to Cardiphonia: Letters to Newton's Adopted Daughter, [6:289]; 4:504

No man hath seen God at any time; the only begotten Son, which is in
the bosom of the Father, he hath declared him.—John 1:18.

I WISH you to have a deep impression on your mind, that your safety, whether abroad or at home, or the continuance of your health from one hour to another, is not a matter of course, but the effect of the care and goodness of him who knows we are helpless as sheep, and condescends to act the part of a shepherd towards us. May you learn to acknowledge him in all your ways, to pray to him for his blessing, and to praise him daily for his mercies; and then you will do well. This is a great privilege which distinguishes us from the beasts of the field; they likewise owe their preservation to his providence: but then they are not capable of knowing him or thanking him. There are many young people who are contented to live without God in the world; but this is not only their sin, but their shame likewise. They thereby renounce the chief honour they are capable of, and degrade themselves to a level with the beasts. But let it not be so with you. Pray to the Lord to teach you to love him; and, when you think of him, fix your thoughts upon Jesus Christ, upon him who conversed on earth as a man. The great God has manifested himself in a way suited to us, as weak creatures and poor sinners. God is everywhere present, but only those who look to him in Christ can attain to love, trust, or serve him aright. When you read our Saviour's discourses, recorded by the evangelists, attend as if you saw him with your own eyes standing before you; and, when you try to pray, assure yourself, before you begin, that he is actually in the room with you, and that his ear is open to every word you say. This will make you serious, and it will likewise encourage you, when you consider that you are not speaking into the air, or to one who is a great way off; but to One who is very near you, to your best Friend, who is both able and willing to give you everything that is good for you.

Sequel to Cardiphonia: Letters to Newton's Adopted Daughter, [6:293]; 4:506

Remember now thy Creator in the days of thy youth, while the evil days
come not, nor the years draw nigh, when thou shalt say,
I have no pleasure in them.—Eccles. 12:1.

YOU are now at the time of life when you are especially called
upon to remember your Creator and Redeemer, and have the
greatest advantages for doing it. But, if your life is spared, to you
likewise the days will come when you will say, 'I have no pleasure
in them.' But I hope long before they come, you will have some
experience of pleasures which do not at all depend upon youth or
health, or any thing that this world can either give or take away. Seek
the Lord, and you shall live; and you have not far to seek for him: he
is very near you; he is all around you; about your bed by night, and
your path by day. He sees, he notices all you say and do. But I do not
wish you to conceive of him so as to make the thought of him uneasy
to you. Think of him according to the account the evangelists give
of him when he was upon earth; how gracious, compassionate, and
kind he was. If he were upon earth now, would you not wish that I
should lead you to him, that he might lay his hands upon you and
bless you, as he did the children which were brought to him?... Go to
him yourself; though you cannot see him, it is sufficient that he sees
and hears you. Tell him, that you hear and believe he is a Saviour to
many, and beg him to be your Saviour too. Tell him it was not your
own choice, but his providence, that removed you from C—, and
put you under my care, which gave you an opportunity of knowing
more of his goodness than you would otherwise have done; and beg
of him to give you his grace, that the advantages you have had may
not aggravate your sins, but lead you to his salvation; and do not let
a day pass without thinking on his sufferings in Gethsemane, and
on Mount Golgotha. Surely his love to poor sinners, in bleeding and
dying for them, will constrain you to love him again.

Sequel to Cardiphonia: Letters to Newton's Adopted Daughter, [6:303]; 4:514

And the Lord came, and stood, and called as at other times, Samuel,
Samuel. Then Samuel answered, Speak; for thy servant heareth.
—1 Sam. 3:10.

I THINK my dear child has told me, that you are often terrified
at the thoughts of death: now, if you seek the Lord, as Mrs.****
did, while you are young, then, whenever you come to die, you will
find that death has nothing terrible in it to them that love the Lord
Jesus Christ. He has disarmed death, and taken away its sting; and
he has promised to meet his people and receive them to himself,
when they are about to leave this world, and everything they loved in
it, behind them... I hope you will do as she did; and the Lord who
was gracious to her, will be gracious to you; for he has promised that
none who seek him shall seek him in vain. Your conscience tells you
that you are a sinner, and that makes you afraid; but, when the Lord
gives you faith, you will see and understand, that the blood of Jesus
Christ cleanses from all sin, then you will love him; and, when you
love him, you will find it easy and pleasant to serve him; and then
you will long to see him who died for you: and, as it is impossible to
see him in this world, you will be glad that you are not to stay here
always; you will be willing to die, that you may be with him where
he is. In the mean time, I hope you will pray to him, and wait for his
time to reveal himself to you; endeavouring to avoid whatever you
know to be wrong and displeasing to him; and sometimes, I hope,
you will feel your heart soft and tender, and serious thoughts and
desires rising in your mind; when you do, then think, 'Now is the
Lord calling me!' And say as Samuel did, 'Speak, Lord, for thy servant heareth.' He does not call with an audible voice, but he speaks to
the heart in a way not to be described by words. When we are grieved
and ashamed for our sins; when we are affected with what we read
and hear of him, of his love, his sufferings, and his death; when we
see and feel that nothing but his favour can make us happy; then we
may be sure the Lord is near.

Sequel to Cardiphonia: Letters to Newton's Adopted Daughter, [6:305]; 4:516

Before I was afflicted I went astray:
but now have I kept thy word.—Psa. 119:67.

INDEED, it is not amiss that you should now and then meet with a balk, that you may learn, if possible, not to count too much on what tomorrow may do for you; and that you may begin to feel the impossibility of being happy any further than your will is brought into submission to the will of God. In order to this, you must have your own will frequently crossed; and things do and will turn out, almost daily in one way or other, contrary to our wishes and expectations. Then some people fret and fume, are angry and impatient; but others, who are in the Lord's school, and desirous of being taught by him, get good by these things, and sometimes find more pleasure in yielding to his appointment, though contrary to their own wills, than they would have done if all had happened just to their wish.

I wish, my dear child, to think much of the Lord's governing providence. It extends to the minutest concerns. He rules and manages all things; but in so secret a way, that most people think he does nothing, when, in reality, he does all... The Lord knows all things; he foresees every possible consequence, and often what we call disappointments, are mercies from him to save us from harm.

If I could teach you a lesson, which, as yet, I have but poorly learned myself, I would put you in a way that you should never be disappointed. This would be the case if you could always form a right judgment of this world, and all things in it. If you go to a blackberry-bush to look for grapes, you must be disappointed; but then you must thank yourself, for you are big enough to know that grapes never grow upon brambles. So, if you expect much pleasure here, you will not find it; but you ought not to say you are disappointed, because the Scripture warned you beforehand to look for crosses, trials, and balks, every day. If you expect such things, you will not be disappointed when they happen.

I have no greater joy than to hear that my children walk in truth.
—3 John 4.

THE other day I was at Deptford, and saw a ship launched: she slipped easily into the water; the people on board shouted; the ship looked clean and bright, she was fresh painted, and her colours flying. But I looked at her with a sort of pity:—'Poor ship,' I thought, 'you are now in port and in safety; but ere long you must go to sea. Who can tell what storms you may meet with hereafter, and to what hazards you may be exposed; how weather-beaten you may be before you return to port again, or whether you may return at all!' Then my thoughts turned from the ship to my child. It seemed an emblem of your present state: you are now, as it were, in a safe harbour; but by and by you must launch out into the world, which may well be compared to a tempestuous sea. I could even now almost weep at the resemblance; but I take courage; my hopes are greater than my fears. I know there is an infallible Pilot, who has the winds and the waves at his command. There is hardly a day passes in which I do not entreat him to take charge of you. Under his care I know you will be safe; he can guide you, unhurt, amidst the storms, and rocks, and dangers, by which you might otherwise suffer, and bring you, at last, to the haven of eternal rest. I hope you will seek him while you are young, and I am sure he will be the friend of them that seek him sincerely; then you will be happy, and I shall rejoice. Nothing will satisfy me but this; though I should live to see you settled to the greatest advantage in temporal matters, except you love him, and live in his fear and favour, you would appear to me quite miserable. I think it would go near to break my heart; for, next to your dear Mamma, there is nothing so dear to me in this world as you. But the Lord gave you to me, and I have given you to him again, many and many a time upon my knees, and therefore I hope you must, and will, and shall be his.

Sequel to Cardiphonia: Letters to Newton's Adopted Daughter, [6:311]; 4:521

I sought the LORD, and he heard me, and delivered me from all my fears.
—Psa. 34:4.

OUR trials are either salutary medicines, or honourable appointments, to put us in such circumstances as may best qualify us to show forth his praise. Usually he has both these ends in view; we always stand in need of correction; and, when he enables us to suffer with patience, we are then happy witnesses to others of the truth of his promises, and the power of his grace in us. For nothing but the influence of God's good Spirit can keep us, at such times, either from despondency or impatience. If left to ourselves in trouble, we shall either sink down into a sullen grief, or toss and rebel like a wild bull in a net.

Our different posts are, as you observe, by the Lord's wise appointment; and therefore must be best for us respectively. Mine is full of trials and difficulties; indeed, I should soon make sad work of it without his continual help, and should have reason to tremble every moment, if he did not maintain in me a humble confidence, that he will help me to the end. He bids me, 'fear not;' and at the same time he says, 'Happy is the man that feareth always.' How to fear, and not to fear, at the same time, is, I believe, one branch of that secret of the Lord which none can understand but by the teaching of his Spirit. When I think of my heart, of the world, of the powers of darkness, what cause of continual fear: I am on an enemy's ground, and cannot move a step but some snare is spread for my feet. But, when I think of the person, grace, power, care, and faithfulness of my Saviour, why may I not say, I will trust and not be afraid, for the Lord of hosts is with us, the God of Jacob is our refuge? I wish to be delivered from anxious and unbelieving fear, which weakens the hands, and disquiets the heart. I wish to increase in a humble jealousy and distrust of myself, and of everything about me; I am imperfect in both respects, but I hope my desire is to him who has promised to do all things for me.

Seq. to Cardiphonia: Letters to Mr. J. F. and Miss M. Barham, [6:338]; 4:543

I am not ashamed: for I know whom I have believed, and am persuaded
that he is able to keep that which I have committed unto him
against that day.—2 Tim. 1:12.

I HOPE you will remember, that all your comfort and prosperity depends upon keeping near to him who is the sun, the shield, the life of his poor children, and that neither experiences, knowledge, nor attainments, can support us, or maintain themselves, without a continual supply from the fountain. This supply is to be kept up by constant prayer, and prayer will languish without continual watchfulness. I trust you will bear me to put you in mind of these things, though you know them. We are yet in an enemy's country, and are directed to exhort one another daily, lest we be surprised by some stratagem and guile of our bitter adversary, who has many thousand snares and instruments to employ against us, and well knows how to use them to the most advantage, and to avail himself of our weak side. Yet we need not fear him, if we take, and keep, and use, the whole armour of God, and remain under the shadow of that Rock which is higher than ourselves.

I am enabled, through grace, to keep myself from the evil of the world, so that I have not been left to bring a blot on my profession. But, alas! my heart is a filthy, defiled heart still. It is well that he only who knows how to bear with me, knows what is within me. My comfort is comprised in this one sentence,—'I know whom I have believed,'—I know that Jesus is mighty to save; I have seen myself lost in every view but the hope of his mercy; I have fled to him for safety; I have been preserved by him thus far; and I believe he will keep that which I have committed to him even to the end. Blessing and honour, and glory and praise, be to his name, who hath loved poor sinners, and washed them in his most precious blood. Amen. For the rest, alas! alas! I am unfaithful and unprofitable to a degree you would hardly believe; yet, vile as I am, I taste of his goodness every day, and live in hope, that in his own time he will enable me to show forth his praise.

Sequel to Cardiphonia: Letters to Several Ladies, [6:16]; 4:284

Who shall lay any thing to the charge of God's elect? It is God that justifieth. Who is he that condemneth?—Rom. 8:33, 34.

WITH respect to my own experience, I have little now to add to what I have formerly offered; at least, little variety: for, in one sense, every new day is filled up with new things;—new mercies on the Lord's part, new ingratitude on mine; new instances of the vileness of my nature, and new proofs of the power of sovereign pardoning grace:—new hills of difficulty, new valleys of humiliation;—and now and then (though, alas! very short and seldom) new glimpses of what I would be, and where I would be. The everlasting love of God; the unspeakable merits of Christ's righteousness; and the absolute freeness of the gospel promises;—these form the three-fold cord by which my soul maintains a hold of that which is within the veil. Sin, Satan, and unbelief, often attempt to make me let go and cast away my confidence, but as yet they have not prevailed; no thanks to me, who am weaker than water: but I am wonderfully kept by the mighty power of God, who is pleased to take my part, and therefore I trust in him that they never shall prevail against me. A vile sinner, indeed, I am; but, since God, who alone has a right to judge, is pleased to justify the believer in Jesus, who is there that shall dare to condemn? I bless the Lord for that comfortable portion of the Scripture, Zech. 3:1-5. When the Lord is pleased to pluck a brand out of the fire to save it from perishing, what power in heaven or earth shall presume or prevail to put it in again? No; he has done it, and who can reverse it? He has said it, and his word shall stand. And I humbly believe (Lord, help my unbelief,) that not one good thing shall fail of all that the Lord my God has, in his word, spoken to me of.

Sequel to Cardiphonia: Letters to Several Ladies, [6:21]; 4:288

The eternal God is thy refuge,
and underneath are the everlasting arms.—Deut. 33:27.

DO not your hearts rejoice in that word, 'The eternal God is thy refuge, and underneath are the everlasting arms?' And if he is pleased and engaged to uphold us, what power or policy can force us from him? No; we may rejoice in it as a certain truth, let Satan and unbelief say what they will to the contrary, that the Lord's afflicted people on earth are as safe, though not so quiet, as his glorified people in heaven. They are embarked on a troubled sea, the tempests often roar around them, and the waves seem ready to swallow them up; but they have an anchor within the veil, sure and steadfast, which can neither be broken nor removed. They have a Pilot, a Guardian, whose wisdom and power are infinite, and who, of his own good pleasure, has engaged his truth and honour, that he will bring them safe through all, to the haven of eternal rest. Let us therefore trust, and not be afraid; let us rejoice, and say, 'The Lord Jehovah is my strength and my song, and he also is become my salvation.'

How happy should we be, could we always believe the glorious things which are spoken to us as children, in the word of him who cannot fail of accomplishing his promise. But are we not fools and slow of heart in this matter? at least, I am, and hence proceed my many complaints.—Alas! what a hard heart have I, that can doubt, and repine, and limit the Lord, after all the great things he has shown me! Wretched heart, that can stand it out still, against oaths, and promises, and blood. Methinks I may sum up all my wants and prayers in one sentence,—Lord, give me faith. Oh, if faith was in daily exercise, how little would the world, and the things of time and sense, seem in my eyes! What a dreadful thing would sin appear, that spilt my Saviour's blood! And how would my very heart rejoice at the sound of Jesus' name?

Sequel to Cardiphonia: Letters to Several Ladies, [6:22]; 4:289

The voice of rejoicing and salvation is in the tabernacles of the righteous: the right hand of the Lord doeth valiantly. The right hand of the Lord is exalted: the right hand of the Lord doeth valiantly.—Psa. 118:15, 16.

WE have, indeed, whereof to glory, but not in ourselves; the right hand of the Lord has been exalted in our behalf; the right hand of the Lord has brought mighty things to pass. When we were utterly helpless and hopeless, he saw and pitied us, and bid us live. He did not cut us off in the midst of our sins, (as is the case of thousands,) but waited to be gracious; and, when his hour was come, his time of love, he revealed himself as our mighty Saviour, he poured oil and wine into our wounds, he gave us beauty for ashes, the garments of praise for the spirit of heaviness; he opened our blind eyes, he unstopped our deaf ears, dispossessed the legion, and brought us to sit at his feet clothed and in our right minds. What a wonder of mercy is this, considered in itself! but much more if we think of the means by which it was effected; that, in order to bring about this blessed change, that mercy and truth might meet together in our salvation, and the righteousness of God harmonize with the sinner's peace, the Lord Jesus, who was rich, humbled himself to become poor; to live an obscure and suffering life, in the form of a servant, and to die a shameful, painful, and accursed death, that we, through his poverty, might be made children and heirs of God; might receive grace to serve him here, and dwell with him in glory forever. For this end he willingly endured the cross, and despised the shame, he hid not his face from shame and spitting, he gave his back to the smiters, his cheeks to them that plucked off the hair, he submitted to wear a crown of thorns, to be nailed by the hands and feet to the accursed tree, to endure the fiercest assaults of Satan, yea, to drink the full cup of the wrath of God when 'it pleased the Father to bruise him,' and to make 'his soul an offering for sin!'

Sequel to Cardiphonia: Letters to Several Ladies, [6:24]; 4:291

Sir, we would see Jesus.—John 12:21.

METHINKS my heart joins with the desire of those who said, 'We would see Jesus.' When we come to heaven, without doubt we shall find great pleasure in communion with the 'general assembly of the church of the first-born;' but the very heaven of all will be to behold him who, for our sakes, was crowned with thorns, and nailed to the cross. All the rest would be but poor company if he were absent. And thus proportionably I find it to be on earth. I delight in his people; but they can only profit me so far as I am enabled to see him in them, and to feel his presence in my own soul. My whole study and desire is comprised in this short sentence,—'To walk with God,'—to set the Lord always before me; to hear his voice in every creature, in every dispensation, ordinance, and providence; to keep him in view as my Portion, Sun, and Shield; my Strength, Advocate, and Saviour. And all my complaints may be summed up in this one,—a proneness to wander from him. This is too frequently the case with me, I hardly know how or why. Through mercy, I am in a measure delivered from the love of this present evil world; the desire of my heart is towards God; I account his loving-kindness to be better than life, and esteem all his precepts concerning all things to be right, and just, and good. I do not even wish for a dispensation to admit any rival into my heart; he richly deserves it all, and I am willing and desirous to be his alone, and to be wholly conformed to him. Yet still I find the effects of a depraved nature; and, notwithstanding all my struggles against inward and outward evil, I am too often carried away from the point of simple faith and dependence. The lively experience of a Christian is not hard to be described; neither is it hard to say much about it. But, to feel what we say, to sit down under the shadow of the tree of life, to abide in Christ, to feed on him in my heart by faith with thanksgiving, this I find a rare attainment, easily lost, and not so soon regained.

Sequel to Cardiphonia: Letters to Several Ladies, [6:28]; 4:295

And I will pray the Father, and he shall give you another Comforter,
that he may abide with you for ever; Even the Spirit of truth ... ye know
him; for he dwelleth with you, and shall be in you.—John 14:16, 17.

I WANT more of the influences of the Holy Spirit under his various characters, as the teacher, quickener, comforter, and sealer of the people of God. I want to know more clearly what the apostle desired for his friends, in those two comprehensive prayers, Eph. 1:17-20, and 3:16-19. How little do I understand of that height and depth, and breadth and length, he there speaks of! How faint are my ideas of the glorious hope of his calling, and the exceeding greatness of his mighty power! Well, blessed be God for the little I have; I trust it is an earnest of more; he has given me to hunger and thirst after righteousness, and he has said I shall be filled. I remember the time when I was easy enough about these things; the language of my heart was, 'Depart from me.' Yea, I resisted his Spirit, despised his mercy, and counted the blood of the covenant an unholy thing. But, oh, he 'was found of me that sought him not!' He passed by me, and bid me live; he saved me in spite of myself; he would not give me up; he appeared in the hour of my distress, snatched the prey from the hand of the mighty, and delivered the lawful captive. And ever since, how good has he been to me! How gently has he led me! How often has he restored me when wandering, revived me when fainting, healed my breaches, supplied my wants, heard my prayers, and set up a seasonable standard against my enemies, when they have been coming in upon me like a flood! And even now he is with me, he is never weary of doing me good, and I believe he will be with me, even to the end, till at length he brings me home to his kingdom to be near him for ever. Hence, indeed, arises a great part of my grief, to think that I should be so cold, and barren, and unprofitable, under such amazing displays of undeserved love. O Lord, touch the rock, and cause the waters to flow; soften and inflame my heart, that I may at length become thy disciple indeed.

Sequel to Cardiphonia: Letters to Several Ladies, [6:30]; 4:296

Yet I will rejoice in the LORD, I will joy in the God of my salvation.
—Hab. 3:18.

FAITH in Jesus prepares us for every event. Though he put forth his hand, and seem to threaten our dearest comforts, yet when we remember that it is *his* hand, when we consider that it is *his* design, *his* love, *his* wisdom, and *his* power, we cannot refuse to trust him. The reluctance we feel is against our judgment; for we are sure that what he chooses for us must be best. Then again, to think how much less our sufferings are than our sins have deserved; how many mercies we still enjoy on every hand; how much heavier burdens are the portion of many around us; to compare the present momentary affliction with the exceeding weight of glory which shall be revealed; to recollect that the time is short, the hour is swiftly approaching when the Lord shall wipe away all tears, and constrain us with wonder and joy to sing, 'He hath done all things well.' Such considerations as these, together with the remembrance of what he suffered for us, are always at hand to compose our souls under troubles, and will be effectual according to the degree of faith. Our faith also is strengthened by affliction; we learn more of our own insufficiency, and the vanity of all things about us; and we discover more of the power, faithfulness, and nearness of a prayer-hearing God. Upon this ground, Habakkuk could sit down and rejoice under the loss of all. He could look at the blasted fig-tree and the withered vine, see the herds and flocks cut off, and every creature-comfort fail; yet, says he, 'I will rejoice in the Lord, and joy in the God of my salvation.' Oh, the name of Jesus, when we can speak of him as ours; this is the balm for every wound, cordial for every care; it is as ointment poured forth, diffusing a fragrancy through the whole soul, and driving away the hurtful fumes and fogs of distrust and discontent!

Sequel to Cardiphonia: Letters to Several Ladies, [6:33]; 4:298

> *What shall we then say to these things?*
> *If God be for us, who can be against us?*—Rom. 8:31.

MANY are the trials and exercises we must expect to meet with in our progress; but this one consideration outweighs them all. The Lord is on our side; and, if he be for us, none can be against us to harm us. In all these things we shall be more than conquerors, through him that has loved us. Afflictions, though not in themselves joyous, but grievous, yet, when sanctified, are among our choice mercies; in due time they shall yield the peaceful fruits of righteousness; and even at present, they shall surely be attended with seasonable and sufficient supports. One great desire of the believer, is to understand the great word of God more and more; and one principal means by which we advance in this knowledge is, the improvement we are enabled to make of our daily trials. The promises are generally made to an afflicted state; and we could not taste their sweetness, nor experience their truth, if we were not sometimes brought into the circumstances to which they relate. It is said, 'I will be with them in trouble;' but how could we know what a mercy is contained in these words, unless trouble was sometimes our lot? It is said to be the believer's privilege to glory in tribulation. But we never could know that this is possible without we had tribulation to glory in. However, this is matter of joy and glory indeed, to find peace and comfort within when things are disagreeable and troublesome without. Then we are enabled to set to our seal that God is true; then we learn how happy it is to have a refuge that cannot be taken from us; a support that is able to bear all the weight we can lay upon it; a spring of joy that cannot be stopped up by any outward events. A great part of the little we know of our God, his faithfulness, his compassion, his readiness to hear and to answer our prayers; his wisdom in delivering and providing when all our contrivances fail; and his goodness in overruling everything to our souls' good; I say, much of what we know of these things, we learnt in our trials, and have therefore reason to say, It was good for us to be afflicted.

Sequel to Cardiphonia: Letters to Several Ladies, [6:35]; 4:300

Then he said unto them, Go your way … neither be ye sorry;
for the joy of the LORD is your strength.—Neh. 8:10.

CAUSES of complaint are, indeed, innumerable; but remember, 'the joy of the Lord is your strength.' Be not surprised that you still find the effects of indwelling sin,—it must and will be so. The frame of our fallen nature is depraved throughout, and, like the leprous house, it must be entirely demolished, and raised anew. While we are in this world, we shall groan, being burdened. I wish you to long and breathe after greater measures of sanctification; but we are sometimes betrayed into a legal spirit, which will make us labour in the very fire to little purpose. If we find deadness and dryness stealing upon us, our only relief is to look to Jesus,—to his blood for pardon,—to his grace for strength; we can work nothing out of ourselves. To pore over our own evils will not cure them; but he who was typified by the brazen serpent is ever present, lifted up to our view in the camp; and one believing sight of him will do more to restore peace to the conscience, and life to our graces, than all our own lamentations and resolutions.

Further, we must expect changes. Were we always alike, we should dream that we had some power or goodness inherent in ourselves; he will therefore sometimes withdraw, that we may learn our absolute dependence on him. When this is the case, it is our part humbly to continue seeking him in his own appointed means, and patiently to wait his promised return. It is a point of great wisdom to know our gospel liberty, and yet not abuse it; to see that our hope stands sure and invariable, distant from all the changes we feel in our experience, that we are accepted, not because we are comfortable or lively, but because Jesus has loved us, and given himself for us; and yet, at the same time, to be longing and thirsting for the light of his countenance, and a renewed sense of his love upon our hearts.

Sequel to Cardiphonia: Letters to Several Ladies, [6:43]; 4:306

He will not suffer thy foot to be moved:
he that keepeth thee will not slumber.—Psa. 121:3.

YOUR warfare, it seems, still continues; and it will continue while you remain here. But he is faithful who has promised to make us more than conquerors in the last conflict—then we shall hear the voice of war no more for ever. Whatever we suffer by the way, the end will make amends for all. The repeated experience we have of the deceitfulness of our own hearts, is a means which the Lord employs to make us willing debtors to his free grace, and teach us to live more entirely upon Jesus. He is our peace, our strength, our righteousness, our all in all. And we learn from day to day, that, though diligence and watchfulness in the use of appointed means is our part, yet we are preserved in life, not by our care, but his. We have a watchful Shepherd, who neither slumbers nor sleeps; his eyes are always upon his people; his arm underneath them; this is the reason that their enemies cannot prevail against them. We are conscious to ourselves of many unguarded moments, in which we might be surprised and ruined if we were left without his almighty defence. Yea, we often suffer loss by our folly; but he restores us when wandering; revives us when fainting; heals us when wounded; and, having obtained help of him, we continue to this hour; and he will be our Guard and Guide even unto death.

The law of sin in my members distresses me; but the gospel yields relief. It is given me to rest in the finished salvation, and to rejoice in Christ Jesus as my all in all. My soul is athirst for nearer and fuller communion with him. Yet he is pleased to keep me short of those sweet consolations in my retired hours which I could desire. However, I cannot doubt but he is with me, and is pleased to keep up in my heart some sense of the evil of sin, the beauty of holiness, my own weakness, and his glorious all-sufficiency. His I am, and him I desire to serve. I am, indeed, a poor servant; but he is a gracious Master. Oh! who is a God like unto him, that forgiveth iniquity, and casteth the sins of his people into the depths of the sea?

Sequel to Cardiphonia: Letters to Several Ladies, [6:51]; 4:313

I will heal their backsliding, I will love them freely:
for mine anger is turned away from him.—Hos. 14:4.

AS to myself, I have had much experience of the deceitfulness of my heart, much warfare on account of the remaining principle of indwelling sin. Without this experience I should not have known so much of the wisdom, power, grace, and compassion of Jesus. I have good reason to commend him to others, as a faithful Shepherd, an infallible Physician, an unchangeable Friend. I have found him such. Had he not been with me, and were he not mighty to forgive and deliver, I had long ago been trodden down like mire in the streets. He has wonderfully preserved me in my outward walk, so that they who have watched for my halting have been disappointed. But he alone knows the innumerable backslidings, and the great perverseness of my heart. It is of his grace and mercy that I am what I am: having obtained help of him, I continue to this day. And he enables me to believe that he will keep me to the end, and that then I shall be with him forever.

I hope your souls prosper, and that all the comforts, employments, cares, and trials of life, are sanctified by his blessing, to lead you to a more immediate dependence upon himself; that he enables you to glorify him in your families and connexions, and conforms you to his image, in love, spirituality, meekness, and resignation. Many things must be attended to in their places; but, oh, the blessing of being taught to do and to bear all things for his sake! The life of faith is, to be continually waiting on him, receiving from him, rendering to him, resting in him, and acting for him. In every other view the present state is vanity and vexation of spirit. But, when the love of Jesus is the leading and constraining motive of our conduct, the necessary business of every day, in the house, the shop, or the field, is ennobled, and makes a part of our religious worship; while every dispensation of Providence, whether pleasant or painful to the flesh, is received and rested in as an intimation of his will, and an evidence of his love and care for us.

Sequel to Cardiphonia: Letters to Several Ladies, [6:55]; 4:316

Wherefore he is able also to save them to the uttermost that come unto
God by him, seeing he ever liveth to make intercession for them.
—Heb. 7:25.

I CONGRATULATE you on that comfortable declaration, 'We have an Advocate with the Father, Jesus Christ the righteous, who now appears in the presence of God *for us.*' An awful cause we had to manage in the court of heaven; and, when we expected to be asked what we could say, that judgment should not be given and executed speedily against us, we were dumb and without plea. We could not deny the fact, or offer the least amends. We could neither stand nor flee. But, since Jesus has been pleased to take our affairs in hand, how are appearances changed! The law is fulfilled, justice satisfied, and heaven opened to those who were upon the brink of despair and destruction. And Jesus did not plead for us once only, but he 'ever liveth to make intercession for us.' Let us then take courage. That word *uttermost* includes all that can be said: take an estimate of sins, temptations, difficulties, fears, and backslidings of every kind, still the word *uttermost* goes beyond them all. And, since he ever liveth to make intercession, since he is the righteous one who is always heard, since his promise and compassions are unchangeable, may his Spirit enable us to apply the conclusion without wavering to our soul's comfort, that he is indeed able and willing, and determined, to save us even to the uttermost.

This point being comfortably settled, that he will neither cast us off himself, nor suffer any to pluck us out of his hands, but that he will surely bring us, through fire and through water, to the wealthy place his love has provided for us; the next important inquiry is, since we may hope for heaven at the end, how may we attain as much of heaven by the way, as is possible to be hoped for in this defiled state of things? Do we indeed, through grace, hope to live with Jesus hereafter? Then surely we desire to walk with him here.

Sequel to Cardiphonia: Letters to Mr. & Mrs. Daniel West, [6:65]; 4:325

For they verily for a few days chastened us after their own pleasure; but
he for our profit, that we might be partakers of his holiness.
—Heb. 12:10.

IT is because I love you that I rejoice to think you are in the Lord's hands, and that I desire to leave you there. Happy is the state of a believer; to such, all things are for good. Health is a blessing, a great mercy, enabling us to relish the comforts of life, and to be useful in our generations; and sickness is a great mercy likewise to those who are interested in the covenant; for it is and shall be sanctified to wean us more from the present world, to stir up our thoughts and desires heaven-ward, to quicken us to prayer, and to give us more opportunity of knowing the sweetness and suitableness of the promises, and the power and wisdom of a promise-performing God. Troubles have many uses when the Lord is pleased to work by them for the good of his children, and are necessary upon this account, among others, that we should miss the time, relish, and meaning of a great part of the Bible without them. I hope the Lord blesses you both with a measure of submission to his will, confidence in his love, and then, with respect to other things you will say, All is well: uncertainty and brevity are written upon all below; therefore may we be enabled both to weep and rejoice as those who know we shall do neither very long here. By the Lord's goodness, it is appointed both for you and for us to have more temporal happiness in possession than the greatest part of mankind have in idea, and yet our best here would be a poor *all*, if it was indeed our *all*. We should be thankful for present things; but, oh, what greater thankfulness for spiritual blessings, for pardon, peace, and eternal life! Our gourds must one day wither; but our portion will be ours for ever. Jesus, the fountain, will be full, when every creature-stream will be dried up. Such discoveries of his presence as we have a warrant to pray for here, are sufficient to comfort us under all the pains, losses, and trials, we can feel or fear.

Rejoice in the Lord alway.—Phil. 4:4.

I HEAR you still continue poorly in health: shall I say I am sorry? I hope this is allowable; we have the best example and authority to sympathize with suffering friends. Yet our sorrow should be mixed with joy, for we are directed to rejoice always in the Lord; always—not only when we are well, but when we are sick; not only upon the mount, but in the valley. I rejoice, therefore, that you are in safe hands; in the hands of him whom you love best and who best loves you... I trust this sickness of your body is, and shall be, for the health of your soul; yea, perhaps even now, if you were able to write, you would tell me that, as your afflictions abound, your consolations in Christ do much more abound. All the fruit shall be to take away sin; therefore be of good courage: behold, we count them happy that endure; yea, blessed are those servants whom the Lord chastiseth. Now he deals with you as a child; he intends this dispensation to revive in you a sense of the uncertainty and vanity of all things here below, to give you a nearer and closer perception of the importance and reality of unseen things; to afford you the honour of a conformity to Jesus, who went through sufferings to the kingdom. But how different were his sufferings from yours? There is no sting in your rod, nor wrath in your cup; your pains and infirmities do not cause you to sweat blood, nor are you left to cry out, 'My God, my God, why hast thou forsaken me?'... When you meditate on these things, I trust you find your heart sweetly composed into a frame of resignation to bear, as well as to do, the will of your heavenly Father; and, though your recovery may be slow, and your physicians shake their heads, as uncertain what to try for you, yet, when the fit time is come, the great Physician who has taken charge of your case, can heal you presently. Diseases hear his voice. To the Lord our God belong the issues from death. I pray as I am enabled for your recovery at the best season, but especially that the rod may be sanctified, and you brought forth from the furnace refined as gold.

Sequel to Cardiphonia: Letters to Mr. & Mrs. Daniel West, [6:71]; 4:330

Nevertheless to abide in the flesh is more needful for you. And having
this confidence, I know that I shall abide and continue with you all
for your furtherance and joy of faith.—Phil. 1:24, 25.

IF we consider this life chiefly with respect to the things which make up a great part of it, as eating, drinking, buying, selling, putting on our clothes, and putting them off, a spiritual mind may well be weary of such a train of necessary trifling. But, besides that even the common actions of life are sanctified, and become a part of our acceptable service, when performed in a spirit of faith, love, and dependence; this life, poor as it is in itself, will become exceedingly important in one view. It is the only opportunity we have to hold forth the power of gospel truth in the midst of a crooked and perverse generation, to show our readiness to bear the cross, and to tread in the steps of a suffering Saviour, and to be subservient to the promoting his cause, and the encouragement of his people. Many of our years were wasted in the service of sin before we knew the Lord; and, though they are happy who are taken out of this vain world soon after their conversion, yet I think they are more honoured who are preserved to bear a testimony to his goodness, and to be useful in their generation for a course of years. Therefore, though, if the Lord had seen fit to remove you, you would have escaped some trials which in this world you will be sure to meet with, and would have had your hungerings after Jesus abundantly satisfied; yet upon the account of dear Mrs. W****, your children, your place in the church and in the world, as well as upon my own account, I cannot but rejoice that there is a prospect of your continuance longer on this side the grave.

It is a happy and most desirable frame to be ready and willing either to live or die, and to be enabled so absolutely to give ourselves up to the Lord's disposal as to have no choice of our own either way, but only intent upon improving today, and cheerfully to leave tomorrow and all beyond it in his hands who does all things well.

Sequel to Cardiphonia: Letters to Mr. & Mrs. Daniel West, [6:77]; 4:334

Watch and pray, that ye enter not into temptation.—Matt. 26:41.

I REMEMBER, when the Lord first set me up (if I may so speak) my heavenly trade lay in a small compass, my views were very narrow; I wanted to be saved, and, alas! I hardly looked further than a bare subsistence and security; but, since the Lord has been pleased in a measure to bless me, I hope I feel a desire of being rich. May I, and all whom I love, be thus minded; not be satisfied that we have life, but labour in his appointed way, that we may have it more abundantly; not only to believe, but to be strong in faith; not only to hope, but to rejoice in hope; not only to desire, but to hunger, and thirst, and pant; to open our mouths wide, that we may be filled with his goodness, as well as taste that he is gracious. Oh, what a happiness is it to be lively and thriving in the ways of God; to drink into the spirit of Jesus, and to walk with that simplicity, dependence, and heavenly-mindedness which become a son or a daughter of the Lord Almighty. I trust the Lord has given me thus to will; but, when I would do good, evil is present with me. On this account, our life is a warfare; and it is never well with us, but when we find it so. But we have a good Captain, good armour, good provisions, infallible balm to heal our wounds, and (what one would think might make even a coward fight) are assured of the victory beforehand.

The Lord has appointed me a sentinel to give the camp notice of the enemy's approach; I am ashamed to say it, but indeed I am such a wretch, that I am sometimes half-asleep upon my post. It is of the Lord's mercy that I have not been surprised and overpowered before now. Such is his condescension, that he comes to awaken me himself, and only says, Arise, watch, and pray, that you enter not into temptation. I have good reason to believe my enemy has been as near to me as David was to Saul, when he took away his spear, and yet I did not perceive him. Well it is for us that there is one who watches the watchmen, a Shepherd who himself neither slumbers nor sleeps, and yet knows how to have compassion on those who are prone to do both.

Sequel to Cardiphonia: Letters to Mr. & Mrs. Daniel West, [6:81]; 4:338

Surely goodness and mercy shall follow me all the days of my life:
and I will dwell in the house of the Lord for ever.—Psa. 23:6.

SURELY his service is perfect freedom; his ways are ways of pleas-
antness, and all his paths are peace. He is a sun and a shield, a
hiding-place, and a resting-place, to them that fear him. May we still
press forward: we have not yet attained. There are larger measures of
grace, establishment, and consolation set forth in the gospel, than all
we have hitherto received. The Lord has set before us an open door,
which no man can shut; he has given us exceeding great and precious
promises; has bid us open our mouths wide, and has said, he will
fill them. He would have us ask great things, and, when we have
enlarged our desires to the utmost, he is still able to do exceeding
more than we can ask or think. May we be as wise in our generation
as the children of this world. They are not content with a little, nor
even with much, so long as there is any probability of getting more.
As to myself, I am but a poor man in the trade of grace; I live from
hand to mouth, and procure just enough (as we say) to keep the wolf
from the door. But I must charge it to my unbelief and indolence,
which have been so great, that it is a mercy I am not a bankrupt. This
would have been the case, but that I have a friend (whom you know)
who has kindly engaged for me. To tell you the plain truth, I have
nothing of my own, but trade wholly upon his stock; and yet (would
you think it possible) though I often confess to him that I am an
unprofitable and unfaithful steward, yet I have upon many occasions
spoke and acted as if I would have people believe that what he has
committed to me was my own property... But he is God and not
man; his ways are not as ours; and, as it has pleased him to receive
us as children, he has promised that we shall abide in his house for
ever. It is our mercy that we have an atonement of infinite value,
and an Advocate who is always heard, and who ever liveth to make
intercession for us.

Sequel to Cardiphonia: Letters to Mr. & Mrs. Daniel West, [6:83]; 4:340

For that ye ought to say, If the Lord will, we shall live,
and do this, or that.—James 4:15.

I WAS balked on the Friday I dined with Mrs. ****, to find you could not be at home. Then I wished I had stayed with you on the Tuesday evening; so ready are we, at least, so ready am I, to want to recall the day that is past, and correct the disposals of Divine Providence. At length I retreated to my acknowledged principles, that the Lord knows where we are, and when it is needful we should meet; that the word *disappointment*, when translated into plain English, means little more or less than the grumblings of self-will against the will of God; and that we should never meet a disappointment in the path of duty, if we could heartily prefer his wisdom to our own. I considered that, though to have had your company would have been more pleasant, yet an opportunity of trying to bow my stubborn spirit to the Lord's disposal, might at that time be more profitable; so I endeavoured to make the best, of it. I am desirous to learn (but I am a slow scholar, and make bungling work at my lessons) to apply the great truths of the gospel to the common concerns of every day and every hour; not only to believe that my soul is safe in the Redeemer's hand, but that the hairs of my head are numbered; not only that those events in life which I call important are under his direction, but that those which I account the most inconsiderable are equally so; that I have no more right or power to determine for myself where or how I would spend a single day, than I had to choose the time of my coming into the world or of going out of it... Oh, would it not be a blessed thing simply to follow him, and to set him by faith always before us? Then we might be freed from anxious cares, and, as I said, out of the reach of disappointment; for, if his will is ours, we may be confident that nothing can prevent its taking place.

Sequel to Cardiphonia: Letters to Mr. & Mrs. Daniel West, [6:86]; 4:342

When Jesus heard that, he said, This sickness is not unto death, but for
the glory of God, that the Son of God might be glorified thereby.
—John 11:4.

WHEN I go into a post-chaise, I give myself up, with the most absolute confidence, to the driver: I think he knows the way, and how to manage better than I do; and therefore I seldom trouble him either with questions or directions, but draw up the glasses, and sit at my ease. I wish I could trust the Lord so; but, though I have given myself up to the care of infinite wisdom and love, and, in my judgment, believe they are engaged on my behalf, I am ready to direct my Guide, and to expostulate with him at every turn, and secretly to wish that I had the reins in my own hand. 'So stupid and ignorant am I, even as a beast before him.' In great trials we necessarily retreat to him, and endeavour to stay our souls by believing he does all things well; but in small ones we are ready to forget him, and therefore we are often more put out by little things that happen in the course of every day, than by the sharpest dispensations we meet with.

The illness under which I have laboured longer than the man mentioned, John 5:5, is far from being removed. Yet I am bound to speak well of my Physician: he treats me with great tenderness; assures me that it shall not be to death, but to the glory of God; and bids me in due time expect a perfect cure. I know too much of him (though I know but little) to doubt either his skill or his promise. It is true, I suffer sad relapses, and have been more than once brought in appearances to death's door since I have been under his care; but this fault has not been his, but my own. I am a strange refractory patient; have too often neglected his prescriptions, and broken the regimen he appoints me to observe. This perverseness, joined to the exceeding obstinacy of my disorders, would have caused me to be turned out as an incurable long ago, had I been under any hand but his. But, indeed, there is none like him. When I have brought myself low, he has still helped me.

Sequel to Cardiphonia: Letters to Mr. & Mrs. Daniel West, [6:87]; 4:343

I am the LORD *thy God, which brought thee out of the land of Egypt:*
open thy mouth wide, and I will fill it.—Psa. 81:10.

YOU are hungering and thirsting to feel the power and savour of the truth in your soul, humbling, quickening, strengthening, comforting you, filling you with peace and joy, and enabling you to abound in the fruits of righteousness, which are, by Jesus Christ, to the glory and praise of God. Are these your desires? He that has wrought them in you is God; and he will not disappoint you. He would not say, Open your mouth wide, if he did not design to fill it. Oh, he gives bountifully; gives like a king. A *little* is too much for our deserts; but *much* is too little for his bounty. Let me tell you a heathen story:—It is said, that a man once asked Alexander to give him some money, I think, to portion off a daughter. The king bid him go to his treasurer, and demand what he pleased. He went, and demanded an enormous sum. The treasurer was startled, said he could not part with so much without an express order, and went to the king, and told him he thought a small part of the money the man had named might serve for the occasion. 'No,' said the king, 'let him have it all. I like that man: he does me honour; he treats me like a king, and proves by what he asks, that he believes me to be both rich and generous.' Come, my friend, let us go to the throne of grace, and put up such petitions as may show that we have honourable views of the riches and bounty of our King. Alas! I prefer such poor scanty desires, as if I thought he was altogether such a one as myself. Speak a word for me when you are near him; entreat him to increase my love, faith, humility, zeal, and knowledge, a thousandfold. Ah! I am poor and foolish; I need a great supply; I cannot dig, and yet am often unwilling to beg.

I find then a law, that, when I would do good, evil is present with me.
—Rom. 7:21.

I WISH my heart was more affected with what my eyes see and my ears hear every day.

And surely, if he were strict to mark what is amiss, I myself might tremble. Oh, were he to plead with me, I could not answer him one of a thousand. Alas! my dear friend, you know not what a poor, unprofitable, unfaithful creature I am. So much forgiven, so little love. So many mercies, so few returns. Such great privileges, and a life so sadly below them. Instead of rejoicing in God, I go mourning for the most part. Not because I am shaken with doubts and fears; for I believe the Lord Jesus, who found me when I sought him not, is both able and willing to save to the uttermost; but because indwelling sin presses me close; because, when I would do good, evil is present with me; because I can attempt nothing but it is debased, polluted, and spoiled by my depraved nature; because my sins of omission are innumerable. In a word, there is so much darkness in my understanding, perverseness in my will, disorders in my affections, folly and madness in my imagination. Alas! when shall it be otherwise? I seem to have a desire of walking with God, and rejoicing in him all the day long; but I cannot attain thereto. Surely it is far better to depart, and to be with Jesus Christ, than to live here up to the ears in sin and temptation; and yet I seem very well contented with the possibility of continuing here a good while. In short, I am a riddle to myself; a heap of inconsistence. But it is said, 'We have an Advocate with the Father.' Here hope revives; though wretched in myself, I am complete in him. He is made of God, wisdom, righteousness, sanctification, and redemption. On this rock I build. I trust it shall be well with me at last, and that I shall by and by praise, and love, and serve him without these abatements.

Behold, I stand at the door, and knock: if any man hear my voice, and
open the door, I will come in to him, and will sup with him,
and he with me.—Rev. 3:20.

THE houses of believers, though most of them called cottages, are truly palaces; for it is the presence of the king that makes the court. There the Lord reigns upon a throne of grace, and there a royal guard of angels take their stand to watch over and minister to the heirs of salvation... Oh, what manner of love, that we, who were like others by nature, should be thus distinguished by grace! We knew him not, and therefore we could not love him; we were alienated from him; sin, self, and Satan, ruled in our hearts; our eyes were blinded, and we were posting along in the road that leads to death, without suspecting danger. But he would not let us perish. Though, when he knocked at the door of our hearts, we repeatedly refused him entrance; he would not take a denial, but exerted a gracious force; made us willing in the day of his power, and saved us in defiance of ourselves. And from the happy hour when he enabled us to surrender ourselves to him, how tenderly has he pitied us, how seasonably has he relieved us, how powerfully upheld us! How many Ebenezers have we been called upon to rear to his praise! And he has said, he will never leave us nor forsake us. And, oh, what a prospect lies before us! When by his counsel he has guided us through life, he will receive us to his kingdom, give us a crown of glory, and place us near himself, to see him as he is, and to be satisfied with his love for ever. How many years did we live before we had the least idea of what we were born to know and enjoy! Many things look dark around us, and before us, but the spreading of the gospel is, I trust, a token for good. Oh, that we might see the work running not only broader as to numbers, but deeper as to the life, power, and experience, in the hearts, tempers, and conversation of those who profess the truth!

Sequel to Cardiphonia: Letters to Mr. & Mrs. Daniel West, [6:109]; 4:360

It is written in the prophets, And they shall be all taught of God. Every man therefore that hath heard, and hath learned of the Father, cometh unto me.—John 6:45.

I AM sure I can say for myself, that I received not the gospel from man. The little instruction I had received in my youth, I had renounced; I was an infidel in the strictest sense of the word. When it pleased God to give me a concern for my soul, and for some years afterwards, I was upon the seas, or in Africa, at a distance from the influence of books, names, and parties. In this space, the Lord taught me, by the New Testament, the truths upon which my soul now ventures its everlasting concerns... These things I am sure of, that the proper wages of sin is death; that I and all mankind have sinned against the great God; that the most perfect character is unable to stand the trial of his holy law. When I saw things in this light, I saw the necessity of a Mediator. And in the account the Scripture gave me of Christ ... I saw a provision answerable to my need. His blood is declared to be a complete atonement for sin; his righteousness, a plea provided for the guilty; his power and compassion are both infinite; and the promise of pardon, peace, and eternal life, is made to them who believe in his name. He himself is exalted to bestow that faith to which the promises belong, and he will give it to all who ask. This I have found to be very different from the assent we give to a point of history. It changes the views, dispositions, desires, and pursuits of the mind; produces that great effect, which is emphatically called, *being born again*; without which, our Lord assures us, no man can see the kingdom of God, whatever his qualifications may be in other respects. Oh, my friend, let us praise the Lord who has enlightened our dark understandings, subdued that natural enmity we felt against his government and his grace, and has given us a hope full of glory! Now we are enabled to trust in him; now we find a measure of stability in the midst of a changing world; now we can look forward to death and judgment with composure, knowing whom we have believed, and that we have an Advocate with the Father, Jesus Christ the righteous.

Sequel to Cardiphonia: Letters to Mr. William Cowper, [6:152]; 4:394

Unto the upright there ariseth light in the darkness.—Psa. 112:4.

I FIND vanity engraven in capital letters, on myself and everything around me; and, while encompassed with mercies, and so thoroughly satisfied with my outward condition, that I could hardly wish a single circumstance altered, I feel emptiness, and groan being burdened.

My preaching seems, in some respects, contrary to my experience. The two points on which I most largely insist, are, the glories of the Redeemer, and the happiness of a life of communion with God. I can often find something to say on these subjects in the pulpit; but, at some other times, my thoughts of Jesus are so low, disjointed, and interrupted, that it seems as if I knew nothing of him but by the hearing of the ear. And answerable to this, is the sensible communion I have with him. Alas! how faint, how infrequent! I approach the throne of grace, encumbered with a thousand distractions of thought, each of which seems to engage more of my attention than the business I have in hand.

To complete the riddle, I would add, that, notwithstanding all these complaints, which seem great enough to forbid my hope, to plunge me in despair, I have peace at bottom. I see, I know, I cannot deny, that he is all-sufficient; can, and does pity and help me, unworthy as I am; and though I seldom enjoy a glimpse of sunshine, yet I am not wholly in the dark. My heart is vile, and even my prayers are sin; I wish I could mourn more, but the Lord forbid I should sorrow as those that have no hope. He is able to save to the uttermost. His blood speaks louder than all my evils. My soul is very sick, but my Physician is infallible. He never turns out any as incurable, of whom he has once taken the charge... Help me to praise him; and may he help you to proclaim the glory of his salvation, and to rejoice in it yourself.

Who is among you that feareth the Lord, that obeyeth the voice of his
servant, that walketh in darkness, and hath no light? let him trust
in the name of the Lord, and stay upon his God.—Isa. 50:10.

I LONG for you to learn to distinguish between what are properly the effects of a nature miserably depraved, and which shows itself in the heart of every child of God, and the effects of Satan's immediate temptations. What you complain of, are fiery darts, but you cannot be properly said to shoot them at yourself; they come from an enemy, and the shield of faith is given you, that you may quench them. Why then are you so ready to throw it away? You seem to think yourself better at one time than at another; now I believe that we, as in and of ourselves, are always alike. Look at the sea; sometimes it rages and tosses its waves, at another time it is calm and smooth. But the nature of the sea is not changed; it is not grown more gentle in itself than it was before; wait but till the next storm, and you will see it rage again as much as ever. Our unrenewed part is as untameable as the sea. When temptations are at a distance, or the Lord is present, it may lie quiet, but it is always deceitful and desperately wicked. Or like a lion, which may be sometimes awake, sometimes asleep; but whether asleep or awake, it is a lion still, and a little matter will rouse it from its slumber, and set it roaring; though, while sleeping, it may seem as harmless as a cat.

If we could muse less upon ourselves, and meditate more upon the Lord Jesus, we should do better. He likewise is always the same; as near and as gracious in the storm as in the calm. Yea, he expresses a peculiar care of those who are tempted, tossed, and not comforted. Though you are sore thrust at that you may fall, he will be your stay. But I wish you could more readily rest upon his word, and rejoice in his righteousness, even in that only.

Unto me, who am less than the least of all saints, is this grace given, that
I should preach among the Gentiles the unsearchable riches of Christ.
—Eph. 3:8.

YOUR judgment in the gospel is sound; but there is a legal something in your experience, which perplexes you. You are capable
of advising others; I wish you could apply more effectually what you
preach, to yourself, and distinguish in your own case between a cause
of humiliation and a reason of distress. You cannot be too sensible of
the inward and inbred evils you complain of; but you may be, yea,
you are, improperly affected by them. You say, you find it hard to
believe it compatible with the Divine purity to embrace or employ
such a monster as yourself. You express not only a low opinion of
yourself, which is right, but too low an opinion of the person, work,
and promises of the Redeemer; which is certainly wrong. And it
seems too, that, though the total, absolute depravity of human nature
is a fundamental article in your creed, you do not experimentally take
up that doctrine, in the length, and breadth, and depth of it, as it lies
in the word of God. Or else, why are you continually disappointed
and surprised that in and out of yourself you find nothing but evil?
A man with two broken legs will hardly wonder that he is not able to
run, or even to stand. Your complaints seem to go upon the supposition, that, though you have nothing good of your own, you ought
to have; and most certainly you ought if you were under the law; but
the gospel is provided for the helpless and the worthless. You do not
wonder that it is cold in winter, or dark at midnight. All depends
upon the sun; just so the exercise of grace depends upon the Sun
of Righteousness. When he withdraws, we find ourselves very bad
indeed, but no worse in ourselves than the Scriptures declare us to be.
If, indeed, the Divine rectitude and purity accepts and employs you,
it is not for your own sake, nor could it be were you ten thousand
times better than you are. You have not, you cannot have, anything
in the sight of God, but what you derive from the righteousness and
atonement of Jesus. If you could keep him more constantly in view,
you would be more comfortable. He would be more honoured.

Sequel to Cardiphonia: Letters to Rev. Mr. Joshua Symonds, [6:185]; 4:421

*And I prayed unto the LORD my God, and made my confession ... We
have sinned, and have committed iniquity, and have done wickedly, and
have rebelled, even by departing from thy precepts and
from thy judgments.—Dan. 9:4, 5.*

I HAD no dread of the Fast-day; for, whether overtures towards
peace had been proposed or not by Lord N****, I should most
certainly not have prayed for havock, but should, both in prayer and
preaching, have expressed my desires and longings for a stop to the
effusion of blood. But I fear we are not yet come to the crisis. The
steps now taking would, humanly speaking, have done something
awhile ago; but they are now too late, and, I think, will be rejected.
But I know not the Lord's secret will. That I am sure will take place.
As to outward appearances, and the purposes of men, *pro* and *con*,
I pay little regard to them. Indeed, they are no more stable than
the clouds in a storm, which vary their shape every moment. It is
enough for us that the Lord reigns, is carrying on his own cause, and
will take care of his own people. The best, the only way in which we
can serve the public, is by praying for it, and mourning for those
sins which have given rise to these calamities. Alas! what signifies
one day of humiliation in a year? When the day is over, everything
goes on just as it did before. The busy world, the carefree world, and
the religious world, are, I suppose, much the same since the fast as
they were before it: buying and selling, eating and drinking, dancing
and playing—and the professing sheep biting and tearing each other
like wolves; or else like decoy-ducks, enticing one another into the
world's snares. And, though I find fault with others, I have enough
to look upon at home. The Lord pardon them and me also! My heart
is deceitful and wicked; my services poor and polluted, my sins very
many, and greatly aggravated; so that I should be one of the last to be
censorious. And yet I cannot help seeing that the profession of many
is cold where it should be warm, and only warm in animosity and
contention. The Lord help us; for we are in a woeful case as a people.

Sequel to Cardiphonia: Letters to Rev. Mr. Joshua Symonds, [6:189]; 4:425

I am the good shepherd, and know my sheep, and am known of mine.
—John 10:14.

WE are his sheep; he is our Shepherd. If a sheep had reason, and were sensible of its own state, how weak to withstand the wolf, how prone in itself to wander, how utterly unable to provide for its own subsistence; it could have no comfort, unless it knew that it was under the care of a shepherd; and, in proportion to the opinion it formed of the shepherd's watchfulness and sufficiency, such would be its confidence and peace. But if you could suppose the sheep had depravity likewise, then it would act as we often do; its reason would degenerate into vain reasoning, it would distrust the shepherd, and find fault with his management. It would burden itself with contrivances and cares; tremble under the thoughts of a hard winter, and never be easy unless it was surrounded with hay-stacks. It would study from morning till night where to hide itself out of the wolf's way. Poor, wise, silly sheep! if thou hadst not a shepherd, all thy schemes would be fruitless; when thou hadst broken thy heart with care, thou art still as unable to preserve thyself as thou wast before: and if thou hast a good shepherd, they are all needless. Is it not sufficient that he careth for thee?

Thus I could preach to such a sheep as I have supposed; and thus I try to preach to my own heart... Till the Lord's purposes by us and concerning us, are fulfilled, we are in perfect safety, though on a field of battle, or surrounded by the pestilence. I trust you will be spared awhile longer to your family, friends, and people. Upon the same grounds, if either of your children should be removed, I shall not so directly ascribe it to the illness, as to the will of God; for, if, upon the whole, it be the most for his glory, and best for you, they likewise shall recover. Should he appoint otherwise, it must be best, because he does it; and a glance of the light of his countenance, the influence of that grace which he has promised shall be afforded according to our day, will enable you to resign them. I do not say it will cost you no pain; but in defiance of the feelings of flesh and blood, you will, I trust, hold nothing so dear that you have received from him as to be unwilling to return it into his hands when he is pleased to call for it.

Sequel to Cardiphonia: Letters to Rev. Mr. Joshua Symonds, [6:191]; 4:426

But Hezekiah rendered not again according to the benefit done unto him; for his heart was lifted up.—2 Chron. 32:25.

I HAVE observed, that most of the advantages which Satan is recorded to have gained against the Lord's servants have been after great and signal deliverances and favours; as in the cases of Noah, Lot, David, and Hezekiah. And I have found it so repeatedly in my own experience. How often, if my history were written by an inspired pen, might this proof of the depravity of my heart be inserted; 'But John Newton rendered not again according to the benefits received; for his heart was lifted up.' May it be far otherwise with you. May you come out of the furnace refined; and may it appear to yourself and all around you, that the Lord has done you good by your afflictions. Thus vile are our natures; to be capable of making the Lord such perverse returns as we often do! How should we blush if our earthly friends and benefactors could bring such charges of ingratitude against us, as he justly might. No; they could not bear a thousandth part; the dearest and kindest of them would have been weary of us, and cast us off long ago, had we behaved so to them. We may well say, Who is a God like unto thee, that pardonest iniquity, and passest by the transgression of the remnant of thine heritage? It seems that the prophet selects the Lord's patience towards his own people, as the most astonishing of all his perfections, and that which eminently distinguishes him from all other beings. And indeed, the sins of believers are attended with aggravations peculiar to themselves. The inhabitants of Sodom and Gomorrah were great sinners, but they did not sin against light, and love, and experience. I see many profligate sinners around me, but the Lord has not followed them with mercies, instructions, and pardons, as he has followed me. My outward life, through mercy, is not like theirs; but, if the secrets of my heart were laid open, they who are favourable to me would not think me much better than the worst of them. Especially at some times and seasons, since I first tasted that he was gracious. And yet he has borne with me, and is pleased to say, he will never leave me nor forsake me.

Sequel to Cardiphonia: Letters to Rev. Mr. Joshua Symonds, [6:194]; 4:429

Then opened he their understanding,
that they might understand the scriptures.—Luke 24:45.

WHEN we begin to know ourselves, and to feel the uncertainty and darkness which are inseparable from our fallen nature, how comfortable and encouraging is it to reflect, that God has given us his infallible word, and promised us his infallible Spirit, to guide us into all necessary truth; and that in the study of the one, and in dependence upon the other, none can miss the way of peace and salvation, who are sincerely desirous to find it. But we are cautioned to keep our eye upon both; and the caution is necessary, for we are too prone to separate what God hath joined together, Isa. 8:20, 1 Cor. 2:10, 11. What strange mistakes have been made by some who have thought themselves able to interpret Scripture by their own abilities as scholars and critics, though they have studied with much diligence!... But, unless our dependence upon divine teaching bears some proportion to our diligence, we may take much pains to little purpose. On the other hand, we are directed to expect the teaching and assistance of the Holy Spirit only within the limits, and by the medium of the written word. For he has not promised to reveal new truths, but to enable us to understand what we read in the Bible: and if we venture beyond the pale of Scripture, we are upon enchanted ground, and exposed to all the illusions of imagination and enthusiasm. But an attention to the word of God, joined to humble supplications for his Spirit, will lead us to new advances in true knowledge. The exercises of our minds, and the observations we shall make upon the conduct of others, and the dispensations of God's providence, will all concur to throw light upon the Scripture, and to confirm to us what we there read concerning ourselves, the world, and the true happiness revealed to sinners in and through Jesus Christ. The more sensible we are of the disease, the more we shall admire the great Physician; the more we are convinced that the creature is vanity, the more we shall be stirred up to seek our rest in God. And this will endear the gospel to us; as in Christ, and in him only, we can hope to find that righteousness and strength of which we are utterly destitute ourselves.

Sequel to Cardiphonia: Letters to Rev. Dr. George Dixon, [6:202]; 4:435

I am come that they might have life, and that they might have it more abundantly.—John 10:10.

I DO not wonder, my dear sir, that, though you are persuaded God will not fail on his part and forsake you first, yet you have sensible fears and apprehensions lest you should forsake him. The knowledge you have of your own weakness, must make your system very uncomfortable, while it leaves your final salvation to depend (as you express it) *entirely upon yourself.* Nay, I must add, that either your heart is better than mine, or at least that you are not equally sensible of its vileness, or your fears would be entirely insupportable; or else, which I rather think is the case, the former part of your letter, wherein you speak so highly of the throne of grace, and confess so plainly that without the grace of Christ you can do nothing, is your experience, and the real feeling and working of your heart, while the latter part, wherein you approve the plan which leaves sinners to depend entirely upon themselves, is but an opinion, which has been plausibly obtruded upon you, and which you find at times very unfavourable to your peace. It must, it will be so. The admission of a mixed gospel, which indeed is no gospel at all, will bring disquiet into the conscience. If you think you are in the same circumstances, as to choice and power, as Adam was, I cannot blame you for fearing lest you should acquit yourself no better than he did. Ah! my dear sir, Jesus came not only that we might have the life which sin had forfeited, restored unto us, but that we might have it more abundantly; the privileges greater, and the tenure more secure: for now our life is not in our own keeping, but is hid with Christ in God. He undertakes to do all for us, in us, and by us, and he claims the praise and honour of the whole, and is determined to save us in such a way as shall stain the pride of all human glory, that he who glorieth may glory in the Lord.

Sequel to Cardiphonia: Letters to Rev. Dr. George Dixon, [6:242]; 4:466;

As sorrowful, yet alway rejoicing.—2 Cor. 6:10.

THE letter we received yesterday from Mr. ****, has given us some painful feelings for you both. He says, you are lower in your spirits than usual. By this time, I hope, the Lord hath raised your spirits again. I wonder not that they sometimes droop. Your part is trying and solitary, affording many handles, which the enemy, if permitted, knows how to take hold of. The pressure of your troubles is further aggravated by their long continuance. It is one thing to stand tolerably in a skirmish, when it is but a brush and away; like a hasty shower in a summer's day, which presently leaves us in full possession of the sun again: it is quite a different thing to endure patiently, when a trial lasts, not for days or months, but from year to year, when expectation seems to fail, and all our scouts return to tell us, there is no perceptible abatement of the waters.

But is this the way to raise your spirits?... Let us try again. Ay, this is it. Read the inscription, 'As sorrowful, yet always rejoicing.' No wonder that we are often sorrowing in such a world as this; but to be always rejoicing, though in the midst of tribulation, this may seem strange, but it is no more strange than true. When I want witness to this truth in open court, I may confidently subpoena you to confirm it.

They who would always rejoice, must derive their joy from a source which is invariably the same; in other words, from Jesus. Oh, that name! what a person, what an office, what a love, what a life, what a death, does it recall to our minds! Come, madam, let us leave *our* troubles to themselves for a while, and let us walk to Golgotha, and there take a view of *his*. We stop, as we are going, at Gethsemane, for it is not a step out of the road. There he lies, bleeding, though not wounded; or, if wounded, it is by an invisible, an almighty hand. Now I begin to see what sin has done. Now let me bring my sorrows, and compare, measure, and weigh them, against the sorrows of my Saviour! Foolish attempt! to weigh a mote against a mountain, against the universe!

A Letter to a Friend in Trouble, [6:377]; 4:581

But know that the Lord hath set apart him that is godly for himself:
the Lord will hear when I call unto him.—Psa. 4:3.

IT pleases me to think, that, though I am much and often sur-rounded with noise, smoke, and dust, my friend, Mrs. C*** enjoys the beautiful scenes of rural life. Oh, how I long sometimes to spend a day or two among woods, and lawns, and brooks, and hedgerows, to hear the birds sing in the bushes, and to wander among the sheep and lambs, or to stand under the shadow of an old oak, upon a hill top! Thus I lived at Olney: how different is London! But, hush, Olney was the place once, London is the place now. Hither the Lord brought me, and here he is pleased to support me, and in some meas-ure, I trust, to own me. I am satisfied. Come, I hope I can make a good shift without your woods, and bushes, and pastures. What is the prospect from the finest hill in Essex, compared with the prospect I have from St. Mary's pulpit? What is the singing of birds, com-pared with the singing our hymn after sermon on a Sunday evening? What the bleating of lambs, compared with the lispings of inquiring souls, who are seeking after Jesus? No, welcome noise, and dust, and smoke; so that we may but be favoured with his gracious presence in our hearts, houses, and ordinances. This will make all situations nearly alike, if we see the Lord's hand placing us in it, are enabled to do his will, and to set him before us, as our Lord and our Beloved... He, in whose presence is life, whose loving-kindness is better than life, be with you all. Though we do not see each other, we are not far asunder. The throne of grace is a centre, where thousands daily meet in spirit, and have real though secret communion with each other. They eat of one bread, walk by one rule; they have one Father and one home. There they will shortly meet, to part no more. They will shine, each one like the sun. They will form a glorious constellation, millions of suns shining together in their Lord's kingdom.

*Sequel to Cardiphonia: Letters to Mrs. C***, [6:365]; 4:563*

If any man among you seem to be religious, and bridleth not his tongue,
but deceiveth his own heart, this man's religion is vain.—James 1:26.

I ALLOW it possible that the best of men, in an unguarded hour, and through the pressure of some sudden and violent temptation or provocation, may occasionally act or speak unsuitably to their habitual character. But I think the apostle must mean thus much at least, that, when grace is in the heart, it will so regulate and control the tongue, that it shall not customarily offend; and that, without some evidence of such a regulation, we are not bound to acknowledge any man to be a Christian, however splendid his profession may be in other respects. Nay, I think we may further say of this *test*, what the magicians of Egypt acknowledged upon another occasion, 'This is the finger of God!' This is, perhaps, the only outward mark of a believer, which the hypocrite cannot imitate. In many things he may seem to be religious; in some, perhaps, he may appear to go beyond the real Christian; but, because his heart is naught, he cannot bridle his tongue.

The man who seems, and who desires to be thought religious, may have many qualifications to support his claim, which may be valuable and commendable in themselves, and yet are of no avail to the possessor if he bridleth not his tongue. He may have much religious knowledge; I mean, of such knowledge as may be acquired in the use of ordinary means. He may have a warm zeal, and may contend earnestly (in his way) for the faith once delivered to the saints. He may be able to talk well on spiritual subjects, to pray with freedom and fervency; yea, he may be a preacher, and acquit himself to the satisfaction of sincere Christians: or he may be a fair trader, a good neighbour, a kind master, an affectionate husband or parent, be free from gross vices, and attend constantly upon the ordinances. Will not such a man seem to himself, and probably be esteemed by others, to be religious? yet if, with all these good properties, he does not bridle his tongue, he may be said to want the one thing needful. He deceiveth his own heart; his religion is vain.

Thoughts on the Government of the Tongue, [6:382]; 4:585

*Let your speech be alway with grace, seasoned with salt, that ye may
know how ye ought to answer every man.—Col. 4:6.*

BUT what are we to understand by bridling the tongue?...
Having seen a glimpse of the holiness and majesty, the glory and
the grace, of the great God with whom they have to do, their hearts
are impressed with reverence, and therefore there is a sobriety and
decorum in their language. They cannot speak lightly of him, or of
his ways. One would suppose that no person, who even but seems to
be religious, can directly and expressly profane his name. But there is
a careless manner of speaking of the great God which is very disgusting and very suspicious. So likewise the hearts of believers teach their
mouths to speak honourably of God under all their afflictions and
crosses, acknowledging the wisdom and the mercy of his dispensations; and, if an impatient word escapes them, it grieves and humbles
them, as quite unbecoming their situation as his creatures, and especially as sinful creatures, who have always reason to acknowledge,
that it is of the Lord's mercy they are not wholly consumed.

In what they say of or to others, the tongues of believers are
bridled by a heartfelt regard to truth, love, and purity. It is grievous
to see how nearly and readily some professors of religion will venture upon the borders of a lie; either to defend their own conduct,
to avoid some inconvenience, to procure a supposed advantage, or
sometimes merely to embellish a story. Admitting the possibility of
a sincere person being surprised into the declaration of an untruth,
yet, where instances of this kind are frequent, I hardly know a fouler
blot in profession, or which can give a more just warrant to fear that
such professors know nothing aright either of God or themselves.
The Lord is a God of truth; and he teaches his servants to hate and
abhor lying, and to speak the truth from their hearts. I may add likewise, with regard to promises and bargains, that, though the law of
the land requires, on many occasions, oaths and bonds to secure their
performance, that person, whose word may not be safely depended
upon without either bond or oath, scarcely deserves the name of a
Christian.

Thoughts on the Government of the Tongue, [6:383]; 4:586

Let no corrupt communication proceed out of your mouth, but that
which is good to the use of edifying, that it may minister grace
unto the hearers.—Eph. 4:29.

WHERE grace is in the heart, the tongue will be likewise bridled by the law of love. If we love our neighbour, can we lightly report evil of him, magnify his failings, or use provoking or insulting language? Love thinketh no evil, but beareth, hopeth, and endureth; and acts by the golden rule, to do unto others as we would they should do unto us. They who are under this influence will be gentle and compassionate, disposed to make the most favourable allowances, and of course their tongues will be restrained from the language of malevolence, harsh censure, and slander, though it be familiar to us as our mother tongue, till we are made partakers of the grace of God.

The tongue is also bridled by a regard to purity. Agreeable to the precepts, 'Let no corrupt communication proceed out of your mouth; neither filthiness, nor foolish talking, nor jesting, which are not convenient,' Eph. 4:29; 5:4. Grace has taught believers to hate these things; how then can their tongues speak of them? There are professors, indeed, who can suit their language to their company. When with the people of God, they can talk very seriously; and, at other times, be well pleased to join in vain, frothy, and evil conversation. But this double-mindedness is of itself sufficient to discredit all their pretences to a religious character.

Upon the whole, though perfection is not to be expected, though true believers may, on some occasions, speak rashly, and have great cause for humiliation, watchfulness, and prayer, with respect to the government of their tongues; yet I think the scripture, and particularly the apostle James ... authorizes this conclusion. That, if the tongue is frequently without a bridle ... then, whatever other good qualities he may seem to possess, his speech betrayeth him... Let us think of these things, and entreat the Lord to cast the salt of his grace into the fountain of our hearts, that the streams of our conversation may be wholesome.

Thoughts on the Government of the Tongue, [6:385]; 4:587

But he that received the seed into stony places, the same is he that heareth the word, and anon with joy receiveth it; Yet hath he not root in himself, but dureth for a while: for when tribulation or persecution ariseth because of the word, by and by he is offended.—Matt. 13:20-21.

MULTITUDES, who had been willing to be thought Christians in a time of peace, renounced their profession when they could no longer maintain it without the hazard of their lives. The terms of safety were to invoke the gods, to offer wine and incense to the statue of the emperor, and to blaspheme Christ, which, Pliny was rightly informed, no true Christian could be prevailed on to comply with: yet, in fact, when the persecution was sharp, so many yielded, that the cause seemed visibly to decline. The temples, which had been almost forsaken, were again frequented, the solemnities revived, and the demand for victims greatly increased. It is plain, therefore, that there were, even in those primitive times, many superficial Christians, destitute of that faith and love which are necessary to perseverance in the face of dangers and death. Of course, it is no new thing for men to desert the profession of the truth, to which they have formerly appeared to be attached; through the fear of man, or the love of the world. These are the stony-ground hearers; and our Lord has assured us, that such would be found, wherever his gospel should be preached. But there were others, who, having experienced this gospel to be the power of God unto salvation, were faithful witnesses, and could neither be intimidated nor flattered into a compliance with evil. It is the same at this day: for though we are mercifully exempted from the terror of penal laws, yet the temptations arising from worldly interest, and the prevalence and force of evil customs, will sooner or later be too hard for all professors who have not received that faith which is of the operation of God, which, by communicating a sense of the constraining love of Christ, is alone able to purify the heart from selfish and sinful principles, and to overcome the world with all its allurements and threatenings.

Remarks on Pliny's Letter to Trajan, [6:390]; 4:591

And my speech and my preaching was ... in demonstration of the Spirit
*and of power.—*1 Cor. 2:4.

WHEN Philip preached, the eunuch rejoiced; when Paul preached, Felix trembled. The power of the truth was equally evident in both cases, though the effects were different. One criterion of the gospel ministry, when rightly dispensed, is, that it enters the recesses of the heart. The hearer is amazed to find that the preacher, who perhaps never saw him before, describes him to himself, as though he had lived long in the same house with him, and was acquainted with his conduct, his conversation, and even with his secret thoughts, 1 Cor. 14:24, 25. Thus, a single sentence frequently awakens a long train of recollection, removes scruples, satisfies doubts, and leads to the happiest consequences, and what we read of Nathaniel and the woman of Samaria, is still exemplified in the conversion of many; while others, who wilfully resist the evidence, and turn from the light, which forces itself upon their minds, are left without excuse. If, therefore, you wish to preach the gospel with power, pray for a simple, humble spirit, that you may have no allowed end in view, but to proclaim the glory of the Lord whom you profess to serve, to do his will, and for his sake to be useful to the souls of men. Study the word of God, and the workings of your own heart, and avoid all those connexions, communications, and pursuits, which, experience will tell you, have a tendency to damp the energy, or to blunt the sensibility of your spirit. Thus shall you come forth as a scribe, well instructed in the mysteries of the kingdom, a workman that needeth not to be ashamed, approved of God, acceptable to men, rightly dividing the word of truth... A just confidence of the truths you speak, a sense of the importance of your message, a love to precious souls, and a perception of the Divine presence, will give your discourses a solidity, a seriousness, a weight, which will impress a sympathetic feeling upon your hearers, and they will attend, as to one who speaks with spirit, demonstration, and power.

Letter to a Young Minister, [6:400]; 4:599

And I, brethren, when I came to you, came not with excellency of speech or of wisdom, declaring unto you the testimony of God.—1 Cor. 2:1.

BEWARE of affecting the orator. I do not advise you to pay no regard to a just and proper elocution; it deserves your attention, and many a good sermon loses much of the effect it might otherwise produce, by an awkward and uncouth delivery. But let your elocution be natural. Despise the little arts by which men of little minds endeavour to set themselves off; they will blast your success, and expose you to contempt. The grand principle of gospel oratory is simplicity. Affectation is displeasing in all persons, but in none is it so highly disgusting as in a preacher. A studied attitude, a measured motion, a nice attention to cadences and pauses, a mimicry of theatrical action, may be passable in the recital of a school declamation, but is hateful in the pulpit. Men never do, never can, speak thus, when they speak from the emotion of their hearts. How is it possible then for a man who professes to speak for God, who addresses himself to immortal souls, who discourses upon the most important subjects, the love of Christ, the joys of heaven, or the terrors of the Lord; how is it possible for this man to find leisure or disposition for such pompous trifling, if he really understands and believes what he says? The truly pious will weep for his ill-timed vanity. And if any seem pleased, it is chiefly because this manner of preaching seldom disturbs the conscience, for it cannot be expected that God will vouchsafe the testimony of his Spirit, even to his own truths, when the poor worm who delivers them, is visibly more solicitous for the character of an eloquent speaker, than for the success of his message.

There is another strain of preaching, which, though it wears the garb of zeal, is seldom a proof of any power but the power of self. I mean angry and scolding preaching. The gospel is a benevolent scheme, and whoever speaks in the power of it, will assuredly speak in love… If we can indulge invective and bitterness in the pulpit, we know not what spirit we are of: we are but gratifying our own evil tempers, under the pretence of a concern for the cause of God and truth.

Letter to a Young Minister, [6:402]; 4:600

For whosoever exalteth himself shall be abased;
and he that humbleth himself shall be exalted.—Luke 14:11.

SPIRITUAL pride and self-complacence will likewise infallibly cause a declension in the divine life, though the mind may be preserved from the infection of doctrinal errors, and though the power of gospel truth may for a time have been really experienced. If our attainments in knowledge and gifts, and even in grace, seduce us into a good opinion of ourselves, as if we were wise and good, we are already ensnared, in danger of falling every step we take, of mistaking the right path, and proceeding from bad to worse, without a power of correcting or even of discovering our deviations, unless and until the Lord mercifully interposes, by restoring us to a spirit of humility and dependence. For God, who giveth more grace to the humble, resisteth the proud; he beholds them with abhorrence, in proportion to the degree in which they admire themselves. It is the invariable law of his kingdom, that everyone who exalteth himself shall be abased. True Christians, through the remaining evil of their hearts, and the subtle temptations of their enemy, are liable, not only to the workings of that pride which is common to our fallen nature, but to a certain kind of pride… We have nothing but what we have received, and therefore to be proud of titles, wealth, or any temporal advantages, by which the providence of God has distinguished us, is sinful; but for those who confess themselves to be sinners, and therefore deserving of nothing but misery and wrath, to be proud of those peculiar blessings which are derived from the gospel of his grace, is a wickedness of which even the fallen angels are not capable. The apostle Paul was so aware of his danger of being exalted above measure, through the abundant revelations and peculiar favours which the Lord had afforded him, that he says, 'There *was given* me a messenger of Satan to buffet me.' He speaks of this sharp dispensation as an additional mercy, because he saw it was necessary, and designed to keep him humble and attentive to his own weakness. Ministers who are honoured with singular abilities and success, have great need of watchfulness and prayer on this account.

Of a Decline in the Spiritual Life, [6:407]; 4:603

*And beginning at Moses and all the prophets, he expounded unto them
in all the scriptures the things concerning himself.*—Luke 24:27.

THE preaching of the gospel being an instituted means of grace,
ought to be thankfully and frequently improved. And books
that have a savour and unction may likewise be helpful, provided we
read them with caution, compare them with the Scripture, and do
not give ourselves implicitly to the rules or decisions of any man or set
of men, but remember that one is our Master and infallible Teacher,
even Christ. But the chief and grand means of edification, without
which all other helps will disappoint us, and prove like clouds without water, are the Bible and prayer, the word of grace and the throne
of grace. A frequent perusal of the Bible will give us an enlarged
and comprehensive view of the whole of religion, its origin, nature,
genius, and tendency, and preserve us from an over-attachment to
any system of man's compilation. The fault of the several systems,
under which, as under so many banners, the different denomina-
tions of Christians are ranged, is, that there is usually something left
out which ought to have been taken in, and something admitted,
of supposed advantage, not authorized by the scriptural standard.
A Bible Christian, therefore, will see much to approve in a variety
of forms and parties; the providence of God may lead or fix him in
a more immediate connexion with some one of them, but his spirit
and affection will not be confined within these narrow enclosures.
He insensibly borrows and unites that which is excellent in each,
perhaps without knowing how far he agrees with them, because he
finds all in the written word.

I know not a better rule of reading the Scripture, than to read it
through from beginning to end; and, when we have finished it once,
to begin it again. We shall meet with many passages which we can
make little improvement of, but not so many in the second reading
as in the first, and fewer in the third than in the second: provided
we pray to him who has the keys to open our understandings, and to
anoint our eyes with his spiritual ointment.

On Reading the Bible, [6:417]; 4:611

For as the sufferings of Christ abound in us, so our consolation
also aboundeth by Christ.—2 Cor. 1:5.

NATURAL fortitude, and cold reasonings, more conformable to the philosophy of the heathens, than to the spirit of the gospel, may stifle complaints; but to rejoice in tribulation, and in everything give thanks, are privileges peculiar to those who can joy in God through our Lord Jesus Christ, by whom they have obtained reconciliation. A cordial belief that he suffered for our sins, that we are accepted in him, that he is our Shepherd, full of care, compassion, and power; who knows the very thoughts and feelings of the heart, and who, having been tempted for us, is able and ready to succour us in all our temptations: a persuasion that his wisdom and love preside over all our dispensations; a liberty of applying to him for strength according to our day, confirmed by a thousand past proofs that, when we have called upon him, he has heard, supported, and delivered us; a humble confidence, which only he can give, that the heaviest afflictions are light, and the longest momentary, compared with that far more exceeding and eternal weight of glory, to which he is leading us by them; and that sense of the demerit of our sins, only fully to be estimated by the value of the necessary atonement, which will always constrain us to acknowledge that our greatest sufferings are less than our iniquities deserve. Considerations of this kind come home to our bosoms, are fully adequate to our wants, communicate a peace passing understanding, and enable those who feel their influence to say, 'It is the Lord, let him do what seemeth him good;' and often they can add, to the astonishment of those who know not the power of their principles, As the sufferings of Christ (those which we endure for his sake or from his hand) abound in us, so our consolation also aboundeth by Christ.

Plain Tests of True Doctrine, [6:424]; 4:617

Blessed is he whose transgression is forgiven, whose sin is covered.
—Psa. 32:1.

AFFLICTIONS are the fruit of sin, and because our sins have been many, our afflictions may be many. 'But where sin has abounded, grace has much more abounded.'

Before our Lord healed the paralytic man who was brought to him, he said, *Be of good cheer, thy sins are forgiven thee.* His outward malady rendered him an object of compassion to those who brought him; but he appears to have been sensible of an inward malady, which only Jesus could discern, or pity, or relieve. I doubt not but his conscience was burdened with guilt. An assurance, therefore, that his sins were forgiven, was sufficient to make him be of good cheer, whether his palsy were removed or not. To this purpose the psalmist speaks absolutely and without exception. 'Blessed is the man,' however circumstanced, 'whose transgression is forgiven, whose iniquity is covered.' Though he be poor, afflicted, diseased, neglected or despised, if the Lord imputeth not his iniquity to him, he is a blessed man. There is no situation in human life so deplorable, but a sense of the pardoning love of God can support and comfort the sufferer under it, compose his spirit, yea make him exceedingly joyful in all his tribulations; for he feels the power of the blood of Jesus cleansing his conscience from guilt, and giving him access by faith to the throne of grace, with liberty to say, Abba, Father; he knows that all his trials are under the direction of wisdom and love, are all working together for his good, and that the heaviest of them are light, and the longest momentary, in comparison of that far more exceeding and eternal weight of glory, which is reserved for him in a better world. Even at present in the midst of his sufferings, having communion with God, and a gracious submission to his will, he possesses a peace that passeth understanding, and which the world can neither give nor take away.

Messiah: The Consolation, [4:11]; 3:16

Now our Lord Jesus Christ himself, and God, even our Father, which
hath loved us, and hath given us everlasting consolation and good hope
through grace, Comfort your hearts, and stablish you
in every good word and work.—2 Thess. 2:16, 17.

SALVATION is wholly of *grace*; not only undeserved, but undesired by us, till he is pleased to awaken us to a sense of our need of it. And then we find everything prepared that our wants require, or our wishes can conceive; yea, that he has done exceedingly beyond what we could either ask or think.

When the Lord God, who knows the human heart, would speak comfort to it, he proposes one object, and only one, as the necessary and all-sufficient source of consolation. This is MESSIAH. Jesus in his person and offices, known and received by faith, affords a balm for every wound, a cordial for every care. If we admit that they who live in the spirit of the world, can make a poor shift to amuse themselves, and be tolerably satisfied in a state of prosperity, while everything goes on according to their wish; while we make this concession, (which, however, is more than we need allow them, for we know that no state of life is free from anxiety, disappointment, weariness, and disgust,) yet we must consider them as objects of compassion... And they are to be pitied indeed, who, when their gourds are withered, when the desire of their eyes is taken from them with a stroke, or the evil which they most feared touches them, or when death looks them closely in the face, have no acquaintance with God, no access to the throne of grace, but, being without Christ are without a solid hope of good hereafter, though they are forced to feel the vanity and inconstancy of everything here. But they who know MESSIAH, who believe in him, and partake of his spirit, cannot be comfortless. They recollect what *he* suffered for them, they know that every circumstance and event of life is under his direction, and designed to work for their good; that though they sow in tears, they shall soon reap in joy; and therefore they possess their souls in patience, and are cheerful, yea comfortable, under those trying dispensations of Providence.

Messiah: The Consolation, [4:12]; 3:17

Forasmuch then as the children are partakers of flesh and blood, he also himself likewise took part of the same.—Heb. 2:14.

T HE Mediator, the Surety for sinful men, must himself be a man. Because those whom he came to redeem were partakers of flesh and blood, he therefore took part of the same. Had not MESSIAH engaged for us, and appeared in our nature, a case would have occurred, which I think we may warrantably deem incongruous to the Divine wisdom. I mean, that while fire and hail, snow and vapour, and the stormy wind, fulfil the will of God; while the brutes are faithful to the instincts implanted in them by their Maker; a whole species of intelligent beings would have fallen short of the original law and design of their creation, and indeed have acted in direct and continual opposition to it. For the duty of man, to love, serve, and trust God with all his heart and mind, and to love his neighbour as himself, is founded in the very nature and constitution of things, and necessarily results from his relation to God, and his absolute dependence on him as a creature. Such a disposition must undoubtedly have been *natural* to man before his fall, as it is for a bird to fly, or a fish to swim. The prohibitory form of the law delivered to Israel from Mount Sinai, is a sufficient intimation that it was designed for *sinners*. Surely our first parents, while in a state of innocence, could not stand in need of warnings and threatenings to restrain them from worshipping idols, or profaning the name of the great God whom they loved. Nor would it have been necessary to forbid murder, adultery, or injustice, if his posterity had continued under the law of their creation, the law of love. But the first act of disobedience degraded and disabled man, detached him from his proper centre, if I may so speak, and incapacitated him both for his duty and his happiness. After his fall, it became impossible for either Adam or his posterity to obey the law of God. But MESSIAH fulfilled it exactly, as a man, and the principles of it are renewed, by the power of his grace, in all who believe on him. And though their best endeavours fall short, his obedience to it is accepted on their behalf; and he will at length perfectly restore them to their primitive order and honour.

Messiah: Immanuel, [4:57]; 3:50

Emmanuel ... God with us.—Matt. 1:23.

AS fallen creatures, we had lost the true knowledge of God, and were unable to form such conceptions of his greatness and goodness, as are necessary to inspire us with reverence, to engage our confidence, or produce obedience to his will. His glory shines in the heavens and fills the earth; we are surrounded by the tokens of his power and presence; yet, till we are instructed by his word, and enlightened by his Holy Spirit, he is to us an *unknown God*. The prevalence of idolatry was early... Men who boasted of their reason, worshipped the sun and moon, yea, the works of their own hands, rather than the Creator. And even where revelation is vouchsafed, the bulk of mankind live without God in the world. But he is known, trusted, and served, by those who know MESSIAH. To them his glory is displayed in the person of Jesus Christ. His agency is perceived in the creation, his providence is acknowledged, and his presence felt as *God with us*.

As fallen creatures, God is against us, and we are against him. The alienation of our hearts is the great cause of our ignorance of him. We are willingly ignorant. The thoughts of him are unwelcome to us, and we do not like to retain him in our knowledge. Guilt is the parent of atheism. A secret foreboding, that if there be a God we are obnoxious to his displeasure; and that if he takes cognizance of our conduct, we have nothing to hope, but everything to fear from him... What a proof is this of the enmity of the heart of man against him! that so many persons who would tremble at the thought of being in a ship, driven by the winds and waves, without compass or pilot, should yet think it desirable, if it were possible, to be assured, that in a world like this, so full of uncertainty, trouble, and change, all things were left at random, without the interference of a supreme governor. But this enmity, these dark apprehensions, are removed when the gospel is received by faith. For it brings us the welcome news, that there is forgiveness with him; that God is reconciled in his Son to all who seek his mercy. In this sense, likewise, MESSIAH is 'Immanuel, God with us,' on our side, no longer the avenger of sin, but the author of salvation.

Messiah: Immanuel, [4:64]; 3:55

For unto us a child is born, unto us a son is given.—Isa. 9:6.

'UNTO us a child is born;' in our nature, born of a woman: 'Unto us a son is given,' not merely a man-child, but, emphatically *a son*, the Son of God. This was the most precious gift, the highest proof and testimony of Divine love. The distinction and union of these widely-distant natures, which constitute the person of Christ, the God-man, the Mediator, is, in the judgment and language of the apostle, the 'great mystery of godliness,' the pillar and ground of truth... It is the central truth of revelation, which, like the sun, diffuses a light upon the whole system, no part of which can be rightly understood without it. Thus the Lord of all humbled himself, to appear in the form of a servant, for the sake of sinners.

'The government shall be upon his shoulder.' In our nature he suffered, and in the same nature he reigns. When he had overcome the sharpness, the sting of death, he took possession of the kingdom of glory as his own, and opened it to all who believe in him. Now we can say, he who governs in heaven and on earth, and whom all things obey, is 'the child who was born, the son who was given for us.'... [Those united to him by faith] have, in one respect, an appropriate honour, in which the angels cannot share. Their best friend, related to them in the same nature, is seated upon the throne of glory. Since he is 'for them, who can be against them?' What may they not expect, when he who has so loved them as to redeem them with his own blood, 'has all power committed unto him, both in heaven and on earth!'

'His name shall be called Wonderful.' In another place the word is rendered 'Secret.' It is true of him in both senses. He is *Wonderful* in his person, obedience, and sufferings; in his grace, government, and glory. So far as we understand his name, the revelation by which, as by a name, he is made known, we may, we must, believe, admire, and adore. But how limited and defective is our knowledge! His name is *Secret*. Who can 'by searching find him out?' His greatness is incomprehensible, his wisdom untraceable, his fulness inexhaustible, his power infinite.

Messiah: Characters and Names of Messiah, [4:106]; 3:87

Christ the power of God, and the wisdom of God.—1 Cor. 1:24.

ANOTHER of his names is 'Counsellor.' The great councils of redemption, in which every concern respecting the glory of God and the salvation of sinners was adjusted, were established with him, and in him, before the foundation of the world. And he is our Counsellor or Advocate with the Father, who pleads our cause, and manages all our affairs in perfect righteousness, and with infallible success; so that no suit can possibly miscarry which he is pleased to undertake. To him likewise we must apply (and we shall not apply in vain) for wisdom and direction, in all that belongs to our duty, and the honour of our profession in the present life. In all our difficulties, dangers, and cares, we must look to him for guidance and support. This is to be wise unto salvation. His secret is with them that consult him; so that, though the world may deem them weak and ignorant as babes (and he teaches them to think thus of themselves), they have a cheering and practical knowledge of many important subjects which are entirely hidden from those who are wise and prudent in their own eyes.

He is 'the mighty God.' Though in the office of Mediator, he acts in the character of a servant, his perfections and attributes are truly Divine. Only the Mighty God could make a provision capable of answering the demands of the holy law, which we had transgressed. Only the Mighty God could be a suitable Shepherd to lead millions of weak helpless creatures to glory, through the many difficulties, dangers, and enemies they are exposed to in their passage. Add to this, the honour, dependence, and obedience, which this great Shepherd claims from his sheep, are absolute and supreme; and they would be guilty of idolatry, if they did not know that he is the *mighty God*.

Messiah: Characters and Names of Messiah, [4:107]; 3:88

The Prince of Peace.—Isa. 9:6.

LASTLY, he shall be called 'the Prince of Peace,' whose sovereign prerogative it is, to 'speak peace to his people;' and there is no peace deserving the name, but that which he bestows. The Scripture expressly declares, 'There is no peace to the wicked.' By whatever name we call that thoughtless security and insensibility, in which mankind generally live, while ignorant of God and of themselves, we cannot allow it to be peace. It is the effect of blindness and hardness of heart; it will neither bear reflection nor examination. Can they be said to possess peace, however fatally regardless they may be of futurity, who are at present under the dominion of restless, insatiable, and inconsistent passions and appetites? But the kingdom of MESSIAH is a kingdom of peace, and in him his happy subjects enjoy 'a peace which passeth all understanding,' such as the world can neither give nor take away. He has made 'peace by the blood of his cross,' for all that come unto God by him. Until they are in trouble and distress, until they feel the bitterness and fear the consequences of their sins, and see the impossibility of helping themselves, they will not apply to him; but whenever they do seek him, thus 'weary and heavy laden,' he hears their prayer. Their minds, for a season, are like the sea in a storm; they are distressed with guilt, fears, and temptations; but when he reveals his mighty name and boundless grace to their hearts, and says, 'Peace, be still,' there is a great calm. 'Being justified by faith, they have peace with God through our Lord Jesus Christ.' He gives them peace likewise in a changing troublesome world, by inviting and enabling them to cast all their cares upon him, and to trust all their concerns in his hands, upon the assurance his word gives them, that he careth for them, and will manage and overrule everything for their good.

Messiah: Characters and Names of Messiah, [4:109]; 3:89

Let me die the death of the righteous, and let my last end be like his!
—Num. 23:10.

ASK death-beds, my friends, they will speak; I know, indeed, that many persons die as they lived, careless and insensible, no more impressed by the thoughts of an eternal state, than the beasts of the field; and I know that others, lest by-standers should suspect them of fear, or question the validity of their infidel principles to support them, have affected to jest in their last hours, and to meet death with a facetiousness utterly unbecoming a wise man. For it is a serious thing to die; and the dignified composure of a true Christian differs so much from the levity of a buffoon, as the sober conduct of a man differs from the mimicry and grimace of a monkey. I have known persons, not in the lowest class for that wisdom and virtue which is taught in the schools of scepticism, tremble, like the boughs of a tree in a storm, when the approach of death has excited an awful sensibility in their conscience, recalled to their remembrance a view of their past lives, and opened to their mind a prospect (till then unregarded) of what was before them. I have had the comfort of seeing many others very differently affected in dying circumstances. I have seen enough to convince me, if the testimony of the word of God needed any confirmation, that the true wisdom of man is most conspicuous (if he retains his senses) when he is about to leave this world; and that his duty, dignity, and happiness, are displayed to the highest advantage, when, like Stephen, he is enabled to commit his departing spirit into the hands of Jesus, and to venture his eternal all upon his faithfulness and ability to save, to the uttermost, those who, renouncing every other ground of hope, confide entirely in his mediation. I have seen them in this situation, in the exercise of a good conscience, possessed of a solid, unshaken peace, and at a loss for words to express their joys, yet humbly sensible of their unworthiness, and the defects and defilements of their best services. I have heard them regret, that their regard to him, and their dependence upon him, had been so faint and so feeble; but I never heard one regret, that he had honoured him too highly, or placed too much confidence in his authority and power.

Plain Tests of True Doctrine, [6:430]; 4:621

Favour is deceitful, and beauty is vain: but a woman that feareth the
LORD, she shall be praised.—Prov. 31:30.

YOU have been sick, nigh unto death, but the Lord has raised you up: may he enable you to consider sin as the source and cause of every sorrow; and that the afflictions the Lord sends, however trying to the flesh, are light, compared with what sin deserves; and designed, if rightly improved, to prevent still worse things which may come upon us, if we despise the chastening of the Lord. It is my heart's desire for you, that you may not only say with gratitude, he hath healed all my sicknesses, but be able to add, he has pardoned all my sin.

An accomplished and well-behaved young woman is an amiable object in the sight of her fellow creatures. She may be sensible and obliging; she may dress and dance genteelly; she may play well upon the harpsichord; she may have much finer work to show than the coats and garments which Dorcas made; and, by her vivacity and good humour, she may become the idol of all her acquaintance: but, if she does not know her state as a sinner; if she admires herself, and is pleased with the admiration of others, while her heart is cold to the love and glory of God our Saviour; if she has no taste for prayer or praise; if her mind is engrossed by the pleasures and prospects of this poor world; she is dead while she liveth. In the sight of God her Maker, she is insensible and ungrateful, she is poor, blind, and miserable.

Your person, I suppose, is formed, your education finished, and your powers expanded. Happy you, if, with these advantages, you should be led to devote yourself to the Lord in early life. Then he will guide and bless you, and make you a blessing in all your connexions. You will live honourably and usefully, and die, whether sooner or later, comfortably. You will have a double relish for every temporal comfort, because you will see his hand providing and bestowing it; and in times of trouble, which you will surely meet with, you will have a refuge, a hiding-place, a present and effectual helper, when the help of man would be utterly in vain.

A Letter to a Young Woman, [6:444]; 4:632

Set your affection on things above.—Col. 3:2.

IF we are, indeed, believers in Christ, and partakers of the power of his resurrection, we are bound by obligation, and required by our rule, to set our affections on the things that are above, not on the things on the earth. He has called us out of the world, and cautioned us against conformity to its spirit. While we are in the world, it is our duty, privilege, and honour, to manifest that grace which has delivered us from the love of it. Christians must indeed eat and drink, and may buy and sell, as other people do; but the principles, motives, and ends, of their conduct are entirely different. They are to adorn the doctrine of God their Saviour, and to do all for his glory. By his wisdom and providence, he places them in different situations, that the power and sufficiency of his grace may appear under a great variety of outward circumstances... Whether they are rich or poor, bond or free, they are so by his appointment; with which, if they cheerfully comply, they shall, in due time, be sensible that he chooses better for them, than they could have chosen for themselves. The language of faith, when in exercise, will not be, 'What is most conducive to my temporal ease and prosperity?' but 'What will give me the fairest opportunity of glorifying him, who has bought me with his blood, and called me out of darkness into his marvellous light? Too much of my time has already been wasted: how shall I improve the little uncertain remainder for his service? I am too short-sighted to judge for myself, but he has thus far determined it. I am where he has placed me; and the calling in which his mercy found me, (if it be a lawful one,) is that in which, for the present, I am to abide, as the best for me. When it ceases to be so, I may depend upon him to appoint me another. But, till then, I desire to be contented with such things as I have, and to be thankful for them. He knows my frame, my feelings, my wants, and my trials; he permits, yea, invites me to cast all my cares upon him; he assures me that he careth for me, and therefore I only wish to do or to suffer according to his will today, and to leave the concerns of tomorrow in his hands. While I live, may I live for him; and when I die, may I go to him! May his grace be sufficient for me, and all shall be well.'

On Covetousness, [6:474]; 4:654

Be thou my refuge, Lord, my hiding-place,
    I know no force can tear me from thy side;
Unmov'd I then may all accusers face,
    And answer ev'ry charge with 'Jesus died.'

Other John Newton titles published by the Trust

THE WORKS OF JOHN NEWTON
4-VOLUME SET | 3,032 pp. | clothbound

This entirely re-formatted edition contains everything that was in the Trust's previously published six-volume edition, with the addition of *An Authentic Narrative,* Newton's autobiography. Ideal as a gift or for personal devotional reading, John Newton's *Works* are a worthy addition to any Christian's library.

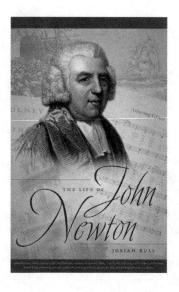

The Life of John Newton
Josiah Bull
paperback, 336pp.

A moving story of God's redeeming and restoring grace, which contains much valuable first-hand material from Newton's diary and letters. This is far from being a 'dry as dust' record of the past. Besides being a worthy memorial to the life and work of John Newton, this biography will also encourage those who love the gospel to consecrate themselves to the Master's service as Newton did.

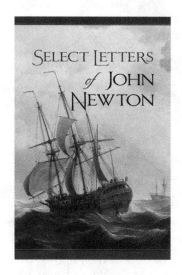

Select Letters of John Newton
paperback, 240pp.

This book of 39 choice letters by John Newton is an excellent place to start exploring the riches of his correspondence. The reader will soon discover why Newton is known as 'the letter writer par excellence of the Evangelical Revival'. His grasp of Scripture and deep personal experience, his many friends (among them, Whitefield, Cowper and Wilberforce), his manifold trials, his country pastorate, his strong, clear, idiomatic style – all these factors combined to prepare him for the exercise of his special gift. These practical letters and cover a wide variety of subjects related to the Christian's life and experience.

Letters of John Newton
Edited by Josiah Bull, with a biographical introduction by Andrew Bonar
clothbound, 416pp.

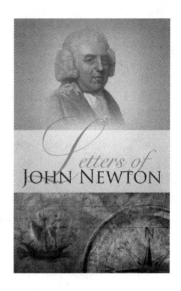

'*In few writers are Christian doctrine, experience and practice more happily balanced than in the author of these Letters, and few write with more simplicity, piety and force.*' – C. H. Spurgeon.

The letters in this volume were selected by Newton's biographer, Josiah Bull. Among them are several that were not previously published in earlier collections of Newton's correspondence. Of particular value and interest are the biographical sketches and historical notes supplied by the editor.

Wise Counsel: John Newton's Letters to John Ryland, Jr.
Edited by Grant Gordon
clothbound, 428pp.

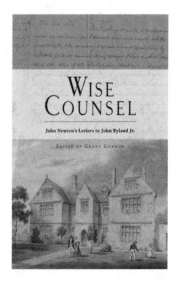

The particular recipient of Newton's 'wise counsel' in this book was John Ryland, Jr. (1753–1825), Baptist pastor and educator, and close friend of Andrew Fuller, William Carey, and all the pioneers of the modern missionary movement. All but ten of the letters in the present volume have been brought out of undeserved obscurity by Dr Grant Gordon. The reader will discover in these letters, not only mature and wise counsel, but a wholesome emphasis on true Christian experience, a great breadth of Christian sympathy, and a strong confidence in the power of the grace of God.

ABOUT THE PUBLISHER

THE Banner of Truth Trust originated in 1957 in London. The founders believed that much of the best literature of historic Christianity had been allowed to fall into oblivion and that, under God, its recovery could well lead not only to a strengthening of the church, but to true revival.

Inter-denominational in vision, this publishing work is now international, and our lists include a number of contemporary authors along with classics from the past. The translation of these books into many languages is encouraged.

A monthly magazine, *The Banner of Truth,* is also published. More information about this and all our publications can be found on our website or supplied by either of the offices below.

THE BANNER OF TRUTH TRUST

3 Murrayfield Road PO Box 621, Carlisle,
Edinburgh, EH12 6EL   Pennsylvania 17013,
UK   USA

www.banneroftruth.org